This book belongs to

....

....

THE COMMONSENSE KITCHEN

The Commonsense Kitchen

500 RECIPES + LESSONS FOR A HAND-CRAFTED LIFE

BY TOM HUDGENS

CHRONICLE BOOKS

SAN FRANCISCO

Library of Congress Cataloging-in-
Publication Data available.

ISBN 978-0-8118-7222-5

Manufactured in China

Design and illustrations by Katie Heit

page 263: "Modern Man" by Ann Applegarth,
originally published in *West Wind Review*,
Spring 1992. Used by permission of poet.

page 608: Excerpt from *Invisible Cities* by Italo
Calvino, copyright 1978, published by Harvest
Books, an imprint of Houghton Mifflin
Harcourt.

10 9 8 7 6 5 4 3 2 1

Chronicle Books LLC
680 Second Street
San Francisco, California 94107
www.chroniclebooks.com

Table
of
Contents

CHAPTER 3

Pancakes, Biscuits, and Cornbread 105

CHAPTER 4

Bread, Butter, Crackers, and Cheese   129

CHAPTER 5

Great Lunches

CHAPTER 9

Beef, Pork, and Lamb

CHAPTER 10

Chicken and Turkey

CHAPTER 13

Sauces and Relishes   411

CHAPTER 14

Pies and Fruit Desserts 439

CHAPTER 15

Cakes   477

Introduction

Welcome to *The Commonsense Kitchen*. Not simply a catalog of the meals I served to the Deep Springs College community of fifty people during my tenure as the chef there, this book was originally conceived to inspire the students' ongoing discovery of the vital craft of cooking as they embarked upon their adult lives. If you are just beginning to cook for yourself and your family, I hope this book will spark your culinary imagination while introducing you, recipe by recipe, to many essential kitchen practices. If you are a seasoned cook, I hope it will inspire you to see a familiar ingredient, technique, or dish in a new light.

The Commonsense Kitchen is an eclectic, working repertoire of dishes and democratic culinary philosophies.

You'll find recipes for many familiar American "comfort food" favorites: big breakfasts with eggs, bacon, pancakes, and grits; Southern and Southwestern dishes, including authentic New Mexico red and green chile sauces; a whole chapter on pies, including a thorough run-down on piecrust and the recipe for my Great-Aunt Lela's famous buttermilk pie. There are recipes for pinto beans, skillet cornbread, steak fried in beef tallow, pork chops marinated with fresh apple, and ten different versions of beef stew. I have included many of my mother's and grand-mother's recipes: baked custard, cornmeal-fried summer squash, chicken enchiladas, Kentucky bourbon balls.

Alongside such old-fashioned dishes, there are many modern, lighter recipes: oatmeal, granola, and other healthful morning grains; lean meats and fish; and vegetables, soups, and salads galore. In fact, two of the largest chapters in the book are devoted entirely to vegetables: Hot Vegetables and Vegetable Soups, and Salads and Dressings. Both are arranged alpha-betically by type of vegetable.

In keeping with the Deep Springs spirit of self-sufficiency, you'll learn how to churn fresh butter, bake homemade crackers, prepare a simple cheese from whole milk and vinegar . . . there's even a recipe for homemade soap.

Most of these recipes were developed in the busy Deep Springs' kitchen, where there is little time for fussy preparations, little money for expensive or exotic ingredients, and little regard for food trends or food snobbery, but where a great appreciation for *any* good, soul-satisfying food abides. Deep Springs is the only place I know where a tobacco-chewing old mechanic from rural Oklahoma might be served black truffle risotto on the same day that a distinguished governmental scholar from France is served cherry Jell-O with canned fruit cocktail.

About Deep Springs

What is Deep Springs? Stated very simply, Deep Springs is a college on a ranch: a very small, fully accredited, two-year college program for academically advanced young men (only twelve are admitted each year), situated on a real, working cattle ranch in an isolated, high-desert California valley. In addition to rigorous academic coursework and the responsibility of self-governance, the students put in about twenty hours of physical labor each week at a variety of jobs on the ranch. Though it's not a vocational school, the young men who attend Deep Springs get a good taste of many professions: rancher, laborer, farmer, mechanic, cowboy, butcher, cook.

Over the years, Deep Springs has been profiled in the *New Yorker*, *Chronicle of Higher Education*, *Los Angeles Times*, *Wall Street Journal*, and many other respected publications. The *New York Times* once called Deep Springs "one of the most selective and innovative colleges in the world." But to describe Deep Springs effectively, it's necessary to first set the scene, to describe the timeless physical place that existed, nameless, eons before human eyes ever traced its contours.

For hundreds of miles along California's eastern side runs the enormous Sierra Nevada mountain range, like a dragon's spine. Yosemite, Kings Canyon, Mount

Whitney, Lake Tahoe: all these renowned places are part of the Sierra Nevada. The western approach to the Sierra peaks is slow and gradual—the Foothills, California's Gold Country. But to approach the peaks from the east is to be astonished: they are sudden, towering, startling. On the eastern side, in the Sierra's "rain shadow," the terrain is desert, with alkali lakes, salt flats, and sagebrush. The beauty here is different, vast, austere, at times brutal, nothing obscuring the near-impossible distances. Death Valley is nearby. You love rocks? You'll love the eastern Sierra.

Deep Springs Valley is small by the standards of the region, roughly twelve miles long and half as wide, running northeast-southwest, ringed by mountains. The weather is extreme—scorching summers, biting-cold winters, violent winds, torrential downpours, snowstorms. From the college you can see several jagged peaks of the Sierra in the distance. At the southern end of the Valley is an alkali lake. Its water is not only bitter but unapproachable, skirted by moonlike acres of salt-crusted alkali mud.

While the land—the lake, the mountains, the canyons, the intermittent streams—is fascinating (botanists, zoologists, and, especially, geologists flock there), it's the sky, the light, that gives the place such a haunting voice. A desert landscape might seem harsh and forbidding to the uninitiated, but with time, experience, and attention, you come to experience the land as a frame for a never-ending, ever-changing show of light.

The light of a clear summer midday in the Valley is overwhelming, so bright your vision dims, colors wash out. You squint, even wearing your darkest sunglasses and widest-brimmed hat. The harsh rays reflect up off the light-colored ground and burn your face. It's almost too much to bear. Or consider the opposite: occasionally a thick cloud cover blankets the Valley. On a moonless night in such conditions, if no artificial light is near, you literally can't see your hand in front of you. It is darker than any closet, as impeccably dark as a deep cave.

Between these extremes, the stark land and light interplay in a perpetual spectacle that is anyone's for the noticing. If you are up early enough, when there are thin, high morning clouds over the Valley, you might see them turn from gray to orange to fierce pink, then settle back to white, all within a ten-minute span.

Some rare winter mornings, a low blanket of fog covers the Valley floor, softly but completely obscuring the low hills, the college buildings, the corrals. You go for a walk and the fog encloses you, allowing only the higher peaks and the sharply clear sky to be seen in a circle above you. The climbing sunlight bounces off the blinding white fog, illuminating the peaks to a dazzling gold that lasts but a moment, saturating the sky's blue to an intensity you never could have imagined. Notice well—the conditions that create this white, blue, and gold may not be repeated for years, or in your lifetime, or ever again.

In the fall, if forest fires are burning in the Sierra, early-afternoon winds often blow a strange, thick haze into Deep Springs Valley. Faraway mountains look like paper cutouts. Sunlight filters coldly through the haze, bathing everything in a wan, white, sad light. If you are happy in that moment, this peculiar light gives you pause, as though sadness lurked nearby, but if you are sad in that moment, this bleached, shadowless light affirms and reinforces your mood, as if happiness abided in some far-off place.

Later in the afternoon, after the haze—and the mood—has dissipated, the angled light brings the mountains near the lake into sharp relief, every canyon and furrow revealing itself. If there has been a rain and the air is freshly charged and super-clear, you can discern individual sagebrush bushes dotting the slopes, ten miles away.

Sunsets delight everyone; never confined to one part of the sky, they stretch all around in a cyclorama of color. Pink columns of mile-high cumulus clouds dwarf the mountains; jet vapor trails crisscross the sky; wispy cirrus clouds break into a geometric pattern, unfolding like a Chinese fan. When afternoon rains dissipate at dusk, the resulting sunsets are extraordinary—charcoal blacks next to indigo, fuchsia impossibly fading into cobalt blue, a melon-colored cloud with a pale-green sky behind it. On rare occasions, there is thunder and lightning; on even rarer occasions, the lightning is pink.

Finally, the full moon over Deep Springs Valley is unlike a full moon anywhere else. The pale-colored Valley floor reflects and intensifies the light. You can see every detail as you walk down the road—pebbles and beetles, the color red. You could read a book without straining your eyes. On moonless nights, the starlit sky is spectacular. Many newcomers to the Valley really see the Milky Way for the first time—its shape, its edges, its gap and spur.

How, you may ask, does all this relate to food and cooking? Well, Deep Springs' landscape and *The Commonsense Kitchen* both repeatedly invite you to *pay close attention*. Whether you are walking a trail in the Valley at sunset or frying eggs, there is a lot going on and a great deal to be learned, simply by noticing and paying attention to all the details. Drift off into a reverie, and your eggs might turn brown and rubbery in an instant, or you might miss that fleeting shaft of light on Mount Nunn.

The College and Ranch

In this austere, spectacular setting, Deep Springs College was founded on an existing cattle ranch in 1917. Twenty-six (yes, only 26) young men attend Deep Springs. Twelve to thirteen arrive each summer for two years of rigorous college coursework and physical labor on the ranch. The students govern themselves and make important decisions in the life of the college, assuming much of the responsibility for hiring faculty, admitting new students, and deciding which courses should be taught.

Students perform a variety of jobs during their two years: irrigating alfalfa fields, feeding livestock, milking cows, answering phones in the office, running the bookstore, maintaining the computer networks, toiling in the gardens and orchard, preparing rooms for guests, butchering meat for the kitchen, washing up after meals, and cooking meals for the entire community.

Meals in the Boardinghouse are an important part of community life, bringing students, faculty, staff, and families together, marking the rhythm of the day. Everyone works hard and comes to meals hungry. A hired chef prepares many of the meals, while the students, rather adventurously, cook the others. Students approach the daunting job of cooking at Deep Springs the same way they approach most of their endeavors—what they lack in practical experience they make up for with enthusiasm, ambition, interest, and intelligence.

Deep Springs can be a wonderful place to cook. Because it is a cattle ranch, free-range, grass-fed beef is always in abundant supply, and a dairy herd of about four cows is milked by student hands twice daily. There are pigs, lambs, and goats. There is a fruit orchard—apples, pears, peaches, plums, and a lone almond tree (though it's a rare year when all these trees manage to bear, due to the harsh winter weather and winds). In summer, the student gardeners harvest onions, garlic, carrots, lettuce, leeks, beets, tomatoes, basil, eggplant, corn, potatoes, cucumbers, and squash. A raspberry hedge thrives. The hen house flanks the garden; students gather about six dozen eggs a day from the chickens and geese.

Among the many unique—and perhaps anachronistic—aspects of Deep Springs is the fact that the college never has admitted women as students (there are female faculty, administrators, and staff). Although many people in the greater Deep Springs "family" have long wished the college were coeducational, many also appreciate the deep camaraderie and gentle nurturing that develops among "the guys." A sense of ease and humility characterizes Deep Springs' all-male student environment. They knit during meetings. They perhaps don't shower or change clothes as frequently as they would elsewhere. They cook for each other; when one student is sick, the others take care of him, bringing him soup or cookies.

In Deep Springs' accredited academic program, there are standard courses in English composition, public speaking, subjects all over the math/science spectrum, history, literature, political science, and philosophy. But there are elective-type courses, too, not only photography, painting, sculpture, pottery, and music, but also, on occasion, saddlery, auto mechanics, bread-making, and culinary arts.

After Deep Springs, most students finish their college degrees at four-year universities such as Harvard, Cornell, Berkeley, Oxford, and Yale. Deep Springers go on to become college professors, teachers, writers, doctors, lawyers, engineers, farmers . . . and chefs.

The Rhythms of a Day

A typical day at Deep Springs starts at 4:30 A.M. A student's alarm goes off; it's time to milk the cows. He rolls out of bed, bleary from too little sleep, and wakes the other "dairy boy." (Deep Springs students in general don't like being called boys, but "dairy boy" endures.) The two silently leave the dorm and walk to the Boardinghouse to collect empty six-gallon stainless-steel milk containers, or "shotguns," from the walk-in refrigerator. They trudge toward the dairy barn, about a quarter-mile from the Boardinghouse, pulling the shotguns on a cart. For much of the year, it's below freezing at this coldest time of day. Frost coats the grass, and a lawn sprinkler's

slow leak has formed an elaborate ice sculpture overnight. Sometimes one of the dogs—there are always several at Deep Springs—will get into the habit of accompanying the dairy boys on their twice-daily labor. The dairy cows are well accustomed to their routine, but the students always have to prompt them. The enormous animals rise from the cold ground and huff and puff a bit, taking their time getting to the barn. Each cow has her own stanchion in the old, low, rock-and-concrete barn (thought to be the oldest building on the ranch). Her head goes through a gap in a whitewashed wooden stand, and the students slide a slat into place to prevent her from backing out. As the dairy boys settle down to work, they invariably put on music—Brahms or Chopin, or maybe some Metallica.

Sitting on low stools, one student on each side of the cow, they first clean the cow's teats and udder with a disinfecting solution, then position a sterilized bucket underneath and begin milking. To milk a cow, you pinch a teat at its top with your thumb and forefinger, then squeeze all the way down the length of the teat with a slight tug: warm milk streams out in a short squirt. After only a short time on the job, the young men develop a fast, skilled, musical rhythm. Sometimes the cows will disrupt things, kicking over the bucket or copiously urinating or defecating, spoiling the milk.

The first milk to emerge is mostly non-fat, but later in the milking, it comes out creamier. Once the pinching-squeezing yields no more milk, they clean the cow's udder and teats again, rub them with Bag Balm (a classic ranch salve the dairy boys don't hesitate to rub on their own chapped hands), and move on to the next cow. When all the cows are milked, the students release them from their stanchions and send them back out into the yard with a pat.

The milk is carefully weighed, the weight recorded in a log. The dairy boys pour the warm milk through a simple device using cooling coils—like an air conditioner—to rapidly cool the milk, then separate the cream using a centrifugal separator. They thoroughly hose down the concrete floor of the milking area, wash and sterilize all the equipment, then finally wheel the milk, sloshing in the shotguns, back to the Boardinghouse in time for breakfast. They greet the Student Cook, who, to the low sounds of classic Chicago blues, is laying bacon out on a sheet pan or cracking brown eggs into a bowl. The dairy boys go to the big refrigerator and empty yesterday's milk into a bucket (this old milk will be fed to the pigs), then fill clean pitchers with fresh milk and set them out on the tables in the dining room.

A quarter-hour before breakfast is served, the cook rings the giant iron bell mounted outside the Boarding-house; this first bell serves as an alarm clock for most of the community. But many people, not just the cook and the dairy boys, are already up. During the summer alfalfa-growing season, the student irrigation team is moving sprinkler lines on the fields, the stu-dent "feed man" is throwing hay to the horses, the student gardeners are harvesting vegetables for that day's meals, the Writer in Residence is preparing for a reading she will give that evening, a designated student is recording the night's high and low temperatures for the National Weather Service, and the art professor is out in the desert, capturing the sunrise on canvas.

The final breakfast bell rings, and students, staff, administrators, faculty, and families gather for pancakes, scrambled eggs, bacon, oatmeal, fruit, coffee, and fresh milk. On Mondays the college president, the academic dean, the ranch manager, and the Student Body president will meet at a back table over breakfast, coordinating all the goings-on in the Valley.

Shortly after breakfast, the morning's classes begin. Some students might spend the whole morning in the biology lab, while others, following an hour of intermediate Spanish or first-year composition class, will be expected to probe deeply into Melville's *Moby-Dick* or de Tocqueville's *Democracy in America*. By the time the final lunch bell rings, everyone's stomach is growling as

the professors wrap up spirited class discussions.

Afternoons at Deep Springs are usually devoted to working: the general labor crew builds fences, mows lawns, and hauls garbage; the butcher blasts Prince's *Purple Rain* as he cuts roasts, steaks, and chops; the cooks hurry to get the meatloaf in the oven so there will be enough time to bake the cookies and rolls. The student "office cowboy" answers the telephone and processes requests for applications to Deep Springs.

Students who don't have afternoon work duties spend their hours studying— or sleeping. The dairy boys typically take a nap before going out for the evening's milking. Sometimes, when there is a surfeit of milk, they will forgo the nap and spend the time in the kitchen, making yogurt or cheese (see page 146 for a basic, easy cheese made from fresh milk, vinegar, and salt).

The last bell of the day—the dinner bell at 6 P.M.—signals for many Deep Springs community members the time to relax and unwind. Everyone loves to linger over dinner, but often the Applications or Curriculum committees must meet, or the morning's class schedule is so tight that some classes must be held in the evenings. On Tuesday evenings, the student dishwashers rush to finish scrubbing the pots so they can attend Public Speaking, a long-standing Deep Springs institution where several students give short speeches to the assembled community, to be critiqued and graded afterward. On Fridays, the entire Student Body gathers for their weekly meeting. These meetings often go late into the night as they democratically tackle the many problems that arise or decisions that must be made in community life.

Many guys find the late-night hours the only time available for studying; to be sleep deprived is a Deep Springs tradition. They spend weekends studying or organizing special work projects (building a grape arbor, painting a mural on the basketball court), but sometimes there is time for relaxing, recharging activities, such as reading for pleasure, riding horses, hiking the many trails in the Valley and surrounding mountains, or just catching up on sleep.

The Author

I've had the good fortune not only to attend Deep Springs as a student, but to work there later as the chef and then return, most recently, to teach a cooking class.

Early in my two years as a student, I signed up for the job of Student Cook, considered the hardest job on the ranch, and loved it. David Tanis, a Deep Springs alumnus and chef at the celebrated Berkeley, California, restaurant Chez Panisse, once visited the Valley during that time and cooked several meals for the community. I hovered at his side as he generously wielded his culinary wizardry, roasting peppers, chopping garlic with anchovies, pitting olives, shaving fennel and Parmesan, butchering lambs, roasting whole chickens, simmering black beans with herbs, peeling apples with a paring knife—all new to me. On the final evening of his visit, David braised thirty pounds of lamb shoulder with Moroccan spices, steamed a mountain of couscous, threw together a salad of grated carrots with fresh ginger and green olives, and baked a round loaf of fennel-seed bread for each table. As the community gathered for dinner, we blasted Umm Kulthum on the Boardinghouse stereo and offered platters of spicy lamb tartare on little toasts. From that point on, I was deliciously hooked on the craft of cooking.

After Deep Springs, while finishing my liberal arts degree at Cornell University, instead of the usual student work-study jobs, I cooked in restaurants and did a good deal of private catering, once even serving a sumptuous wedding banquet to a hundred guests. My friend Elge and I met in a class called "The Social History of Food and Eating" and became fast friends. We cooked for each other: we'd make tangerine-juice-injected leg of lamb, steak tartare, fresh egg noodles, gazpacho, Greek salad, and almond-crusted cherry pie when perhaps we should have been studying for exams. No matter—in a broader sense, we were still pursuing our education. After graduation I moved to Berkeley, where, thanks to my experience at Deep Springs with David Tanis, I got a job washing lettuce and rolling out pasta dough at the extraordinary Chez Panisse, the famous, influential restaurant that emphasizes beautiful, fresh ingredients and simple, classic techniques. Later, with new skills and experience, I lived and cooked in Hawaii. I was excited and inspired by the rich patchwork of island cultures and culinary traditions.

Several years after I graduated, I returned to the Valley for a three-year stint as Deep Springs' chef, feeding the community and working closely with students every day. Once, early on, someone asked me for a couple of my recipes, so I wrote them down, plus a few others. At the end of that year, I compiled a small volume, called simply, *The Deep Springs Cookbook*, and gave a copy to each of the graduating students. Each year, with each graduation, the cookbook expanded. A few years later, I returned to Deep Springs once more to teach a course in culinary arts, using the old cookbook as a reference and ultimately working it into what you are reading today.

For more information on Deep Springs College:

MAILING ADDRESS
HC 72 Box 45001
Dyer, NV 89010

TELEPHONE
(760) 872-2000

WEB SITE
www.deepsprings.edu

CHAPTER 1

Kitchen Basics

Learning to Cook

Learning to cook is a lifelong process. Every time I mix a batter, slice an onion, or peel an apple, I'm learning to cook, provided I'm paying attention. You want to learn to cook? Go into the kitchen and start cooking. Keep cooking. Let your hunger and appetite guide you; cook what you want to eat. Pay close attention to every step in the process, and to your results.

Food is our primary, fundamental connection to nature. Even urban dwellers who rarely see the sun or set foot on soil must still eat food grown in the sun, in soil. What is the most highly processed food you can think of? Whatever it is, it is still ultimately based on plants, grown in a field somewhere under the sun. Cooks perform a kind of alchemy, transforming natural products—plants, animals, water, salt—into food that builds and nourishes the body and soul. I believe the dawn of human civilization occurred not at the moment we learned to build a fire, nor at the moment of killing and butchering an animal, but rather at the moment we learned to carefully cook bits of that animal's flesh over the fire without burning it, to brown, smoky, juicy perfection.

Learning to cook, like learning any craft or skill, is a matter of learning to pay attention, to ask questions. The best first step in learning to cook is *developing close attention to what you eat.*

What tastes good to you? Why? What we eat affects not only our bodies, but ultimately the whole, interconnected world. To open a can of green beans creates a different result, both in your body and in the world, than if you bought and cooked a handful of fresh green beans. Each choice, no matter how small, makes a difference.

Appreciate your food before eating it. Take a moment to be aware of the colors and aromas. Be aware of all the people who worked to produce the food. Use whatever has been made available to enhance your experience of eating. Sprinkle a little salt, if it makes the food taste better. Pepper. Condiments. Squeeze the lemon or lime. Help yourself to any sauce the cook has provided. Spread a little butter on your bread. Be aware of how the different foods offered complement one another. Relish every bite. Lick your fingers. Stop when you're full. Compliment the cook.

Pay attention to your food likes and dislikes. With time, they may change. Foods I once hated I now love. When I was a kid, each summer my mother would implore me to taste *just one* cherry tomato she had grown in our New Mexico backyard: "Just try it," she'd say, "they're sweet as candy!" I'd dutifully pop one in my mouth, bite into it . . . and gag. Now, as an adult, I love tomatoes of every size, stripe, and hue. A friend once insisted on *his* dislike for cherry tomatoes—until he tasted them simply cut in half with a knife, and then he loved them. He didn't like the way the little tomatoes squirt their juice when they are bitten whole. Halved, their good flavor was more accessible. "I never knew anything so simple could make such a difference," he said. Welcome to the craft of cooking.

The second step in learning to cook is *developing close attention to ingredients.* Notice their qualities, their properties, their inherent beauty. I can't decide which is more beautiful, the finished pot of Gumbo (page 175) or the gleaming bell peppers, fat yellow onions, celery like temple columns, fuzzy okra pods, bits of thyme and dried hot red pepper, raw pink chicken with yellow skin, smoked hot sausages, and vibrant bunch of parsley, all laid out on the counter.

Develop the habit of asking yourself, *"Where do these ingredients come from?"* For those of us living in modern, industrialized society, answering that question can be extraordinarily complex. Parts of virtually any modern

American meal could come from all over the globe. Nonetheless, as we take a greater interest in preparing our own food, the question naturally arises. Each summer at Deep Springs a new group of students arrives. It doesn't take long before some of them recognize, innately, the possibility of a meal composed entirely of Deep Springs–grown ingredients. This always excites them greatly, as it excited me. Once, when I was first learning to cook as a Deep Springs student, I made a shepherd's pie from a James Beard recipe, containing lamb, onions, garlic, rosemary, potatoes, milk, and butter—all grown or produced in the Valley. It was a revelatory moment: the rich, homely, old-fashioned dish came out well, but it also possessed a kind of deep authority. It belonged right there, where we were. It tasted appropriate and immediate.

Ingredients are infinitely variable. Food is nature, it is life, it is plants and animals, and therefore it is ever changing, dynamic. Food is always a product of its place and time and circumstance; *food is always in the present moment*. Cooking, by its concrete nature, resists overintellectualization. Rather than thinking about it conceptually, ask yourself what is happening right there in the moment: sometimes the lettuce is sweet, sometimes it's bitter, so the sharpness of the dressing has to be adjusted accordingly. The tomatoes were watery last year, needing vinegar to perk up their flavor; this year they are deeply colored, plummy and concentrated, needing nothing but salt. Last week's burgers were deliciously beefy, but these today are a little flat, needing more black pepper and hot sauce.

The third step in learning to cook is, simply, to do it: *cook, cook, cook, and keep cooking*. Work to satisfy your hunger. Follow recipes. Each recipe in this or any other cookbook offers a lesson and will contribute to your growing culinary knowledge. When following a new recipe, it's important to sit down and *read the recipe through*—every word, from beginning to end—before you begin. Sometimes, while cooking, things happen very quickly and there is no time to leave the stove and check the recipe. When the dish is finished, and the actual, physical experience of having cooked it is under your belt, it's always a good idea to go back and read the recipe through again. Take notes in the margins.

It's important to remember that a recipe is not a guarantee that the result will be exactly what you imagine.

A recipe is to the finished dish as a written invitation is to the party itself. Anything could happen. Even the simplest recipe is subject to a host of variables, including your own expectations.

Consider a dish as simple as a grilled cheese sandwich. Many questions arise, should you care to ask them. First, what are your expectations? Did you eat and love grilled cheese sandwiches as a child? Were it possible to exactly replicate those grilled cheese sandwiches today (it isn't), would you still love them? Is the bread white, wheaty, soft, chewy; the cheese sharp, mild, grainy, creamy? Will it be Cheddar, bouncy American, or something more "sophisticated," whatever that means? Will the cheese melt creamily, or will it separate and release some of its oil? What fat, if any, will you use to toast the sandwich? Butter? Olive oil? Mayonnaise? Do you spread the outside of the bread thinly with butter and very slowly toast it over low heat in a pan until the bread is golden and the cheese is just melted? Or will you cook it more quickly, over higher heat, and then finish melting the cheese for a few moments in the microwave? Is there another element to the sandwich, a slice of onion, a slice of tomato (do you salt the tomato?), the slightest smear of mustard? Is the bread toasted to a deep brown or just a pale gold? Are you going to sit down and eat your sandwich by yourself as soon as it comes out of the pan, or are you making several for a crowd? Is the sandwich cut in half or in quarters, diagonally or crosswise? What, if anything, will accompany your grilled cheese sandwich? Tomato soup? From a can or homemade? Applesauce? A fresh, crisp apple? A shaved fennel and radish salad? Will you serve the sandwich on a room-temperature plate, a warmed plate, or just a napkin or paper towel? Each option will affect your grilled cheese sandwich experience. Since each question could have any number of answers, an infinite variety of grilled cheese sandwiches is possible. My recipe for a grilled cheese sandwich (page 159) reflects my own bias and answers a few of these questions, but it still leaves plenty of them up to you. Successfully following a recipe not only requires your attention, it requires your good judgment and common sense.

You will find lots of rules in this or any other cookbook, but I hasten to point out that for every cooking rule, there exist several delightful, delicious exceptions. "Be lamps unto yourselves," the dying Buddha told his students. *Paying close attention to your own experience* as you cook is far more important than following rules just because they are printed on a page.

Ruining food is a tiny tragedy and is almost always the result of a lapse of attention somewhere along the way. Simply resolve to pay closer attention the next time, and keep cooking. Learn from your mistakes, and learn how to correct your mistakes whenever possible. If you are given to improvisation, know that the more adept you are with the basics, the more successful your improvisations will be. Cooking is not so much a systematically acquired body of knowledge as a series of intricate, interwoven understandings of ingredients and procedures, each taken on its own terms, each its own idiosyncratic universe.

Finally, learning to cook well is learning how to coax the best out of a few ordinary ingredients, developing the knack for making "something out of nothing." *Constraints and limitations often stimulate creativity and new ideas.* All good cooks remember a time when, faced with a poorly equipped kitchen and a virtually bare cupboard, they nonetheless produced something

delicious. Once I had a job where I cooked vegan dinners in a squalid little café kitchen equipped with only a glass-topped electric stove, an electric oven, and a few poor-quality pots and pans. The stove was no good for anything but boiling water, so I did most of my cooking in the oven—slowly roasting onions instead of sautéing them—and managed to turn out some really good food.

Keep cooking. Honest, nourishing, delicious food is a universal right, not a luxury reserved for the privileged, the greedy, or the righteous. Food, though perhaps not all-important, is still important. Remember: if you're irritable, you're probably hungry. Food may strengthen, embolden, invigorate, empower, restore, refresh, recharge, comfort, balance, collect, soothe, gratify, entertain, cheer, amaze, surprise, and delight us.

May you find this book instructive and inspiring. May it help you discover your own, unique culinary principles and philosophies, helping you to write, as it were, your own cookbook.

Culinary Terms

Someone once said that the essence of education is learning new words. A bit reductive, perhaps, but every art, craft, or discipline comes with its own vocabulary; a single word may efficiently connote a complex process or product. Whether you aspire to highly skilled chefdom or simply to putting an honest meal on your family's table, knowing these words will help you on your path.

boil *(noun or verb)*:
Put tap water into a pot, put the pot on a stove burner, and turn the burner to its highest setting. The water will come to a boil, with many large bubbles briskly breaking the surface of the water. (Contrast with **simmer**.)

How long will it take for water to come to a boil? That depends on many things: the thickness and material of the pot, the size and shape of the pot, whether the pot is covered, the intensity of the burner's heat, the pot's proximity to the flame, the initial temperature of the water, the amount of water, and the altitude. At higher altitudes (such as Deep Springs' altitude of 5,200 feet), water boils at a lower temperature and remains at that lower temperature while it boils. Therefore, certain foods, such as beans, take longer to cook at higher altitudes. Added pressure raises the boiling point, so foods will cook faster. This is the principle behind pressure cookers.

A **low boil** is characterized by a few large bubbles rapidly breaking the surface of the water here and there. A **rolling boil**, by contrast, is characterized by many large bubbles very rapidly breaking everywhere on the surface of the water.

braise *(noun or verb)*:
A cooking method whereby food is cooked slowly in a small amount of flavorful liquid. See the recipes for Herbed Braised Chicken, page 355, and Beef Stew, page 315.

brine *(noun or verb)*:
A saltwater solution, often also containing sugar and aromatic ingredients, that penetrates, flavors, and tenderizes meat. See the recipe for Tender Cured Pork Chops, page 336. Brining produces a more radical transformation than **marinating**. See also **cure**.

chiffonade *(noun or verb)*:
To cut an herb or a leaf into fine ribbons with a sharp knife.

chile *(noun; pronounced "CHEE-lay")*:
The proper Spanish term for what are commonly called "hot peppers." Chile is all-important in Southwestern cooking, particularly in the traditional cooking of New Mexico, used either green (typically roasted, peeled, and seeded) or red (typically dried and ground).

chili *(noun; rhymes with "silly")*:
A stew containing beans (or meat, or both), onions, and a hefty quantity of **chile**. "Chili powder" is usually a spice blend containing cumin, oregano, and other spices in addition to ground chile.

chunk *(noun or verb)*:
To cut into large, cube-shaped pieces, from ½ inch to 1 inch. See also **dice**.

cream *(verb)*:
To whip or beat butter or other fat, either alone or in combination with sugar, until much air is incorporated into the butter. Creamed butter is light in color and texture, very pliable, and fluffy. When sugar and butter are creamed together, the water in the butter partially dissolves the sugar.

crush *(verb)*:
In this book, *crush* means to finely mash until the food (usually garlic) is reduced to a purée or, in the case of dry foods such as crackers, to crumbs.

cure *(verb)*:
To transform a food's original texture or structure using salt—either dry salt

or a saltwater solution. When a food is **brined**, it is said to be cured. Salting a piece of meat or fish, and allowing the salt to penetrate the meat completely over time, is another method of curing (see the recipe for Gravlax, page 374).

deglaze *(verb)*:
To dissolve, using a small amount of liquid (water, wine, or stock), the flavorful, caramelized brown residue (see **fond**) that forms in a pan when sautéing meat, mushrooms, onions, or other savory foods.

dice *(noun or verb)*:
To cut into small, cube-shaped pieces. **Fine dice** means to cut into about ¼-inch cubes, and **medium dice** means to cut into about ½-inch cubes.

emulsify *(verb;* **emulsion** *is the noun)*:
To smoothly combine two substances that wouldn't normally mix, usually a water-based mixture (for instance, vinegar in salad dressing) with an oil-based one. This is done by means of an **emulsifier**—such as mustard, garlic, egg yolks, or potatoes. Mayonnaise (page 426) is a familiar example of an emulsion.

fillet *(noun)*:
A boneless piece of meat or fish.

fold *(verb)*:
To gently combine a mixture that contains a lot of air (usually whipped egg whites or whipped cream) with another, heavier mixture, so that relatively little of the air is lost from the first mixture. To fold, place the lighter mixture on top of the heavier one. Using a whisk or a rubber spatula, gently sweep large folds of the heavier mixture up from the bottom of the bowl. Continue until the mixture is uniform. The whisk or spatula is held almost parallel to the vessel's bottom. Mere stirring, by contrast, involves holding the utensil perpendicular to the vessel's bottom.

fond *(noun)*:
The flavorful, caramelized brown residue that forms in the pan when sautéing meat or other foods. The fond is an important source of the finished dish's flavor. See Beef Stew, page 315, or Sautéed Chicken Breast, page 348. See also **deglaze**.

julienne *(noun or verb)*:
To cut into small, uniform matchstick-shaped pieces (see Kohlrabi-Apple Slaw, page 289).

knead *(verb)*:
To stretch and fold a mixture, usually bread dough, repeatedly for the purpose

of activating the elastic wheat protein known as gluten. The basic motion involves stretching the dough out, then folding it over, rapidly, again and again. Kneading may be done in a sturdy electric mixer or by hand.

macerate *(verb)*:
To soak shallots or onions in vinegar with salt, flavoring the vinegar. Also to sprinkle sugar over cut fruit in order to draw out the fruit's juices.

marinate *(verb;* **marinade** *is the noun)*:
To flavor food by letting it sit submerged in, rubbed with, or tossed with flavorful ingredients.

mince *(verb)*:
To chop very finely.

mirepoix *(noun; pronounced "meer-eh-PWA")*:
Classically, the trio of aromatic vegetables—onion, carrot, and celery—that gives a fundamental "structure" to the final flavor of many a dish (see the recipe for Brown, White, and Wild Rice Pilaf with Mirepoix, page 400).

nonreactive *(adjective)*:
In this book, *nonreactive* always refers to a vessel made of (or lined with) a material that will not react with acidic foods: glass, ceramic, or enamel, and in some cases, plastic or stainless steel.

poach *(verb)*:
To cook food in very hot, but not boiling, water (or wine, or other flavorful liquid). Typically, the water is brought to a boil, the food is put into the water, and then the pot is taken off the heat; the residual heat of the water cooks the food. See the recipes for Poached Eggs, page 101, and Boiled (technically poached) Shrimp, page 382.

roast *(noun or verb)*:
To cook food in the oven, uncovered, for a sufficient length of time and at a sufficiently high temperature to produce an appetizing brown exterior. "Bake," by contrast, simply means to cook food in the oven.

roux *(noun; pronounced "ROO")*:
A blend of flour and fat (vegetable oil, lard, butter, or bacon grease) that is cooked together for the purpose of thickening and enriching liquid. See the recipes for Biscuits and Gravy, page 115, and Gumbo, page 175.

sauté *(noun or verb)*:
Means "jump" in French, evoking the intensity of the heat and the way

skilled chefs toss ingredients around in a pan with a deft flick of the wrist. *Sauté* means to quickly cook food in an uncovered pan over high heat in a little oil or butter. The pan must be wide enough so the meat or fish browns appetizingly. If the cook attempts to sauté too great a volume of food at a time relative to the surface area of the pan, the food will not brown; in this case, the action is closer to **stewing**.

season *(verb;* **seasoning** *is the noun)*
1. To salt food.
2. To apply salt and/or other flavorings to food.
3. To prepare a cast-iron pan for use by applying a thin coat of oil or fat and heating it in the oven (see page 56). The oil hardens and fuses to the pan, creating a nonstick coating.

shave *(verb)*:
To slice food paper-thin.

simmer *(noun or verb)*:
A specific heat level for a deep pot of liquid, at which small bubbles appear here and there intermittently on the liquid's surface. (Contrast with **boil**.)

sponge *(noun)*:
In breadmaking, a sponge is made by combining the recipe's liquid (water or milk), yeast, and only a portion of the flour, mixing it to a batterlike consistency, and allowing it to sit so the yeast naturally proliferates. After the sponge has developed sufficiently, the recipe's salt, fat, and remaining flour are mixed in, resulting in a dough.

stew *(verb)*:
To slowly cook food in a covered pan without allowing the food to brown. Steam plays a significant role in the cooking. (Contrast with **sauté**.)

whip *(verb)*:
To beat a substance rapidly in such a way that air is incorporated into it. Examples: whipped cream (page 447), whipped egg whites, and whipped butter.

zest *(noun or verb)*:
The flavorful, oil-rich, pigmented outer skin of citrus fruits, used to give bright flavor to many dishes. Usually removed by means of a fine grater, **zester**, or rasp (see page 56); zest may also be taken in long strips with a vegetable peeler. Care is usually taken to avoid the bitter white pith between the zest and the fruit's juicy flesh.

Essential Equipment

Extraordinary food does not depend on extraordinary kitchen equipment, and extraordinary kitchen equipment does not guarantee extraordinary food. People often assume that my kitchen drawers and cupboards are filled with the finest, most expensive culinary gadgets. Actually, I have quite ordinary stuff, most of it battered from years of use: a few good knives (and some not-so-good ones); heavy, heat-conducting pots and pans; various utensils; and a few basic time-saving electric appliances. On one hand, I don't place too much emphasis on tools and equipment. Once you develop good knife skills and attention to temperatures and timing, many manufactured kitchen thingamajigs become superfluous.

On the other hand, it's important to remember that "no job is difficult if you have the right tool." To that I might add "and the right skill." A few good tools are important if you want to learn to cook well. *Your hands are always your primary kitchen tool.* The physicality of all your kitchen skills resides in your hands—your strength, your gentle touch, your delicate control. A steady hand, a light hand, a practiced hand— these can all be cultivated. Tactile sensations always tell you a great deal about the food you are working with. Tools are just extensions of your hands. So, assuming you have a good pair of hands, and that your kitchen has a stove, an oven, a sink, and a refrigerator, what tools do you need to begin cooking, to follow the recipes in this book? Well, you need a couple of knives, a cutting board, and a steel to keep the knives sharp. You need a few sturdy pots and pans that conduct heat evenly, and a few utensils: spoons, spatulas, sieves. . . .

Quality kitchen equipment might be expensive, but in some cases the expense is well justified. I once saw a sign in a shop window in Reno, Nevada, that read, "The burden of poor quality far outlasts the thrill of the bargain." Considering something as simple as cooking your morning oatmeal, the recipe in this book calls for lightly toasting the oats in the pan in a little butter before adding the water and milk. In an inexpensive, thin-bottomed pot, if you keep the flame very low and stand over the stove, constantly and patiently stirring the oats, you just might be able to toast them successfully without scorching them, but it won't be easy. On the other hand, a thick-bottomed pot diffuses the stove's heat well; toasting oats in such a pot will demand much less of your attention—the oats will gently toast and acquire flavor without burning, thanks to the quality of the pot. I know folks who routinely burn food in their inexpensive pans, necessitating the pans' frequent replacement. If you take all that ruined food into account, as well as the expense of new pans, paying $100 for a pan of excellent quality that will last a lifetime doesn't seem so outrageous.

On the other hand, sometimes the cheaper item is every bit as good. I have a few different vegetable peelers, but I bought my favorite one at a grocery store fifteen years ago for $1.75—it peels thinly; its blade has stayed razor-sharp.

KNIVES AND CUTTING IMPLEMENTS

It would be difficult to argue that any kitchen tool is more essential than a good, sharp knife. If I were forced to use only one knife, it would be a **chef's knife** (also sometimes called a cook's knife) with an 8- to 10-inch blade. A chef's knife of excellent quality will last for a very long time. To learn about knives before you invest in one, go to a knife store, look at your various options, *hold them in your hand*, and ask questions. Stainless-steel knives are the easiest to use, though in Europe, carbon-steel knives are more common—they sharpen readily, but they pit and discolor easily and may react with acid foods. I've always used stainless-steel knives.

When I first cooked as a student in the Boardinghouse kitchen at Deep Springs, I asked the ranch manager, Geoff Pope, if we could order a new knife—all the existing knives were hopelessly dull. The new knife was a revelation: suddenly, kitchen tasks were easy, even pleasurable. I sailed through piles of onions, easily trimmed beef for stew, chopped herbs with abandon. I remember the joy of making a giant batch of salsa—every tomato, onion, and jalapeño finely diced by hand. Around that time, my mother gave me my own German chef's knife for my birthday, a knife I used steadily for ten years.

Knives are made by one of two processes: forged or stamped. Fully forged knives are crafted one at a time and are better balanced in the hand. They are also more expensive. Stamped knives are made by cutting a knife shape from a sheet of stainless steel, then sharpening it. Stamped knives are cheaper, typically about half the price of forged knives, though some brands are still well balanced and sturdy enough to withstand heavy use. Pay attention to all parts of any knife you are considering purchasing. Look closely at the blade, how it curves. Pay attention to how the handle feels in your hand, how easy it is to grip.

Notice the overall weight and balance of the knife—a good knife will balance when held at the point where blade and handle meet, or will tip slightly toward the handle. Look closely, too, at the back edge of the knife blade. On sturdy, well-made knives, this right-angled back edge is sharp, good for crushing small amounts of garlic to a smooth, juicy purée.

After your chef's knife, the next most used knives are smaller **paring knives**, with 4- to 5-inch blades, both straight and serrated. These need not be forged. Once I bought an expensive forged paring knife and promptly lost it—I swept it into the garbage along with a pile of lettuce trimmings while washing salad at Chez Panisse. I realized my mistake only when retrieving it would have meant sifting through the entire day's garbage. I find most stamped paring knives to be perfectly adequate.

I rely on **serrated knives** a good deal: a smaller one (with a 4- to 5-inch blade) for cutting tomatoes or sectioning citrus fruit, and a larger one for bread. On the large serrated bread knife, an offset handle is preferable, enabling you to cut all the way through a loaf of bread without smashing your knuckles.

A **sharpening steel** is necessary for keeping your knife sharp. A steel won't put a new edge on a dull knife, but it will maintain an existing good edge for a long time. You can acquire the skill necessary for using the steel. Ask the person at the knife store—or a chef—to show you how. Some cooks prefer a wide angle for steeling their knives, creating a sturdier edge that will last longer, while others prefer a narrower angle, creating a very sharp edge that won't last as long. Find your own balance between these two, and stick with it; changing angles will wear your knife blade away more quickly. If you love sharp knives and intend to use yours a lot, you may also want to get—and learn to use— a **sharpening stone**. I prefer water-lubricated stones (also called whetstones); they are cleaner and easier to maintain than those lubricated with oil. When to use a sharpening steel and when to use a stone? The steel maintains the edge on your knife, while a stone restores it. Your steel is for everyday use—it's a good idea to steel your knife every time you use it. But for household cooks, stone sharpening is necessary only occasionally. If you need to create an entirely new edge on your knife, it's time to take it to a professional knife sharpener who uses an electric stone wheel. Knife stores or kitchen-supply stores often offer sharpening services.

An important, constant companion to your knife is a **wooden cutting board**. Maple, thanks to its hardness, is the best wood for cutting boards. Like a knife, a good-quality cutting board might be expensive, but also like a knife, with care it may last a lifetime or longer. *Cutting boards should never be submerged in water.* They should be nice and big; I have an 18-by-24-inch one that always sits on the counter (caveat: clean underneath it frequently, and ensure that it never gets wet underneath). Smaller cutting boards that fit in a drawer are good to have for tasks like slicing a tomato for a sandwich. Flexible plastic cutting mats are handy (I often use them when trimming meat), especially when cut down with scissors to more manageable sizes, but these should not take the place of a larger cutting board.

Kitchen **shears** are essential for many tasks, and shears whose blades come apart are the easiest to clean.

Vegetable peelers are also essential and come in many designs. I prefer a peeler that peels quite thinly.

Finally, the citrus **zester** is a favorite tool of mine; many recipes in this book call for citrus zest. A now-common kitchen tool introduced fairly recently, the **"fine-plane" rasp** is like a grater, except with a grating surface of tiny, precisely sharpened cutting holes. It was originally manufactured and used as a woodworking tool, but chefs discovered its keen ability to finely grate citrus zest, Parmesan cheese, and chocolate. Such a grater is also very good for reducing a clove of garlic to a smooth mush, or horseradish to a sinus-clearing cloud, though lots of the latter will quickly dull the tiny blades. But a fine, sharp, regular **box grater** will still produce good results.

POTS AND PANS

Many recipes in this book specify a *heavy* skillet, saucepan, or pot. Why? Heavier cookware conducts heat more evenly; you want the heat from the stove burner to evenly distribute over the cooking surface of the pan. You don't want pans that have hot spots; thin, cheap pans make the cook's job much harder. Any cookware that has an aluminum core clad in stainless steel will likely perform well; there are many brands—and prices. Though sturdy, these are still lighter weight

(and a bit easier on the wrists) than most alternatives.

French-style **enameled cast iron** is beautiful and performs well, but it's especially heavy and the enamel is prone to chipping. If the inner enamel surface becomes stained, you might be tempted to bleach it, but too much bleach will make the enamel porous. I especially enjoy using low-tech **American cast iron**. Antique cast-iron skillets are readily found, and you have to wonder, while you are cooking your dinner in them, what stories they could tell, what histories they have mutely witnessed. New (or long-neglected) cast-iron cookware must first be "seasoned" before it is used: wash with soap and water, dry thoroughly, then rub the entire surface—inside and out—with a very light film of cooking oil. Put the skillet upside down in a 300°F oven for about an hour, then turn off the oven and let the skillet cool overnight. The oil coating should now be "fixed" and dry on the surface of the pan. If it seems tacky or sticky, heat it again. Acidic foods may disintegrate the seasoning and react with the pan, so I usually cook tomato sauces and other acidic foods in stainless-steel or coated cookware. I occasionally give a cast-iron skillet a brief scrub with a soapy dishcloth, but most often the skillet needs only to be wiped out with a paper towel. Deep-frying is excellent for maintaining the seasoning on cast iron. When food is burned onto a cast-iron pan, scrub the residue with salt. If you end up scrubbing the seasoning off, you can easily reseason it.

A couple of **nonstick-coated skillets** are nice to have, especially for cooking eggs, but I have found that the coating disintegrates after several years of use, regardless of how well made the pan itself is.

Many of your pots and pans should have **well-fitting lids**, and ideally, most of them—and their lids—should be able to withstand oven heat. It is a great convenience to be able to start cooking a dish on top of the stove and finish it in the oven, in the same pan.

UTENSILS, ET CETERA

Wooden spoons are indispensable—they will not mar the surfaces of your cookware, and they just get better looking with use. The **heatproof rubber spatula** is my mother's favorite kitchen tool (her mother called them "child cheaters" because they get all the cake batter out of the bowl, with

none left to lick!). An **instant-read thermometer** is a very useful tool, especially for beginning cooks. It's essential for roasting whole chickens, turkeys, roast beef, pork loin, or other large cuts of meat, and if you bake bread, it helps you tell when the bread is done. The old-fashioned meat thermometers, the kind you stick in the roast and leave there during baking, are not as useful.

As for electric appliances, a **toaster** makes better toast than a toaster oven, but the toaster oven is more versatile—you decide. A **blender** purées liquids, while a **food processor** purées more-solid substances. A blender is necessary for silky puréed soups, but a food processor is necessary for certain other things—pulverizing soaked chickpeas for falafel, for instance. Pressed to choose, I'd go with the blender. If you love pesto, a **heavy stone mortar and pestle** (if you are a city dweller, look for these in well-stocked Asian food stores) will coax the truest flavors out of the garlic and basil, but it's practical only for working with small quantities. A food processor makes a large batch of pesto in a jiffy, or if you don't mind adding a great deal of oil, so will a blender, but the violent mechanical action of these devices may subtly diminish some flavors—the flavor of good olive oil, for instance. If you bake a lot, a **stand mixer** is convenient, especially a sturdy one that will knead bread dough.

Supplies needed for the kitchen, and called for in this book, are most conveniently thought of as items that come in rolls: **paper towels**, **plastic wrap**, **aluminum foil**, **baking parchment paper**, **wax paper**, **cheesecloth**, and **butcher's twine**. Of these, parchment paper is the newcomer to home kitchens. It's very good for baking cakes and other items that tend to stick to their pans. A sheet may be lightly crumpled, then reflattened and placed over stewing vegetables, permitting just the right amount of steam to escape. Certain acidic foods will eat holes in aluminum foil, but a sheet of parchment between food and foil will prevent this.

EQUIPMENT LIST

The following list of equipment encompasses everything you will need to cook all the recipes in this book.

Items with ● *are nice to have but not essential.*

Items in [ ] *are necessary only for making the dish in question (ice cream maker, meat grinder, doughnut cutter . . .).*

Blades, steels, and boards

* chef's knife

* paring knife

* small serrated knife

* offset bread knife

* boning knife ●

* [oyster knife]

* kitchen shears

* pizza cutter (not just for pizza—also for cutting fresh pasta noodles or homemade crackers)

* zester or modern "fine-plane" grater ●

* vegetable peeler

* sharpening steel

* sharpening stone ●

* hardwood cutting board

* small cutting board(s) or flexible plastic mats •

Pots and pans

* large (about 4-quart capacity) saucepan with tight-fitting lid

* 2 small (about 1½-quart capacity) saucepans with tight-fitting lids

* smaller saucepan •

* stockpot (deep, 8-quart capacity)

* steamer insert •

* braising pot or soup pot (oven safe; about 4 quarts), with tight-fitting, oven-safe lid

* small nonstick • sauté pan (omelet pan), 6 to 8 inches in diameter

* medium (9- to 10-inch) nonstick • skillet

* large (10- to 12-inch) nonstick • skillet (with tight-fitting lid)

* griddle • (flat, like a skillet, but no sides, for cooking pancakes and such)

* teakettle (metal or glass; for boiling water)

* [teapot] (ceramic or glass; for brewing tea)

* pressure cooker • (great for cooking beans at high altitudes)

* roasting pans (with sides about 2 inches high, one of sufficient capacity to hold a whole chicken, another larger one to hold a whole turkey •)

* baking dishes (9 by 13 inches, 8 by 8 inches)

* 2 round cake pans (9 inches in diameter)

* 1 springform pan • (10 to 12 inches in diameter)

* [1 large tube-style cake pan]

* 2 or 4 • loaf pans

* 2 sheet pans (12 by 17 inches, with rim)

* 2 baking sheets • (also called cookie sheets, without rim)

* [pie plates] (10 inches in diameter, one regular for single-crust pies, one deep for double-crust pies)

Utensils

* 4 or 5 wooden spoons, assorted sizes
* heatproof rubber spatulas
* skimmer (wide, perforated spoon)
* slotted or perforated spoon
* wire whisk
* ladle
* metal spatula (pancake turner)
* tongs
* wooden rolling pin
* instant-read thermometer (powered by a small battery; range should be from freezing to 400°F)
* candy/deep-fry thermometer •
* perforated colander
* screen sieves, one fine-mesh •
* sifter • (screen sieves work well)
* pastry brush •
* [nutcracker and picks]
* corkscrew/bottle opener
* potato masher •

Other equipment

* pepper grinder
* cruet for olive oil •
* 4 or 5 stainless-steel mixing bowls (assorted sizes)
* box grater (with two or three sizes of blade-type holes)
* large stone mortar and pestle • (good for many things, but especially if you love garlic)
* wire cooling racks
* measuring spoon set, two •
* measuring cup set, two •
* salad spinner (not just for salad— good for spin-drying leafy herbs, and shaved potatoes for potato chips)
* toaster and/or toaster oven •
* [ice cream maker]
* blender (more essential than a food processor)
* food mill • (can take the place of a food processor and blender in many cases)

* potato ricer• (a food mill is more versatile)

* food processor (necessary for some recipes)

* [pasta roller-cutter] (hand crank)

* stand mixer•

* electric hand-held mixer•

* [meat grinder with interchangeable blades]

* spatter screen• (to reduce the mess in high-heat stovetop cooking)

* [ramekins] (individual porcelain custard cups, necessary for crème brûlée)

* propane blowtorch• (for crème brûlée)

* coffee grinder•

* another coffee grinder for grinding whole spices•

* jars with lids, various sizes

* terrycloth kitchen towels

* flour sack–type kitchen towels

* [doughnut cutter]

* [coffee cone] (for holding filters)

* kitchen scale, accurate to the quarter-ounce, up to 5 pounds•

* sealable storage containers (plastic, or glass with sealable plastic lids; assorted sizes)

Essential Ingredients

Author Mark Kurlansky, in his book *Salt*, tells of a thousand-year-old Chinese children's song listing the seven necessary kitchen staples needed every day: firewood, rice, oil, salt, soy sauce, vinegar, and tea. What a great list! Can we modern Westerners come up with a similar one? What are the minimal pantry staples needed to cook in North America? Narrowing down the possibilities (for instance, flour and sugar are certainly staples in the Deep Springs kitchen, where baked goods are prepared every day, but not when I cook just for myself or my family), here is an easy-to-remember list of seven items I always have on hand, and that are called for in this book constantly: *salt, pepper, olive oil, butter, lemons, garlic, and onions*. With these items, you can prepare virtually any fresh food (vegetables, fruit, nuts, grains, meat, eggs, dairy) simply but deliciously, whether you are making appetizers, soup, salad, a main course, dessert . . . or all of the above. Many meats need no seasoning besides salt and pepper; fish and shellfish usually need only salt and perhaps a little lemon; garlic and onions enhance virtually any savory food; butter and lemon are the foundation for many sauces and desserts.

These fundamentals, plus several other common ingredients frequently called for in this book, deserve further mention and explanation.

BAKING POWDER AND BAKING SODA

See page 106.

BUTTER

When people ask me what my favorite food is, I love to say, "Butter." For a lavish Christmas party, my friend Elge and I once offered a "butter bar"—a black marble slab with several different kinds of "artisan" butter for guests to taste on plain French bread. If you love butter, try some of these more expensive butters—they're delicious. Or, best of all, make your own, as we do at Deep Springs (see page 141).

A few of the recipes in this book specify salted or unsalted butter, but most simply say "butter," and you may use whatever you have on hand. Are there any differences between salted and unsalted butter, other than the obvious? Yes: unsalted butter, also known as "sweet butter," has a shorter shelf life, so if you purchase it within the "sell by" date printed on the package, you will usually have fresher butter. Salted butter, with its slightly longer shelf life, usually has a more intense butter flavor. Sometimes you might find "European-style" butter, with a lower moisture content (and a correspondingly higher fat content) than American butter. The cream

used to make it is first cultured, like sour cream.

Butter is not pure fat, but clarified butter is, and so is Indian **ghee**. Melt a stick of unsalted butter over a low flame, undisturbed. As soon as the butter is completely melted and a thick white foam has formed on top, carefully skim off all the foam with a wide spoon (save this in a bowl; it's very good on toast). What remains in the pan is a thick layer of pure butterfat over a thin layer of milk solids and water. Were you to pour off the pure fat and heat it again in a clean pan, again skimming the foam to remove residual water, you would have **clarified butter**, which is excellent for pan-frying (see page 375). To make ghee, continue heating the butter after you have skimmed off the foam. As the layer of water evaporates out of the fat, you will hear a merry sizzling sound. Once all the water cooks off, the sizzling quiets. The milk solids remaining on the bottom of the pan will then toast to a nutty brown and flavor the butter. At this point, when the butter releases a nutty, toasted aroma, pour the ghee out of the pan and into a metal bowl to cool. If you simply melt a pat of butter in a wide pan until it turns toast brown, you have made **brown**

butter, great on Brussels sprouts (see page 220).

For a good alternative to pure butter for your toast, just whisk up to ¼ cup of canola or other flavorless vegetable oil into a stick of softened butter until there are no lumps (the blender will do this easily and quickly). While this blend won't work well for baked goods in which butter plays a significant role, it may be used in any recipe that calls for a small quantity of butter.

Unless you use butter infrequently or your kitchen is hot, store your table butter in a covered container at room temperature.

BUTTERMILK
See page 106.

CANNED FOOD
Canned food was hailed as a miracle when the technology was first developed in the late 1800s and early 1900s. Nowadays it receives a great deal of disdain, but we needn't turn up our noses at canned food completely; some of the recipes in this book call for various canned tomato products, a couple of lunch dishes call for canned condensed soup, and canned tuna is, of course, a convenient American staple. But for the most part, the high-heat canning

process causes the flavor and nutritive quality of foods to deteriorate to such an extent that manufacturers must add enormous quantities of sugar, salt, and other substances to make them taste good. Fresh or frozen food is almost always better.

CITRUS
Lemons, oranges, limes, and other citrus are essential for lively-flavored food, as important for the intense oils in their zest, or outer colored skin, as for their sweet or tart juice. Though major varieties of citrus fruit are available in supermarkets year-round, the season for the best citrus is December through March, peaking in January. Some citrus varieties, such as blood oranges, have even shorter seasons. The juiciest specimens are heavy for their size and have smaller pores. I use lemons and limes year-round, but I make a practice of avoiding oranges and other citrus during summer and early fall, when many other fruits are in season to be enjoyed. Then, in the darkest, coldest time of the year, the sweet, vibrant taste of the first oranges seems like a gift.

CHOCOLATE
Theobroma, food of the gods! Visiting an arboretum, I once saw a cacao (chocolate) bush and a coffee bush

growing side by side; they are clearly botanical cousins.

The dessert chapters in this book contain recipes for chocolate pudding, chocolate cakes, chocolate sauce, chocolate cream pie, brownies, and several different kinds of chocolate chip cookies, all relying on the most readily available and least expensive forms of chocolate: unsweetened cocoa powder and chocolate chips. But chocolate has developed a winelike connoisseurship recently; many varieties are available, some quite expensive. If you wish to use bars of high-quality chocolate in place of chocolate chips in any of these recipes, you will not be disappointed. Try chocolate chip cookies made with bittersweet Belgian or Swiss chocolate, hand-chopped with a knife into rough, uneven "chips." A little of the chocolate may melt and ooze out, showing a different character.

In Mexico and the rest of Latin America, chocolate has always been thought of primarily as a beverage, what we call hot chocolate, rather than as a solid candy. Solid sweet Mexican chocolate, usually flavored with cinnamon and almonds, is rough and grainy with sugar crystals, designed to be dissolved in rapidly boiling water. Once dissolved, the brew is whipped with a traditional wooden whip called a *molinillo* until an appealing froth forms on the top (chocolate naturally contains a bit of starch, enabling this froth to form). In some parts of South America, a hot drink of chocolate is customarily served unsweetened, with sugar packets on the side for those who like it sweet, and milk for those who like it creamy. In this form, and in the caffeine jolt you will quickly receive, chocolate's kinship with coffee once again becomes apparent.

Chocolate is composed of two substances, chocolate liquor and cocoa butter. Unsweetened cocoa powder is mostly chocolate liquor (the name has nothing to do with alcohol), containing most of the pigments and characteristic flavor compounds we know as "chocolate." Cocoa butter, on the other hand, contains all the fatty richness we associate with solid chocolate but few of the flavor compounds. White chocolate, devoid of chocolate liquor, is made of cocoa butter, sugar, and vanilla. Many of the chocolate dessert recipes in this book call for unsweetened cocoa powder, and all will be perfectly good if made with a leading brand. However, sometimes you may find other cocoa powders that are richer and darker than the leading supermarket brands—

"Dutch-processed" cocoa, for example. These yield excellent results.

In a practice reaching far back into pre-Columbian times, chocolate is also occasionally treated as a spice, deepening the roasty-toasty flavor of chiles—a little is called for in some of this book's Mexican and Southwestern recipes. Conversely, a pinch of cayenne pepper (or other hot chile) curiously piques and enhances the flavor of many a chocolate dessert.

COFFEE

A couple of the cake recipes in the book call for brewed coffee, and the breakfast chapters mention it frequently. If you love coffee, it would be a worthwhile experiment to purchase green coffee beans to roast and grind yourself, as was the common practice of yesteryear. Roasting, during which myriad flavor compounds are formed, is simple enough to do but exceedingly complex chemically. Since many of these compounds are quite unstable, the most flavorful coffee is made of very freshly roasted beans. The darkest roast is not necessarily the most flavorful; medium-roast coffee often has a wonderful complexity of aromas and flavors. Store your coffee, whether ground or whole-bean, in an airtight container in the freezer.

To make a great cup of coffee, consider the following ideal scenario: toast your green coffee beans slowly in a pan in a 300°F oven, tossing and redistributing them every 5 minutes, until they are a color that pleases you. Finely grind your beans in a coffee grinder and put a kettle of cold water on to boil. Position a paper filter in a filter cone over your favorite mug. Put 2 heaping tablespoons of ground coffee in the filter (more if your mug is abnormally large). The moment the water reaches a boil, pour the water over the coffee, thoroughly moistening the grounds. You will see tiny rainbowy bubbles coming off the grounds as the water seeps through; this is called "bloom." Once the first pour of water has filtered through, pour another, enough to fill your cup. Stir the grounds gently with a spoon, being careful not to rip the filter. Once your second pour has filtered through, your coffee is ready to enjoy.

GARLIC AND ONIONS

Cook your way through the savory chapters of this book, and you will be reaching for onions and garlic constantly. Both have been very successfully grown at Deep Springs for years—and used with abandon by the Student Cooks. Chopping and sautéing **onions** are fundamental kitchen tasks—it's the first thing I teach Student Cooks, and when I taught a culinary arts class, the first thing I demonstrated was dicing an onion (afterward, the students liked to say, "Tom made us cry on the first day of class."). Actually, if your knife is quite sharp, fewer fumes will be released, whereas a dull knife crushes more of the onion's cells, releasing more fumes. To lessen the effect of the fumes, light a candle nearby. Watch out for onions with any soft or rotten parts—cut these away entirely.

Garlic is an almost addictive ingredient—it not only tastes good in its own right, but it enhances the flavors of everything else. To peel fresh garlic, separate the head into cloves, and then with a small knife, cut the stem end off a clove. Often the skin will peel right off—lightly crushing the clove helps release the skin. If the clove of garlic seems dry, shrunken, or yellowed, or has a granulated surface, it has not stayed fresh—throw it out. Cut out any brown spots. For garlic that will be used raw, cut each clove in half and pry out the tough little sprout in the center. This part tastes especially harsh and bitter. If the garlic will be cooked, it's okay to leave the sprout in. Garlic may be minced with a knife, but crushing it allows more of its flavor to

be released and dispersed throughout the dish. Many good cooks swear by a garlic press. A heavy stone mortar and pestle does a beautiful job of crushing a small handful of garlic to a smooth, flavorful purée. When a recipe calls for just a clove or two or three, you can easily crush the split cloves to a juicy purée with the back edge of your chef's knife, and there's no extra equipment to wash.

Shallots have a finer, smoother, more intense savor than onions—some cuisines of the world use them exclusively. Use shallots in recipes that call for them—then try the same recipe with onion and note the difference. A small shallot, grated into a cup of yogurt, with a little salt and pepper stirred in, makes a superlative sauce for any simple food (see page 424).

Avoid using prepeeled, prechopped onions, garlic, or shallots. Since the flavor compounds in these vegetables are so volatile, such products must be heavily treated with preservatives. For the same reason, don't be tempted to chop your onions and garlic far ahead of time. There simply is no substitute or shortcut for peeling and chopping fresh onions and garlic yourself, as you need them—all that is required is your knives, a little practice, and patience.

The flavors in your cooking will have a deep, complex sweetness and savor.

FLOUR

Wheat flour is the staple grain of half the world, playing a fundamental role in European-derived cuisines. As grains go, wheat is high in protein and sustained many of our forebears. There are numerous types of wheat flour on the market: all-purpose, unbleached, whole wheat, white whole wheat, bleached, bread flour, cake flour, semolina flour, self-rising flour. Choosing flour can be confusing to a beginner.

What we commonly know as "white flour" is more properly known—and labeled—as **all-purpose flour**. To keep things simple, all the recipes in the book have been tested using this basic flour. If you like, you may use **bread flour** in the bread recipes (bread flour has a higher protein content than all-purpose; wheat's elastic protein gives bread its characteristic springy texture). You can also use **cake flour** in the cake and quick bread recipes (cake flour has a lower protein content than all-purpose, and so makes for lighter, softer-textured baked goods). I highly recommend choosing **unbleached all-purpose flour** (not to be confused with whole-wheat flour) over flour labeled "bleached." In my experience,

name-brand flour will perform more consistently than bargain brands or store brands. In the American South, **self-rising flour** is popular for biscuits and such. It is made of softer wheat than all-purpose flour, and has baking powder and salt already mixed in. The recipes printed on packages of self-rising flour should yield good results, but don't use self-rising flour for the recipes in this book.

Semolina flour is made from pale yellow, high-protein durum wheat (the same wheat used in macaroni, spaghetti, and other dried pasta) and has a sandlike texture. This granular texture makes it good for dusting fresh pasta noodles, and it can be added to bread doughs (see Pizza, page 155).

Learning to make fresh pasta (see page 388) is a particularly good, direct way to learn about the properties of flour. Knowledge thus gained will carry over into breadmaking and the baking of quick breads, piecrust, and cakes.

OLIVE OIL

While olive oil is much touted for its health benefits, it's important to remember that other, cheaper vegetable oils contain many of the same beneficial compounds. Olive oil is good to use because it tastes so delicious.

Extra-virgin olive oil is pressed from olives using only mechanical extraction—no heat or solvents are used. Extra-virgin olive oil has the deepest olive flavor. **Pure olive oil** is extracted from olives using heat or solvent extraction methods—it doesn't have as strong an olive flavor, but it's fine for frying. Sometimes in food-service settings, you will see something labeled "olive pomace oil." This flavorless oil is extracted from olive pits and the residue left over from olive oil pressing; under international law it is not allowed to be labeled as olive oil. **Extra-light olive oil** has emerged on the market recently. It costs the same as regular olive oil but has no flavor or aroma. If you want a lighter-tasting oil, just blend a little extra-virgin into a larger quantity of canola oil. Even among extra-virgin oils, you'll find many varieties and prices. I tend to buy less-expensive extra-virgin olive oil and use it for both cooking and salads. When I have a bottle of great extra-virgin olive oil, I use it where its flavor will be most appreciated: in delicate green salads, on hot pasta with garlic, in mashed potatoes in place of the butter, or simply drizzled on bread.

PEPPER

Black pepper is by far the most commonly used spice in European-derived cooking. History books say that demand for it ultimately led to the Europeans' "discovery" of the Americas. It not only provides a little spicy kick, but actually acts as a flavor enhancer, too. Even foods rich with other hot spices, such as chili or curry, often reach their balance with a touch of black pepper. Black pepper is made by soaking and drying unripe pepper berries after harvest. A naturally occurring enzyme causes the outer skin to shrivel and blacken (you have probably noticed that the inside of a peppercorn is white). This process creates many complex flavor compounds. These, in turn, enhance other flavors. **White pepper** is made by soaking off the peppercorn's outer skin in water, leaving only the inner seed. The peppercorns undergo a slight fermentation in this process, so their flavor is different, a bit cheese-like. White pepper is much used in Chinese cooking. **Green peppercorns** are freeze-dried and have a mild, fresh, almost floral scent. They are the least processed form of pepper, being neither fermented nor soaked.

As pepper is an essential kitchen seasoning, so a pepper grinder is an essential kitchen tool. Many of those aforementioned complex flavor compounds evaporate when ground pepper sits around for too long; *only freshly ground pepper fulfills pepper's full promise*. In addition to grinding pepper, I sometimes even sieve it: using a fine-mesh wire strainer and a regular-mesh strainer, I sift the pepper into three grades: fine, coarse, and cracked. I always try to use the coarse grind in egg salad (see page 166) and other preparations where the powdery fine grind would turn the dish gray.

What is "red pepper"? It's a common name for **cayenne**—small, very hot, bright red chile pods that are dried and then used whole, or crushed coarsely, or finely ground. Many recipes in this book call for a pinch. Its intense heat is bright, clean, and forward, without lingering in the mouth the way many other hot chiles do. When small, hot, red chile pods are crushed coarsely, they are referred to as **hot red pepper flakes** and are important in Italian cooking.

SALT

In the first terrifying, frustrating, but ultimately rewarding weeks of cooking for the entire Deep Springs community when I was a student, I remember learning two extremely important things: (1) to turn the stove burner down, and (2) to add salt until the food tasted good.

Why do we, like many animals, crave salt? Why does it taste so good to us? I have a theory: it has to do with trace minerals. Pure salt, or sodium chloride, is relatively rare in nature. A host of other minerals, many of which are essential to our body chemistry, exist in trace quantities alongside the sodium chloride in seawater and salt deposits (which are ancient dried seawater). This same mineral balance exists in our blood; we are, literally, the salt of the earth or, more directly, the salt of the oceans. Until quite recently in our evolutionary history, we humans consumed unrefined salt from these natural sources. Nowadays, industries extract and use the minerals, one reason why pure salt—the leftover—is so cheap. Virtually all salt on the market today is refined, even if it's labeled "sea salt." And so, even if we consume a lot of refined salt, we continue craving salt because our bodies require the trace minerals that always accompany salt in its natural state.

The salt craving reaches a zenith with professional cooks (especially men), who, tasting food all day, typically become inured to the taste of salt, and so tend to oversalt their food. Many years ago, I started using truly unrefined sea salt in all my cooking at home. Of course, such salt is more expensive than refined salt, though not prohibitively so. Most varieties are pale gray and somewhat moist. I've found that when I use this salt consistently, I don't use too much—I enjoy under-salted or even unsalted food much more than I used to.

Judicious use of salt is fundamental to good cooking. Salt is the great balancer—it offsets acidity (for example, tomatoes need a lot of salt) and balances sweet-ness (most of the dessert recipes in this book call for a pinch). If you have oversalted a dish, you can sometimes correct your error by adding an acidic component—lemon juice or tomatoes. When sautéing many vegetables together, add them to the pan one at a time, beginning with the one that needs the longest cooking. With each addition, add a pinch of salt to the pan—this is called "salting from the bottom up" and allows the individual flavors to remain distinct. Many recipes in this book direct you to do this. It is important to salt all or most of the elements in composed dishes—all the components of lasagna, for instance, are individually seasoned, and potatoes to be added to soup taste best when boiled separately in well-salted water.

A note on kosher salt: A very few recipes (for pickles and brines) in this book specify kosher salt. This is especially pure, refined salt with a unique crystalline structure that makes it lighter than other kinds of salt; a tablespoon of kosher salt weighs much less than a tablespoon of regular table salt. Use kosher salt in recipes that specify it—the minerals in other salts could adversely affect the recipe.

SPICES (AND HERBS)

By **"spice,"** we mean dried, intensely aromatic plant material, usually used in small quantities, such as seeds (mus-tard, fennel, coriander), berries (pep-per), fruits (cayenne, paprika), buds (cloves), flowers (saffron), and bark (cinnamon). Aromatic leaves, fresh or dried, are, of course, called **herbs**. With herbs, fresh is most often better, though dried forms of some (such as bay, oregano, thyme, and sage) are traditional in many a dish. I tend to use dried spices sparingly, to enhance, not dominate, a food's inherent flavors. Even spice-heavy preparations such as Indian curry must be carefully bal-anced to be good.

Dried spices are best stored in a dark cabinet; they lose their flavor and aroma over time, especially if exposed to heat and light. I think standard spice jars are too big. Whenever pos-sible, buy spices in quantities you are likely to use up within a year. Most of my spice jars are quite small, and I keep larger quantities of spices—and lesser-used ones—well wrapped and sealed in the freezer, to better preserve their volatile aromas. I usually buy whole spices, grinding them as needed in a coffee grinder designated for the purpose. Here is a list of all the spices (and dried herbs) called for in this book:

Whole spices and herbs

* black peppercorns (used very frequently if you have a pepper grinder)
* caraway seed (occasional)
* cardamom (occasional)
* celery seed
* cinnamon sticks (occasional)
* cloves
* coriander
* cumin
* fennel seed
* juniper berries (occasional)
* marjoram (occasional)
* mustard seed (yellow or black)
* nutmeg
* oregano
* red pepper flakes

* saffron (occasional)
* thyme
* white pepper

Ground or powdered spices and herbs

* black pepper (used very frequently if you do not have a pepper grinder)
* cayenne pepper (used frequently)
* cinnamon
* cloves
* cumin
* curry powder (see page 358 for a recipe)
* ginger
* mace (occasional)
* dry mustard
* paprika
* sage
* turmeric (for blending curry powder)
* white pepper

VINEGAR AND OTHER FLAVORFUL THINGS IN BOTTLES

The word *vinegar* comes from the French *vinaigre*, literally meaning "sour wine." Alcohol in wine (or hard cider) may, when exposed to air over a long period, convert into acetic acid. Whatever characteristics the wine or cider had will contribute to the character of its corresponding vinegar. Vinegar, even vinegar of good quality, is relatively cheap, and a little goes a long way, so I like to have several varieties on hand. This book frequently calls for the following three vinegars: **red wine vinegar**, **balsamic vinegar** (made by a more complex process than other vinegars), and **apple cider vinegar**.

Other types of vinegar, such as **sherry vinegar**, **champagne vinegar**, or **malt vinegar**, are also worth experiencing. Vinegars flavored with herbs or fruit may be appealing, but I find that they are not as versatile as the three above. I keep **white distilled vinegar** under the kitchen sink, with the cleaning products—I prefer vinegar with more character for use in food.

Alongside the vinegars in my kitchen pantry, I keep a few other flavorful bottled items: **Worcestershire sauce**, a timeless, curious blend of molasses, tamarind, anchovies, and shallots; **soy sauce**, occasionally used in non-Asian recipes; **Tabasco** or other fiery hot

sauce; and various pure extracts— **vanilla**, **almond**, and **lemon** are all called for in this book's dessert recipes. Finally, I'm particularly fond of flower waters, frequently used in Middle Eastern cookery, particularly **rosewater** and **orange flower water**. These intensely perfumy waters are best used sparingly—sprinkled lightly over food just before serving. They are delicious on sweet summer melon (see page 464). Rosewater is called for in some very old American baking recipes; there is a little in this book's pound cake (see page 482). And I find that a few drops of rosewater or orange flower water often improve the taste of a glass of cheap wine.

Measuring

MEASURING FLOUR

When a recipe in this book specifies "sifted flour," it means that the flour must be sifted prior to measuring. Since we in the United States prefer our volume measurements (cups and teaspoons and tablespoons) to the more accurate weighing common in Europe, sifting flour before measuring will ensure that you get the same amount each time. But I cheat a little—I simply "fluff up" any flour I'm about to measure by sifting it through my hand or with a spoon. Then I gently spoon the flour into the measuring cup and level the cup off with a straight-edged object such as the back of a knife. Don't tap the cup or pack the flour down into the cup. This is especially important when multiplying a recipe—I always advise Deep Springs Student Cooks to measure the flour for cakes cup by cup, or to weigh it.

MEASURING OTHER INGREDIENTS

Liquids are best measured in glass or plastic liquid measuring cups, with clearly marked gradations. Dry ingredients are best measured in metal or plastic measuring cups that can be leveled off. Substances like brown sugar must be firmly packed into the cup. Sticks of butter as usually packaged are easy to measure with the aid of the markings on the wrapper and your good eye. If you have butter that is not conventionally packaged, use the displacement method: to measure ½ cup of butter, take a 1-cup liquid measuring cup and put ½ cup of cold water in it. Add butter, pressing the butter just below the surface of the water. When the water reaches the 1-cup mark, pour off the water and you have ½ cup of butter.

When a recipe calls for ⅛ teaspoon of a dry ingredient (usually salt), measure out ¼ teaspoon of the ingredient onto a plate, then divide the pile in half evenly with a knife.

Useful equivalents

1 cup = 16 tablespoons

1 cup (liquid) = 8 ounces

2 cups = 1 pint

1 pint = 1 pound; "A pint's a pound the world around."

4 cups = 2 pints = 1 quart

4 quarts = 1 gallon

—

1 tablespoon = 3 teaspoons

4 tablespoons = ¼ cup

1 ounce butter = 2 tablespoons

1 stick butter = ½ cup

1 cup grated cheese = about 4 ounces, or ¼ pound

2 cups sugar = 1 pound

2 cups butter = 1 pound

4 cups sifted flour = 1 pound

4 jumbo eggs = about 1 cup

5 large eggs = about 1 cup

—

1 cup whole almonds = 4½ ounces

1 cup walnut halves and pieces = 3¼ ounces

1 cup chopped walnuts = 3¾ ounces

2 cups dry beans = about 1 pound

1 cup chocolate chips = 6 ounces

—

6-ounce portion of meat = about the size of two decks of cards

1 ounce of cheese = about the size of your thumb

METRIC EQUIVALENTS OF U.S. MEASUREMENTS

Volume

U.S. MEASURE	METRIC EQUIVALENT	ROUND TO
¼ tsp	1.2333 ml	1 ml
½ tsp	2.4645 ml	2.5 ml
1 tsp	4.929 ml	5 ml
1 tbsp	14.787 ml	15 ml
2 tbsp	29.574 ml	30 ml
3 tbsp	44.361 ml	45 ml
¼ cup	59.148 ml	60 ml
⅓ cup	78.815 ml	80 ml
½ cup	118.30 ml	120 ml
⅔ cup	157.63 ml	160 ml
¾ cup	177.44 ml	175 ml
1 cup	236.59 ml	240 ml
1 pint	473.18 ml	475 ml
1 quart	946.08 ml	950 ml
2 quarts	1.89 L	1.9 L
3 quarts	2.838 L	2.85 L
1 gallon	3.784 L	3.8 L

Weight

U.S. MEASURE	METRIC EQUIVALENT	ROUND TO
¼ oz	7.0874 g	7 g
½ oz	14.175 g	14 g
1 oz	28.35 g	28 g
4 oz	113.4 g	113 g
6 oz	170.1 g	170 g
8 oz	226.8 g	227 g
12 oz	340.19 g	340 g
1 lb	453.59 g	454 g
2 lb	907.19 g	907 g
3 lb	1.3608 kg	1.4 kg
4 lb	1.8144 kg	1.8 kg
5 lb	2.2680 kg	2.25 kg
10 lb	4.5359 kg	4.5 kg

Length

U.S. MEASURE	METRIC EQUIVALENT	ROUND TO
¼ inch	6.35 mm	6.5 mm
½ inch	1.27 cm	1.25 cm
¾ inch	1.905 cm	1.9 cm
1 inch	2.54 cm	2.5 cm

continued . . .

Length *continued...*

U.S. MEASURE	METRIC EQUIVALENT	ROUND TO
6 inches	15.24 cm	15.25 cm
8 inches	20.32 cm	20 cm
9 inches	22.86 cm	23 cm
10 inches	25.4 cm	25 cm
1 foot	30.48 cm	30.5 cm

Temperature

U.S. MEASURE	METRIC EQUIVALENT	ROUND TO
0° F	-17.78° C	-18° C
40° F	4.4444° C	4° C
100° F	37.778° C	38° C
125° F	51.667° C	52° C
135° F	57.222° C	57° C
140° F	60° C	60° C
150° F	65.556° C	66° C
154° F	67.778° C	68° C
160° F	71.111° C	71° C
170° F	76.667° C	77° C
175° F	79.444° C	79° C
180° F	82.222° C	82° C
190° F	87.778° C	88° C
200° F	93.333° C	93° C
212° F	100° C	100° C

U.S. MEASURE	METRIC EQUIVALENT	ROUND TO
225° F	107.22° C	107° C
250° F	121.11° C	121° C
275° F	135° C	135° C (Gas Mark 1)
300° F	148.89° C	149° C (Gas Mark 2)
325° F	162.78° C	163° C (Gas Mark 3)
350° F	176.67° C	177° C (Gas Mark 4)
375° F	190.56° C	190° C (Gas Mark 5)
400° F	204.44° C	204° C (Gas Mark 6)
425° F	218.33° C	218° C (Gas Mark 7)
450° F	232.22° C	232° C (Gas Mark 8)
475° F	246.11° C	246° C
500° F	260° C	260° C
525° F	273.89° C	274° C
550° F	287.78° C	288° C
575° F	301.67° C	302° C
600° F	315.56° C	316° C
700° F	371.11° C	371° C
800° F	426.67° C	427° C
900° F	482.22° C	482° C

CHAPTER 2

Breakfast: Oats, Grits, Bacon, and Eggs

Deep Springs students have legendarily hearty appetites, even for young men, thanks to all the hard physical work and long periods of mental concentration. Therefore, the big, cholesterol-laden American ranch breakfast is alive and well every day at Deep Springs; eggs, bacon, quick breads, and pancakes are all mainstays. However, at the behest of older, more sedentary, health-conscious community members, the cooks often make a pot of oatmeal and set out yogurt and a tray of cut fresh fruit. While much of the oatmeal may go uneaten, ending up as slop for the pigs, no matter how much bacon the cooks make, there is rarely any left over.

In this chapter, you'll find recipes for wholesome, lighter, every-day breakfasts for adult metabolisms alongside old-fashioned ranch breakfast recipes for young hard workers and hard thinkers.

Oatmeal

SERVES 2

A bowl of piping-hot oatmeal, cooked with a little milk, topped with butter, and augmented with dried fruit, seeds, and other flavorful accompaniments, is a breakfast of particular savor.

1 teaspoon butter

1 cup rolled oats (regular or old-fashioned, not quick or instant)

2 cups water

¼ teaspoon salt

1 cup milk

FOR SERVING (ANY COMBINATION)

butter

milk, half-and-half, or cream

buttermilk or yogurt

brown sugar, honey, maple syrup, jam or jelly, fruit preserves

bananas, blueberries, peaches, pears, Fuyu persimmons, or other fresh sweet fruit (acidic fruit doesn't marry well)

dates, raisins, dried cherries, dried cranberries, or other dried fruit, cut small

stewed fruit (prunes simmered with orange slices, dried pears simmered with a cinnamon stick, dried apricots simmered with ginger)

almonds, walnuts, pecans, or other nuts

sunflower, sesame, or flax seeds

Melt the butter in a medium-sized, heavy saucepan over medium-high heat. Add the dry oats and *lightly toast the oats*, stirring and tossing constantly, keeping everything moving, until a nutty smell emerges from the pan. (The butter adds flavor, and the fat in the butter aids in the toasting, but it may be omitted—just toast the oats in a dry pan.) Some of the grains may turn pale gold, but otherwise *the grains should not visibly darken*. Immediately add the water, salt, and milk, and cook until the mixture comes to a boil. Reduce the heat to medium-low and cook, stirring frequently, until thick and creamy, about 10 minutes. Add more milk or water if you like a soupier consistency. For richer oatmeal, use half water, half milk. If you like raisins cooked with your oatmeal, add them when you add the liquid. Serve with any combination of the suggested toppings.

Steel-Cut Oats

If you love oatmeal but have never tried steel-cut oats, you are in for a treat. Steel-cut oats are used for the classic "porridge" of Ireland and Scotland. Rolled oats (the type most familiar in the United States) are made by steaming oat berries before they are flattened by rollers, whereas steel-cut oats, as the name suggests, are simply unprocessed oat berries cut into small pieces with powerful steel cutters. Steel-cut oats, being less processed, are more nutritious and delicious. What's more, this type of oatmeal can be reheated with almost no loss of integrity.

Follow the directions for regular oatmeal (see facing page), using the following slightly different proportions, and simmer the oatmeal for about 20 minutes, rather than 10. Taste to determine if the grains are tender to your liking or if they need more time. Stir frequently, going over the bottom of the pan with your wooden spoon to make sure nothing is sticking.

1 teaspoon butter

⅔ cup steel-cut oats

2 cups water

¼ teaspoon salt

⅔ cup milk

(For convenience, I often cook steel-cut oats in a rice cooker. First toast the oats with the butter in a skillet, then add them to 2 cups water and the salt in the cooker, and stir frequently as the oatmeal comes to a boil—this helps prevent bubbling over. After the cooker switches off, let the oatmeal sit undisturbed for about 20 minutes. Then thoroughly stir in the cup of milk, turn the cooker on again, let it come back up to a simmer, and serve.)

OTHER COOKED BREAKFAST CEREALS

Oats are naturally sweet, readily releasing their unctuous starch in the cooking—hence oatmeal's perennial popularity. You might also find rolled *rye flakes* or *barley flakes* or *spelt flakes,* or the steel-cut or cracked form of these grains. These can be cooked like oats and have their own unique nutty flavors and degrees of starchiness. Just like rye bread, cooked rye cereal is excellent with a touch of orange zest. Polenta (page 404) also makes a satisfying breakfast porridge (especially in its perishable whole-grain form) that is particularly tasty with dried cherries. Quinoa (page 407), a grain uniquely high in protein, is especially fortifying for breakfast, but I think its unique, vegetal flavor is best with savory accompaniments, such as tomatoes, chiles, cheese, and nuts, rather than sweet fruits, sugar, or syrup.

Grits

SERVES 4 TO 6

Dear to the heart of many a Southerner. Serve with syrup, sausage, and fried eggs.

  2 cups water

  2 cups milk

  1 cup quick grits

  ½ teaspoon salt

  2 tablespoons butter

Bring the water and milk to a boil in a medium-sized, heavy saucepan, being careful not to let it boil over. Reduce the heat a bit and slowly whisk in the grits. Let cook, stirring frequently, until thickened, about 5 minutes. Cover the pan, remove from the heat, and let sit for about 5 minutes. Add the salt and butter.

Fried Grits

Follow the procedure for Fried Polenta (page 405), to which grits are a close cousin. This puts a grin on longtime Deep Springs mechanic Chuck Teel's face every time, no matter how bad a day it is.

Elaine's Baked Grits

SERVES 6 TO 8

Chuck Teel's wife (see the Fried Grits variation at left) gave me the recipe for this savory breakfast casserole.

  4 cups water

  2 cups milk

  3 teaspoons salt

  1¾ cups quick grits

  4 tablespoons butter

  ¼ teaspoon black pepper

  pinch of paprika

  pinch of cayenne pepper

  dash of Worcestershire sauce

  3 cups (12 ounces) grated sharp Cheddar cheese

  3 eggs, lightly beaten

  one 4-ounce can chopped green chiles, mild or hot, drained slightly

  about ½ cup mild or hot salsa

Heat the oven to 375°F. Bring the water and milk to a boil in a medium-sized, heavy saucepan, add 2 teaspoons of the salt, and then whisk in the grits. Bring to a boil again, and lower the heat. Cook, stirring frequently with a wooden spoon, for about 10 minutes. Let the grits cool for about 15 minutes. Add the butter, remaining 1 teaspoon salt, black pepper, paprika, cayenne, Worcestershire, cheese, eggs, and chiles. Pour into a buttered 9-by-13-inch pan. Sprinkle salsa on top. Bake for about 1 hour, or until set. Let cool for 10 minutes before serving.

Granola

MAKES ABOUT 12 CUPS

My longtime friends (excellent home cooks who once worked as librarians at Deep Springs) make a version of this delicious, basic, not-too-sweet granola once a month. If you want to add raisins, stir them in after the granola has cooled. Sometimes, in summer, I make a triple batch of granola for breakfast at Deep Springs, serving it alongside fresh home-made yogurt.

½ cup vegetable oil

¾ cup honey

10 cups rolled oats

½ cup unsweetened flaked coconut

½ cup raw sunflower seeds

¼ cup sesame seeds

1 heaping cup coarsely chopped raw almonds

¼ cup wheat germ

½ teaspoon salt

FOR SERVING

fresh fruit

yogurt, milk, or buttermilk

continued...

. . . continued

Heat the oven to 275°F. Warm the oil and honey together to a simmer in a small pan, and toss thoroughly with the oats in a large mixing bowl. Add the coconut, sunflower seeds, sesame seeds, almonds, wheat germ, and salt, and toss thoroughly. Spread the mixture onto 2 large rimmed baking sheets and toast slowly in the oven, tossing and redistributing every 15 minutes, until the oats and coconut are an appealing golden color, about 1 hour. Watch the granola carefully, especially toward the end. Let cool completely on the sheets (tossing a few times as it cools), then carefully transfer to zipper-lock bags or a storage container.

Serve with fresh fruit and yogurt, milk, or buttermilk.

Griddle Toast

SERVES 1

Just set a skillet over a medium flame (or use the pancake griddle as we do at Deep Springs), generously butter a thick slice of bread on both sides (the basic dinner bread recipe in this book is excellent for toast), and toast the bread in the skillet, checking it carefully and turning it a few times, until it is golden brown.

Milk Toast

Cut a slice of Griddle Toast (recipe above) into quarters, and put the pieces in a bowl. Heat a cup of milk until hot and steaming, and pour it over the toast. Salt lightly and serve with a spoon. Sometimes this is all you want.

Bready Egg

The childhood stay-home-sick-from-school favorite. Tear a piece of Griddle Toast (recipe at top) into bite-sized pieces, dropping them into a warmed bowl. Scoop a fresh, warm soft-boiled egg (page 102) out of its shell and over the toast. Mix to coat the bread with egg. Salt lightly and serve.

Gashouse Egg or One-Eyed Egyptian

Cut a 2-inch round hole in the center of a slice of bread with a cookie cutter, or cut a diamond-shaped hole with a knife. Toast on one side as for Griddle Toast (recipe at left), then flip the bread. Put a very small pat of butter into the bread's hole, then immediately crack an egg into the hole. Cook carefully to set the underside of the egg, and flip again to cook the white of the egg through, letting the yolk remain runny. Salt and pepper to taste. Serve with ham or sausage.

This egg-and-toast dish goes by many other names, including moon egg, egg in a nest, chicken in a basket, knothole egg, and one-eyed jack.

French Toast

SERVES 2 TO 3

The plain Dinner Bread recipe (page 134) works beautifully for French toast; the richer variation—with eggs and extra butter in the dough—is even better, but the Sweet Potato Bread (page 139) just might be the best of all.

2 eggs, lightly beaten

1 cup milk

¼ teaspoon sugar

¼ teaspoon vanilla extract

pinch of salt

6 or 7 thick slices bread

butter for cooking

FOR SERVING (CHOOSE ONE)

butter and maple syrup

jam and powdered sugar

yogurt and fresh fruit

In a wide, flat-bottomed dish (I use an 8-by-8-inch glass baking dish), whisk together the eggs, milk, sugar, vanilla, and salt. Submerge the slices of bread in the

continued...

. . . continued

milk mixture and let them soak for 10 to 15 minutes. Melt a pat of butter in a wide skillet over medium-high heat, swirling to coat the bottom. When the butter's sizzling subsides, lay in 2 to 3 slices of the saturated bread. Cook until brown on one side, then flip and cook the other side, turning the flame down to medium to allow the French toast to cook all the way through without burning on the outside. Wipe out the skillet with a paper towel, raise the heat again, add another pat of butter, and cook the remaining pieces in the same manner.

Serve with butter and maple syrup, or jam and powdered sugar, or yogurt and fresh fruit.

Simple Breakfast Potatoes

SERVES 3 TO 4
LARGE QUANTITY RECIPE: SERVES 30 TO 40

This is an easy method for delicious, crispy potatoes to accompany your bacon and eggs. This recipe can be increased to feed a crowd—alternate amounts are provided, as they are for large-quantity recipes throughout the book.

1½ pounds medium red potatoes
30 medium red potatoes

1 tablespoon salt, plus more for seasoning
½ cup salt, plus more for seasoning

2 to 3 tablespoons vegetable oil
½ to ¾ cup vegetable oil

1 small yellow onion, finely diced
3 large yellow onions, finely diced

1 tablespoon butter
4 tablespoons butter

black pepper

Scrub the potatoes and put them in a large pot. Cover with water 1 inch over the tops of the potatoes, add 1 tablespoon *[½ cup]* salt, and bring to a boil. Cook until the potatoes are soft throughout but not falling apart. Drain the potatoes well and put them on a large sheet pan. Using 2 forks, quickly break up the hot potatoes into rough ½-inch chunks, taking care not to mash them. Let the potatoes cool and release steam for a few minutes.

Heat a griddle (for smaller quantities, a large nonstick skillet works well, or a seasoned cast-iron skillet) over a medium-high flame. Oil the griddle with some of the vegetable oil. Throw the onion onto the griddle, with a good sprinkling of salt. Using a pancake turner or spatula *[2 spatulas if you're cooking a large quantity]*, toss the onions around and let it cook until just beginning to brown. Add a bit more oil to the griddle and dump the potatoes over the onion. Toss everything around with the spatula. Melt the butter into the potatoes. Continue cooking, tossing occasionally, until the potatoes are browned and crisped to your liking. Add thin streams of oil as necessary (more oil will help the potatoes brown and crisp). Salt and pepper well to taste, transfer to a serving dish, and serve immediately.

BAKED BACON

What could be better than a cast-iron skillet of slowly cooking bacon, mingled with the sweet, heady scents of pancakes and biscuits and the "drip-drip" of strong coffee? I love bacon cooked a bit unevenly, with crisp spots and chewy spots all on the same strip. The skillet does a lovely job, provided you pay close attention as the bacon slowly browns, poking and turning the strips as necessary. But what if the skillet, or your attention, is already well occupied? What if you are cooking lots of bacon, or you want to avoid the sputtery stovetop mess? Here's what to do:

Heat the oven to 350°F. Cover a large sheet pan (with a 1-inch rim) with aluminum foil (shiny side up), and lay out strips of bacon, leaving a 2-inch zone free on one end of the sheet pan. Put the pan in the oven and place 2 small metal measuring cups or other small heatproof objects under the other end of the pan, so the pan is tilted and the grease flows into the empty space as the bacon cooks. Bake slowly in this manner for about 30 minutes, or until the bacon is as crisp and golden as you like; the cooking time will depend on the thickness of the bacon. For thicker bacon, turn the strips over with tongs and *continued . . .*

. . . continued

cook for a few minutes more. If you like
your bacon very crisp, it's best to buy
thinner bacon, or to let thick bacon cook
longer and slower, in a 300°F oven. When
the bacon is cooked to your liking, carefully pour off the grease into a metal cup
(reserving it for cooking vegetables, if you
like), and serve the bacon hot, on a platter
well lined with paper towels.

If you have a wire rack that fits into your
sheet pan, you can bake the bacon on the
rack, so that the grease drips onto the
sheet pan below. But cleaning the rack
afterward is a chore.

Fresh Breakfast Sausage

MAKES 1 POUND; SERVES 5 TO 6

This is one of the simplest sausages to
make, and it's an ideal opportunity to
make Biscuits and Gravy (page 115).
As with any meat grinding, make sure
both the meat and the grinder are very
cold. Cold meat grinds more cleanly and
retains more juice when cooked. If you
do not have a meat grinder but do have a
large, sharp knife, you can still make this
sausage, with even better, juicier results.
Chill your cutting board as well as the
meat, shore up your patience, and chop
the meat very finely, to roughly ⅛-inch
dice, in small batches.

EQUIPMENT/SUPPLIES

meat grinder

ice

rock salt

---

1 pound boneless pork butt,
30% to 40% fat

1 teaspoon salt

¼ teaspoon sugar

1 teaspoon black pepper

1 teaspoon dried sage

1 teaspoon ground ginger

Cut the pork butt into chunks small enough to fit through the feed tube of your meat grinder, and toss with all the seasonings in a medium bowl. Put in the freezer for up to 30 minutes while you ready the grinder. Chill the grinding apparatus, disassembled, including the grinding plate with the largest holes (coarsest), in a bath of 1 gallon of cold tap water, up to 1 gallon of ice, and a cup of rock salt. Mix these well, then completely submerge all parts of the grinder. Let the grinder chill for about 20 minutes, then assemble it and grind the sausage.

Heat a big skillet over medium heat, gently form the sausage into small patties, about ½ inch thick, and fry slowly on both sides until the patties are cooked through and appealingly browned.

Chicken-Fried Steak

SERVES 3 TO 4

Early German settlers brought their beloved schnitzel with them to Texas, where it gradually became chicken-fried steak, a dish emblematic of Texas and readily found on breakfast, lunch, and dinner menus in informal restaurants all over the American West.

Once, when I was the Deep Springs chef, the Student Cooks wanted to make chicken-fried steak for dinner. They told me they'd set some steaks aside, and I gave them this basic recipe. I had to miss that dinner—I was spending the evening in town. The next morning, I came in to make lunch and found a pan of leftover *chicken-fried rib-eye* steaks! I hadn't thought to ask what cut of steak they intended to use—rib-eyes are luxurious, tender, fatty steaks that are best suited to the simplest cooking methods, not for breading and frying. No doubt it was the best chicken-fried steak ever served! Although this recipe specifies round steak, you may use any lean, flavorful, tough cut of steak.

continued . . .

. . . *continued*

about 1 pound round steak

½ teaspoon salt, plus more for seasoning

black pepper

1 cup flour

pinch of cayenne pepper

1 cup buttermilk

about 2 cups safflower oil, peanut oil, or other oil appropriate for frying

FOR SERVING

gravy from Biscuits and Gravy recipe (page 115)

Fried Eggs (page 97)

Cut the steak into 3 or 4 portions. Using a meat pounder, pound the steaks well, until very thin and translucent (hold them up to the light to check). Using paper towels, pat the steaks dry, then salt and pepper them generously. In a shallow bowl, season the flour with ½ teaspoon salt, black pepper to taste, and the cayenne. Pour the buttermilk into another shallow bowl. Dip the steaks in the buttermilk, shaking off the excess, then dredge them well in the flour. Put the steaks on a rack set over a tray and refrigerate for about 30 minutes. This allows the coating to set.

Fill a large cast-iron skillet halfway with oil, and set it over a medium-high flame. When the oil is very hot and just beginning to smoke, put the steaks in the skillet. Don't crowd the steaks in the pan, lest you cool down the oil too much—fry one at a time if necessary. Fry to a golden brown, 1 to 2 minutes, then turn carefully and cook the other side. Drain the steaks on a couple of brown paper grocery bags, or on paper towels. Serve hot with fried eggs and sausage gravy. Make the gravy first, keeping it hot, then cook the steaks, and finally quickly fry the eggs, and serve everything immediately.

Eggs

Here are essential methods and preparations for breakfast eggs in all their glory. I say "breakfast eggs," keeping in mind that eggs may be served at any meal: an omelet is very good for lunch or dinner, and scrambled eggs with lots of butter and salt are the classic midnight snack, perfect for settling the body when you've arrived home late from a party and you're still too giddy to sleep. For more egg recipes, including a run-down on hard-boiled eggs, egg salad, and deviled eggs, see the Great Lunches chapter (beginning on page 149). You'll find a savory soufflé and Italian *frittate* there, too.

Egg cookery is exacting. To make good eggs requires attention and precision, whatever the cooking method. Furthermore, if people are finicky about a single food in their diet, it is invariably their morning eggs. Among cooking professionals, short-order breakfast cooks are in a class of their own—their position is inescapably unglamorous, yet their skills and timing are put to the test every day.

For scrambled eggs, fried eggs, or omelets, I observe three rules:

1. **The eggs must be at room temperature.** Cold eggs will cool down your pan, making them stick. To warm refrigerated eggs, put them in a bowl of hot tap water for a few minutes.

2. **The pan must be hot enough.** If it's not, the eggs will likely stick, even with plenty of butter. But it should not be so hot that the eggs brown immediately. Let the butter be your guide: when butter melts, first it sizzles and foams, then the sizzling quiets and the foam begins to subside, and soon the butter will brown. For most egg methods, put the eggs in the pan as soon as the foam subsides. For omelets, you want the pan a bit hotter: add the eggs the moment the butter begins to brown. If you put butter in the pan and it immediately sizzles, foams, and browns before it's even finished melting, the pan is too hot.

continued ...

. . . continued

Egg pans (also called omelet pans) are small sauté pans with sloped sides, about 8 inches in diameter, usually nonstick, preferably of a sturdy, heat-conducting material. A nice, new nonstick pan makes all these egg preparations easier.

3. Don't let eggs brown. Browned egg is indigestible and a sure indicator of overcooking. Omelets are frequently browned, in an attempt to cook the center through, but they are much more delectable when they are finished on gentler heat.

Scrambled Eggs

SERVES 1

Eggs need a good sprinkle of salt, but due to the nature of the protein in egg white, adding the salt at the end of cooking will help keep the egg tender.

2 large, fresh eggs

2 teaspoons buttermilk (yogurt or sour cream may also be used)

2 teaspoons butter

salt

———

FOR SERVING

black pepper

hot sauce, such as green Tabasco sauce

Warm the eggs to room temperature before cracking them: put them in a bowl of hot tap water for a few minutes, or leave them at room temperature for an hour. Crack the eggs into a small bowl, add the buttermilk, and beat briefly with a fork, just enough to break up the yolks—the mixture need not be uniform.

Heat a small, heavy omelet pan or skillet over medium-high heat. It is important that the pan is hot enough. Melt the butter—it should melt quickly and bubble without burning—and swirl it to coat the bottom of the pan. As soon as the butter's foam subsides, pour in the eggs. Move the eggs about with your spatula constantly as they cook. Do not let them brown.

Cook just until the eggs have set—the mass should be moist but not liquidy.

Scrambling 2 eggs takes about 30 seconds once the eggs go into the pan. Season judiciously with salt (eggs need a good amount of salt), and turn out onto a plate or warmed serving dish immediately. *Do not let the eggs sit in the pan,* or they will overcook. Some people prefer their eggs cooked drier, until the curds have lost their sheen of moisture.

Let diners season to taste with additional salt, black pepper, or hot sauce (a Deep Springs favorite is green Tabasco).

Fried Eggs

SERVES 1

2 large, fresh eggs

1 tablespoon butter

Warm the eggs before cracking them: put them in a bowl of hot tap water for a few minutes, or leave them at room temperature for an hour. Heat a small, heavy omelet pan or skillet over a medium-high flame. It is important that the pan is hot enough. Melt the butter in the pan, swirling it around, until the sizzling quiets and the foam subsides. At that point, break open the eggs very close to the surface of the pan (this will help keep the yolks from breaking). Jostle and swirl the pan gently to keep the eggs moving smoothly on the film of butter as they cook. Cook the eggs in this way for about 30 seconds, then remove the pan from the heat.

For **sunny-side-up eggs,** put a lid on the pan, and let the eggs continue cooking in the residual heat of the pan until the whites have just set, about 1 minute more. Return to a low flame if necessary. Gently slip the eggs out of the pan, or lift them out carefully with a spatula. The yolks will be very runny, the whites tender.

continued...

... *continued*

For **over-easy (or over-medium) eggs**, flip the eggs, and continue cooking in the pan's residual heat to the desired yolk texture, about 30 seconds more for over-easy or about 1 minute for over-medium. Check and return the pan to a low flame if necessary. Flipping an egg without a utensil, only a flick of the wrist, requires the right pan shape—an omelet-style pan with gently sloping sides—and practiced skill. If you are lacking either of these, use a spatula, be gentle, and accept a broken yolk.

Though I usually consider it the cook's responsibility to season food, breakfast fried eggs are an exception; people customarily salt and pepper fried eggs themselves.

Fried Egg Sandwich

An over-medium egg is best for a sandwich; the yolk should be gooey, not runny. When you flip your egg, salt and pepper it generously, then place a thin slice of cheese on top to soften while the egg finishes cooking. I like wheat bread, sharp cheese, a generous amount of mayonnaise, just a little mustard, and lettuce, tomato, and thinly sliced onion. Fried egg sandwiches are excellent fare for a Sunday afternoon hike.

Omelet

SERVES 1

Omelets take practice to make well— several steps happen in quick succession, so don't be discouraged if your first attempts don't meet your expectations. An omelet could be considered a sophisticated variation on scrambled eggs. You can make an omelet without a filling and it would still be an omelet, but omelets are usually filled. A nonstick pan is highly recommended for omelets.

There are three rules for omelet fillings:

1. **Don't overfill your omelet.**
   For a 3-egg omelet, about ⅓ cup of filling is about right; for a 2-egg omelet, use ¼ cup.

2. **Fillings should be precooked and well seasoned, and should go into the omelet warm** (except for cheese; see rule 3). Throwing a heap of cold filling into your partly cooked omelet will cool everything down. Even if you manage to turn out a solid-looking omelet, a tepid, unappetizing mix of raw egg and filling will run out when you cut into it. Vegetables—onions, peppers, mushrooms—should be sautéed until completely cooked and seasoned well with salt before being used in an omelet.

3. Cheese for omelets should be grated and at room temperature. This ensures that the cheese will not cool down the eggs. An ounce of cheese per omelet is ample.

3 large, fresh eggs, at room temperature

½ teaspoon milk

pinch of salt, plus more as needed

2 to 3 teaspoons butter (most for the pan, a small pat for the finish)

⅓ cup filling of your choice (see the following list)

Warm the eggs before cracking them: put them in a bowl of hot tap water for a few minutes, or leave them at room temperature for an hour. Crack the eggs into a small bowl, add the milk and a big pinch of salt, and beat briefly with a fork, just enough to break up the yolks.

The total cooking time for an omelet, once the eggs go into the pan, is about 2 minutes. Therefore, have everything in position before you begin: butter, a spatula, your prepared (warm) filling, and the serving plate (warming it is a nice touch) nearby.

Heat a small, heavy omelet pan over medium-high heat. Melt about 2 teaspoons butter—it should melt quickly and bubble without burning—and swirl it to coat the bottom of the pan. As soon as the foam has subsided and the butter is just beginning to brown, pour in the eggs.

Let the eggs cook undisturbed for a few seconds, then start pushing folds of cooked egg to the center of the pan, allowing uncooked egg to run under.

After about 20 seconds, when half the volume of egg is cooked, add about ⅓ cup of warm filling, scattering and spreading it in the center of the omelet. Fold the omelet in half, with the aid of a spatula, if necessary, and remove it from heat. Let the omelet cook in the pan's residual heat for a moment to set its folded shape, then flip to cook the other side. You may peer into the center of the omelet with a small knife—the egg should be solid but still creamy inside. Return it to a low flame if necessary. Try not to let it brown. Give the omelet another light sprinkle of salt. Turn the omelet onto a warmed plate, then run a small pat of butter over the surface; this gives a wonderful aroma, flavor, and shine. Serve immediately.

Traditional omelet filling ingredients; use your favorite combination

* sautéed diced onion

* sautéed diced sweet peppers (bell peppers, pimentos, and other sweet varieties)

* Sautéed Mushrooms (page 237)

* sautéed tomatoes (take care to cook most of the moisture away)

* crumbled cooked bacon or sausage

* chopped ham

continued . . .

... *continued*

* grated cheese (such as fontina, Cheddar, jack, Swiss, feta, Gruyère, or smoked Gouda)

Special omelet fillings and presentations

* chopped fresh herbs (such as parsley, chives, sage, thyme, or dill) beaten into the eggs, and the omelet filled with delicate cheese

* cream cheese with sautéed bacon and minced jalapeños

* chopped green chile (canned or freshly roasted, page 423) and grated Jack cheese (scatter cubes of avocado over the finished omelet)

* feta cheese (include a little chopped fresh dill in the eggs; in summer serve with slices of ripe tomato on the side)

* Ratatouille (page 258), heated (finish with a drizzle of good olive oil)

* smoked salmon and chives or dill (for a special occasion, garnish with sour cream and a bit of salmon caviar)

Sorrel Omelet

SERVES 2

A special springtime dish, this omelet is an excellent way to appreciate the gentle, tart flavor of this unusual herb. Because sorrel cooks and readily softens at a low temperature, it can be mixed into the eggs raw. For a great lunch, toss a mixed green salad, rub hot toast with a cut clove of fresh garlic, and cook up a sorrel omelet.

5 large, fresh eggs

2 heaping cups coarsely chopped sorrel leaves (from 1 small bunch)

½ teaspoon salt

1 tablespoon butter, plus more for finishing

freshly grated Parmesan cheese

Warm the eggs in a bowl of hot tap water. Crack them into a bowl, beat them lightly, and mix in the sorrel and salt.

Heat a small, heavy omelet pan over a medium flame. Melt 1 tablespoon butter—it should bubble without burning—and swirl it to coat the bottom of the pan. As soon as the foam has subsided, pour in the eggs. Let the eggs cook undisturbed for a few seconds, then start pushing folds of cooked egg to the center of the pan, allowing uncooked egg to run under. There is no need to fold this omelet; it can simply be flipped flat when the first side is cooked. As sorrel cooks, it turns a dull green—using a small knife, peek inside the omelet and look for telltale patches of bright green sorrel and undercooked egg. Continue cooking gently, flipping as necessary, until the omelet is cooked through. The total cooking time will be about 5 minutes. Turn the finished omelet onto a plate, run a pat of butter over the surface, then sprinkle lightly with Parmesan. Cut in half and serve.

Poached Eggs

SERVES 1

Poached eggs are "shreddy" by nature. I don't bother to trim or otherwise neaten their appearance. Bring 4 cups of water to a boil in a saucepan. When the water is at a *full rolling* boil, break in 2 large eggs, holding them right above the surface of the water. Slap on the cover and remove the pan from the heat. Let the eggs cook in the hot water for exactly 3 minutes, gently jostling the pan once or twice, then remove the eggs with a slotted spoon. The yolks will be runny; for firmer eggs, leave them in the water for another minute. Drain the eggs for a moment, then place on hot buttered toast, crispy-browned corned beef hash, your *salade de frisée aux lardons,* or whatever they are to be served with, and serve immediately.

Soft-Boiled Eggs

SERVES 1 OR 2

A soft-boiled egg is the most direct egg experience—you eat it right out of its shell. If you come by the pastel blue-green eggs produced by black-and-white Araucana chickens, this is the best way to serve them, so the beauty of their shells can be appreciated. To serve soft-boiled eggs in the traditional manner, you need egg cups and small spoons.

On occasional Saturday mornings at Deep Springs, I'll forgo the usual student-cooked breakfast, instead opting to walk across the road to the henhouse and reach under an obliging bird for a couple of freshly laid eggs for my breakfast: two salt-and-peppered soft-boiled eggs, nothing else. Put on some old blues records, and I'm ready to clean the whole house.

Put 2 large eggs in a saucepan and cover with cold water. (For smaller or larger eggs, adjust the cooking time in 20-second increments.) Bring to a boil over high heat. When the water comes to a boil, immediately remove from the heat, slap on the cover, and let the eggs sit in the hot water for 3 minutes and 15 seconds for a cooked but tender white and a warm but runny yolk. (This is the correct time for sea-level kitchens; at Deep Springs' altitude, to compensate for the lower boiling point of water, I leave the eggs in the water for about 25 seconds longer, for a total of 3 minutes and 40 seconds.) Dump the hot water out of the pan and cover the eggs with cold tap water to stop the cooking. Remove after several seconds, lest they cool down too much, and serve immediately. Place the egg, pointy side up, in an egg cup.

To eat, have salt and pepper nearby. Tap the side of the pointed end all around to break the shell. Lift off the top part of the egg and scoop out the bit of white. Eat the remainder of the egg from the shell in small bites, salting and peppering each bite. The yolk will be your favorite degree of runniness. In a perfectly cooked egg, the yolk sauces the white.

Shirred Eggs

SERVES 6

This is perhaps the easiest way to prepare eggs, provided you watch them carefully to prevent overcooking. The same procedure can be used whether you are preparing just a few eggs for an intimate breakfast or several dozen for Sunday brunch.

2 tablespoons melted butter, for greasing tin

½ cup heavy (whipping) cream or half-and-half

12 eggs

Heat the oven to 325°F. Grease the cups of a muffin tin well with melted butter. Into each cup, pour about 2 teaspoons of heavy cream or half-and-half (I've also successfully used a mixture of equal parts sour cream and buttermilk). Break an egg into each cup. Bake until the whites of the eggs are set but the yolks are still runny, 10 to 12 minutes: *check frequently.* Don't overcook—once the yolks cook solid, they have lost much of their saucy savor. Run a small knife around the edge of each egg, then use a wide soup spoon to lift out the eggs.

CHAPTER 3

Pancakes, Biscuits, and Cornbread

Many of the recipes in this chapter call for buttermilk; its gentle tanginess and full dairy flavor make for tender, tasty baked goods. In the Deep Springs kitchen we use 3 gallons of it each week, for breakfast baking, for cornbread and biscuits for lunch, for dinner dessert cakes, and for creamy salad dressings. People who don't like to drink buttermilk by itself may be reluctant to commit to a whole quart of it (pints are rare outside the South). Keep in mind, however, that a quart is 4 cups—two or three recipes' worth—and that it has a much longer refrigerator shelf life than milk. If you like plain yogurt, you may easily acquire a taste for buttermilk—it's tangy and refreshing, but fortifying. Like yogurt, it's very good for you, more easily digested than milk. Can you substitute plain yogurt for buttermilk in these recipes? Not always—yogurt contains less liquid than buttermilk, so it could yield a drier product. See the Cakes chapter for more recipes containing buttermilk.

Most of these recipes also contain *baking powder* or *baking soda*. What is the difference? When baking soda, called bicarbonate of soda in old cookbooks, is combined with an acid ingredient such as buttermilk, little bubbles of gas form, thereby leavening the dough or batter. Baking powder is simply baking soda combined with a powdered acid. As soon as baking powder comes into contact with moisture, the chemical reaction begins. Over time, especially in moist climates, baking powder's leavening capability may deteriorate, so it's wise to buy small containers of baking powder and use them within a year of purchase. Always use a perfectly dry measuring spoon to measure baking powder—the moisture from a wet spoon could ruin the whole container. If you are in doubt as to the potency of your baking powder, just drop a spoonful into a glass of hot water—if this results in an immediate, lively fizz, it's still good.

If you detect a metallic taste in biscuits, cornbread, and other plainly flavored preparations that use baking powder, try substituting home-mixed baking powder, using the following ratio: 1½ teaspoons cream of tartar (a powdered acid), 1 teaspoon baking soda, and ¼ teaspoon salt. This is best mixed as needed—its leavening power deteriorates over time. Use the same measurements you would use for regular baking powder.

Bread recipes containing flour and baking powder or baking soda are usually categorized as "quick breads." (Yeast breads, on the other hand, take considerable time to rise and have an entirely different character.)

There are three rules to keep in mind with any quick bread (including pancakes):

1. *Mix the dough or batter just until blended, and treat it gently.* Overmixing results in dry, tough bread. With biscuits and scones, this requirement is even more extreme: mix just until the flour is barely moistened, no more.

2. *Bake or cook quick breads just until cooked through.* These breads lack the moisture-retaining properties of yeast breads, and so are prone to drying out.

3. *Serve savory quick breads (such as biscuits and cornbread) immediately.* Sugar retains moisture in baked goods; therefore low-sugar quick breads are especially prone to dryness.

Jack's Buttermilk Pancakes

SERVES 6 TO 7

Here is the all-time favorite, everyday classic, from my predecessor in the Boardinghouse kitchen. These pancakes have been a part of Deep Springs breakfasts for many years.

3 cups sifted all-purpose flour

½ cup sugar

1 tablespoon baking powder

1½ teaspoons baking soda

1½ teaspoons salt

3 eggs, at room temperature, beaten

4 cups buttermilk, at room temperature

4 tablespoons butter, melted

vegetable oil for cooking the pancakes

FOR SERVING

softened butter

warmed maple syrup

Thoroughly whisk together the flour, sugar, baking powder, baking soda, and salt in a medium bowl. Whisk together the eggs, buttermilk, and melted butter in a large, deep bowl. Over a medium-high flame, heat a griddle (or a wide skillet) for several minutes. Add the dry ingredients to the wet ingredients and combine just until mixed.

Oil the griddle lightly with vegetable oil, and begin cooking: gently drop spoonfuls of batter onto the griddle. For the easiest dispensing of the batter, transfer it to a pitcher or other vessel with a spout. I like to make pancakes that are on the small side, using about ¼ cup of batter, the better to make a tall stack. Let the pancakes cook until the impressions of bubbles remain in the uncooked top surface, then flip and cook on the other side for a few moments more. Press lightly on the top of a pancake—if your finger leaves an impression, it needs a bit more time. If it springs back, it's done. The side cooked first is considered the more attractive "top" side. Serve immediately with soft butter and warm maple syrup.

Cowboy Pancakes

Instead of serving them with syrup, roll up the buttered pancakes with brown sugar and a hot slice of bacon. Eat like a taco.

Whole-Wheat Pancakes

For the tastiest 100 percent whole-grain pancake, spelt, an ancient form of wheat, delivers a sweeter taste and none of the bitterness of whole wheat. Simply substitute whole-grain spelt flour for the all-purpose flour in the master recipe, adding 3 to 4 tablespoons of wheat germ. Alternatively, use half whole-wheat flour, half all-purpose, plus 3 to 4 tablespoons wheat germ and a tablespoon or two of honey.

Buckwheat Pancakes

These are especially good in cool weather, with marmalade or another citrusy topping. Substitute 1½ cups buckwheat flour for 1½ cups of the all-purpose flour in the master recipe.

Blueberry or Huckleberry Pancakes

Proceed with the master recipe, adding 1 to 2 cups fresh or frozen blueberries or huckleberries (if using frozen, do not thaw) when combining the wet and dry ingredients. Or sprinkle the berries directly on the wet batter of each pancake before flipping it. Huckleberries are a wild delicacy: tiny berries, intensely pigmented, with a distinctively intense sweet-zingy flavor.

Eloise's Cornmeal-Buttermilk Pancakes

SERVES 4 TO 5

My friend Eloise once ran a breakfast café in San Francisco; these Southern-style pancakes—the centerpiece of her menu—go superbly with sausage, syrup, and good, strong coffee.

One morning, I had a whole batch of these cornmeal-buttermilk pancakes cooking on the griddle, when the Deep Springs president's wife ran into the kitchen, pale and shaken, asking, "Have you heard the news?" While I flipped the pancakes, she told me what had happened on the East Coast that morning of September 11, 2001.

1 cup sifted all-purpose flour

1 cup medium-grind cornmeal

1 teaspoon baking soda

1 teaspoon salt

¼ cup firmly packed brown sugar

3 large eggs, at room temperature, beaten

2 cups buttermilk, at room temperature

½ cup plain whole-milk yogurt

4 tablespoons butter, melted

vegetable oil for cooking the pancakes

continued . . .

. . . continued

FOR SERVING

softened butter

warmed maple syrup

Whisk together the flour, cornmeal, baking soda, and salt in a medium bowl. In a large, deep bowl, mix together the brown sugar, eggs, buttermilk, yogurt, and melted butter. If the wet ingredients are cold, place the bowl in a basin of hot water to bring the contents to room temperature.

Over a medium-high flame, heat a griddle (or wide skillet) for several minutes. Oil the griddle with a bit of vegetable oil. Whisk the dry ingredients into the wet mixture just until there are no lumps of flour left, and begin cooking: carefully drop spoonfuls of batter onto the griddle. Or transfer the batter to a pitcher or other vessel with a spout, and pour measures of batter onto the griddle. These cook a bit faster than regular pancakes and are rather delicate; I think it's easiest to make them on the small side, using about ¼ cup batter. When the impressions of bubbles remain in the uncooked top surface of the pancakes, they are ready to flip. After flipping, to determine whether they are cooked through, press lightly on top of a pancake—if your finger leaves an impression, it needs a bit more time. If it springs back, it's done. The side cooked first is considered the more attractive "top" side. Serve immediately with soft butter and warm maple syrup.

Ricotta Pancakes

SERVES 2

These rich little pancakes have a lovely brown exterior and a delicate, custardy interior. Ripe pears are a natural choice, but sliced, sugared strawberries or other juicy fruit are good, too. If you are serving these pancakes as a dessert, add a few drops of vanilla extract to the wet ingredients for the batter.

3 tablespoons all-purpose flour

2 tablespoons sugar

¼ teaspoon baking powder

¼ teaspoon salt

¾ cup ricotta cheese

1 egg

¼ cup milk

___

TOPPING

½ cup ricotta cheese

2 teaspoons sugar

___

2 to 3 tablespoons butter for cooking the pancakes

slices of ripe pear, or sliced, sugared strawberries, for serving

In a small bowl, whisk together the flour, sugar, baking power, and salt. In a pitcher or other spouted vessel, whisk the ricotta, egg, and milk together until uniform. Add the dry ingredients, whisk the two mixtures together thoroughly, and let *rest for 20 minutes* to allow the flour to absorb liquid.

For the topping, mix together the ricotta and sugar in a small bowl and keep at room temperature.

Heat a griddle or wide skillet over a medium-high flame. Melt a small pat of butter on the griddle and begin cooking, using about 2 tablespoons of batter for each pancake. Let the pancakes cook until deep golden brown on one side, then flip and cook on the other side for a few moments more. Serve immediately, topped with the sweetened ricotta and fruit.

Biscuits

SERVES 4 TO 6

This recipe yields buttery biscuits with a layered texture. For especially fluffy, delicate biscuits, use a blend of cake flour and all-purpose flour. For a good, nutty flavor, use a blend of whole-wheat and all-purpose flour.

> 2 cups sifted all-purpose flour
>
> 2½ teaspoons baking powder
>
> ½ teaspoon baking soda
>
> ½ teaspoon salt
>
> 6 tablespoons cold unsalted butter
>
> ¾ cup cold buttermilk

Heat the oven to 450°F. Sift together the flour, baking powder, baking soda, and salt into a medium bowl. Cut the butter into slices and rapidly work the butter into the dry mixture with your hands. Work until the flour is somewhat moistened and there are no large, but many small, pieces of butter in the mixture. Pour in the buttermilk and gently combine with a wooden spoon just until mixed.

Turn the dough out on a floured board and knead (in other words, flatten, fold over, flatten, fold over) *only four or five times*, sprinkling flour on the board as necessary to prevent sticking. In flattening and folding, work the dough into a

continued . . .

rectangle, about 8 by 6 inches. Gently roll the dough, using flour as necessary to keep it from sticking, to a ¾-inch thickness and cut with a sharp, round cutter dipped in flour or into squares with a long, sharp knife dipped in flour. (To the irritation of traditionalists, I almost always make square biscuits, as it uses 100 percent of the dough with no scraps to bother with.) Place 1 inch apart on an ungreased baking sheet, and let rest for a few moments. Once the biscuits are cut and placed on the baking sheet, they may be refrigerated until you are ready to bake them. Bake in the center of the oven until golden brown on the bottom and top, 8 to 10 minutes. *Biscuits must be consumed warm from the oven.* "Take two and butter 'em while they're hot!" my mother likes to say as she passes the napkin-lined basket of biscuits.

Whole-Wheat Cheddar Biscuits

These are good with brothy soups. Replace the flour in the master recipe with 1 cup whole-wheat flour, ¾ cup all-purpose flour, and ¼ cup wheat germ. Work 1 cup (4 ounces) grated sharp Cheddar cheese into the dry ingredients along with the butter, using only 4 tablespoons butter.

Cream Biscuits

These are more cakey and less flaky than regular biscuits, with a creamy, tender flavor.

   2 cups sifted all-purpose flour

   2½ teaspoons baking powder

   ½ teaspoon salt

   1 cup heavy (whipping) cream

Proceed as for regular biscuits, except, of course, there is no butter to work in. As this dough is a bit stickier, bake the biscuits on a greased baking sheet.

Sour Cream Biscuits

   2 cups sifted all-purpose flour

   1½ teaspoons baking powder

   ¾ teaspoon baking soda

   ½ teaspoon salt

   1¼ cups natural sour cream
   (no binders or thickeners)

Proceed as for Cream Biscuits (above).

Cornmeal Biscuits

For when you can't decide whether to make biscuits or cornbread.

   1½ cups sifted all-purpose flour

   ½ cup medium-grind cornmeal

   2 teaspoons baking powder

   ½ teaspoon baking soda

¾ teaspoon salt

6 tablespoons cold butter

¾ cup buttermilk

Follow the instructions in the master recipe.

Griddle Biscuits

Any of these biscuits may be "baked" on a hot griddle set at pancake temperature or a little cooler. The outer texture will be crispier and the insides more dense than oven biscuits. Roll them ½ inch thick rather than ¾ inch, and gently turn them after they are nicely browned on the first side. In my experience they are cooked when both sides are brown; this will depend, of course, on the thickness of the biscuits and the temperature of the griddle. Cornmeal Biscuits are my favorite for griddle cooking; serve with gravy or maple syrup.

Drop Biscuits

If you are really in a hurry, make drop biscuits; they eliminate the rolling and cutting step. Use any of the recipes here, adding about ¼ cup more liquid than is called for—the dough will be wet and sticky. Using an ice cream scoop (a small one—1 ounce—if possible), drop neat, uniform scoops of dough 1½ inches apart on *well-greased* baking sheets. I like to serve drop biscuits with their attractive browned undersides facing up.

Biscuits and Gravy

SERVES 4 TO 6

Biscuits and gravy with sausage and fried eggs—some brisk mornings, nothing else will do for breakfast. If you have a meat grinder, you could even make your own breakfast sausage (see page 92). Don't make these with whole-wheat flour; this traditional Southern dish proclaims the soothing taste of white flour.

SAUSAGE GRAVY

3 tablespoons fat in skillet from cooking breakfast sausage or bacon

3 tablespoons all-purpose flour

3 cups milk

½ teaspoon salt

¼ teaspoon freshly ground black pepper

1 or 2 pinches of cayenne pepper

about ½ cup crumbled cooked breakfast sausage *(optional)*

—

1 recipe Biscuits (page 113), split and buttered

Cook breakfast sausage (or bacon, though I prefer the substantial taste and heft of sausage in this setting) in a cast-iron skillet, retaining all the browned bits and

continued . . .

. . . continued

3 tablespoons fat in the skillet. Stir the flour into the fat with a wooden spoon, scraping up any stuck browned bits. Cook this roux over medium-low heat for a few minutes, stirring constantly, until it bubbles well and has begun to turn a shade darker. Remove from the heat, continuing to stir for a moment more as the roux cools. Let stand for 10 minutes, then return to medium-high heat and add the milk slowly, whisking constantly. Cook until thickened, then reduce the heat to low and simmer, whisking frequently, for 2 to 3 minutes. Season carefully with salt, black pepper, and cayenne. If you like, stir in a handful of crumbled cooked breakfast sausage.

Ladle the gravy generously over piping-hot, split, buttered biscuits.

Skillet Cornbread

SERVES 6 TO 8

I've tried many Southern cornbread recipes over the years: Southern cornbread tends to be savory, not sweet, and has a greater proportion of cornmeal, while Northern, or "Yankee" cornbread, very good in its own right, is cakier and sweeter. Though some recipe writers insist that "true" Southern cornbread contains only cornmeal, no flour, most recipes of this kind do indeed call for a small amount of all-purpose flour. This recipe uses both polenta, or coarse-grind cornmeal, and medium-grind cornmeal. The polenta adds a little extra toothsome texture. If you don't have polenta, just eliminate the first step of soaking it in buttermilk, and use 1½ cups cornmeal. Fresh stone-ground cornmeal is very perishable and difficult to find outside the South, but it makes heavenly cornbread.

Sugar is controversial: some Southern cooks shun it entirely, while others pour it in with abandon. I think a small amount is necessary for its moisture-retaining properties. As for the cheese, this recipe is good without it, but it enhances the flavor of the corn. Butter gives the cornbread a round, full flavor, but vegetable oil may stand in for some of the butter. Bacon drippings can be used for part of the fat, too, resulting in a slightly drier but delicious cornbread. Perhaps the most important part of this recipe is the hot cast-iron skillet. I never bake cornbread in anything else. The crusty exterior is a great part of the charm, much like the skin on a roast chicken. A deep golden, steaming-hot round of skillet-baked cornbread is a beautiful sight to behold.

½ cup polenta (coarse cornmeal)

1 cup buttermilk

1 cup medium-grind cornmeal (white has a subtly finer taste, but yellow is prettier)

½ cup sifted all-purpose flour

2 teaspoons baking powder

1 teaspoon baking soda

1 teaspoon salt

½ cup (2 ounces) finely grated sharp white Cheddar cheese (optional)

2 eggs, lightly beaten

2 tablespoons brown sugar

½ cup sweet corn kernels (optional; 1 small ear's worth)

5 to 6 tablespoons butter (3 or 4 tablespoons for the batter, 2 tablespoons for the skillet)

Heat the oven to 400°F. For best results, have all ingredients at room temperature. In a medium bowl, stir the polenta into the buttermilk and set aside. Sift the cornmeal, flour, baking powder, baking soda, and salt together into a large bowl. If you are using the cheese, toss it with the dry ingredients.

Into the polenta-buttermilk mixture, stir the eggs and the sugar (and the corn, if you are using it). Meanwhile, in the oven, melt the butter in a well-seasoned, 10-inch cast-iron skillet. Stir all but 2 tablespoons of this melted butter into the wet ingredients, returning the hot skillet, with the remaining 2 tablespoons of butter, to the oven. Carefully add the wet ingredients to the dry, stirring just until the dry ingredients are moistened—do not overmix.

When the butter in the skillet is just beginning to brown, spoon the thick batter into the skillet—it should sizzle happily. Bake for 15 minutes, or just until a toothpick inserted in the center comes out clean. Let the cornbread rest in the skillet for a moment, then invert it onto a plate. Since the skillet will retain a great deal of heat, it's best not to leave the cornbread in the skillet, lest it overcook and dry out. Serve immediately.

Dutch Babies

SERVES 2 TO 4

My mother used to make Dutch babies, or German pancakes, for the occasional weekend breakfast when I was a kid. Inevitably, I asked, "Why are they called Dutch babies?" We imaginatively figured it was because the pancake, puffed as it emerges from the oven, looks somewhat like a roasted baby, all golden and crispy in the skillet.

> 3 large eggs (or 4 smaller ones)
>
> ¾ cup milk
>
> ¾ cup sifted all-purpose flour
>
> ½ teaspoon salt
>
> 3 tablespoons butter
>
> ―
>
> **FOR SERVING (CHOOSE ONE)**
>
> butter and maple syrup
>
> butter and powdered sugar
>
> fresh fruit with jam or jelly

Heat the oven to 450°F. Bring all the ingredients to room temperature. Beat the eggs, milk, flour, and salt in a medium bowl until very smooth. Melt the butter in a heavy 10-inch or 12-inch oven-safe skillet. As soon as the butter is hot and bubbling, pour in the batter and put the skillet into the oven. After 15 minutes, lower the oven temperature to 350°F and continue baking for another 8 to 9 minutes. The pancake will be a deep golden brown, with crisp edges. If the pancake puffs up in large bubbles in the first 10 to 15 minutes, pierce the bubbles with a fork.

Cut the pancake into wedges and serve immediately with more butter and maple syrup, or butter and sifted powdered sugar, or a quick compote of fresh fruit tossed with melted jam or jelly.

Apple Dutch Babies

This traditional variation is superb with "frizzled" ham (thick slices of ham steak quickly sizzled in a little oil in a hot skillet) and plenty of strong drip coffee. Pears are good, too, with nutmeg or ginger.

> 4 tablespoons butter
>
> 3 tart apples, cored, peeled if you like, and thinly sliced
>
> ½ teaspoon ground cinnamon
>
> ⅛ teaspoon salt
>
> 1 tablespoon sugar
>
> batter for Dutch Babies

Heat the oven to 450°F. In a cast-iron skillet over a medium-high flame, melt the butter. When it is hot and bubbling, throw in the apples, cinnamon, salt, and sugar. Cook the apples, stirring frequently, until soft but still holding their shape, about 10 minutes. Whisk the batter ingredients together, pour over the apples in the skillet, and bake as directed in the master recipe. This is delicious cooled to room temperature; the apple flavor becomes stronger as it sits.

Oatmeal Scones

MAKES 8 LARGE SCONES

You need not serve butter and jam with these great scones—they are perfect just as they are, with a cup of tea or strong coffee. They're sweet and buttery enough to remain delectable even hours out of the oven.

  2 cups sifted all-purpose flour

  ⅓ cup firmly packed brown sugar

  1½ teaspoons baking powder

  ¾ teaspoon baking soda

  ¾ cup rolled oats, plus ¼ cup more for shaping and cutting the scones

  ¾ cup cold salted butter (1½ sticks), cut into thick slices

  ½ cup currants or raisins

  ½ cup buttermilk, or more as needed

Heat the oven to 425°F. Combine the flour, brown sugar, baking powder, baking soda, and ¾ cup of the oats in a large bowl. Rapidly work the butter into the dry mixture with your hands, lightly smearing the slices between your palms. Break the butter into smaller pieces, dispersing it throughout. The flour will become somewhat moistened, and the visible pieces of butter will resemble small peas. Stir in the currants. Pour in the buttermilk and mix the dough until just combined. If the dough still seems very dry, sprinkle in a tablespoon or so more buttermilk.

Scatter the remaining ¼ cup oats on a cutting board. Gather the dough into 2 equal-sized balls. On the oat-strewn board, gently pat each ball into a 1-inch-thick disk. With a sharp knife, cut each disk into 4 wedges. Place the scones about 1 inch apart on an ungreased baking sheet and bake in the center of the oven until they are a rich golden brown on the outside and are cooked in the center, 12 to 15 minutes.

Let the scones rest on the sheet for a few minutes before removing them to a cooling rack—they are very crumbly when they emerge from the oven.

Cream Scones

MAKES 8 MEDIUM SCONES

Flavored with orange zest and studded with currants, these scones are very English, perfect with tea. Made with the extra-thick, double-rich cream from the Deep Springs cows, they won a blue ribbon at the regional Tri-County Fair.

2 cups sifted all-purpose flour

⅓ cup sugar

1 tablespoon baking powder

½ teaspoon salt

¾ cup dried currants

1 teaspoon grated orange zest

1¼ cups heavy (whipping) cream

Heat the oven to 425°F. Lightly grease a baking sheet. Whisk the flour, sugar, baking powder, and salt together in a medium bowl. Stir in the currants and zest. Mix in the cream *just until the dry ingredients are moistened*. Gather the dough into a ball, transfer it to a lightly floured surface, and pat into an 8-inch round, about ¾ inch thick. Cut into 8 wedges and place at least ½ inch apart on the baking sheet. Bake until the tops are golden brown, 12 to 15 minutes. Transfer the scones to a rack and let cool slightly before serving.

Joan's Irish Soda Bread

MAKES 2 MEDIUM LOAVES

If you've never tasted caraway seeds in anything but rye bread, you'll be surprised at their entirely different character when combined with raisins in this lightly sweetened soda bread. For the most tender texture, don't over-mix the batter—combine the dry and wet ingredients just until there is no dry flour left. (My friend Joan, who makes many loaves of this soda bread every St. Patrick's Day, mixes for only as long as it takes to say an "Our Father," a "Hail Mary," and a "Glory Be.")

3 cups all-purpose flour

⅔ cup sugar

1 teaspoon baking soda

2 teaspoons baking powder

1 teaspoon salt

2 cups buttermilk

2 eggs

2 tablespoons caraway seeds

2 tablespoons canola oil or other vegetable oil

1½ cups raisins

Heat the oven to 350°F. Grease and flour 2 medium (4-cup) loaf pans. Whisk the flour, sugar, baking soda, baking powder, and salt together in a large bowl. Whisk the buttermilk, eggs, caraway seeds, and oil together in a medium bowl. Pour the wet ingredients into the bowl with the dry ingredients, and sprinkle the raisins over. Sweeping your whisk thoroughly over the bottom of the bowl, mix the batter only until uniform; do not overmix. Scrape into the prepared pans and bake for 30 to 35 minutes, until a toothpick inserted in the center comes out clean. Let the soda bread rest in the pans for 10 minutes, then turn out onto a rack to cool. A toasted, buttered slice is delicious the next day.

Grandma Z.'s Coffeecake

SERVES 8

This cake is somehow much more than the sum of its parts. It is based on a recipe from the grandmother of my oldest friend, whose name is also Tom.

1 cup granulated (white) sugar

1 cup firmly packed brown sugar

3 cups sifted all-purpose flour

1 cup cold butter (2 sticks)

¼ teaspoon salt

½ teaspoon baking powder

½ teaspoon baking soda

2 eggs, beaten

1 cup buttermilk

½ teaspoon vanilla extract

Heat the oven to 375°F. Grease and flour a 9-by-13-inch baking dish. In a large bowl, mix the granulated sugar, brown sugar, and flour. Cut the butter into thin slices and toss the slices in the flour-sugar mixture. With your hands, rapidly work the butter into the mixture, smearing the butter slices between your palms, to the point that the mixture is somewhat moistened and only small pieces of butter are visible.

continued...

. . . continued

Reserve 1 firmly packed cup of this mixture for the topping. Mix the salt, baking powder, and baking soda into the remainder.

Combine the eggs, buttermilk, and vanilla in a medium bowl. Add to the flour mixture and, with a rubber spatula, fold together both mixtures *just until smooth*. Scrape into the prepared baking dish. Sprinkle the reserved topping evenly over the top. Bake just until a toothpick inserted in the center comes out clean, 20 to 25 minutes. Let cool for at least 15 minutes before cutting into squares.

Blueberry Coffeecake

Omit the brown sugar and use 2 cups granulated sugar. Include ¼ teaspoon ground nutmeg and/or 1 tablespoon finely grated lemon zest in the batter. After spreading the batter in the pan, but before you sprinkle on the topping, scatter 2 cups fresh or frozen (if frozen, do not thaw) blueberries over the top. Sprinkle the topping over the berries and bake. Frozen blueberries will cool everything down, so allow an extra 5 to 10 minutes of baking time.

Sweet Potato Cinnamon Rolls

MAKES ABOUT 28 CINNAMON ROLLS

The Sweet Potato Bread dough, made simply by adding flour, yeast, and a little butter to mashed sweet potato, tastes as rich and moist as traditional egg dough. Once the cinnamon rolls are assembled, they may be refrigerated overnight, to be baked the next morning.

1 heaping cup pecans (about 3¼ ounces), lightly toasted (see page 301) and coarsely chopped

½ cup golden raisins

1 cup firmly packed brown sugar

1 tablespoon ground cinnamon

4 tablespoons butter, at room temperature

2 tablespoons all-purpose flour

1 recipe dough for Sweet Potato Bread (page 139), ready for second rise

---

GLAZE

¼ cup water

4 tablespoons butter

1 cup powdered sugar, sifted

¼ teaspoon vanilla extract

½ teaspoon grated orange zest or a few drops orange extract

Generously butter 2 large baking sheets. Mix half the pecans together with the raisins, brown sugar, cinnamon, butter, and flour in a medium bowl. Set the remaining pecans aside for the final topping. Divide the dough in half, and thinly roll each half into a long, even rectangle (aim for about 18 by 14 inches). The thinner the dough, the better your swirl. Distribute the brown sugar–pecan filling evenly over both rectangles, leaving a strip of bare dough along one long side of each piece. Roll tightly, starting from the side opposite the bare edge. Lightly moisten the bare edge with water to seal the roll.

With a sharp slicing knife, cut off slices 1 inch thick, placing them flat on the sheets so their edges touch. Cover with plastic wrap and let rise at room temperature for 1 hour. Or immediately cover the pans with plastic wrap and refrigerate. Bring them out the next morning and let them come to room temperature and rise for about 1½ hours. Have the oven at 350°F.

Bake the rolls until they are browned on top and lightly browned on the bottom, 20 to 25 minutes. Carefully test a center roll to make sure the dough is cooked all the way through. Let the rolls cool to warm.

To make the glaze, heat the water and butter together in a small saucepan until the butter is melted. Gradually add the hot butter-water mixture to the powdered sugar in a medium bowl. Add the vanilla and orange zest. Drizzle the warm glaze over the rolls and top with the extra pecans.

Pumpkin Bars

MAKES ABOUT 24 SMALL BARS

At Deep Springs, these moist, sweet, cakey treats herald the holiday season. To make your own pumpkin purée, see Pumpkin Pie (page 455). You can also use a 15-ounce can of pumpkin.

2¾ cups sifted all-purpose flour
(up to 1 cup whole wheat may be used)

1½ teaspoons baking powder

1¼ teaspoons salt

1½ teaspoons ground cinnamon

½ teaspoon ground nutmeg

¼ teaspoon ground cloves

½ cup golden raisins

½ cup walnuts or pecans, lightly toasted
(see page 301) and coarsely chopped

2 eggs, lightly beaten

1 cup firmly packed brown sugar

¾ cup canola oil or other vegetable oil

2 cups pumpkin purée

½ teaspoon vanilla extract

1 teaspoon finely grated orange zest

GLAZE

½ cup powdered sugar, sifted

1 tablespoon fresh lemon juice

1 tablespoon orange juice

continued . . .

. . . continued

Heat the oven to 350°F. Grease and flour a
12-by-17-inch baking sheet with a ½-inch
rim. In a medium bowl, whisk together
the flour, baking powder, salt, cinnamon,
nutmeg, and cloves. Toss in the raisins and
nuts. In a large bowl, whisk together the
eggs, brown sugar, oil, pumpkin, vanilla,
and orange zest until well combined.

Add the flour mixture to the pumpkin
mixture, folding with the whisk *just until
the batter is uniform.* Using a rubber spatula,
spread the batter evenly into the prepared
baking sheet, smoothing the top. Bake until
a toothpick inserted in the center comes out
clean, about 20 minutes. Let the cake cool
completely in the pan.

To make the glaze, combine the powdered
sugar with the lemon and orange juice
in a small bowl, whisking until smooth.
Drizzle over the top of the cake, using all
the glaze. Let stand for 1 hour before cutting into bars.

Banana Bread

MAKES 2 LOAVES OR 1 LARGE CAKE

This is a bread in name only; with a cup
each of butter and sugar, it is really a
cake. Your bananas should be fully ripe—
thoroughly yellow with many brown
speckles.

2½ cups mashed ripe bananas (4 or 5)

2 teaspoons fresh lemon juice

1 cup butter (2 sticks), at room
temperature

½ cup granulated (white) sugar

½ cup firmly packed brown sugar

3 large eggs

1 teaspoon vanilla extract

1 cup pecans or walnuts (about
3¼ ounces), lightly toasted (see page 301)
and coarsely chopped

2½ cups sifted all-purpose flour

1 teaspoon salt

2 teaspoons baking soda

Heat the oven to 350°F. Grease and flour
2 loaf pans or 1 large tube pan. Stir the
lemon juice into the mashed bananas.

In a large bowl, using an electric mixer,
cream the butter until light. Add both
kinds of sugar and cream again. Add the
eggs, one at a time, beating after each one.

Mix in the banana–lemon juice mixture, the vanilla, and the nuts. Sift together the flour, salt, and baking soda, and fold into the wet ingredients. Mix just until the batter is uniform.

Pour the batter into the prepared pans. Bake for about 45 minutes, until a toothpick inserted in the center comes out clean. Let cool for 10 minutes in the pan, then remove and cool on a rack.

Doughnuts

MAKES ABOUT 30 MEDIUM DOUGHNUTS

Deep-frying requires a large amount of oil, so that the oil's temperature will remain stable when the doughnuts are dropped in. If the oil cools down too much, the doughnuts will absorb more of it. A candy or frying thermometer, the glass kind that clips over the rim of the pot and stays there throughout the cooking, is useful for maintaining the oil's temperature.

As far back as I can remember, I was fascinated by the transformation of ingredients. When I was a toddler, we had an old refrigerator with the freezer compartment on the bottom. I often froze the milk left in my breakfast cereal bowl—I loved to come back later and find the bowl of frozen milk, with a few stray Froot Loops or Cocoa Puffs embedded in it. A bowl of milk, looking almost the same, but cold and rock-hard: extraordinary. When I was six or seven, I made my mother breakfast in bed for Mother's Day. The first thing I did was make the coffee, but I didn't serve it until the French toast and blueberries were finished: she drank it stone-cold, dutifully, and waited decades to tell me. On my eleventh birthday, I made a batch of these cake doughnuts from a recipe in *The Betty Crocker Picture Cookbook*. I ate most of them and had a stomachache

continued . . .

. . . *continued*

by evening. It was worth it, though; they were the best doughnuts I'd ever had. Making the recipe twenty years later at Deep Springs, I discovered they still are.

EQUIPMENT/SUPPLIES

doughnut cutter

deep-fry thermometer (or instant-read thermometer)

———

1 cup sugar

2 tablespoons butter, melted

4 egg yolks

½ cup buttermilk

¼ cup plain yogurt

1 teaspoon vanilla extract

3½ cups sifted all-purpose flour

2 teaspoons baking powder

1 teaspoon baking soda

½ teaspoon salt

¼ teaspoon ground mace

———

5 to 6 cups safflower oil, peanut oil, or other appropriate oil for frying

———

FOR DUSTING (OPTIONAL)

¾ cup sugar

1 tablespoon ground cinnamon

Beat the sugar and melted butter into the egg yolks in a large bowl. Beat in the buttermilk, yogurt, and vanilla until the mixture is uniform. Sift together the flour, baking powder, baking soda, salt, and mace, and add to the wet ingredients, stirring just until thoroughly combined. Cover the dough and refrigerate for at least 1½ hours, preferably overnight.

On a generously floured surface, gently roll out the dough to a ⅓-inch thickness, handling it as little as possible. It is a very delicate dough and easy to overwork. Dip the doughnut cutter in flour before cutting each doughnut. Using a thin metal spatula, transfer the cut doughnuts to a floured plate, the holes to another. Reroll the scraps gently, and cut a few more doughnuts. If you will be coating the doughnuts in cinnamon sugar, combine the sugar and cinnamon in a wide, shallow dish.

In a large, heavy saucepan over a medium-high flame, heat 5 to 6 cups of fresh oil (oil that has not been previously heated) to about 360°F—it's best to keep the oil between 350° and 375°F. Fry the doughnuts in small batches, turning once, until they are a medium-deep golden brown on both sides. The timing will depend on the size of the doughnuts. Break open a doughnut to be sure they are cooked all the way through. Allow the oil to return to the correct temperature before frying the next batch. Fry the holes and any remaining scraps of dough separately. Drain briefly on plenty of paper towels, then dredge them in cinnamon sugar, if desired, while still warm. I like to make half the doughnuts cinnamon-sugared and leave half plain.

Funnel Cakes

SERVES 6

Funnel cakes, another utterly gratifying deep-fried treat, are much simpler than doughnuts: the batter can be mixed and ready by the time the oil is hot. As with doughnuts, you need to keep a large amount of oil at a stable temperature, to ensure that the funnel cakes don't absorb too much of it.

At home, it is easiest to fry the funnel cakes one at a time in a heavy, 6- to 8-inch-deep saucepot, filled at least 3 inches deep with oil. At Deep Springs we fit four large food service–sized cans, both ends removed, into our commercial deep-fryer to achieve the round shape. As for the funnel, one that holds ½ cup is ideal—that's about how much batter you'll need for each cake.

EQUIPMENT/SUPPLIES

deep-fry thermometer (or instant-read thermometer)

funnel

—

4 to 5 cups safflower oil, peanut oil, or other appropriate oil for frying

2 cups sifted all-purpose flour

¼ cup granulated (white) sugar

1 teaspoon baking powder

½ teaspoon salt

¼ teaspoon ground mace

2 eggs

1½ cups whole milk

1½ teaspoons vanilla extract

powdered sugar for dusting (optional)

In a deep, heavy saucepan over a medium-high flame, heat the oil to 375°F. Meanwhile, sift together the flour, sugar, baking powder, salt, and mace. Whisk the eggs, milk, and vanilla together in a large bowl. Whisk the dry mixture into the wet mixture just until uniform.

Ladle ½ cup of batter into a funnel, your finger stopping the hole. Release the batter into the hot oil, "scribbling" the stream of batter evenly over the surface of the oil. The frying batter will rise to the top in a tangled mass. After about a minute, when the cake is golden brown on the underside, gently flip it and cook the other side until golden brown, about a minute more. Drain on plenty of paper towels for a few moments. Allow the oil to return to 375°F before frying the next funnel cake.

I like funnel cakes unsugared, but most people prefer them dusted lightly with powdered sugar: put a spoonful of powdered sugar in a sieve and tap the sieve over the warm cakes. Consume immediately.

CHAPTER 4

Bread, Butter, Crackers, and Cheese

Deep Springs students have always loved making and eating bread. Once, an experienced baker, the wife of a Deep Springs professor, taught a very popular course, "Breads of Europe and the Middle East," in which each student baked many, many loaves of bread, including some made with sourdough cultures they had "caught" themselves. Breadmaking can become wonderfully complex, but don't forget that it's also quite simple. I'll always remember one of my classmates at Deep Springs, making bread for that evening's dinner in the Boardinghouse kitchen, being struck with an epiphany: "You just take powder and germs, mix in some water, and you get bread!"

A warm loaf of home-baked bread makes the simplest meal quite special. In the world of food and cooking, bread occupies its own sovereign kingdom. Making good bread requires a different sort of attention: precisely timed moments between long periods of simply leaving it alone. The few recipes here provide a good, basic introduction to breadmaking. If memories of past bread failures still haunt you, begin afresh with the easy recipes in this chapter.

Like other arenas of cookery, breadmaking requires close attention to timing and temperature. Making bread takes time. *When bread dough rises slowly, a more delicious yeasty, wheaty flavor develops.* These recipes presuppose an *ambient kitchen temperature of about 70°F;* your dough will rise more quickly in a warmer kitchen. I have found that it's easy, when making bread on warm days, to inadvertently let the dough rise for too long, to the point that the yeast is exhausted and the loaf emerges denser and not as well textured. At Deep Springs we always make our tastiest loaf bread in the colder months. Focaccia, an olive oil–rich flatbread with a quicker rise, is a great choice for warmer weather.

Bread's characteristic structure comes from the protein in wheat, called gluten. You knead bread dough for a long period of time to fully develop this gluten into long, elastic strands. In contrast, the quick bread recipes in the previous chapter, leavened with baking powder or baking soda, require very brief mixing, so little elastic gluten is formed. See Butter Piecrust (page 443) or Handmade Egg Noodles (page 388) for further perspective on gluten.

All these breads are superb warm from the oven and stay good and moist for the rest of the day. Left at room temperature, they are good as toast the next day. *Never refrigerate bread*; it goes stale in the refrigerator faster than at room temperature. Once cooled completely, wrap extra whole loaves of bread well with plastic wrap. Immediately freeze any loaves you will not be using that day. Thaw the bread, wrapped, for several hours at room temperature, then unwrap, brush with water, and heat in a 400°F oven for about 5 minutes, until the crispiness of the crust is restored. It will taste almost fresh-baked.

Don't let bread get moldy. At Deep Springs we put stale bread scraps in a deep pan that sits on the back of our big convection oven. The bread dries quickly and is easily pulverized to make fine breadcrumbs, good for frying. Sometimes, using a food processor, I pulse chunks of moister, day-old bread to coarse crumbs and toast them until golden in a 325°F oven with olive oil and salt, as a topping for pasta. See Italian Meatballs, page 322, for more about breadcrumbs. Make crumbs, croutons (page 300), or French Toast (page 89) out of bread that is more than two days old. If bread develops mold, toss it in the compost.

Dinner Bread

MAKES 4 LOAVES, 1¼ POUNDS EACH

Warm bread at dinner. A talented bread enthusiast developed this easy, basic recipe for the Deep Springs kitchen. It fits perfectly into our cooking schedule: we make the "sponge" right after breakfast and mix the dough first thing when we come in to prepare dinner. Each step takes only minutes.

The use of a sturdy, large-capacity electric mixer is specified in this recipe, but if your strength and stamina are good, you can knead your bread dough by hand. The recipe may be halved.

SPONGE

2 cups warm low-fat milk (bath temperature—110° to 115°F)

2 cups warm water

4 cups all-purpose flour, preferably unbleached, or 2 cups whole-wheat flour and 2 cups all-purpose flour

2 tablespoons brown sugar

1½ tablespoons active dry yeast (2 packets, or ½ ounce)

DOUGH

2 tablespoons salt

6 tablespoons butter, at room temperature

7 to 8 cups all-purpose flour

melted butter for brushing the tops (optional)

7:30 A.M.: MAKE THE SPONGE

Thoroughly combine the warm milk, warm water, 4 cups flour, brown sugar, and yeast in a large bowl, or in the bowl of a large-capacity electric mixer. Cover the bowl and let the sponge develop at *room temperature* (about 70°F—not in a particularly warm place) for 5 to 7 hours.

2:00 P.M.: MIX THE DOUGH

Add the salt, butter, and 7 cups flour to the sponge. Mix with the paddle attachment until the dough is uniform—it should leave the sides of the bowl. If the dough is still very soft and sticky, add another cup of flour. (Some of the variations will produce a stickier dough; these are more difficult to knead by hand.) Switch to the dough hook and knead the dough at low speed for about 10 minutes, stopping the mixer and turning the dough over once or twice to ensure even kneading. Lightly oil a large bowl and put the dough in it, turning it over once. Cover with plastic wrap (or enclose in a large, clean garbage bag) and let the dough rise at room temperature until doubled in bulk, a little over an hour.

3:30 P.M.: SHAPE THE LOAVES

Grease 4 loaf pans, or dust 2 flat baking sheets well with cornmeal. Punch down the dough and divide evenly into 4 pieces.

Take a piece of dough and gently flatten it into a rectangle. Choose its smoothest side and fold the dough in on itself in thirds, smooth side out, pinching the seam closed on the bottom. Place smooth side up in one of the bread pans, or on the cornmeal-dusted sheet. Shape the other 3 loaves. Cover the loaves with plastic wrap (or enclose in the inflated garbage bag) and leave them at room temperature for the second rise. Ensure that the oven will be at 400°F by baking time.

5:00 P.M.: BAKE THE BREAD

Have the oven at 400°F. (*Optional:* using a *razor-sharp blade,* slash the tops of the loaves lengthwise—this will help the bread expand in the oven and make for a lighter texture. A regular knife is not sharp enough and will just deflate the bread.) For a crispy crust, spray the loaves well with a water mister before putting them in the oven, and spray once or twice during the first 10 minutes of baking. Bake the bread in the hot oven for 25 to 30 minutes, until deep golden brown all over and lightly browned on the bottom. When done, the loaf will sound hollow when thumped on the bottom. If you have an instant-read thermometer, the internal temperature of the bread should be about 190°F. Remove from the pans and put on a rack to cool. (*Optional:* for a softer crust, brush the tops of the hot loaves with melted butter.) Let cool for at least 20 minutes before slicing.

Rich Dinner Bread

Follow the master recipe, reducing the water in the sponge by ½ cup. Add 2 tablespoons more butter and 2 whole eggs when you mix the dough.

Wheaty Dinner Bread

In a covered saucepan, combine 1 cup bulgur wheat and 2 cups water. Bring to a boil and let boil for 2 minutes. Drain well, saving the water, and let cool. Use the water as part of the liquid in the sponge in the master recipe, and stir the bulgur into the sponge. In the sponge, use all whole-wheat flour. When you mix the dough, add ½ teaspoon more salt and 2 tablespoons honey.

Sesame Bread

With its haunting sesame flavor, this is a good bread to accompany beef. Use half whole-wheat flour and half white flour in the sponge in the master recipe. When mixing the dough after the sponge has developed, replace half the butter with 3 tablespoons of strong, dark Asian sesame oil. After the first rising, shape the loaves into rounds, then press the tops of the loaves into a wide bowl of sesame seeds, coating the tops thoroughly with the seeds. The seeds will toast as the bread bakes.

continued . . .

. . . continued

Potato Bread

Scrub a small russet potato and cut into cubes. Put in a small saucepan with 2 cups water, and bring to a boil. Reduce the heat, cover, and boil gently until the potato is completely soft and falling apart. Drain, saving the liquid. Rub the potato chunks through a screen sieve back into the liquid, and use this warm liquid for the 2 cups of water in the sponge in the master recipe. The potato's starch will produce a stickier dough, but it gives the bread a wonderfully moist texture.

Bread for Lunch

Using the master Dinner Bread recipe or any of the variations, make the sponge the night before, using only 1½ teaspoons of yeast. Let it develop, covered, at room temperature overnight. Mix and knead the dough right after breakfast at 8:00, shape the loaves at 10:00, then bake at 11:30—the loaves will be finished and ready to slice at 12:30, when lunch is served.

Bread for the Next Day

Often, this 2-day process is much more convenient—and the bread that results has a deeper yeasty flavor but is perhaps a little denser. Using the master Dinner Bread recipe or any of the variations, cover and refrigerate the dough *immediately*

after mixing/kneading. The following day (12 to 24 hours later), take out the dough and shape it into loaves. Cover (or put in an inflated garbage bag) and let come to room temperature and rise for about 2 hours. Bake as usual.

Hamburger Buns

For good, soft, homemade hamburger buns, follow the master recipe or (if you like) any of the above variations, keeping the dough on the wet and sticky side. After the first rise, using well-floured hands (and a rolling pin, if necessary), form the dough into disks about 6 inches in diameter and about ½ inch thick. Thoroughly dredge the buns in flour before placing them on a baking sheet about 2 inches apart. Let rise, and bake the buns at 400°F for about 15 minutes, until golden on the outside and light and springy throughout. Brush off the excess flour and let the buns cool on a rack. Carefully split the buns with a sharp bread knife. Use them the same day you make them, or if they are a day old, butter and toast them first.

Focaccia

MAKES 2 FLATBREADS; SERVES 6 TO 8

For years, easy, forgiving focaccia was the only bread I made. The soft, olive oil–rich dough is rolled or stretched into a sheet and baked on a sheet pan, somewhat like a pizza with much simpler toppings. This master recipe can be started and baked in a single afternoon. It's a good yeast bread to make in hot weather—the Dinner Bread is a little more heat sensitive. Once you gain experience, the potato and longer-rise variations are as instructive as they are delicious. Substituting white wine for some of the water adds a subtle dimension to the yeastiness. You can use whole-wheat flour for part of the all-purpose flour if you prefer.

SPONGE

2 tablespoons yeast (2½ packets)

¼ teaspoon brown sugar

2 cups warm water (bath temperature—110° to 115°F)

2 cups all-purpose flour, preferably unbleached

DOUGH

2 teaspoons salt

6 tablespoons extra-virgin olive oil

1 tablespoon finely chopped fresh rosemary

about 3 cups all-purpose flour

TOPPING

4 tablespoons extra-virgin olive oil

1 tablespoon coarse sea salt

To make the sponge, in a large mixing bowl, stir the yeast and brown sugar into the water. Mix in 2 cups flour, and cover the bowl tightly with plastic wrap. Let the sponge develop at room temperature for 30 to 40 minutes.

To make the dough, mix the salt, olive oil, and rosemary into the sponge, then add enough flour to make a dough that just leaves the sides of the bowl, about 3 cups. Knead the dough for about 7 minutes, or until it is soft, shiny from the oil, and elastic. Put the dough in a large bowl coated with olive oil, turn once, cover with plastic wrap, and set aside to rise at room temperature for about 30 minutes.

Heat the oven to 450°F. Punch the dough down and cut it in half. Oil 2 baking sheets (about 12 by 17 inches) not too skimpily with olive oil. Gently stretch the halves of dough into rough rectangles of similar size, placing each onto a baking sheet. Cover loosely with plastic wrap (or place in an inflated garbage bag) and let rise for 30 minutes. Uncover and dimple the dough heavily, all over, by pressing your oiled fingers all the way down into the dough, almost piercing it.

continued . . .

. . . continued

Drizzle each focaccia with about 2 tablespoons of olive oil, and sprinkle evenly with the coarse sea salt. Cover and let rise again for about 30 minutes.

Bake in the hot oven until the bread is golden brown all over and light brown underneath, about 20 minutes. Rotate the pans once or twice during baking to ensure even browning. When done, remove the focaccia from the pans and place on a rack to cool.

Potato Focaccia

Scrub a russet potato and cut into chunks. Cover with water in a small saucepan and gently boil, covered, until the potato is completely soft. Pass the potato and its water through a food mill or a sieve. Add enough water to this thin potato purée to measure 2 cups. Let cool to warm bath temperature, if necessary, and proceed with the master recipe, substituting the purée for the water in the sponge. You will still need a total of about 5 cups flour, but this potato dough should be a little stickier than a regular dough—it will probably stick to the sides of the mixer bowl.

You may top this focaccia with paper-thin slices of unpeeled potato—use various sizes and colors—blanched in lightly salted water just until tender. After you dimple the dough, place the potato slices between the dimples, pressing them lightly into the dough, and brush each with olive oil. Make sure each slice gets some sea salt. This is one of the ways we celebrate our abundant Deep Springs potato crop.

Longer-Rise Focaccia

A longer rise promotes the development of more-complex wheat flavor and a springier texture. Following the master recipe or the potato variation, use only 1 tablespoon of yeast. Let the sponge develop for 3 hours. Let the finished dough rise for 1 hour.

Other Variations

Substitute sage for the rosemary. Or strew sautéed onions, thyme, and pitted oil-cured black olives over the dough. Or lightly press thin slices of red, ripe tomato into the dough after you dimple it. Beautiful.

Sweet Potato Bread

MAKES 3 LOAVES, 1 POUND EACH

This moist bread has a terrific orange color. In common usage, yams are orange-fleshed and sweet potatoes are yellow-fleshed, but the two are essentially interchangeable, and to my ear, "sweet potato bread" sounds more euphonious than "yam bread." The yams provide all the moisture in this bread—there is no added water. It's perfect for Thanksgiving (make extra for turkey sandwiches the next day) or in a menu with pork or chicken and cool-weather vegetables. I often bake half the dough as a loaf and make cinnamon rolls (see page 122) for the next morning out of the other half. Once the cinnamon rolls are assembled, they may be refrigerated overnight, to be baked the next morning. If cinnamon rolls seem too ambitious, this bread also makes excellent French toast (see page 89).

SPONGE

2¼ pounds orange-fleshed yams

1 tablespoon yeast (1½ packets)

1 cup all-purpose flour

DOUGH

1 tablespoon salt

3 tablespoons butter, at room temperature

about 4½ cups all-purpose flour, preferably unbleached

To make the sponge, first bake the yams on a foil-covered baking sheet in a 400°F oven until they are *completely soft*, about 1 hour and 20 minutes (longer for really fat yams). The foil is specified because yams expel syrup as they cook, which burns and permanently lacquers whatever surface they are baked on. Allow the yams to cool until you can handle them, about 35 minutes. Peel off the skins, but retain any syrup. Mash the yams (and syrup), making sure they are soft throughout (pass through a food mill or sieve if there are hard lumps). Measure out *2 ⅔ cups* of yam purée and place in a large mixing bowl. At this point the yams should be around 110°F, about the temperature of a warm bath. Heat a bit if necessary. Stir in the yeast and 1 cup of flour to make a rather stiff sponge. Cover with plastic wrap and let the sponge develop at room temperature for about 5 hours.

To make the dough, mix in the salt, butter, and enough flour to make a soft dough—it should be a little on the sticky side, and consequently will be easier to knead in a sturdy mixer than by hand.

continued . . .

. . . continued

Knead for 10 minutes—the dough should
be soft and elastic and the color of an
orange Creamsicle. Put the dough in an
oiled bowl, turn once, cover with plastic
wrap (or place in an inflated garbage bag),
and let rise at room temperature until
doubled in bulk, 1 to 1½ hours.

Dust 2 baking sheets well with flour.
Divide the dough evenly into 3 pieces,
and shape into round loaves. Dredge the
loaves in flour, coating them lightly but
thoroughly, and place on the baking sheets
(you may also bake this bread in 3 greased
loaf pans). Re-cover the dough and let
rise again at room temperature until it has
expanded by about a third, about 1 to
1½ hours. Heat the oven to 400°F.

Using a razor-sharp blade, slash the tops
of the loaves—this helps the bread expand
while baking. Bake the bread, rotating
it in the oven a couple of times during
baking, for 40 to 45 minutes, depending
on the thickness of the loaves. The bread
is done when it is well browned on top
and golden brown on the bottom. When
cooked through, the loaf sounds hollow
when thumped on the bottom. On an
instant-read thermometer, the loaf should
reach an internal temperature of 190°F.
Remove the bread from the pans to a cooling rack. Let cool for at least 20 minutes
before slicing.

FARM BUTTER

Much equipment has come and gone from the Deep Springs Boardinghouse kitchen over the years, but the same old wooden 1-pound butter mold, its corners rounded from many decades of use, is still used to shape small quantities of Deep Springs' own butter. Occasionally we bake with it, but most often it is reserved simply for lavishing on freshly baked bread.

Cream to be churned into the most delicious butter must first be ripened, or cultured. Mix ¼ cup of fresh, cultured yogurt or buttermilk into each quart of fresh cream. A quart of cream will yield a scant pound of butter. Put the cream in a jar with a well-fitting lid, and put the jar in a larger basin of hot water, sloshing the cream around in the jar occasionally. Heat the cream gently in this way until it reaches 80°F, barely lukewarm to the touch. Wrap the jar in towels to insulate it, and let stand overnight. When the cream is cultured, it should have a light, yogurty tanginess.

Once cultured, cool the cream to about 60°F. Put the cultured cream in the bowl of an electric mixer and whip on medium-low speed. At first, the cream will thicken as for whipped cream. Continuing to whip, you will begin to see flaky granules of butter. When the granules stick together in clumps the size of corn kernels, stop the churning. Immediately drain off the liquid. This liquid is the original buttermilk, quite different from the cultured-milk product we buy at the store.

Wash the butter in a large bowl, in water that is about 50°F. Use only as much water as necessary to wash out the excess buttermilk. Take handfuls of the butter and squeeze gently to remove as much water as possible.

Finally, knead the butter 20 or 30 times to give it a good texture. Pack the butter into a mold lined with plastic wrap, and chill. Remove from the mold and wrap well. To serve, bring to room temperature.

Cheese Crackers

MAKES ABOUT 30 CRACKERS; SERVES 6

This recipe and those that follow make enough crackers to generously serve 6 people as a soup or cheese accompaniment. These crackers are also good with Quince Jam (page 437).

1 cup all-purpose flour

½ teaspoon salt, plus more for sprinkling

½ teaspoon dry mustard

¼ teaspoon cayenne pepper

1 tablespoon butter

1½ cups (6 ounces) grated extra-sharp Cheddar cheese, at room temperature

1 egg

1 egg yolk

In a medium mixing bowl, whisk together the flour, salt, mustard, and cayenne. Work in the butter and cheese with your hands very well, until the mixture is crumbly and uniform. Mix in the egg and yolk, and knead the dough a few times, until it is uniform. Wrap tightly and let rest, refrigerated, for at least 1 hour, to allow the flour to absorb the liquid.

Heat the oven to 375°F. Lightly grease a baking sheet. Divide the dough into fourths. Working with one piece of dough at a time, on a lightly floured board with a lightly floured rolling pin (or using the rollers of a hand-crank pasta machine), roll the dough thin. Prick all over with a fork, cut into squares or diamonds (a pizza cutter works well), and carefully place on the baking sheet. Sprinkle the crackers lightly with salt. Bake until they are pale golden brown, 8 to 10 minutes. The crackers will crisp as they cool on a rack.

Black Pepper Cheese Crackers

Add coarsely ground black pepper, about 1 teaspoon, to the dry ingredients, and reduce the cayenne to a pinch. These are excellent with fresh corn soup.

Whole-Wheat Crackers

MAKES ABOUT 30 CRACKERS; SERVES 6

These crackers and the Puffy Salties on page 144 are based on recipes from Diana Kennedy's cookbook *Nothing Fancy*—one of my favorites. Try them with a generous schmear of soft home-made cheese (see page 146).

¼ cup fine bulgur wheat

1 cup whole-wheat flour (whole-grain spelt flour may also be used)

1 cup minus 2 tablespoons sifted all-purpose flour

3 tablespoons wheat germ

1 teaspoon salt

¼ teaspoon baking powder

6 tablespoons cold butter

½ cup buttermilk

Toast the bulgur wheat in a small dry skillet over a medium-high flame, tossing constantly, until light brown with an appealing nutty scent. Transfer to a small plate to cool. Mix the bulgur with the whole-wheat and all-purpose flours, wheat germ, salt, and baking powder in a medium bowl, then thoroughly work in the butter until evenly dispersed throughout the mixture. Add the buttermilk and blend just until the dough is uniform. Wrap tightly and let rest, refrigerated, for 30 minutes.

Heat the oven to 375°F. Lightly grease a baking sheet. Divide the dough into fourths. Working with one piece of dough at a time, on a lightly floured board with a lightly floured rolling pin (or using the rollers of a hand-crank pasta machine), roll the dough thin—as thin as the bulgur will allow. Prick all over with a fork, and cut into squares (a pizza cutter works well). Carefully place on the baking sheet. Bake just until light brown, about 10 minutes; watch carefully. The crackers will crisp as they cool on a rack.

Puffy Salties

MAKES ABOUT 75 SMALL CRACKERS; SERVES 6

These simple crackers are good with soups of all types. You will need a clean spray bottle filled with water.

2 cups sifted all-purpose flour

½ teaspoon salt

3 tablespoons butter, at room temperature

½ cup cold water

coarse sea salt or kosher salt for sprinkling

In a medium bowl, thoroughly mix the flour, salt, and butter. Mix in the cold water and *knead the dough well, until it is very elasticized.* Wrap and let rest for 10 minutes.

Heat the oven to 400°F. Divide the dough into fourths. On a lightly floured board with a lightly floured rolling pin (or using the rollers of a hand-crank pasta machine), roll the dough *very thin*—a little thinner than a tortilla. Spray lightly with water, then evenly sprinkle sea salt or kosher salt over the dough—not too much! Using a pizza cutter, cut the dough into 1-inch squares. Transfer to a lightly greased baking sheet. Bake until puffed and light brown, 5 to 6 minutes; watch carefully.

Thyme Crackers

MAKES ABOUT 20 LARGE CRACKERS; SERVES 6

These large crackers, with their beautiful scattering of whole thyme leaves baked right into the dough, go well with clam chowder (or any kind of chowder), but they are also superb with soft goat cheese and honey for dessert. You will need a clean spray bottle filled with water for spraying the surface of the crackers.

7 or 8 sprigs fresh thyme

2 cups sifted all-purpose flour

2 tablespoons wheat germ (optional)

1 tablespoon sugar

1 teaspoon salt

2 tablespoons butter, at room temperature

⅔ cup milk

coarse sea salt or kosher salt for sprinkling

To prepare the thyme, carefully strip the tiny individual leaves and clusters of leaves off the stems. Pick apart any large clusters of leaves. You should have about 1 tablespoon.

In a large bowl, blend the thyme, flour, wheat germ (if using), sugar, and salt. Thoroughly work in the butter with your hands—it should be evenly dispersed throughout the mixture. In this process you will bruise many of the thyme leaves, releasing their scent into the dough. Mix in the milk, enough to make a pliable dough, and mix the dough just until it is uniform. Wrap the dough well with plastic wrap and let rest in the refrigerator for at least 1 hour.

Heat the oven to 400°F. On a lightly floured board with a lightly floured rolling pin (or using the rollers of a hand-crank pasta machine), roll one-third of the dough at a time into an oblong or rectangle, a little thinner than a tortilla. With a sharp knife or pizza cutter, cut into long strips 1 to 2 inches wide.

Place the strips on a lightly greased baking sheet, spray lightly with water, and sprinkle lightly with coarse or kosher salt. Bake the crackers in the center of the hot oven for 5 to 6 minutes. *Watch them carefully*—they should have many golden brown spots but not be browned throughout. They burn easily because of the sugar in the dough and the high heat of the oven. Remove the crackers from the sheet to cool on a rack.

SERVING CHEESE

Cheese is a universe unto itself. Western Europe is a cheese lover's paradise, with many hundreds of traditional varieties still made there today, each a unique expression of its place. Happily, many of these European cheese traditions are gradually taking root in North America.

Serve cheese on a wooden board, with a small knife of appropriate strength and sharpness for the type of cheese being served. Cut slices of cheese to go on good bread or crackers, or just cut or break cheeses into chunks to eat by themselves. The French love a bite or two of cheese after a meal, before or instead of dessert. Here are some guidelines for serving cheese:

Serve cheese at room temperature. The fat in cheese carries much of its flavor, but cold fat doesn't accomplish this as well.

Serve cheese simply. The simple cracker recipes in this chapter (the ones that don't contain cheese) beautifully accompany cheese, as would a loaf of home-baked bread. Apples, pears, grapes, and dates complement the flavor of many cheeses, while citrus and most other acid fruit may detract from it. Nuts—especially sweet nuts right out of the shell—are also a good accompaniment.

continued . . .

. . . continued

Many fine cheeses may be expensive, but a little goes a long way. An ounce of cheese is about the size of your thumb. Though it's very easy to eat more, an ounce per person is usually enough, especially of cheeses high in fat. If you wish to serve an inexpensive cheese in an elegant way, feta cheese is a great possibility: let a block of white feta come to room temperature for an hour or two, then drizzle it with fragrant olive oil and grind black pepper over it. This is marvelous in summer with fresh ripe figs, or at other times of year with sweet dates (Medjool, Khadrawi, and Black Sphinx are all good date varieties).

Queso Blanco

MAKES ABOUT 2 CUPS

This is the simplest cheese you can make. When all the Deep Springs dairy cows are in full production, there is more milk than the community can drink, so naturally cheesemaking enters everyone's mind. There is always a lot of talk of Roquefort and Gouda and Brie, but this milk cheese, known in Latin American cooking as *queso blanco* (and in Indian cookery as *paneer*) is what usually gets made.

Keep in mind that cheesemaking is a form of food preservation. As such, for best results, *make sure your raw ingredient (in this case, milk) is absolutely fresh, and that your surfaces and utensils are absolutely clean.* This simple cheese will keep, refrigerated, for a few days if made with whole milk, longer if made with skim. If you make it with whole milk, a soft, creamy, almost spreadable cheese results. With nonfat milk, you will have a much firmer, slightly rubbery product (also delicious, but different). It does not readily melt in either case, but if made with lower-fat milk, it can be crumbled and browned in a nonstick skillet in a little oil. The whey, the by-product, may be made into a tasty and unusual lemonade (recipe follows).

instant-read thermometer

cheesecloth (or clean cotton "flour sack" towel)

———

8 cups (½ gallon) very fresh whole, low-fat, or skim milk

¼ cup vinegar (cider vinegar or red wine vinegar; the label should specify 5% acidity)

1 teaspoon salt

Heat the milk in a heavy pot over a medium-high flame, stirring and scraping the bottom frequently with a wooden spoon, until the milk reaches 180°F. Stir in the vinegar—the milk will curdle; in other words, the soft curds will separate from the liquid whey. Set a colander over a large stockpot. Wet the cheesecloth with cold tap water, and wring it out. Line the colander with cheesecloth. Pour the hot curds and whey through the cheesecloth, using a rubber spatula to scrape any bits of stuck curd off the bottom of the pot. If you like, pour the hot whey into a pitcher and make whey lemonade.

Drain the curds for a moment, then turn them back into the pot. Stir in the salt thoroughly, then pour the cheese back into the cheesecloth-lined colander. If necessary, arrange the cheese into a nice round shape. Cover the top with plastic wrap, put the colander, set over a bowl, in the refrigerator, and let the cheese continue to drain for 1 to 2 days, turning once. When the cheese has drained sufficiently, remove it from the cloth and wrap it tightly. Keep refrigerated.

This cheese has many uses. Its fresh, uncomplicated flavor is best enhanced by other flavorful elements: on little toasts with ripe tomatoes and herbs, or crumbled into spicy dishes. It is particularly good crumbled and sizzled in a little hot olive oil in a nonstick skillet until it browns. Serve immediately by itself, or alongside a salad, or topped with a relish . . . possibilities abound.

Whey Lemonade

The Queso Blanco recipe will yield about 8 cups of milky whey. While it is still warm, stir in 1 cup of sugar. Add the juice and grated zest of 3 lemons and a big sprig of fresh mint. Let cool, then let steep and chill in the refrigerator for several hours. Strain into ice-filled glasses, garnish with slices of fresh lemon, and enjoy.

Great Lunches

Enthusiastic class discussions often spill over into the lunch hour, and afternoon ranch work begins immediately after lunch, so Deep Springs lunches must deliver a powerful, quickly consumed nutritional punch, satisfying the hunger that comes after a morning of intense classes and fueling the body for an afternoon of sweaty outdoor work.

What constitutes a great lunch is limited only by your taste, appetite, and imagination. Of course, dishes for many other great lunches may be found in several neighboring chapters; this one gives a sampling of dishes—usually meals in themselves, inexpensive to prepare and appealing in hot or cold weather—that I rely on most heavily at Deep Springs: pizza, pasta, macaroni and cheese, enchiladas, sandwiches. . . .

Lunch, served at the hottest time of the day, is when Deep Springers like to consume vast quantities of cool, refreshing beverages such as iced tea and lemonade; you will find recipes for those at the end of the chapter.

continued . . .

Reatha's Macaroni and Cheese

SERVES 6 TO 8

My friend Reatha, originally from South Carolina, is a great Southern cook. This is my written-down version of her renowned "mac & cheese." I've adapted and changed a couple of things over the years, but it still evokes her generous spirit.

This macaroni and cheese is rich. Serve it with something tart and refreshing, like a green salad, sliced summer tomatoes, or Apple and Pear Salad (page 277), and follow with a nice nap. The crumb topping is optional but excellent—we all love something creamy underneath something crunchy.

1 pound dry large elbow macaroni

4 tablespoons butter

12 ounces extra-sharp Cheddar cheese, grated (about 3 cups)

4 ounces mozzarella cheese, grated (about 1 cup)

4 ounces Muenster cheese, grated (about 1 cup)

two 12-ounce cans evaporated milk

3 eggs, beaten

1 teaspoon salt

1 teaspoon dry mustard

⅛ teaspoon cayenne pepper

¾ teaspoon white pepper

CRUMB TOPPING (OPTIONAL)

1½ cups unseasoned breadcrumbs

3 tablespoons butter, melted

1 or 2 pinches salt

black pepper

paprika for sprinkling on top

Heat the oven to 350°F. Cook the macaroni in a large pot in plenty of boiling salted water (the water should taste lightly salty) until soft but not falling apart. Drain well, shaking the colander, but do not rinse. Dump the hot macaroni into a large bowl or, if there is ample room to mix, back into the pot, and toss it gently with the butter. Combine the cheeses in a medium bowl, and toss three-quarters of the cheese with the hot buttered macaroni. In a medium bowl, whisk together the milk, eggs, salt, and spices to make a savory custard. Dump the macaroni mixture into an ungreased 9-by-13-inch baking dish and pour the custard over it. Top with the remaining cheese.

Make the topping, if you opt for it, while the macaroni bakes: combine the crumbs, melted butter, salt, and pepper to taste in a medium bowl and toast carefully in

continued . . .

. . . *continued*

the oven on a baking sheet, or toss in a medium-hot skillet, until the crumbs are golden brown, about 5 minutes.

Bake the macaroni and cheese for 7 to 8 minutes, then bring the dish out of the oven and quickly stir the whole thing around to evenly distribute the heat. Immediately return the dish to the oven and bake for another 7 to 8 minutes, then take it out and stir it again. When the cheese is melted and the sauce is smooth and creamy, remove it from the oven. Do not overbake: if the cheese gets too hot it will separate and the creaminess will turn to greasiness. You can check the temperature of the sauce with an instant-read thermometer; at 140°F, the cheese will be melted and the eggs cooked. Sprinkle lightly with the optional topping and paprika, and serve.

Baked Potatoes

SERVES 6

These baked potatoes emerge with a light, fluffy texture and tender, flavorful skin. Alongside baked potatoes and the array of toppings, I like to serve an abundant green salad and something rich in protein: hard-boiled eggs or chicken salad.

More than toddlers love candy, Deep Springs rancher/cattlewoman Iris Pope loves baked potatoes. "My mouth is watering!" she always yells into the kitchen after seeing "Baked Potatoes" on the lunch menu board.

6 large russet potatoes

1 tablespoon vegetable oil

1½ teaspoons salt

½ teaspoon black pepper

FOR SERVING

butter

sour cream

thinly sliced green onions or chives

crumbled cooked bacon

grated Cheddar cheese

Sautéed Mushrooms (page 237)

chopped cooked broccoli

Heat the oven to 450°F. Scrub the potatoes under running water with a clean cloth and let them briefly air-dry. Combine the oil, salt, and pepper and rub this mixture all over the potatoes with your hands: the abrasion of the salt tenderizes the skin. Prick each potato in two places with a small knife. Arrange the potatoes on a baking sheet and bake for 40 minutes to an hour, or until thoroughly soft inside. Slit the top of each potato. Let people add the toppings of their choice.

Pizza

SERVES 3 TO 4

You could easily find more sophisticated recipes for pizza, but this, baked in a rectangular sheet pan and cut into squares, evokes the perennial lunch-time favorite of generations of Deep Springs students. Green salad with abundant creamy dressing is a good accompaniment.

To accommodate the rising time for the dough, start 3 hours before you intend to serve the pizza. A little semolina flour, made from high-protein durum wheat, makes a good crust with a nice straw color, but you can successfully use more all-purpose flour in its place.

Many suggestions for toppings are given below, both with and without tomato sauce. A list giving a quick over-view of the assembly instructions is also provided.

SPONGE FOR CRUST

1 cup warm water (bath temperature—115°F)

pinch of brown sugar

1 cup semolina flour

½ cup whole-wheat flour

2¼ teaspoons active dry yeast (1 packet)

continued...

. . . continued

DOUGH FOR CRUST

1¾ cups all-purpose flour, or more as needed

1 tablespoon extra-virgin olive oil

1½ teaspoons salt

GARLIC OIL

2 cloves garlic, crushed to a purée

pinch of salt

2 tablespoons olive oil

ASSEMBLY

about 1 cup Thick Tomato Sauce (page 417)

2 to 2½ cups (8 to 10 ounces) grated mozzarella cheese

about 2 cups toppings of choice (see the list on facing page)

FOR SERVING

freshly grated Parmesan cheese

hot red pepper flakes

To make the sponge, pour the warm water into a large bowl and stir in the brown sugar, semolina flour, whole-wheat flour, and yeast. Cover the bowl and let the sponge develop for 1 hour.

To make the dough, mix the all-purpose flour, olive oil, and salt into the sponge. If it seems overly sticky, add a bit more all-purpose flour, enough to produce a soft,

silky dough. Knead for 8 to 10 minutes. Put the dough in a large, oiled bowl, turn to coat with oil, cover, and let rise for 45 minutes. This is a good time to grate the cheese and make the sauce.

Heat the oven to 450°F. Position a rack near the center of the oven. Line a sheet pan with parchment paper well rubbed with olive oil and dusted with semolina flour or cornmeal; if you have no parchment, just oil the pan well and dust generously. On a floured surface, gently stretch and shape the dough to an evenly thick rectangle (it's okay to use a rolling pin), and lay it in the pan. Lightly press the dough to fill out the sides and corners of the pan, making a rim. Cover (an inflated garbage bag works well) and let rise for 20 minutes while you ready the toppings.

To make the garlic oil, in a small bowl, mix the garlic with a pinch of salt and the olive oil. Brush over the surface of the crust.

To assemble the pizza, top it first with the sauce, then with about a third of the grated mozzarella cheese, then the topping of your choice, and finish with the remaining mozzarella.

Bake the pizza for about 20 minutes, or until the crust is cooked through and browned on the bottom and the cheese is bubbly and brown on top.

Let the pizza rest and "set up" for about 5 minutes before cutting. Serve with Parmesan and hot red pepper flakes.

Assembly, bottom to top

* oiled pan, or pan lined with oil-rubbed parchment paper

* dusting of semolina or cornmeal

* dough

* garlic oil

* sauce

* one-third of the grated mozzarella

* topping

* remaining grated mozzarella

Favorite traditional thin-sliced toppings with tomato sauce

* pepperoni

* mushrooms and parsley

* zucchini (lightly salted/peppered) and red onion

* fresh tomato (lightly salted/peppered) and oil-cured olives (use less sauce)

* sausage and sautéed Greens (page 232) (precook loose Italian sausage and pour off the excess fat)

* fresh tomato (lightly salted/peppered) and fresh basil (use less sauce)

Favorite unusual toppings without tomato sauce

* lightly sautéed fennel, oil-cured olives, lemon zest, a little mozzarella, and Parmesan at the end (cool weather)

* cream-simmered leeks, a scraping of nutmeg, and Gruyère cheese (good with cornmeal in the crust instead of semolina—excellent in cooler weather, when leeks are in season)

* fresh, raw spinach tossed with olive oil, salt, pepper, and grated mozzarella, topped with dollops of ricotta cheese (the spinach wilts and cooks in the oven)

* small cubed boiled potatoes, pesto, mozzarella and Parmesan cheeses (warm weather)

* ripe pear with blue cheese and dollops of ricotta seasoned with nutmeg (cool weather)

* chopped cooked bacon, chopped fresh escarole tossed with olive oil, and mozzarella, topped after baking with grated hard-boiled egg

EGG PIZZA

Americans are often surprised to discover Europeans eating pizza that has had an egg cracked over it during the last 5 to 6 minutes of baking—the white just set, the yolk still gooey.

Clam Chowder

SERVES 6 TO 8

This is not a proper New England clam chowder. Given good fresh clams, I make chowder with them containing little beyond onion, salt pork, potatoes, milk, and cream. We can't easily get good, fresh clams in the eastern Sierra, but this version using canned clams, a thick, cafeteria-style clam chowder, never fails to please. It is especially popular with the over-60 crowd at Deep Springs. I always make corn chowder (see the variation following) at the same time and serve both chowders with homemade crackers (such as Thyme Crackers, page 144).

6 tablespoons butter

½ cup all-purpose flour

1 large yellow onion, cut into small dice

2 stalks celery, cut into small dice

3 teaspoons salt, or more as needed

2 teaspoons fresh thyme leaves, coarsely chopped, or ½ teaspoon dried thyme

3 cups whole milk

two 8-ounce bottles clam juice

three 6.5-ounce cans chopped clams with juice

1 pound boiling potatoes (gold, white, or red), peeled only if you insist, cut into chunks

½ cup heavy (whipping) cream

¼ cup chopped parsley

freshly ground black pepper

In a heavy soup pot, melt 5 tablespoons of the butter over medium-high heat, and stir in the flour to make a roux. Stirring with a wooden spoon, let the mixture come to a full, bubbly boil. It will be a pasty white color at first; continue cooking, stirring constantly, until the color turns to a pale beige. Remove from the flame and let cool for about 10 minutes.

Meanwhile, in a smaller saucepan, melt the remaining tablespoon of butter over medium-high heat. When it sizzles, add the onion and celery with a teaspoon of the salt and cook, stirring frequently, for about 5 minutes. As the vegetables become translucent, stir in the thyme, cover the pan, and reduce the heat to low, cooking until the vegetables are tender.

Add the milk, bottled clam juice, and all juice from the canned clams (but not the clams themselves) to the pot with the roux, stir well, and bring to a simmer over a medium-high flame. Go over the bottom of the pan frequently with your wooden spoon. When the mixture thickens, reduce the heat and stir in the cooked onion and celery. Keep warm.

Put the potatoes into the same small saucepan in which you cooked the onion and celery. Cover with water, add the remaining 2 teaspoons salt, and bring to a boil. Boil gently until the potatoes are soft. Drain well and add the potatoes to the chowder (this separate cooking of the potatoes keeps the flavors of the chowder in balance).

Add the clams, cream, and parsley. Add salt to taste (this will depend on the saltiness of the clams) and freshly ground pepper. Heat the chowder gently—do not let it boil. It is excellent reheated the next day.

Corn Chowder

Replace the clams and clam juice in the master recipe with 4 cups fresh sweet corn kernels, cut off the cob, and 2 cups chicken or vegetable stock (page 364 or 261). Proceed as directed, simmering the corn and other ingredients for about 5 minutes before adding the cream. Since the flavors go so well together, I often can't resist adding a can of chopped roasted green chiles to corn chowder, or a good dollop of Green Chile Relish (page 423). Serve with Black Pepper Cheese Crackers (page 142). Compare this old-fashioned corn chowder with the sleeker, more modern Catherine's Corn Soup on page 229.

Grilled Cheese Sandwich

SERVES 1

This dish fulfills, perhaps more than any other, that primal gastronomic desire for something crisp on the outside and creamy within. It is delicious with a crisp, spicy-tart apple, or a beer, or a bowl of tomato soup.

Lightly butter 2 slices of good brown bread on one side. Place sharp white Cheddar cheese between them, buttered sides out, and toast on both sides in a skillet over the lowest heat. It takes about 10 minutes to cook properly, so the cheese is perfectly melted and the bread perfectly toasted. Cut in half diagonally and serve immediately.

Good Sandwiches

Whole books have been written about sandwiches, and many more could be. At Deep Springs we rarely use purchased bread or presliced deli meat, so sandwiches for lunch are a labor of love: I'll be roasting extra beef the night before (which takes hours; see page 313); hand-slicing the beef paper-thin (the old electric meat slicer has sat in the repair shop for years); starting the bread dough; mixing, rising, shaping, baking, and cooling the bread; and then slicing it by hand, along with tomatoes, onions, lettuce, and cheese. Furthermore, the lunch line in the Boardinghouse moves with excruciating slowness on sandwich day, as each person must assemble his or her own sandwich. Nonetheless, the results are a dream; how often do you get such a fresh sandwich? The lesson to be learned here is that *even something as simple as a sandwich benefits from the same care and close attention as any other food.* Even a "boring"-sounding sandwich—wheat bread, sliced turkey, Cheddar, mayonnaise, mustard, lettuce, tomato, and onion—will be startlingly good if all elements are fresh and treated with care. Here are a few pointers for very good sandwiches:

Fresh bread: choose bread that is soft, flavorful, and baked that day. Chewy, artisan-style breads, baguettes, large rolls—all these are wonderful to eat on their own, but they are rarely my first choice for a sandwich. Sliced packaged bread is often pointedly sweet. Focaccia is an ever-popular sandwich bread in upscale cafés, but I find it overly rich and oily. The basic Dinner Bread recipe in this book, and all variations, makes good sandwiches. If your bread is not fresh, just put on a little more spread.

Flavorful spread: mayonnaise carries flavors beautifully and also helps keep moisture from your filling (tomatoes are often the culprit) from soaking into the bread and making it soggy. Mustard enhances the flavor of virtually any cold meat. A little apricot jam mixed into mayonnaise is great with ham, pork, or turkey. Also consider chutney, or any type of relish, or soft cheese. Whatever your choice, take care to spread it all the way to the edges of the bread.

Green: a little fresh, tender greenness is essential to a sandwich. Like any salad, it needs to be washed and dried (see page 270). If you want a lot of lettuce on your sandwich, and you intend to eat it immediately, consider tossing it with vinaigrette or other dressing first. Choices are legion—leaf lettuce, watercress, arugula, even herbs (I like a few mint leaves on a sliced lamb sandwich).

Tomato: I confess: in the colder months of the year, when tomatoes are definitely not in season, I still keep a few Roma tomatoes on hand for sandwiches. For the best flavor, salt the tomato, but if you're wrapping the sandwich for later, wait to salt it until just before you eat it, or else the tomato will throw off much of its juice, sogging the bread. On a ham sandwich, try a few slices of leftover fried green tomato (see page 255).

Onion: thinly sliced red onion is beautiful, a health tonic, and a flavor enhancer.

Meat/cheese: meat and cheese for sandwiches should be thinly sliced. Try a vegetable peeler, rather than a knife, to dispense cheese onto a sandwich, if a block of cheese is all you have. Home-roasted meats make sandwiches with singular character, especially roast beef, but good-quality ham, turkey, and other deli meats—prepared specifically for use in sandwiches—rarely disappoint.

Finally, enjoy your sandwich at *room temperature, not refrigerator-cold*—it will taste much better.

Tuna Salad

SERVES 3 TO 4

When Deep Springs students wander into the Boardinghouse kitchen and notice I'm mixing up a giant bowl of tuna salad, they know that tuna melts will be on the menu for lunch: generous scoops of tuna atop thick slices of homemade bread, with mild, creamy Muenster cheese melted over the top.

two 5-ounce cans solid white tuna packed in water

¼ cup finely diced red onion

juice of ½ lemon, plus more as needed

½ teaspoon red wine vinegar

½ teaspoon Dijon mustard

⅛ teaspoon salt, plus more as needed

⅛ teaspoon freshly ground black pepper

⅓ cup finely diced celery (optional)

pinch of cayenne pepper

3 to 4 tablespoons mayonnaise

Remove the tuna from the can and drain well in a screen sieve. Put the tuna in a medium bowl and flake it not too finely with a fork, then toss with the onion, lemon juice, vinegar, mustard, salt, black pepper, celery (if using), and cayenne, and let marinate for 10 minutes. Mix in the mayonnaise. Taste for salt and acidity, adding more salt and another squeeze of lemon, if necessary.

Mediterranean Tuna Salad

In place of the mayonnaise in the master recipe, use 2 to 3 tablespoons olive oil. Add a handful of coarsely chopped green olives, a few chopped capers, some coarsely chopped parsley, and an extra squeeze of lemon. This mixture is delightful and healthful atop a green salad.

Tuna Salad with Pickled Vegetables

Another delicious tuna salad is flavored simply with a big handful of chopped pickled vegetables (see page 429). Add a spoonful or two of the pickling liquid and a little chopped parsley, and bind with mayonnaise.

Curry Tofu Salad

SERVES 4 TO 6

This makes an excellent sandwich filling, but I also like it piled on cucumber slices or stuffed in celery sticks. Nothing else but tofu works for this recipe—its light, mellow character is the perfect foundation for building an intense and lively curry flavor. I first devised it to have something to serve the non–tuna eaters when I make tuna melts for lunch at Deep Springs, but it became popular with everyone, even people who thought they didn't like tofu.

1 pound firm tofu

¾ teaspoon salt, plus more as needed

1-inch piece fresh ginger, peeled and thinly sliced

2 cloves garlic

2 tablespoons canola oil or other vegetable oil

6 large white mushrooms, wiped clean, trimmed, halved, and sliced

1½ teaspoons mild or hot Curry Powder (page 358)

1 small carrot, peeled and finely shredded

2 green onions, thinly sliced

1 medium stalk celery, finely diced

¼ cup mayonnaise, plus more as needed

1 tablespoon yellow mustard

1 teaspoon soy sauce

1 tablespoon fresh lemon juice, plus more as needed

freshly ground black pepper

3 to 4 tablespoons chopped fresh dill, parsley, or cilantro (optional)

Crumble the tofu finely in a medium bowl, sprinkle with ¾ teaspoon salt, and mix well.

Finely mince together the ginger and garlic. In a wide skillet over a medium-high flame, heat the oil. Throw in the garlic and ginger with a pinch of salt and sauté, stirring, for 20 to 30 seconds. Add the mushrooms with a pinch of salt, then add the curry powder and cook, stirring, for another minute. Add the tofu, continuing to stir as the tofu heats through and excess water evaporates, 4 to 5 minutes. When there is no more excess water, remove from the heat and let the tofu cool completely in the pan, about 30 minutes. Add the remaining ingredients: carrot, green onion, celery, mayonnaise, mustard, soy sauce, lemon, black pepper to taste, and optional herbs. Taste for seasoning, adding more salt, pepper, lemon juice, or mayonnaise to balance. Serve immediately or refrigerate.

HARD-BOILED EGGS

This method produces an egg that is cooked through, but no more; the yolk is bright colored and creamy, with no gray ring, and the white is firm but tender.

Very fresh eggs, when hard-boiled, can be difficult to peel. If your eggs are very fresh, age them at room temperature for a day. Place eggs gently in a saucepan and cover with cold water. Quickly bring to a boil over high heat. The moment they come to a boil, slap on the lid and remove them from the heat. Let sit, undisturbed, for exactly 7 minutes (for large eggs), 7½ minutes (for extra-large eggs), or 8 minutes (for jumbo eggs). At high altitudes, add 30 seconds to the sitting time.

If you are cooking a large quantity of eggs in a large pot over a small burner, it will take a long time for the water to reach a boil. In this case, the eggs may need to cook for only a minute or two after the water starts to boil: break open an egg to check, and judge how much more time is needed to cook the yolk through.

Pour off the hot water and run cold water over the eggs for a minute, then dump enough ice into the pan to cover the eggs. Chill thoroughly in the ice bath for about 10 minutes. To peel, gently crack the shell all over, then start removing the shell at the blunt end. The shell and the filmy membrane should easily peel away.

Hard-boiled eggs are excellent in your lunch for any kind of outdoor excursion, but don't forget to pack some salt and pepper—simply fold a little into a small sheet of aluminum foil. The best hard-boiled eggs I ever ate were enjoyed in the company of good friends on the 14,246-foot summit of White Mountain Peak near Deep Springs.

Deviled Eggs

MAKES 1 DOZEN; SERVES 4 TO 6

Deviled eggs are among the most popular hors d'oeuvres. A little-kid joke: why does Grandma call them deviled eggs? Because they smell like sulfur. But hard-boiled eggs get that sulfury smell only when Grandma overcooks them. For deviled eggs, you need a firm white, but you still want the yolk to be tender and buttery.

6 large eggs

¼ cup mayonnaise

1 teaspoon Dijon mustard

pinch of salt

⅛ teaspoon cayenne pepper

⅛ teaspoon paprika

TOPPINGS

paprika

freshly ground black pepper

minced fresh chives (optional)

Cover the eggs with water in a saucepan and set on a high flame. Bring to a boil, reduce the heat to low, and cook, covered, for 30 seconds. Remove the pan from the heat and let stand, still covered, for 10 minutes. Drain and run cold water over the eggs for a few minutes. Plunge the eggs into an ice-water bath, leaving them for several minutes, to chill thoroughly. Carefully peel the eggs, first tapping the egg all over on a hard surface to evenly break the shell, then peeling from the blunt end. Rinse each one to remove tiny specks of shell. Cut the eggs in half lengthwise, carefully removing the yolks to a medium bowl and placing the whites on a tray. Mash the yolks with the mayonnaise, mustard, salt, cayenne, and paprika. Put the mixture in a sturdy plastic bag, cut a small hole in a corner of the bag, and pipe the yolk mixture into the whites, almost touching the egg with the tip of the bag as you squeeze. Dust with more paprika and some black pepper, and sprinkle with chives, if you like.

Egg Salad

SERVES 6 TO 8

A Deep Springs classmate of mine, now a rabbi and teacher, married with children, makes this egg salad for his wife when she is in need of gustatory comfort. She is always *very* appreciative.

1 dozen perfectly cooked Hard-Boiled Eggs (page 164), cooled and peeled

2 tablespoons finely diced red onion

½ cup finely diced celery (optional)

3 tablespoons fresh lemon juice, plus more if needed

¾ to 1 cup mayonnaise

½ teaspoon salt, plus more if needed

¼ teaspoon coarsely ground black pepper

Chop the eggs in large dice or put them through a large wire grid (I use a cooling rack). Place in a medium bowl and gently blend in the onion, celery (if using), lemon juice, mayonnaise, salt, and pepper. Taste, and add more salt and lemon juice if necessary. This is best served immediately.

Variations

Chopped fresh dill is wonderful and traditional in egg salad. Coarsely chopped green olives are also good. In both instances, I don't bother including the celery.

Asparagus-Mushroom Frittata

SERVES 4 TO 6

There are many kinds of frittata, or Italian baked omelet, but asparagus, mushrooms, and eggs make an especially good partnership. Have all the vegetables cut and ready to go before you start cooking. This is good at room temperature and so makes ideal picnic food. Serve a big green salad alongside.

1 bunch fresh asparagus

3 tablespoons olive oil

1 medium yellow onion, finely chopped

2 large cloves garlic, finely crushed

about ½ teaspoon salt

8 ounces white or brown mushrooms, wiped clean, trimmed, halved, and thinly sliced

8 large eggs, at room temperature

freshly ground black pepper

pinch of hot red pepper flakes

2 tablespoons chopped parsley

3 tablespoons freshly grated Parmesan cheese

Heat the oven to 300°F. To prepare the asparagus, rinse it, then peel the bottom 3 to 4 inches of each stalk with a vegetable peeler. Snap the tough bottom off each stalk (peeling it first yields a greater quantity of tender asparagus), and diagonally slice the asparagus, tips and all, as thinly as possible.

In a 10-inch oven-safe skillet (if you wish to unmold the frittata onto a platter, a nonstick skillet is recommended), heat 2 tablespoons of the olive oil over a medium-high flame. Add the onion and garlic with a couple of pinches of salt and sauté, stirring frequently, until the onion is translucent—it shouldn't brown. Add the mushrooms with a generous pinch of salt and sauté for a few moments more. Once the juice from the mushrooms begins to subside, add the asparagus with a generous pinch of salt, and sauté until the asparagus is tender (adding salt with each addition keeps the various flavors distinct). Crack the eggs into a large bowl and beat lightly, just enough to break up the yolks. Stir the warm mushroom-asparagus mixture into the eggs. (Keep the skillet nearby—it will be used to cook the frittata.) To the egg mixture, add freshly ground pepper to taste, ¼ teaspoon salt, a pinch of red pepper flakes, and the parsley and Parmesan. Beat lightly just until everything is combined.

Clean the skillet, and in it, warm the remaining 1 tablespoon olive oil over a medium flame for a minute. Dump in the egg mixture and put the skillet in the oven. Bake until the mixture is set in the center, about 20 minutes. Remove from the oven and let the frittata "set up" for about 5 minutes before turning it out onto a plate or a board. Serve warm or at room temperature, cut into wedges.

Chard and Mushroom Frittata

Substitute a bunch of chard for the bunch of asparagus in the master recipe. Remove the leafy green part from the chard and slice the stems finely. Sauté the stems with the onion, then chop the leaves and add them at the end. Cook until the vegetables are just tender, then mix as directed in the recipe. This variation is good with crumbled feta cheese substituted for the Parmesan.

Tortilla Española

SERVES 4 TO 6

In Spain, *tortilla* is a slowly cooked omelet of onions and potatoes fried in olive oil, usually served as a tapa, or hors d'oeuvre. Since we use the same word for the delectable staple of Mexican cooking, the name of this Spanish dish confuses the uninitiated, and the clunky name "potato omelet" never sounds good. Despite these nomenclatural difficulties, *tortilla española* is one of the touchstones of a good cook, transforming cheap, humble ingredients into something that even ardent carnivores will happily devour as the main dish of a meal. I make *tortilla española* for lunch at Deep Springs several times a year, served always with a plentiful green salad and, in summer, with Gazpacho (page 287).

The Spanish recipes I've seen call for no pepper, garlic, or thyme, and they always call for the *tortilla* to be cooked entirely on top of the stove and flipped once or many times in the cooking. Unless strict authenticity is my goal, I find it much easier to use the oven, and as for the extra seasonings, they taste delicious. I have even included such things as mushrooms and anchovies in *tortilla española*.

2 cups olive oil for frying

2 large white or yellow onions, diced

1½ to 2 teaspoons salt

3 medium russet potatoes, peeled, halved lengthwise, and sliced in ⅛-inch-thick slices

1 large clove garlic, crushed

7 large eggs, at room temperature

2 teaspoons chopped fresh thyme (3 to 4 sprigs' worth) or ¼ teaspoon dried thyme

½ teaspoon white pepper

Heat the oven to 325°F. Heat the olive oil in a 10-inch heavy, oven-safe skillet (if you wish to unmold the *tortilla* onto a platter, a nonstick skillet is recommended) over a medium-high flame until a bit of onion bubbles excitedly when dropped in. Gently drop in the onions with ¼ teaspoon salt, and fry gently until the onions are almost translucent, 3 to 4 minutes. Stir in the potatoes with about ½ teaspoon salt and fry-sauté the mixture, stirring from time to time. When the potatoes are nearly tender, stir in the garlic with another pinch of salt. Continue to cook until the potatoes are cooked through, 6 to 7 minutes. Using a screen sieve set over a metal bowl or pot, drain the potatoes and onions of all excess oil for several minutes, reserving the oil: it will impart its delicate potato and onion scent to almost anything else you cook (store it in the refrigerator).

Wipe out the skillet and add back about 1 tablespoon of the olive oil.

Using a whisk, beat the eggs briefly in a large bowl, just to break up the yolks, then stir in the thyme, pepper, and about ¾ teaspoon salt. Fold in the hot drained potatoes and onions. Dump the mixture into the warm skillet, smoothing the top if necessary, and bake until the eggs are set, 10 to 12 minutes. Let the *tortilla* rest in the skillet for about 5 minutes, then invert it onto a plate. Let cool for a bit longer before cutting it into wedges. Serve slightly warm or at room temperature.

Goat Cheese, Spinach, and Green Chile Soufflé

SERVES 4 TO 6

This rich soufflé makes a splendid lunch when accompanied by a light green salad; for a more substantial meal, it goes well with simple, lean roast meats, warm or cold. It's very good, too, with ham for brunch. The cream is an authentic Deep Springs touch, but if it seems too extravagant, yogurt may take its place.

One spring, a friend in town ("town" meaning Bishop, an hour's drive from the college) gave Deep Springs a young milk goat, named Tinker-bell. Though her nasty temperament inspired us to rechristen her "Stinker-smell," she gives abundant milk, which we make into fresh, flavorful white cheese.

2 tablespoons butter

¼ cup fine breadcrumbs

8 large eggs

10 large white or brown mushrooms, wiped clean, trimmed, halved, and thinly sliced

several pinches of salt

continued . . .

. . . continued

1 bunch green onions, thinly sliced diagonally

1 small can (4 ounces) chopped fire-roasted green chiles, drained briefly and chopped, or ½ cup chopped freshly roasted green chiles (see page 423)

2 bunches fresh spinach, washed well and drained

8 ounces fresh goat cheese

2 tablespoons freshly grated Parmesan cheese

½ cup heavy (whipping) cream or yogurt

freshly ground black pepper

Heat the oven to 375°F. Generously butter a large (9-by-13-inch) baking dish with a tablespoon of the butter and dust with the breadcrumbs, shaking out the excess. Carefully separate the eggs, making sure not a speck of yolk gets into the white. Reserve the whites in a very clean bowl.

In a large skillet, melt the remaining 1 tablespoon butter over medium-high heat. Sauté the mushrooms with a generous pinch of salt until they are a medium golden brown, about 5 minutes. If the mushrooms throw off liquid shortly after you add them to the pan, just cook until the liquid boils away; then the mushrooms will brown. Add the green onions and chiles and cook for a few moments more. Transfer this mixture to a large bowl, and let cool.

Re-heat the skillet over a medium-high flame and throw in the washed spinach. Toss quickly until it wilts. Let it continue to cook for a moment, then transfer to a plate to cool. Over the sink, once the spinach has cooled sufficiently to handle, take it up in handfuls and lightly squeeze out the excess water. Chop coarsely and add to the bowl with the mushroom mixture. Crumble the goat cheese and add to the bowl. Add the Parmesan, cream, and egg yolks to the bowl along with a generous pinch of salt and freshly ground pepper to taste, and combine.

In a large bowl, using an electric mixer or a whisk, beat the egg whites to soft peaks with a generous pinch of salt. Fold half of the whites into the yolk mixture to lighten it, then very gently fold in the remainder. Scrape into the prepared baking dish and gently place in the oven. Bake until the soufflé is risen and the center is set, about 30 minutes. Serve immediately.

My Mother's Enchiladas

SERVES 4 TO 6

Between this recipe and the two that follow, the imaginative cook will see a world of possibility in the enchilada. The word *enchilada* means "imbued with chile"—the thing imbued with chile being, of course, corn tortillas. Enchiladas may be rolled, stacked, baked like a casserole, or "built" directly on the plate; the tortillas may be fried in oil or just heated on a burner; enchiladas may have a savory, meaty filling or no filling but cheese; the cheese may be a traditional variety, such as Jack, or may be borrowed from another ethnic tradition, such as feta or fontina; the chile sauce may be red or green, creamy or lean, mild or hot.

For many years, mostly in Texas and New Mexico in the 1970s, this recipe was one of my mother's most prized company dishes. It is elegant, rich, distinctive, and universally loved. Accompany with a big tossed green salad and a bowl of radishes chilled in ice water.

This recipe calls for frying the tortillas, an authentic New Mexico touch. A brief dip in boiling oil helps the tortillas retain their texture, and the end result is succulently rich. However, for a leaner dish, I often merely heat the tortillas in a hot, dry skillet until they take on appealing brown spots. Sometimes I brush them with a little oil first (see the next recipe, Green Chile Enchiladas). If you use tortillas cold, they will disintegrate, and the enchiladas will emerge too puddingy.

SAUCE

2 teaspoons vegetable oil or lard

1 medium yellow onion, diced

pinch of salt

2 cloves garlic, crushed

¾ teaspoon ground cumin

¾ teaspoon dried oregano

one 14-ounce can cream of chicken soup

one 8-ounce can diced fire-roasted green chiles (or use 1 cup chopped, freshly roasted chiles, see page 423)

¼ teaspoon freshly ground black pepper

1 to 2 cups diced cooked well-seasoned chicken (optional; to cook chicken, see Green Chile Enchiladas, page 172)

1 cup safflower oil or other light vegetable oil for frying

12 corn tortillas

2 cups (8 ounces) grated Jack cheese

Heat the oven to 375°F. To make the sauce, warm the oil or lard in a medium-sized, heavy saucepan over a medium-high flame. Add the onion and sauté with a pinch of salt for 3 to 4 minutes, stirring frequently, until mostly translucent. Add the garlic, cumin, and oregano and cook slowly without browning, stirring frequently, for 2 to 3 minutes. Add the can of soup, ½ can of water, and the green *continued . . .*

. . . continued

chiles. Heat, stirring frequently, until the mixture reaches a simmer. Reduce the heat and let simmer for 5 minutes, stirring occasionally. Stir in the black pepper (and the chicken, if you opt for it) and remove from the heat, but keep warm.

To fry the tortillas, heat the oil in a deep, heavy pot over a medium-high flame until a bit of tortilla dropped in sizzles and bubbles fiercely. Drop in a tortilla, using a slotted spoon or tongs to immerse it completely, and fry for about 10 seconds, or only until softened. Lift the tortilla out of the oil and allow to drain over the pot for a few seconds. Lay it on a thick bed of paper towels to drain further. Continue with the remaining tortillas. Blot the tortillas with more paper towels.

Spread a ladleful of the sauce on the bottom of a 9-by-13-inch baking dish. Arrange a single layer of tortillas over the sauce, top with a little more sauce, then sprinkle lightly with cheese. Repeat layers of sauce, tortillas, more sauce, and cheese until everything is used up. Finish with a generous amount of sauce and cheese, with no tortilla exposed. Bake until the cheese is melted and the top is bubbly, 20 to 25 minutes. Let rest for about 10 minutes, then cut into squares or wedges and serve.

Green Chile Enchiladas

SERVES 4 TO 6

This superb dish from New Mexico is more laborious than the previous recipe, but it tastes more authoritatively of green chile. Since the flavor is so haunting, a simple green salad is all you need alongside. To save time on the day you want to serve, you may make the sauce and cook the chicken a day ahead. For a meatless variation, try filling the enchiladas with sautéed fresh summer corn, cut off the cob (see page 228).

In this recipe, the tortillas are lightly rubbed with oil and heated in a skillet. If you want a rich, authentically New Mexican flavor, fry the tortillas briefly in oil as described in the previous recipe.

12 ounces boneless, skinless chicken breast (2 medium-sized breast halves)

pinch of dried oregano

¼ teaspoon salt

black pepper

vegetable oil or lard for heating tortillas

12 corn tortillas

1 recipe New Mexico Green Chile Sauce (page 422)

1½ cups (6 ounces) grated Jack cheese

1 cup (4 ounces) grated sharp white Cheddar cheese

1 medium onion, finely chopped

Season the chicken with oregano, salt, and pepper. Rub with a little vegetable oil and cook in a medium skillet over medium heat until browned on both sides and cooked through, about 4 minutes on each side. Let cool to room temperature on a plate, then chop into small dice.

To assemble and bake the enchiladas, heat the oven to 350°F. Heat the green chile sauce. Heat the tortillas by rubbing them lightly on one side with vegetable oil (or melted lard, or a mixture) and heating them in a hot, dry skillet until they get appealing brown spots here and there. Place a tortilla in the skillet, flip, place another on top, flip both, place another on top of that, flip all three, and so forth, building up the stack and giving each tortilla its moment of direct contact with the heat. The accumulated heat will steam and soften the tortillas. When all are heated, cut the stack in half with a sharp knife to make half-moons.

Spread a little warm green chile sauce on the bottom of a 9-by-13-inch baking dish. Put down a layer of tortillas, top with more sauce, a little cheese, a bit of chicken, and a little chopped onion. Repeat until the tortillas and chicken are used up, and finish with a generous amount of sauce and cheese. Bake for about 30 minutes, until the cheese is browned and bubbly. Let rest for about 10 minutes, then cut into squares or wedges and serve.

Red Chile Enchiladas

SERVES 3 TO 4

Here is another approach to enchiladas: rather than assembling the elements into a casserole and baking it, the tortillas, sauce, cheese, and filling are assembled "to order" on individual plates. In New Mexico, these enchiladas are often topped with a fried egg. Yellow Cheddar cheese on enchiladas may seem unsophisticated or inauthentic, but it's what our mothers often used, and it tastes delicious with red chile.

1 recipe New Mexico Red Chile Sauce (page 420)

1½ cups filling of choice: cooked seasoned ground beef, or cooked turkey or chicken, or summer corn cut off the cob

8 or 9 corn tortillas

vegetable oil or lard for heating tortillas

1 small onion, finely diced

1½ cups grated cheese of choice: sharp yellow Cheddar, jack, fontina

3 or 4 Fried Eggs (page 97; optional)

Warm the sauce and the filling, if necessary. Heat the corn tortillas in either of the ways described in the previous two recipes: fry them briefly in oil or rub them lightly with oil and heat in a hot, dry skillet. Or you can merely heat them directly on the gas flame of your stove until they develop brown spots here and there.

On each plate, put a dab of chile sauce. Lay a hot tortilla over the sauce. Put a spoonful of filling on the tortilla. Drizzle more sauce over. Sprinkle with some chopped onion and a little cheese. Repeat with another tortilla, more filling, sauce, onion, and cheese. For each person, a 2- or 3-tortilla stack is usually ample.

Top each serving with a fried egg, if you like, and more chopped onion. Serve immediately.

Gumbo

SERVES 6 TO 8

I grew up eating gumbo. My grandfather, from Louisiana (gumbo's "home"), was a mess cook in World War I, volunteering for the position shortly after he enlisted, when he saw that no one else would. He certainly didn't want to eat the food of an unwilling cook! Later, when my mother was a girl, he ran a restaurant, the Silver Grill in Clovis, New Mexico. Much later, when I was a baby, I'm told he'd dip my toes in the butter and nibble it off.

Gumbo is a way of life, a unique cultural expression—a bit of France and a bit of Africa, cultivated in the soil of the American South. It's best defined as a stew of peppers, tomatoes, onions, celery, and usually okra, thickened with roux or filé powder, flavored with thyme, parsley, and cayenne, and enriched with poultry, sausage, or shrimp. I believe the heart and soul of good gumbo resides in the roux, vegetables, and herbs; meatless gumbo is still delicious. Smoked turkey necks, wings, drumsticks, and even fatty tails are available in supermarkets wherever there is a large African American population. Andouille sausage, seasoned with hot dried red peppers and thyme, is the real thing, but try any medium-spicy smoked sausage.

Six cups of chicken stock or water will make a thick, soupy gumbo, to be served in a bowl, over a little rice—this is how I like it best. Four cups of chicken stock or water will make a thicker, more stewlike gumbo, to be served over a larger amount of rice. Either way, gumbo is a meal in itself; no accompaniment is needed.

Green bell peppers are required for gumbo—red or yellow bell peppers will make the dish too summery-sweet.

½ cup canola oil or other vegetable oil

½ cup all-purpose flour

2 medium onions, finely chopped

3 to 4 stalks celery, finely chopped

salt

2 green bell peppers, finely chopped

¾ teaspoon dried thyme, or 2 to 3 teaspoons chopped fresh thyme

½ teaspoon hot red pepper flakes

6 cups chicken stock or water (use 4 cups for a thicker gumbo)

1 smoked turkey neck or ham shank

one 14-ounce can whole plum tomatoes, chopped

2 to 3 fresh red tomatoes, chopped

about 1 pound andouille sausage

12 ounces fresh young, tender okra, sliced ¼ inch thick (see page 238 for how to detect tough okra pods)

½ cup chopped parsley

continued . . .

. . . continued

½ teaspoon black pepper

Tabasco or other hot sauce

———

FOR SERVING

⅛ teaspoon filé powder for each serving (optional)

steamed long-grain white rice (see page 398)

First make the roux. In a large, heavy saucepan over medium-high heat, blend the oil and flour with a wooden spoon. Stir constantly as the mixture heats and begins to bubble. When it is vigorously bubbling, turn down the heat to medium-low, and keep stirring. The roux will turn from pasty white to pale ivory, then will darken by degrees to the color of peanut butter. At this point, and not a moment later, throw in the onions and celery with a large pinch of salt. Raise the heat to medium and cook, stirring constantly, for about 5 minutes, then throw in the bell pepper with a pinch of salt. Cook for another 7 to 10 minutes, stirring constantly, until the vegetables are tender. Taste a bit of the onion—there should be no crunch left.

Add the thyme, pepper flakes, chicken stock, turkey neck, canned and fresh tomatoes, and whole sausage to the pot. If you used water instead of chicken stock, add a teaspoon of salt. Bring to a simmer and cook for about 30 minutes, stirring frequently. Add the okra and simmer for another 10 minutes, stirring frequently,

until the okra is tender. Remove the turkey neck, pick the meat off the bones, chop the meat coarsely, and return it to the pot. Remove the sausage, slice it thickly, and return to the pot. Stir in the parsley and black pepper. Taste for salt and add Tabasco to taste; gumbo should be warmly spicy, never hot.

Both the roux and the okra thicken the gumbo, but filé powder will also provide a little thickness. If you like, stir ⅛ teaspoon of filé into each bowl just before serving.

Serve the gumbo in wide bowls over a small amount of hot steamed long-grain white rice.

Variations

Add a pound of shrimp, shelled or not (the shells will impart more flavor, but your guests will get their fingers messy peeling them), in the last 10 minutes of simmering. Or add a pound of picked crabmeat at the very end (for the liquid, use half water, half chicken stock). Or, follow the recipe up to the point of adding the sausage, and use this "base" as a medium for braising chicken (see page 355). Add the okra after the chicken is tender.

If you opt for a meatless gumbo, eggplant, surprisingly, tastes right at home and helps make it more substantial. Omit all meat from the recipe and throw a coarsely chopped eggplant into the pot along with the peppers.

Gunhild's Chicken Curry

SERVES 4 TO 6

Indian food is a wholly different and exciting culinary idiom. Fresh ginger, basmati rice, and whole spices are no longer hard to find, as they were early in my cooking days. Once you learn a few of the basic dishes and procedures, Indian food lends itself to flights of improvisation, especially when you have access to a variety of vegetables. Vegetables are closer to the heart and soul of Indian food than meat; in fact, it may be perfectly expressed without any meat at all. For an added touch of authenticity, use ghee, a kind of clarified butter (see page 63), instead of vegetable oil.

I learned to make this curry early in my days as Student Cook at Deep Springs. One of my classmates had a Danish mother and a father from northern India; soon after they married, she went to India to take cooking lessons from his family. When they visited Deep Springs during my tenure as Student Cook, my classmate's mother enthusiastically showed me how to make their basic family curry, with all the accompaniments. She didn't use a written recipe. All her spices were from India, and very freshly ground. She used two blends: a simple mix of ground cumin and coriander,

and a complex *masala* (meaning "spice blend") that was red from hot chiles. I never knew which spices constituted her red masala, but a good, fresh American masala, known to us as curry powder, is perfectly good in this curry.

The lemon and red onion, served separately on a plate, are meant to be eaten like a relish with everything else; an occasional strong crunch of onion or zingy burst of lemon only makes the curry taste better.

This may be made well ahead of time, up to the point of adding the spinach. For the spinach to retain its vivid green freshness, stir it into the hot curry just before serving.

RICE

2 cups uncooked basmati rice

1 teaspoon vegetable oil or ghee

1 teaspoon salt

3 cups plus 2 tablespoons water

CURRY

1 tablespoon vegetable oil or ghee

1 large yellow onion, thinly sliced lengthwise

¼ teaspoon plus several pinches salt, or more as needed

4 cloves garlic

1 ounce (a 2- to 3-inch piece) fresh ginger, peeled

continued . . .

. . . *continued*

½ teaspoon ground cumin

½ teaspoon ground coriander

4 teaspoons curry powder (to grind your own, see page 358)

¼ teaspoon black pepper

8 boneless, skinless chicken thighs (about 2 pounds)

one 14-ounce can condensed cream of chicken soup

1 large bunch fresh spinach, washed well and coarsely chopped

———

FOR SERVING

1 lemon, thinly sliced

1 small red onion, thinly sliced

Indian naan or other flatbread, warmed and brushed lightly with ghee or oil (sometimes I use whole-wheat tortillas)

raita (see facing page)

To make the rice, put the rice, oil, salt, and water in a medium-sized, heavy saucepan with a well-fitting lid. Set the pan on high heat, bring to a boil, reduce to a simmer, slap on the lid, and let the rice cook, undisturbed, for about 20 minutes, or until all the water is absorbed. To tell if the rice is done without lifting the lid, tilt the pan slightly and listen carefully: if you hear the hissing, sizzling sound of water hitting the sides of the pan, it needs more time. If you don't hear anything, the water is all absorbed and the rice is done.

To make the curry, heat the tablespoon of vegetable oil in a large, heavy soup pot over a medium flame. When the oil shimmers, throw in the onion with ¼ teaspoon salt and sauté, stirring frequently, until the onion is translucent, 5 to 6 minutes. Chop together the garlic and ginger until very fine—this is quick work with a food processor. Add the garlic and ginger to the onions with a pinch of salt and cook, stirring frequently, for another minute. Stir in the spices, then the chicken, with a final big pinch of salt. Cook for about 5 minutes, stirring frequently, while your kitchen fills with a wonderful aroma. Add the can of soup and about ½ can of water. Bring the mixture to a simmer. Reduce the heat and cover the pan. Simmer slowly, stirring occasionally, until the chicken is tender, about 20 minutes. Stir in the spinach, and let cook for 3 to 4 minutes more. Taste for salt—the curry should be well seasoned. Serve with the hot basmati rice, and the thinly sliced onion and lemon on a platter. Serve warmed flatbread and a raita on the side.

Mushroom Curry

For a meatless curry, I like to substitute thick-sliced mushrooms for the chicken in the recipe (sometimes sautéing them first in a little ghee, sometimes not), using cream of mushroom soup instead of cream of chicken.

Cucumber Raita

SERVES 4 TO 6

Raitas—cool yogurt salads—aid in the digestion of a spicy Indian meal. Use whole-milk, low-fat, or nonfat yogurt, as you prefer.

1 English cucumber

1½ cups plain yogurt

½ teaspoon salt

3 tablespoons chopped fresh mint

Grate the cucumber into a medium bowl, using the coarse holes of a box grater. Squeeze out the excess liquid (I love to drink this). Mix in the yogurt, salt, and mint. Chill and stir again before serving—I like raita cooler than room temperature but not refrigerator-cold.

Cantaloupe and Black Pepper Raita

SERVES 4 TO 6

If you like your curry especially spicy, the sweet melon in this raita will temper the heat most agreeably.

½ sweet cantaloupe, peeled and seeded, cut into small dice, and chilled

1½ cups plain yogurt, chilled

½ teaspoon salt

½ teaspoon coarsely ground black pepper

2 tablespoons chopped fresh mint

Mix everything in a medium bowl. Serve.

Falafel

SERVES 4 TO 6

Everyone—even meat eaters—loves a meal of falafel, hummus, and pita bread. Despite the frying, it is a simple meal to put together; the result is somehow more beautiful and festive than one would imagine, given the ordinary ingredients.

FALAFEL

1 cup dry chickpeas, soaked overnight in 4 cups water, drained

½ cup chopped onion

¼ cup coarsely chopped parsley

1 large clove garlic

½ teaspoon ground cumin

½ teaspoon ground coriander

1 teaspoon salt

¼ teaspoon baking powder

pinch of cayenne pepper

1 egg

2 teaspoons sesame seeds (optional)

TAHIN SAUCE

½ cup roasted sesame tahini

½ cup cold water

2 tablespoons fresh lemon juice

⅛ teaspoon salt

ACCOMPANIMENTS

½ bunch flat-leaf parsley

½ bunch fresh mint

¼ small onion

about 1 cup sliced cucumber

about ½ cup chopped fresh ripe tomato

about ½ cup chopped green onion

1 to 2 cups shredded lettuce

sliced fresh oranges (optional; good in winter)

Hummus (optional; recipe at right)

about 8 yeasted flatbreads (pita or other type; sometimes in a pinch I just use whole-wheat flour tortillas)

safflower oil, peanut oil, or other light oil for frying

To make the mix for the falafel, in a food processor, pulse the soaked chickpeas, onions, parsley, garlic, cumin, coriander, salt, baking powder, cayenne, and egg to a grainy, uniform mush. The bits of chickpea and onion must be very fine if they are to cook through. Stir in the sesame seeds, if desired.

To make the tahin sauce, whisk the tahini, cold water, lemon juice, and salt together in a small bowl until smooth. Whisk together again, if necessary, just before serving.

Before frying the falafel, have all the accompaniments chopped and ready: very finely chop the parsley, mint, and onion together. Put the herb-onion mixture, cucumber, tomato, green onion, and lettuce in small dishes on the table—these all are better at room temperature than chilled. In winter, a platter of sliced oranges enhances everything. If you are also serving hummus, make sure it's at room temperature, and heat the flatbreads while frying the falafel.

Heat 1 inch of oil in a wide, heavy skillet over medium-high heat until a dab of batter sizzles merrily when dropped in. Slip neat spoonfuls of the falafel mix into the oil (I use a small ice cream scoop). I like falafel made on the small side, with 2 to 3 tablespoons of batter—the more crispy surface area, I think, the better. Smaller falafel are also easier to cook through. Fry, turning once, until the falafel are a deep brown, 2 to 3 minutes per side. Break one open to make sure they are cooked through—they will look doughy and be lighter colored in the centers if they are not (sometimes I finish them in a 350°F oven if I have made the falafel large or gotten the oil too hot). Drain on paper towels. Serve immediately or keep warm.

To eat, stuff pockets or pieces of flatbread with falafel and vegetables (and hummus, if you opt for it), moistening well with spoonfuls of tahin sauce. Falafel is the most forgiving of fried foods and can be held, eaten at room temperature, or even reheated.

Hummus

SERVES 4 TO 5

I admit that sometimes I just buy prepared hummus, enlivening it with a few pinches of powdered New Mexico red chile. But fresh, homemade hummus is delicious enough to not require that inauthentic addition. This popular dip may be made with canned chickpeas, but if you wish to cook them yourself, start with 1 heaping cup of dry chickpeas, and follow the guidelines for cooking beans on page 187.

2 cups cooked chickpeas

2 to 3 tablespoons chickpea cooking water

¼ cup roasted sesame tahini

1 clove garlic, crushed

1 teaspoon salt, plus more as needed

pinch of cayenne pepper

juice of 1 large lemon

⅓ cup extra-virgin olive oil, plus 2 to 3 tablespoons more as needed

TOPPING

1 tablespoon extra-virgin olive oil

paprika

continued...

CHAPTER 5: Great Lunches — 181

... continued

Purée the chickpeas, 2 tablespoons of the cooking water, tahini, garlic, salt, and cayenne in a food processor, scraping down the sides of the bowl as necessary, until you have an ultra-smooth paste. Stir in the lemon juice and ⅓ cup olive oil. Adjust the consistency and richness with more olive oil or more of the chickpea-cooking water, if needed. Taste for seasoning, adjusting if necessary—this will depend on the saltiness of the chickpeas. Transfer to a serving dish and swirl the surface so there are deep furrows and ridges. Drizzle with 1 tablespoon more olive oil, and sprinkle a bit of paprika over.

Minted Iced Tea

MAKES 1 GALLON

Here we have fresh mint both used in the brewing of the tea and added with lemons to flavor the tea as it cools. This tea is barely sweetened with honey—add sugar to taste to make "sweet tea."

2 lemons, washed and thinly slilced

1 large bunch mint, washed thoroughly

6 cups water

5 English Breakfast or Earl Grey teabags

⅓ cup honey

lots of ice

Take a large square of cheesecloth, and tie the lemons and half of the mint together into a bundle.

Bring the water to a boil in a large saucepan. Throw in the teabags, immediately remove the pot from the heat, and add the loose mint. Let steep for 5 minutes, then gently remove the mint and the teabags and discard—without squeezing them. Immediately stir the honey into the brew to fix the fresh tea flavor. Pour the tea into a gallon pitcher.

Add the bundle of lemons and mint to the pitcher to further infuse the tea. Once cool, squeeze a little of the lemon juice from the bundle into the tea, then discard the bundle. Add sufficient ice and cold water to fill the pitcher. Stir and serve.

Hibiscus Iced Tea

MAKES 1 GALLON

A favorite in Mexico, this deep ruby-red brew has a unique, pleasant, tart flavor. The Spanish word for hibiscus is *jamaica*.

3 cups packed dried hibiscus flowers (4 ounces)

8 cups cold water

zest of ½ orange, taken in strips with a vegetable peeler (optional)

1 cup sugar, plus more as needed

lots of ice

Put the hibiscus flowers into a large saucepan. Add 4 cups of the water (and the orange zest, if you opt for it) and bring to a boil. Remove from the flame and let steep for 10 minutes. Strain the tea into another container, leaving the hibiscus flowers in the pan. Add 4 more cups cold water to the pan with the flowers, and bring to a boil. Let steep for 10 minutes, then strain the second batch of tea into the container with the first. Add the sugar, stirring to dissolve. Taste—if the brew is still very tart, add more sugar to taste, just enough to balance the tartness and sweetness. Let cool to room temperature.

Pour the tea into a gallon pitcher filled with ice, adding more ice or cold water as necessary to fill the pitcher, and serve. If you are making the tea ahead of time, add the ice just before serving.

Lemonade

MAKES 1 GALLON

You want a big glass of this good, tart, refreshing lemonade in the late afternoon, when you've been working out in the sun. For an unusual whey lemonade, see page 147.

7 medium lemons

1 cup plus 2 tablespoons sugar

6 cups water

lots of ice

Wash and dry the lemons. In a medium saucepan, stir together the sugar with 3 cups of the water, bring to a boil, and remove from the heat. Finely grate the zest of 3 of the lemons into the hot syrup. Let cool to room temperature. If you wish, strain the zest out of the syrup (I like the little bits of zest). Squeeze about 1¼ cups of lemon juice from 6 of the lemons, and mix into the syrup. Fill a gallon pitcher with ice. Pour the lemonade base over the ice. Add about 3 cups cold water to fill the pitcher. Stir well and taste the lemonade, adjusting with more lemon juice if necessary. Slice the remaining lemon and immerse the slices in the lemonade. Serve.

Limeade

For some delightfully zippy limeade, follow the above instructions, using the juice and half the zest of 8 to 9 limes instead of the lemons. Where's the tequila?

CHAPTER 6
Beans

Beans, a staple of Deep Springs cooking, are nutritious, inexpensive, and among the tastiest of foods. It is easy to cook beans badly, which is not necessarily to say that it is difficult to cook beans well. Having a good dish of beans is simply a matter of following a series of steps. Selecting beans in the market is the first step; try, whenever possible, to buy and cook beans, lentils, or split peas *from the current crop—no more than a year old*. For about a year after harvest, beans retain a trace amount of moisture. When they are old and bone-dry, they not only take forever to cook but have also lost some of their flavor. Supermarkets that have a large Latin American clientele will have fresh, good-quality beans. Don't buy beans containing a lot of splits.

I often simmer beans in the oven, especially when preparing a large quantity. The oven provides indirect, even heat—no frequent stirring required. Beans are rich in starch, which sticks to the bottom of your pot and readily burns over direct heat.

The following guidelines work for virtually any type of dry bean: pinto, black, pink, chickpeas, navy, dry lima, or, for a proper New Year's Day in the American South, black-eyed peas.

Guidelines for Cooking Beans

1. Before measuring, pour the beans out on a clean counter or into a wide bowl and run through them with your fingers, meticulously picking out stones, dirt clods, moldy or discolored beans, and splits. Moldy beans will muddy the flavor of the whole pot, and split beans are especially dry and flavorless. *Rinse* the beans in a colander, then put them in a large container or in the *heavy-bottomed, preferably oven-safe pot* in which you intend to cook them. To allow room for expansion, they should fill the pot by no more than a third.

2. Fill the pot with cold water (2 to 3 inches above the level of the beans) and *soak the beans, refrigerated,* for at least 6 hours, or overnight. If left at room temperature, soaking beans will occasionally start to ferment, especially in warm weather. *Drain the beans of their soaking water* and return them to the pot.

3. Fill the pot with fresh water, covering the beans by about 2 inches, and bring to a boil, skimming off any light-colored foam that rises to the surface. Reduce the heat to a *low boil* (not a simmer). Add bay leaf or other flavorings *except salt.* After several minutes of cooking, the skins of the beans will start to wrinkle. Add oil or fat.

continued . . .

. . . continued

Cover the pot and continue cooking over medium-low heat at a gentle simmer. I often put the whole thing in a 300°F oven at this point. Cook for 1 to 3 hours, according to your altitude and the type of bean you have, stirring occasionally. Because the boiling temperature of water lowers with higher altitude, beans take considerably longer to cook (up to 3 hours) at Deep Springs' altitude of 5,200 feet (a pressure cooker may be a great time and energy saver if you frequently cook beans at high altitudes). Check the water level occasionally—*the beans should always stay well covered.* If you need to add water, bring it to a boil first.

When the beans are done, they should be completely soft and yielding. Most recipes say "until soft but not mushy" and I concur, but I am always happy to err on the side of mushy if error is unavoidable.

4. *Once the beans are completely soft, add salt.* Stir the salt in well and taste the broth—it should taste savory enough to be eaten on its own—perhaps a tiny bit on the salty side, as the beans will absorb some salt. Return the beans to the oven for ½ hour more. Taste the beans again for salt. They are now ready to be served plain, with hot sauce and vinegar, or made into chili or soup. If you are using the beans in a room-temperature bean salad, *cool them in their broth*, then drain them well and make the salad. If you let hot beans cool out of their broth, they will dry out.

5. Beans' combination of protein and starch makes them very perishable—they "hold onto their heat," providing a ready medium for potentially harmful microorganisms to grow. *Cool the beans quickly* if you will not be using them right away: at home, I put the pot of beans into a shallow sink of cool tap water, just deep enough to come two-thirds up the side of the pot, sometimes with ice added. Stir the beans from time to time; they are usually cool enough to refrigerate in under an hour. With larger quantities of beans, pour them into large, shallow pans (at Deep Springs we use food-service "hotel" pans) and let cool on a rack to room temperature, stirring occasionally, then promptly refrigerate. *Reheat leftover beans thoroughly.*

Lentil cookery is similar to bean cookery, but these smaller legumes require no soaking and cook in less time. Cook lentils in water until they are soft, and then, off the heat, add salt to taste and a glug of olive oil. Stir the pot frequently as it cools. The lentils will absorb salt and oil richness from the broth. They may be used for soup, or well drained and added to a salad.

Pinto or Black Beans

SERVES 4 TO 6

Not only are beans an indispensable part of any Mexican or Southwestern meal, they may be the meal itself, along with a couple of warm corn tortillas. A bowl of plain, freshly cooked pinto beans in their broth is surprisingly good.

Generally speaking, black beans are served in the southern states of Mexico, while pinto beans are served in the northwestern states of Mexico and throughout the southwestern United States. Black beans were completely unfamiliar in my Texas–New Mexico growing-up years but were a great discovery in early adulthood. Black beans appeal in summer, whereas pinto beans are often exactly what you crave when the weather is cold. Pink beans are quite similar to pintos and may be used in these recipes.

3 cups dry pinto or black beans (about 1½ pounds)

1 cup finely chopped white onion

2 tablespoons vegetable oil or lard

1 tablespoon salt

Follow the guidelines for cooking beans on page 187, stirring in the onion at the same time as the oil, when the skins of the beans start to wrinkle.

Variations

Sometimes I include meat, a small, bony cut of fresh beef or pork, to add richness and flavor. Or, using pinto beans, you may throw in a couple of strips of raw bacon once the beans settle to a simmer, and Texans will feel right at home (these are known as *Texas beans*). In both cases, the fat on the meat will suffice to enrich the beans, and the oil may be omitted. Or, using black beans, you may dump in a cup of beer in the last 20 minutes of cooking; then you will have *frijoles borrachos* (drunken beans).

Refried Beans

SERVES 4 TO 6

Here's an old New Mexico joke: Why do we have refried beans? Because we didn't get it right the first time! "Refried beans" does not mean that the beans were fried once and are now being fried again. The term is a direct, if misleading, translation of the Spanish *frijoles refritos*, meaning cooked pinto beans that have been not merely reheated but cooked down with a generous amount of fat, richly concentrating their flavor.

> 1 recipe Pinto Beans (see page 191)
>
> 3 to 4 tablespoons vegetable oil or lard
>
> salt
>
> black pepper

Cool the pinto beans in their broth and refrigerate overnight. Drain off and reserve any bean broth above the level of the beans.

Heat the oil in a wide cast-iron skillet over a medium-high flame. When hot but not smoking, spoon in the beans. Cook the beans, mashing them (a potato masher with a flat bottom is ideal) and stirring them constantly until some of the liquid is evaporated away and the beans are richer tasting. Reduce the heat to low. To develop the flavor, *allow the beans to gently brown on the bottom, then scrape the crust up into the rest of the mass, using a wooden spoon*. Repeat this a few times, but do not let the beans burn or become too dry—add reserved bean broth as necessary to keep them almost pourable.

Season the beans with salt, if necessary, and pepper. For a good Mexican touch, if you feel the flavor needs piquing, stir in the juice of half a lime.

You may also refry your beans in the oven. Heat the oil in an oven-safe skillet on the stovetop, add the beans, and stir until the beans are thoroughly hot and bubbly. Put the skillet in a 350°F oven. Stir every 15 minutes or so, scraping up the crust that forms on the bottom, for a total of 30 to 45 minutes. This method requires much less of your time and attention.

Mama Nell's Chili con Carne

SERVES 10 TO 12

This is my version of my grandmother's chili; the square of chocolate is her beautiful and fascinating touch. *Chili* (spelled with an "i" at the end) is a thoroughly Anglo-American stew flavored with *chile* (spelled with an "e" at the end) and other ingredients, sometimes meat, sometimes beans, sometimes both.

For nicely hot chili, use 14 chile pods; for medium-hot chili, use 10. For mild chili, use California dry chile pods. For a more streamlined preparation, substitute ½ to ¾ cup chili powder (mild or hot) for the chile pods. Just add the chili powder to the meat when you add the oregano and cumin. Chili powder is not pure ground chile; it's a spice blend containing cumin and oregano and sometimes salt in addition to mild ground red chile. If you use chili powder, taste before adding the final tablespoon of salt—it may need less. You may also use pure ground red chile. The rather laborious method below, starting with whole pods, delivers a wonderfully pure, clean chile flavor. Though spicy, it's easier on the stomach, as ground chile and chili powder contain tiny glasslike shards of chile skin. Here, the skins are discarded.

My mother writes (referring to my grandmother), *"Mama served this one of two ways: (1) In bowls, with grated cheese, chopped green onion, and chopped dill pickle on top. Or (2) she used corn tortillas, grated longhorn cheese, and more chopped white onion and made stacked enchiladas, using the chili as the sauce. Daddy liked a fried egg on top of his."*

3½ cups dry pinto beans
(about 1¾ pounds)

5 teaspoons salt, plus more as needed

10 to 14 dry New Mexico chile pods

2½ cups water

1 tablespoon vegetable oil

2 pounds ground beef, lean but not "extra-lean"

1 large yellow onion, cut into medium dice

6 large cloves garlic, smashed

2 teaspoons ground cumin

1 teaspoon dried oregano

one 28-ounce can diced tomatoes in juice

1 ounce (1 square) unsweetened baking chocolate

1 tablespoon cornmeal

½ teaspoon black pepper

FOR SERVING

grated Jack cheese

chopped onion or sliced green onion

cornbread

chopped tomatoes

saltine crackers

continued . . .

. . . continued

Cook the beans according to the guidelines on page 187, adding 2 teaspoons of the salt in the last 20 minutes of cooking. While the beans are cooking, rinse the chiles if they're dusty. Open the pods and remove the seeds, stems, and veins (the light-colored veins are the hottest, harshest-tasting part). Tear the flesh into 2-inch pieces. In a medium saucepan, bring 2 cups of the water to a boil and throw in the chile pieces. Stir to submerge the chiles, bring the pot back to a boil, cover, and remove from the heat.

Meanwhile, in a large, deep saucepan, heat the oil over a medium-high flame and add the beef. (If your beef is not lean, you should, of course, omit the oil. If it is very lean, use more oil.) Stir to break up the meat, add the onion and 1 teaspoon of the salt, and cook, stirring frequently, until the beef begins to lose its pink color and the onion is becoming translucent. Add the garlic with a pinch of salt and the cumin and oregano. Cook, stirring, until the meat is cooked and the onion is clear.

Put the soaking chiles and their water into the jar of a blender. Blend at low speed for about 5 seconds, just to break the chiles up slightly—don't purée them. Don't wash the blender yet. Put a screen sieve over the saucepan with the meat, and pour in the chile slurry. Using the back of a ladle, press as much chile pulp as possible through the sieve and into the meat.

Return the chile skins left in the sieve to the blender, add the remaining ½ cup water, blend for 5 seconds more, then pour through the sieve again, pressing as much flavorful chile pulp from the skins as possible. Add the can of tomatoes and 2 teaspoons more salt to the pan with the meat and chile. Lower the heat and let simmer until the beans are finished cooking.

Drain 2 cups of the broth off the beans, and reserve. Stir the meat mixture into the beans. Add the chocolate and cornmeal and simmer the chili over low heat for ½ hour more, stirring frequently. If necessary, adjust the consistency of the chili with the reserved bean broth. Add the black pepper and taste for salt. Serve with grated cheese, sliced green onions, cornbread, and chopped tomatoes. Or serve all by itself, with saltine crackers. This is even better the next day, after the chile flavor has permeated the beans.

Black Bean Chili

SERVES 6 TO 8

This modern classic is based on a recipe in a book I've always loved, Deborah Madison's *The Greens Cookbook*. A favorite standard Deep Springs lunch consists of a big pot of this chili, a big pot of Pork and White Bean Chili (page 200), condiments, green salad, and huge Skillet Cornbreads (page 116).

2 cups dry black beans (about 1 pound)

1 bay leaf

2½ teaspoons salt, plus more as needed

2 teaspoons ground cumin

2 teaspoons dried oregano

1 tablespoon paprika

2 tablespoons canola oil or other vegetable oil

2 medium yellow onions, cut into small dice

4 cloves garlic, crushed

2 to 3 tablespoons ground dry chile: ancho (medium-hot), pasilla (medium-hot), New Mexico (hotter), or California (milder), or 2 to 3 tablespoons chili powder

2 to 3 teaspoons chopped canned chipotle chile

pinch of ground cinnamon

pinch of ground cloves

1 ounce (1 square) unsweetened baking chocolate or 2 triangles Mexican chocolate

one 28-ounce can diced tomatoes

1 to 2 teaspoons red wine vinegar

black pepper

¼ cup chopped cilantro

FOR SERVING (TWO OR THREE ARE AMPLE)

chopped green onions

diced ripe tomatoes

minced jalapeños

sour cream thinned with milk

lime wedges

onion chopped with cilantro

grated pepper Jack cheese

Soak the beans overnight and cook with the bay leaf, following the guidelines on page 187. Once the beans are soft, add 2 teaspoons of the salt and simmer for about 20 minutes more. Remove the bay leaf. Leave the beans in their broth.

Toast the cumin in a small, dry skillet over high heat, stirring constantly, until fragrant. Add the oregano and toast for a few seconds more. Add the paprika, and immediately remove from the heat. Stir the mixture for a few more seconds as the skillet cools. Transfer the spices to a bowl.

Heat the oil in a large, heavy pot over a medium-high flame and throw in the onions with ½ teaspoon salt. Cook, stirring frequently, until the onions have begun to wilt. Reduce the heat to
continued...

. . . continued

medium, cover the pot, and cook until the onions are soft, about 10 minutes, lifting the lid to stir from time to time. Add the garlic with a pinch of salt, the toasted spices, the ground chile, chipotle chile, cinnamon, cloves, and chocolate. Cook for a minute, stirring constantly, then stir in the tomatoes. Bring to a simmer, and let cook for 5 minutes.

Pour 2 to 3 cups of the bean broth out into a separate pot and set aside. Add the tomato mixture to the beans, and adjust the consistency with the reserved broth. Allow the chili to simmer for 10 minutes to allow the flavors to combine, then remove from the heat and add enough wine vinegar to enliven the flavors. Add black pepper to taste, together with the cilantro. Taste for salt and serve with the accompaniments of your choice.

Chickpeas with Tomatoes, Lemon, and Mint

SERVES 4 TO 6
LARGE QUANTITY RECIPE: SERVES 30 TO 40

This nice summer Mediterranean salad is excellent with Cumin Roast Chicken (page 346). Serve Melon with Rosewater (page 464) for dessert. To cook the chickpeas, see the guidelines for cooking beans, page 187.

1 tablespoon olive oil
¾ cup olive oil

½ red onion, diced
4 large red onions, diced

1 clove garlic, crushed
10 cloves garlic, crushed

salt

2 cups cooked chickpeas, well drained
*about 24 cups cooked chickpeas
(two #10 cans, each containing 6 pounds
12 ounces), well drained*

about 1 cup diced ripe red tomatoes, drained
9 to 10 cups diced ripe red tomatoes, drained

juice and grated zest of ½ lemon
juice and grated zest of 4 lemons

pinch of hot red pepper flakes
1 teaspoon hot red pepper flakes

½ cup loosely packed mint leaves, coarsely chopped
4 cups loosely packed mint leaves, coarsely chopped

¼ cup coarsely chopped parsley

2 cups coarsely chopped parsley

black pepper

extra-virgin olive oil

lemon slices for garnish

In a large skillet, heat the olive oil over a medium-high flame until it shimmers. Add the onion and garlic with a little salt and sauté for 1 to 2 minutes. When the onion is mostly cooked, add the chickpeas and cook until the chickpeas are dry. They are now ready to absorb moisture and flavor from the other ingredients. Turn the chickpeas out onto a shallow serving dish to cool to room temperature. Just before serving, gently toss in the tomatoes, lemon, pepper flakes, mint, parsley, and plenty of salt and pepper to taste. Drizzle well with extra-virgin olive oil, and arrange lemon slices over the top.

Lima Bean and Ham Soup with Kale

SERVES 6 TO 8

Big buttery beans, ham, bacon, and vitamin-loaded greens—this is February food. Serve with brown bread and green salad. You can make this soup in stages, cooking the beans and ham hock the day before. Though the kale will lose its vibrant color, this soup is very good reheated. The ham shank is cooked separately from the beans because the salt it releases while cooking will slow the softening of the beans.

1 smoked ham shank

2 cups dry large lima beans (about 1 pound), soaked overnight and drained (see steps 1 and 2 of the guidelines for cooking beans, page 187)

1 bay leaf

salt

2 to 3 strips thick-sliced bacon, cut into medium dice (or 2 to 3 tablespoons olive oil)

1 medium yellow onion, cut into medium dice

1 small carrot, peeled and cut into medium dice

2 stalks celery, cut into medium dice

continued . . .

. . . *continued*

1 large bunch kale, thickest stems removed, washed and chopped or torn into bite-sized pieces

2 cloves garlic, crushed

one 14-ounce can diced tomatoes in juice

black pepper

1 to 2 teaspoons cider vinegar or fresh lemon juice

Cover the ham shank with water in a large saucepan. Bring to a boil, skim off any scum that rises to the surface, and reduce the heat to a simmer. Let simmer for 1 hour, or until the meat is tender and can be easily removed from the bone.

Meanwhile, put the soaked beans in a large, heavy soup pot with the bay leaf and fresh water to cover the beans by about 2 inches. Bring to a boil, skim off the scum that rises to the surface, and reduce the heat to a simmer. Cook the beans until they are completely buttery-soft and yielding, 30 to 40 minutes (longer at high altitudes). Carefully add salt until the broth tastes good, like a thin soup. Cook over low heat for about 20 minutes longer so the salt penetrates the beans. Remove the bay leaf.

When the ham shank is tender, remove it to a plate to cool, saving the broth. Discard the bones, fat, and gristle.

Break up the meat into chunks, and add the meat and ham broth to the beans.

In a large saucepan, cook the bacon over medium-low heat to render out the fat. When the bacon is beginning to brown and there is ample fat (2 to 3 tablespoons; you may replace some of this fat—or the bacon altogether—with olive oil), throw in the onion, carrot, and celery with a good pinch of salt and cook, stirring occasionally, until the onion is no longer translucent, about 10 minutes. Add the kale in batches—it will cook down—and the garlic. When everything is simmering, add the tomatoes and their juice. Bring the mixture back to a simmer and cook, stirring every so often, until the kale is tender, about 20 minutes.

Stir the vegetable mixture into the beans, and simmer for about 10 minutes more. Taste for salt. Add pepper to taste. To brighten the flavors, add 1 to 2 teaspoons of cider vinegar or lemon juice.

This soup is also excellent sans meat, using olive oil to stew the vegetables.

White Navy Beans

The next four recipes all use white navy beans. Taken together, they are not necessarily meant to sing the praises of that particular, rather bland bean, but rather to show how versatile beans can be in general. Between a bean casserole, a rich and spicy chili, and two elegant but different soups, inspired cooks will see a world of possibility in one humble bean. Consider these recipes as templates for imaginative use of the many bean varieties available.

White Bean Gratin with Fennel

SERVES 6 TO 8

This casserole is superb served with fish or any simple, hearty meat such as pork or chicken, or by itself with fresh brown bread and a big, vegetabley salad.

2 cups dry white navy beans (about 1 pound)

1 bay leaf

4 tablespoons extra-virgin olive oil

2 teaspoons salt, plus more as needed

1 fennel bulb, cut into medium dice, reserving the feathery fronds for topping

1 large yellow onion, cut into medium dice

2 tablespoons coarsely chopped fresh sage

1½ teaspoons red wine vinegar, plus more if needed

¼ teaspoon hot red pepper flakes

black pepper

—

TOPPING

¾ cup dry breadcrumbs

2 tablespoons extra-virgin olive oil

feathery fennel fronds, coarsely chopped

salt and black pepper

continued . . .

. . . continued

Soak and cook the beans with the bay leaf, following the guidelines for cooking beans on page 187. When the beans are tender, remove from the heat and stir in 2 tablespoons of the olive oil and the salt. Taste the broth: it should be pleasantly seasoned, like soup. Let the beans sit in the broth while you prepare the vegetables and the topping.

Heat the oven to 350°F. In a medium saucepan, in the remaining 2 tablespoons olive oil, cook the fennel and onions with a pinch of salt over a medium flame until tender. Add the sage and cook for 1 minute more.

Drain off sufficient liquid so that the beans are still very moist, but not soupy. Add the onion-fennel mixture, vinegar, red pepper flakes, and salt and pepper to taste. Taste; the flavors may need brightening with a judicious touch more vinegar.

Combine the ingredients for the topping— breadcrumbs, olive oil, chopped fennel fronds, and salt and pepper to taste—in a small bowl. Spread the beans in a 9-by-13-inch baking dish, and sprinkle the topping evenly over the surface. Bake until the topping is golden brown, 20 to 25 minutes.

Pork and White Bean Chili

SERVES 6 TO 8

A Deep Springs student brought this recipe from his mom. I adapted it and adopted it immediately. What's the secret? It's the cheese.

2 heaping cups dry white navy beans (a little over a pound)

1 bay leaf

2½ teaspoons salt, plus more as needed

2 teaspoons ground cumin

2 teaspoons ground coriander

1½ teaspoons dried oregano

2 pounds ground pork (on the lean side, if possible)

¼ teaspoon black pepper, or more as needed

2 medium yellow onions, cut into small dice

4 cloves garlic, minced

pinch of ground cloves

pinch of hot red pepper flakes

three 4-ounce cans chopped fire-roasted green chiles

1½ cups (6 ounces) grated jack cheese

½ cup coarsely chopped cilantro

chopped green onions

diced ripe tomatoes

minced jalapeño

sour cream thinned with milk

lime wedges

white onion chopped with cilantro

Soak and cook the beans with the bay leaf, following the guidelines on page 187. When the beans are tender, add 2 teaspoons of the salt and simmer for ½ hour more. Remove the bay leaf. Leave the beans in their broth.

Over medium heat, toast the cumin and coriander in a small skillet (or in the skillet in which you'll cook the pork) until their fragrance is released. Add the oregano and toast for a few seconds more. Transfer the spices to a small bowl.

In a large skillet over medium-high heat, cook the pork with ½ teaspoon salt, ¼ teaspoon pepper, and the reserved toasted spices until it is no longer pink, 6 to 7 minutes. If your pork is fatty, drain off as much of the fat as you like. Add the onions with another pinch of salt and cook for 10 minutes, or until the onions are soft.

Add the garlic, cloves, red pepper flakes, and green chiles with their juice, and cook for a few minutes more.

Drain and reserve 3 cups of broth from the beans. Stir the pork mixture into the beans, adding back enough broth to achieve a thick, soupy consistency. Simmer for 10 minutes to allow the flavors to combine, then remove from the heat and add the cheese and cilantro, stirring to melt and incorporate the cheese. Add salt and pepper to taste and serve immediately with the accompaniments of your choice. You can make the chili, up to the point of adding the cheese and cilantro, well ahead of time.

White Bean Soup with Fried Sage

SERVES 4 TO 6

While I think of chili and heartier bean soups as meals in themselves, this is an example of a more refined, lighter, puréed bean soup, easier to fit into a menu with other foods.

2½ cups dry white navy beans
(about 1¼ pounds)

1 bay leaf

4 tablespoons extra-virgin olive oil

2 teaspoons salt, plus more as needed

1 medium yellow onion, cut into small dice

2 stalks celery, cut into small dice

3 cloves garlic, crushed or minced

chicken stock, vegetable stock, or water for thinning the soup, if needed

1 to 2 teaspoons fresh lemon juice

freshly ground black pepper

TOPPING

¼ cup olive oil for frying

12 to 16 large sage leaves

Soak and cook the beans with the bay leaf and a tablespoon of the olive oil, following the guidelines on page 187. Since the beans are for soup, use ample water when cooking them. When the beans are soft,

add 1½ teaspoons salt and simmer for about 20 minutes more. Leave the beans in the broth.

In a small, heavy saucepan over a medium flame, heat 2 tablespoons of the olive oil. Gently sauté the onion, celery, and garlic with a few pinches of salt until the vegetables are soft and sweetened, about 5 minutes—do not let them brown. Add the vegetables to the beans and simmer for about 10 minutes more. Purée the soup in batches in a blender. *Be careful when blending hot liquids: fill the blender jar only half full, hold the lid in place with a kitchen towel, and start the blender on lower speeds.* For the smoothest texture, pass the soup through a screen sieve, using the back of a ladle. Add some chicken stock, vegetable stock, or water if the soup needs thinning. Stir in a teaspoon or two of lemon juice to brighten the flavor. Add more salt to taste, and pepper. Enrich with a final tablespoon of olive oil.

To fry the sage, heat ¼ cup olive oil in a small skillet over medium-high heat until the tip of a sage leaf sizzles when dipped in. Fry the sage leaves until crisp, 5 to 10 seconds—they will turn a darker shade of green and release a puff of fragrance. *Remove immediately* with a slotted spoon and drain on paper towels. Reserve the sage-scented oil for a marinade or dressing. Break the leaves into small pieces and strew over the soup just prior to serving.

Rosemary Oil

Instead of fried sage, you can garnish this soup with rosemary oil. Strip the needles off a small branch of rosemary until you have about 2 tablespoons of needles. Put the needles in a blender jar with ½ cup olive oil and blend on high speed until the herb is completely pulverized. Pour the mixture into a small cup and allow it to sit for an hour. Strain through a sieve, and drizzle ½ teaspoon of the scented oil over each bowl of soup just prior to serving. (Use the remaining rosemary slurry to marinate chicken or scent focaccia bread or, with garlic, nuts, and Parmesan added, to garnish pasta, pizza, or rice.)

White Bean and Escarole Soup

SERVES 6 TO 8

This simple, elegant soup contains escarole, a lettucelike green that tastes pleasantly bitter and satisfyingly crunchy raw, but nutty and fortifying cooked. Like all members of the chicory family, escarole is especially tasty with savory beans. Once you have chicken stock and cooked beans on hand, the soup is practically already made. We served it at Deep Springs one Christmas to begin a sumptuous Italian dinner featuring glazed Deep Springs–raised ham.

1 large head escarole

2 teaspoons olive oil

1 medium yellow onion, cut into small dice

1 medium carrot, peeled and cut into small dice

1 small stalk celery, cut into small dice

2 pinches of salt, plus more as needed

6 cups good chicken stock

3 cups cooked, well-seasoned white navy beans in their liquid (start with 1½ cups of dry beans, and follow the guidelines on page 187)

continued...

. . . continued

Remove any wilted or blemished outer leaves of the escarole; remove the remainder of the leaves from the core and cut into bite-size squares. Briefly immerse the escarole in a basin of cold water and drain.

Heat a teaspoon of the olive oil in a large, heavy soup pot over medium heat. Add the onion, carrot, celery, and a good pinch of salt and cook slowly, covered, stirring occasionally, until the vegetables are completely tender, about 5 minutes—they shouldn't brown. Add the chicken stock, and bring to a simmer. Let this soup base simmer gently for about 5 minutes while you wilt the escarole.

Heat another teaspoon of olive oil in a large saucepan. When it just begins to smoke, add half the escarole with a pinch of salt and immediately stir. It will quickly wilt and turn a vivid green. Let the escarole cook, stirring two or three times, for about 1 minute, or until nutty and tender. Add it to the soup, and repeat with the remaining escarole.

Drain the beans, saving their flavorful liquid for another purpose, and add them to the soup. Bring to a simmer. If the chicken stock was well seasoned, the soup should not need salt—taste. Serve immediately, stirring the pot from the bottom when ladling up each serving.

Split Pea Soup

SERVES 4 TO 6

This hearty split pea soup contains marjoram, a flowery herb similar to oregano. Lacking marjoram, you may approximate its flavor with a couple of pinches of oregano and a pinch of dried mint. Why the rice? It somehow lightens the peas' starchiness, invisibly. You can make this soup with yellow or green split peas—I often use a combination. Serve with a warm loaf of wheat bread.

2½ cups dry green or yellow split peas (about 1¼ pounds)

½ cup uncooked brown rice

9 cups water

1 bay leaf

2 to 3 pinches of hot red pepper flakes

1 tablespoon butter

1 medium carrot, peeled and cut into medium dice

1 medium yellow onion, cut into medium dice

1½ teaspoons salt, plus more as needed

1 teaspoon dried marjoram, or 1 tablespoon chopped fresh marjoram

2 tablespoons soy sauce

freshly ground black pepper

2 teaspoons red wine vinegar

In a large, heavy soup pot, soak the split peas and rice in 9 cups water for about 1 hour. Bring to a boil over high heat, skim off the foam that collects on the surface, and add the bay leaf and pepper flakes. Reduce the heat to a lively simmer. Cook, stirring frequently, until the peas and rice have dissolved into a purée, about 50 minutes. Watch carefully at the end—as it thickens, it will tend to stick to the bottom and burn. Remove the bay leaf.

In a medium saucepan, melt the butter over medium-high heat. Add the carrot and onion with the salt and cook, stirring frequently, until the onion is soft, 8 to 10 minutes. Add these vegetables to the peas and simmer slowly for 20 minutes more. Add the marjoram, soy sauce, and pepper to taste. Stir in the vinegar to brighten the corners. Taste for salt and serve. This soup is very good reheated.

If you want ham in your split pea soup, either cut up a packaged ham steak and throw it into the soup near the end or separately braise a ham shank to tenderness, adding the chunks of meat and broth to the soup in the last 20 minutes of cooking.

CHAPTER 7

Hot Vegetables and Vegetable Soups

Each vegetable has its own natural history. Over millennia, people encouraged certain traits such as sweetness and tenderness, very gradually transforming wild plants into modern cultivars. The bunch of green chard sitting on your kitchen counter mutely contains within its cells epochs of human history. Because some of chard's modern cultivars were developed in fertile cattle-grazing valleys in northern Italy and Switzerland, chard tastes especially good cooked with a little cream and Parmesan or Gruyère cheese. That zucchini squash tastes "truest" when cooked quickly in a little olive oil is a clue that it developed in warmer southern European climates, where olives thrive. Chilly weather brings out the natural sugars in cabbage, and cooks know that cabbage tastes best when braised slowly in a little butter or pork fat, with maybe a chopped apple thrown in. So we might hazard a guess that what we know today as cabbage developed in colder northern climates. Each vegetable, each embodying its own individual story, must be considered on its own terms; there aren't many universal vegetable-cookery rules.

I know many people who, like me, are not vegetarians but who nurture a great love for vegetables. It's the produce section, not the meat counter, that most inspires me when I'm shopping to cook a meal. Any vegetable can be delicious, especially if grown with care, bought fresh, and cooked thoughtfully. It's gratifying to serve people vegetables they thought they hated—beets or Brussels sprouts or cabbage—and see them discover for the first time how good they can be.

Technically, there are three vegetable chapters in this book. Beans are certainly a vegetable, and their chapter precedes this one. This chapter contains recipes and ideas for hot vegetable dishes, including many soups (the preceding Beans chapter also contains several soup recipes). The next chapter deals with salads and cold vegetable preparations, including a terrific approach to gazpacho, a chilled soup.

continued . . .

. . . continued

Artichokes

SERVES 6

Artichokes are traditional in the spring, but they grow well in California's cool coastal climate in all but the hottest months. When I serve artichokes at Deep Springs, I often give a demonstration of how to eat them, since there are always one or two students who have never encountered them before. An interesting fact: one of the flavor compounds in artichokes causes some people to perceive sweetness in plain water, or even in inhaled air. Lemon Vinaigrette (page 296) is also excellent with artichokes and is a bit lighter than butter.

6 large globe artichokes

1 strip lemon zest, taken with a vegetable peeler

juice of ½ lemon

½ small onion, cut into large dice

1 carrot, peeled and coarsely chopped

1 stalk celery, thickly sliced

1 bay leaf

10 peppercorns

3 tablespoons olive oil

salt

LEMON BUTTER

½ cup butter (1 stick)

juice of ½ lemon

Rinse the artichokes well. With a large bread knife or other serrated knife, cut off the top inch of the artichokes, revealing the lighter-colored inner leaves. Pull off the outer layer of leaves from around the base, and then, using kitchen scissors, snip the sharp thorn off the remaining outer leaves. Cut the stems off at the base so the artichoke sits straight. Trim the brown tips from the stems. As you finish, plunge the artichokes and stems into water with a little vinegar added—this will keep them from browning.

Arrange the artichoke stems on the bottom of a large, heavy pot. Throw in the lemon zest, lemon juice, onion, carrot, celery, bay leaf, peppercorns, and olive oil. Add enough salt to the water to make it taste slightly salty. Arrange the artichokes on top, adding just enough water to submerge the bottom thirds of the artichokes. Cover the pot and bring to a boil. Lower the heat slightly and cook the artichokes at a low boil for 20 to 30 minutes, or just until a knife can be inserted into the base with no resistance. Drain the artichokes.

To make the lemon butter, melt the butter in a small saucepan, add the lemon juice, and serve in small cups with the artichokes. Provide a large bowl for the discarded leaves.

continued...

. . . continued

To eat an artichoke, begin with the outer leaves. Pull a leaf off with your fingers, dip the lower, pale-colored tip into the butter, then scrape off the edible flesh from the bottom of each leaf with your teeth. The leaves become more tender the closer you get to the heart. When all the leaves are consumed, scoop out the bristly "choke" with a spoon. Take up your knife and fork and enjoy the succulent heart, dipping slices into the remaining lemon butter. The stems, when peeled, are as tender and flavorful as the heart.

Simplest Artichokes

Cooking at home, I often won't bother with onion, carrot, celery, or other flavorings in the artichoke cooking water. These add an extra layer of savoriness, but when cooking very simply it is fine to omit them. I just use water, salt, olive oil, and a bit of lemon juice or vinegar to counter the artichokes' characteristic bitterness.

Stuffed Artichokes

SERVES 6

This special-occasion dish is lots of work for the cook but heaven for the eater. These are especially good served with vinegar butter: rather than lemon juice, the richness of melted butter is cut with a little red wine vinegar.

6 large globe artichokes

1 strip lemon zest, taken with a vegetable peeler

juice of ½ lemon

½ small onion, cut into large dice

1 carrot, peeled and coarsely chopped

1 stalk celery, thickly sliced

1 bay leaf

10 peppercorns

3 tablespoons olive oil

salt

FILLING

3 cups pea-sized crumbs of good-textured bread

2 medium onions, finely diced

2 tablespoons butter

salt

4 or 5 cloves garlic, crushed

½ cup chopped parsley

freshly ground black pepper

—

VINEGAR BUTTER

½ cup butter (1 stick)

1 tablespoon red wine vinegar or other vinegar with character

Cut off the top third of each artichoke, revealing the lavender inner leaves. Pull out these inner leaves and scrape out the fibrous choke. These will take a bit less time to cook than artichokes with their chokes intact.

Arrange the artichoke stems on the bottom of a large, heavy pot. Throw in the lemon zest, lemon juice, onion, carrot, celery, bay leaf, peppercorns, and olive oil. Add enough salt to the water to make it taste slightly salty. Arrange the artichokes on top, adding just enough water to submerge the bottom thirds of the artichokes. Cover the pot and bring to a boil. Lower the heat slightly and cook the artichokes at a low boil for 10 to 20 minutes, or just until a knife can be inserted into the base with no resistance.

To make the filling, while the artichokes are cooking, heat the oven to 325°F. Toast the breadcrumbs on a large baking sheet, tossing and redistributing them every so often, until they are a uniform golden brown, 7 to 8 minutes. In a small saucepan, slowly cook the diced onion in the butter with a little salt until tender, 5 to 6 minutes. Add the garlic and cook for a few minutes more.

Heat the oven to 350°F. Drain the artichokes and arrange them in a baking dish. Remove the stems from the artichoke cooking pot, peel off their fibrous outer layer, and chop them fine. In a medium bowl, combine the breadcrumbs, chopped stems, onion and garlic, parsley, and salt and pepper to taste. Taste—the mixture should be rich and savory. Fill each artichoke cavity with the breadcrumb mixture. Bake for about 20 minutes to heat through. If necessary, you can hold the artichokes for up to half an hour in the turned-off oven.

To make the vinegar butter, melt the butter with the vinegar in a small saucepan; serve in small cups alongside the artichokes.

Eat the artichoke leaves with your fingers, dipping the pale-colored tip into the butter, then scraping the edible flesh from each tough leaf with your teeth. When all the leaves are consumed, pour the rest of the butter over the stuffing, take up your knife and fork, and eat the prized artichoke heart with the stuffing.

Pan-Roasted Asparagus

SERVES 2 TO 4

Asparagus, its little shoots popping up out of the ground, is the quintessential spring vegetable. I cook, eat, and serve lots of asparagus in spring and otherwise do without. Air shipping and prolonged cold storage rob asparagus of much of its flavor and character. I read some-where that legendary architect Frank Lloyd Wright (who visited Deep Springs in the early days) would sometimes have nothing for dinner but a heap of spring asparagus with butter and lemon.

Pencil-thin asparagus is not necessarily the best. If you take the time to peel the stalks before snapping off the bot-toms, even the thickest asparagus turns out tender and succulent. I used to boil asparagus in salted water, but I have come to prefer slowly pan-roasting the whole spears on top of the stove, or simply broiling them.

1 pound asparagus

1 tablespoon butter or olive oil

salt

black pepper

Rinse the asparagus. Using a vegetable peeler, peel each stalk, starting about 3 inches away from the tip and going down. Then, grasping only the bottom inch of the stalk, snap off the bottom part of the stalk—the asparagus will break where its tenderness and toughness meet.

Heat a wide skillet over a medium-high flame. Melt a tablespoon of butter or olive oil and lay the asparagus in the skillet in a uniform line. Sprinkle lightly with salt. Let the asparagus cook—it will gently sizzle—for 2 to 3 minutes. Using tongs, turn the spears and cook on the other side for about 1 minute, until tender but still crisp. Sprinkle with pepper to taste.

Broiled Asparagus

Peel spears of asparagus as described, then toss in olive oil and salt, arrange on a baking sheet, and put the sheet under a hot broiler for about 5 minutes, or until there are appealing brown spots here and there. If the spears are thick, they will need to be turned and broiled on the other side.

Asparagus Pasta

Peel spears of asparagus as described, then thinly slice on the diagonal. Sliver the tips. Sauté with a little crushed garlic and salt in plenty of olive oil just until tender, then toss with freshly cooked medium shell pasta or another similar pasta shape. When draining the pasta, save a little of the pasta cooking water, in case moisture is needed in the finish. Add salt and pepper, grated lemon zest, and Parmesan. Taste and adjust. Lemon Butter Sauce (page 425) is also superb on asparagus pasta, perhaps with a few Sautéed Mushrooms (page 237). See the entry for Snap Peas (page 244) for a similar pasta.

Sautéed Green Beans

SERVES 2 TO 4

These sautéed beans are slightly wrinkly in appearance, and bright green. They are almost as good cold as freshly cooked. Though green beans are a year-round supermarket staple, they are at their sweetest and best in summer.

> 1 pound fresh summer green beans
>
> 2 tablespoons olive oil
>
> 1 small red onion, thinly sliced lengthwise (optional)
>
> 2 cloves garlic, crushed fine (optional)
>
> ½ small red bell pepper, sliced into long, thin strips (optional)
>
> salt
>
> black pepper

Rinse the beans well in a colander and snip the tops and tails off. I arrange handfuls of green beans, aligning the ends to be cut off against the counter surface and cutting the lot with my chef's knife, but it takes only a little more time to sit at the kitchen table and top and tail them one by one, getting a fast rhythm going.

continued . . .

. . . continued

In a wide skillet with a well-fitting lid, heat the olive oil over a medium-high flame. When it shimmers, add the optional onion, garlic, or red bell pepper with a pinch of salt and sauté quickly for a few seconds. Throw in the green beans with another pinch of salt. There should be just a little water left on the beans from rinsing, which will help them to cook. Stir everything around to distribute a light coating of oil on the beans, then slap on the lid. If the pan seems very hot, reduce the flame a little. If the pan seems dry, add a tablespoon or so of water. Keep cooking the beans, stirring every so often, until they are tender but still crisp (taste one). Very fresh young beans could take only a minute, while large, mature beans could take almost 20 minutes to tenderize enough. On average, pencil-sized beans are tender after 8 to 10 minutes of sautéing. Don't stir them constantly; they are especially good if they brown lightly here and there. Grind a little black pepper over the beans and serve.

FRESH SHELL BEANS

Virtually any variety of bean cultivated for use as a dry bean may be eaten fresh, as a shell bean. When beans have just matured but the pods are still green, pop them out of the pods and simmer them in water, as you would dry beans. A strictly summer crop, shell beans are sometimes available at farmer's markets and well-stocked produce markets. Japanese *edamame* are fresh soybeans in the pod—simply boil the whole pods in well-salted water until the beans within are tender. Cranberry shell beans are beloved by Italians, and American Southerners dote on fresh shell black-eyed peas and runner beans, but lima beans are the best-known shell bean. I am sure millions of children still grow up eating mixed vegetables made from frozen packages: always those same cubed carrots, inch-long green beans, peas, corn, and a lima bean here and there. And I'm sure many of those millions still hate the lima beans and pick them out, or swallow them whole with milk, as I once did. But I also remember discovering that the smaller, greener lima beans were actually quite good.

I have occasionally seen fresh garbanzo, or chickpea, shell beans. I bought a large bunch once, with only one or two beautiful green garbanzo beans to each pod. After more than an hour of work, I had produced a preciously small amount of light and fresh-tasting green hummus.

If you find shell beans, sit at your kitchen table and remove the beans from the pods. Put the beans in a heavy saucepot, and cover with cold water by about 1 inch. Bring to a boil and skim off any scum that collects on the surface. Reduce the flame, maintaining a lively simmer. Add half an onion to the pot, plus a bay leaf and a small peeled carrot. Depending on the variety, shell beans will be tender after 30 to 40 minutes of cooking—taste one to determine doneness. When the beans are soft, remove the pot from the flame and immediately stir in enough salt to season the liquid well. Also add a good shot of olive oil. Stir frequently as the beans cool—they will absorb salt and oil from the broth. Cooked shell beans are quite perishable: refrigerate them promptly after they are cool.

Cooked shell beans and their flavorful broth may form the backbone of a delicious, hearty vegetable soup (see Soupe au Pistou, page 260). Or add sautéed corn, freshly cut from the cob, and stewed onion to drained shell beans, with perhaps a little chopped fresh savory or other herb, and you have a wonderful succotash. Or toss shell beans and some of their broth with fresh tomatoes, herbs, an appropriately shaped pasta, and golden-toasted breadcrumbs.

BROCCOLI

Bursting with vitamins and calcium, broccoli, a cool-weather crop, is one of the most popular vegetables in the United States. Many people steam broccoli; I usually find steamed vegetables bland, but I admit, sometimes I just artlessly throw a crown of broccoli whole into my smallest saucepan with a splash of water and turn the heat up high. Often, I am amazed at how sweet it tastes with no salt or seasoning.

Most of the time I "steam-sauté" broccoli. Cut the florets off the central stem, and then, with a paring knife or peeler, peel the tough outer skin from the stem. (Broccoli stems, usually thrown away, are tender if peeled.) Cut the smaller florets in half, the larger ones in quarters. Cut the stem into uniform pieces; all the cut broccoli should cook at about the same rate.

For each pound of broccoli, melt a tablespoon of butter or olive oil and 2 tablespoons of water in a large saucepan with a well-fitting lid over a medium-high flame. When the water begins to boil, throw in all the broccoli with ¼ teaspoon salt, and stir to coat. Cook, stirring frequently but otherwise keeping the lid on, until the broccoli is as tender as you like. Some like it soft; others prefer a little crunch remaining.

continued...

. . . continued

If you want to use cooked broccoli in a salad, use olive oil in the cooking, spread the cooked broccoli on a tray to cool, and dress it at the last minute—the acidic vinegar will turn broccoli a dull army green. For an excellent picnic salad, toss broccoli with Aioli (page 427) and halved cherry tomatoes. Broccoli to be served warm is enhanced by dark Asian sesame oil and a sprinkle of lightly toasted sesame seeds, or by sizzling crushed garlic in the oil before throwing in the broccoli. Or toss cooked small-cut florets with pasta, hot red pepper flakes, olive oil, toasted breadcrumbs, and grated Parmesan.

Broccoli, Roasted Red Peppers, and Walnuts

For this festive early-fall dish, arrange a pound of just-cooked broccoli in a warm serving dish. Scatter evenly over the top ½ cup Roasted Red Peppers (page 244), first cutting the peppers into strips and dressing them with a teaspoon of olive oil, a pinch or two of salt, a twist of black pepper, and 2 drops of balsamic vinegar. Scatter over the peppers and broccoli ½ cup lightly toasted walnuts (see page 301), tossed with a drop or two of olive oil and a pinch of salt. Finish with a few twists of black pepper and serve immediately while the broccoli is still warm.

Brussels Sprouts with Brown Butter

SERVES 4 TO 6

Brussels sprouts and brown butter were made for each other, as my friend Adra taught me while we were still in high school. Making a frequent appearance on my Thanksgiving table, they are always everyone's surprise favorite, even the alleged Brussels sprout haters. The toastiness of the butter enhances the naturally meaty, cabbagey flavor of the Brussels sprouts.

Once you get the hang of it, brown butter is one of the easiest sauces there is. The French call it *beurre noisette*— "hazelnut butter." You simply take the butter to within a few seconds of burning, then pour it over hot food.

Brussels sprouts are strictly a winter crop. Sometimes you may find them on their stalk, resembling 2-foot-tall Muppet-trees. Precut Brussels sprouts, ideally, should have no yellow. I have eaten Brussels sprouts that had yellowed on the outside, but I peeled them down to the green before cooking. Lots of brown butter on those, please, and I hope your kitchen has good ventilation.

1 pound Brussels sprouts, stems trimmed, tough or discolored outer leaves removed

1 cup water

¼ teaspoon salt, plus more as needed

2 to 3 tablespoons butter

freshly ground black pepper

Cut each sprout in half lengthwise. Put the water and ¼ teaspoon salt in a medium saucepan and bring to a boil over a high flame. Throw in the sprouts, stirring well to distribute. Let the water come back to a boil, slap on the lid, and let the Brussels sprouts cook for about 4 minutes, stirring once or twice. To test for doneness, rinse a sprout in cold water and bite into it. When they are just tender to the bite, they are done. Avoid undercooked, crunchy sprouts or overcooked, mushy sprouts. Drain the liquid from the pan and transfer the sprouts to a serving dish. Give the pan a quick rinse and set it back on the burner.

To make the brown butter, turn the flame to medium-high and let the pan dry for a few seconds, then throw in the butter. When the butter melts and bubbles and the foam subsides, swirl the pan and watch carefully until the butterfat (the liquid on the bottom) and the remaining foam turn a toast brown. It will first smell raw and dairylike, then it will take on a toasty and savory aroma as it browns.

When the butter is well browned and smells tantalizing, dump in the Brussels sprouts, tossing gently to distribute. Let the sprouts sizzle in the butter for a moment. Add a pinch or two of salt, if necessary, and a few twists of pepper, then slide them back into their serving dish. Serve immediately.

Cabbage with Juniper

SERVES 2 TO 3

This splendid, unusual combination makes an elegant accompaniment to a winter dinner. In the fall, I harvest blue juniper berries from the tree in front of the Deep Springs faculty duplex; they are the size of peppercorns and very fragrant.

½ small green cabbage

¼ teaspoon juniper berries

pinch of salt, plus more as needed

1 tablespoon water

2 tablespoons butter

1 tablespoon dry white wine

freshly ground black pepper

Cut the core from the cabbage, and cut the leaves into bite-size strips. In a small bowl, crush the juniper berries well with a pinch of salt. Add the tablespoon of water. In a medium saucepan over medium heat, melt 1 tablespoon of the butter with the juniper-water mixture. When the water boils, add the cabbage and the wine. Cook the cabbage, stirring frequently, until tender, 6 to 8 minutes. Stir in the remaining tablespoon of butter, and add salt and pepper to taste.

Honey-Glazed Carrots

SERVES 4 TO 6

Carrots are at their sweetest and best in the colder months of the year. Once, the gardeners pulled a bumper crop of carrots from the Deep Springs garden when an early hard freeze threatened. The Boardinghouse walk-in refrigerator was filled with crates and crates of carrots, dirt still clinging to the fat orange roots—the smell was powerfully fresh, sweet, and earthy.

1 pound sweet carrots

1½ tablespoons butter

salt

1½ tablespoons honey

coarse black pepper

Peel the carrots, trim the ends, and cut them into small bite-size pieces on the diagonal, rotating the carrot a bit each time you cut, producing uniform, attractive, jewel-like chunks. Melt the butter over medium heat in a wide skillet. When it is bubbling, throw in the carrots with a good sprinkling of salt and cook them, tossing frequently, until they are cooked on the outside but still raw on the inside, about 2 minutes. Raise the heat to medium-high and add the honey, tossing the carrots to coat. Cook quickly, tossing frequently, until the liquid in the pan reduces to a syrup and a few of the carrots have lightly caramelized, about 10 minutes. Sprinkle the carrots lightly with coarsely ground pepper. If necessary, these may be held briefly in a warm oven.

Italian Tzimmes

One of the traditional dishes served at a Jewish Passover dinner, or seder, *tzimmes* usually consists of a sweet vegetable, such as carrots or sweet potatoes, with dried fruit and spices. In Yiddish, *tzimmes* means "mess." I found this particular combination in an Italian-Jewish cookbook. Plump ¼ cup golden raisins in hot chicken stock or water, and lightly toast ¼ cup pine nuts (see page 301). Add ¼ teaspoon ground cinnamon to the pan when adding the honey, and sprinkle the raisins and pine nuts over the finished dish just before serving. This was good with lemon-and-rosemary roast lamb at a Passover seder I hosted at my house one year at Deep Springs. We used pine nuts we had harvested the previous fall up in the White Mountains.

Carrot Soup with Ginger

SERVES 4

Found on the menus of socially progressive cafés, this simple soup is a modern classic. This version ends up thick, with a clean, subtle ginger flavor. For a richer, more elegant soup, dress it up with ½ cup of heavy cream at the end. Or for an entirely different effect, use half a can of coconut milk. If your carrots are ordinary, you may slip a small red bell pepper (seeded and chopped) in with the carrots—it will perk up their flavor without announcing its own presence. Similarly, a teaspoon or two of curry powder (see page 358) harmonizes well, added at the same time as the carrots. But if you have super-fresh, sweet carrots, these amendments are unnecessary.

2½ pounds sweet, crisp, tender carrots

about 2 tablespoons butter

1 large yellow onion, cut into medium dice

4 cloves garlic, minced

2-inch piece of fresh ginger, peeled and finely chopped

about 1 teaspoon salt

black pepper

continued . . .

Peel the carrots and cut on the diagonal into even ½-inch slices. In a large, heavy pot with a well-fitting lid, melt a tablespoon of the butter over a medium-high flame. Throw in the onion, garlic, and ginger with ¼ teaspoon of the salt, and stew, stirring frequently but keeping the pot covered between stirrings, until the onion is almost tender, about 5 minutes. Add the carrots with another ¼ teaspoon of salt and stew, stirring frequently, for about 5 more minutes. Add enough cold water to cover the carrots by 1 inch, and add another ½ teaspoon salt. Bring to a boil, and simmer gently until the carrots are completely soft, about 15 minutes. Purée the soup in batches in a blender, adding a small pat of cold butter to each batch while blending. *Be careful when blending hot liquids: fill the blender jar only half full, hold the lid in place with a kitchen towel, and start the blender on lower speeds.* Pass the soup through a screen sieve using the bottom of a ladle to press on the solids. Discard any stringy material left in the sieve. Thin the soup with water, if necessary. Taste for salt—it will probably need a pinch more. Reheat gently, and garnish each bowl with a light twist of black pepper.

Cauliflower

SERVES 4 TO 6

Cauliflower, a cool-weather vegetable, has its own particular savor, more delicate yet somehow meatier than broccoli or other cruciferous vegetables. It may be "steam-sautéed" like broccoli (see page 219); however, unlike broccoli, it tastes very good when allowed to brown slightly in hot oil.

1 medium head cauliflower (about 1 pound)

2 tablespoons butter or olive oil

salt

freshly ground black pepper

Rinse the cauliflower thoroughly and drain, then halve lengthwise. Cut off all dark or blemished leaves. I include any unblemished pale green leaves in whatever I'm cooking, and often the tender core as well. Cut the cauliflower into thin wedges lengthwise, then cut each wedge into attractive, uniform bite-sized pieces.

Over a medium-high flame, melt 1 tablespoon of the butter in a large skillet. When it sizzles, add half the cauliflower with a big pinch of salt. Stir to coat, and cook, stirring and tossing frequently for about 5 minutes, or until the cauliflower is as tender as you like—check the doneness by tasting a small piece. Very freshly picked cauliflower will cook more quickly. Allow the cauliflower to brown slightly in the pan. I like it cooked until it has just lost its crunch but is not mushy. Add freshly ground pepper, for which cauliflower has a particular affinity. Transfer to a serving dish, wipe out the skillet, and repeat with the remaining butter and cauliflower.

Mashed Cauliflower

SERVES 4 TO 6

This is like mashed potatoes, only made with cauliflower.

1 medium cauliflower (about 1¾ pounds)

¼ cup heavy (whipping) cream (or half-and-half or sour cream), warmed

1 tablespoon butter

salt and freshly ground black pepper

Cut the cauliflower in half, and boil both halves in a large saucepan in lightly salted water until quite soft, 12 to 15 minutes (poked with a knife, it should offer no resistance). Drain well. Gently mash the cauliflower to a purée with a potato masher, adding the cream and butter. If the mixture isn't as smooth as you'd like, purée a portion of it in a blender or food processor, then fold this purée back into the remainder of the cauliflower. Add salt and, of course, freshly ground black pepper to taste.

BROILED CAULIFLOWER

Cut cauliflower uniformly into small bite-size pieces. Toss with a little olive oil, salt, and pepper. Arrange on a baking sheet so the pieces are not too crowded, and stick under a hot broiler for 8 to 10 minutes, or until some edges are beginning to deliciously blacken here and there. Serve immediately.

Chayote

SERVES 4 TO 6

Chayote is a hardy member of the squash family, usually sold in Latin American markets. It grows like a weed in temperate climates. A little bland by nature, it is good company to many other more highly flavored vegetables. Here is a basic recipe, with garlic and a whisper of cayenne.

2 chayotes (about 5 ounces each)

1½ tablespoons olive oil

2 or 3 cloves garlic, crushed fine

½ teaspoon salt, plus a pinch

2 or 3 pinches of cayenne pepper

Peel the chayotes carefully—they exude a unique, slippery liquid that makes them hard to hold onto. Use a towel if necessary. Cut into medium dice. If the seed within offers little resistance to your knife, it is tender and need not be removed—just cut right through it. If it feels tough, cut it out. Heat the olive oil in a medium saucepan over medium-high heat, add the garlic and ½ teaspoon salt, and cook, stirring rapidly, just until the garlic turns opaque—do not let it brown. Add the chayote with the cayenne and the pinch of salt, reduce the heat to medium, and cook, covered, stirring frequently, until the chayote is tender, 6 to 8 minutes.

CORN ON THE COB

Fresh corn on the cob is a summer ritual dear to the heart of many an American. Is there a point to all that fuss about freshness? Yes, when the corn in question is any of the old heirloom varieties, such as Golden Bantam or Silver Queen. The sugars support a rich, milky corn flavor, but you must cook the corn very soon after it is picked, before the sugars turn to starch. My grandmother always said you should bring your big pot of water to a boil and then, and only then, send "your fastest boy" out to the cornfield and have him pick the corn and "shuck it as he runs back to the kitchen." I'm not sure who my grandmother's "fastest boy" was, as she had three daughters.

In recent decades, new "supersweet" varieties of corn have emerged, and now almost nobody grows anything else. Though these varieties are indeed sweet and stay sweet through prolonged storage, their flavor is not as rich and nuanced as the old varieties. If your corn isn't as sweet as you'd like, add a bit of sugar to the boiling water.

Like asparagus and summer tomatoes, corn is quite particular to its season. Eat lots of corn in the summer, but don't be tempted by corn your supermarket offers in the colder months, when you know it grew halfway around the world. Just wait until next summer—the corn will taste all the sweeter for your patience.

Get as many ears of corn as will fit in your largest pot—it's fine if they are crowded. Peel back the husks and remove the silks. Rub off any excess silk with a damp kitchen towel. Fold the husks back over the kernels. The husks will intensify the corn flavor and, peeled back after cooking, offer a convenient, if funny-looking, handle by which to hold the ear.

Fill your largest pot about half full with water. Don't add salt; it will toughen the corn. Bring to a boil, and plunge in the corn. Let the water return to a boil, then boil for 3 to 4 minutes. Drain and serve.

As much as I like butter and salt, I love corn unadorned. However, fresh lime juice, salt, and powdered chile is delicious on corn, as you will discover on any trip to Mexico. Sometimes, remembering those flavors, I make the following butter.

Jalapeño-Lime Butter

Mix in a bowl the finely grated zest and juice of a lime, a stick of room-temperature butter, a minced jalapeño (seeds and light-colored pith removed if you want it mild), and ¼ teaspoon each salt and pepper. Keep stirring—the butter and lime juice will eventually emulsify. Serve with hot corn on the cob.

Sautéed Corn

SERVES 4 TO 6

Corn sweetens any plate; this sauté goes well with meat, seafood, or cheese dishes and is easy company with many other vegetables. It may even induce people to eat kale and other greens (see page 232).

6 ears fresh sweet corn

3 tablespoons butter

1 small onion, finely diced

¼ teaspoon salt, plus more to taste

freshly ground black pepper

Shuck the corn and rub the silks off with a damp kitchen towel. Using a chef's knife, cut the kernels off the corn. Cut away from you onto a large cutting board. Once the kernels are cut off, scrape the bare cobs with the back of the knife to extract all the germ and milk.

Melt the butter in a wide skillet over medium-high heat. When it sizzles and foams, throw in the onion and ¼ teaspoon salt. Sauté the onion for about a minute, stirring and tossing frequently, until it is mostly transparent. Do not let the onion

brown—remove the pan from the heat for a moment if necessary. Throw in the corn kernels with all their liquid and sauté, keeping everything moving. After a minute or two, reduce the heat to medium and continue to cook for about 5 minutes, or until the onion is tender and the corn kernels are cooked but still a little crisp. Season with pepper to taste and additional salt, if necessary. Serve immediately.

Variations

Throw in some Jalapeño-Lime Butter (page 227) or a little cooked, crumbled bacon. For elegant *creamed corn*, add ½ cup heavy cream to the pan along with the corn. Cook until the cream is reduced somewhat and is coating the corn. Or pep things up with a handful of chopped Roasted Red Peppers (page 244) and a pinch of cayenne to further the red pepper flavor.

Catherine's Corn Soup

SERVES ABOUT 6

This soup is pure essence of corn.

12 large ears fresh, sweet summer corn

about 6 tablespoons butter

1 large onion, diced

salt

freshly ground black pepper

GARNISH (CHOOSE ONE)

1 tablespoon chopped basil or cilantro
sprinkled over each bowl

some Jalapeño-Lime Butter (page 227)

chopped Roasted Red Peppers (page 244)

a spoonful of Green Chile Relish
(page 423)

a swirl of either the New Mexico Red or
Green Chile Sauce (page 420 or 422)

Shuck the corn, and rub the silks off with a kitchen towel. Using a chef's knife, carefully cut the kernels off the cobs into a wide bowl. With the back of your knife, scrape all the juice and germ out of the cobs into the bowl with the corn. Put the cobs in a large pot, cover with cool water, and bring to a boil. Reduce the heat to a simmer.

Meanwhile, heat 4 tablespoons of the butter in a heavy soup pot over medium-high heat, and throw in the onion with a good pinch of salt. Cook the onion for a few minutes, stirring frequently, until it begins to soften. Stir in the corn with all its accumulated juice and stew for several minutes, stirring frequently, until the corn is thoroughly heated. Pour in enough of the hot corncob water to barely cover the corn kernels. Bring the soup to a boil, reduce the heat, and boil gently for about 5 minutes.

Adding a small pat of cold butter to each batch, purée the soup in batches in a blender. *Be careful when blending hot liquids: fill the blender jar only half full, hold the lid in place with a kitchen towel, and start the blender on lower speeds.* If you would like a little texture to remain in the soup, purée only about two-thirds of it. Let the blender run for a full minute for each batch. Press the soup through a screen sieve, using the bottom of a ladle and extracting as much liquid as possible. Discard the dry, fibrous material remaining in the sieve. Salt the soup lightly, tasting it carefully, and add freshly ground black pepper to taste. Reheat gently, ladle into warmed bowls, garnish, and serve.

ROASTED EGGPLANT

Always an abundant summer staple, eggplant needs a blast of dry, high heat to taste silky and succulent; I always roast or broil or grill it. In the past, I followed recipes that instructed the cook to salt and drain the eggplant prior to cooking to remove the bitter juices, but I'm not convinced this is necessary, especially with fresh summer eggplant. Do not peel eggplant—too many vitamins and nutrients reside in the richly pigmented skin.

Heat the oven to 450°F. Cut eggplant into 1-inch chunks, and toss with a little olive oil in a large bowl. Exercise judgment when adding oil: eggplant will readily absorb and retain any oil you throw its way, and too much will make the eggplant heavy. Sprinkle with salt and toss again, then arrange the chunks in a single layer on a baking sheet and put in the oven, roasting the eggplant until deep brown and soft throughout, 15 to 20 minutes.

Eggplant thus cooked is delicious mashed up with a little fresh garlic, coarsely chopped cilantro, and more olive oil and served as a dip or relish; or tossed with penne or other similar sturdy pasta, spicy tomato sauce, lots of fresh basil, and Parmesan or feta cheese.

One Deep Springs summer, despite the heroic efforts of the student gardeners in battling ferocious winds, dust devils, late frosts, and gophers, a huge crop of eggplant was the only successful harvest. In the Boardinghouse kitchen, as Student Cook, I developed the habit of throwing a couple of whole eggplants and whole unpeeled heads of garlic into whatever simmering meat stock I had on the back stove burner, and letting them cook until soft. The eggplant and garlic gave something to the stock, and vice versa. I'd drain and quickly peel and mash the eggplant and garlic together with salt, and serve it as a sauce with whatever was for dinner that night. Did I put in olive oil, herbs, and pepper? I hope so, but I don't remember—and though boiled eggplant doesn't sound like something I'd approve of today, I remember it as a light, delicate, flavorful condiment.

ROASTED GARLIC

Garlic is one of Deep Springs' most dependable crops. As long as we plant it at the correct time, it seems to thrive in the hot sun, winds, and temperature extremes, and the rapacious gophers and birds leave it alone. Most garlic is harvested in midsummer, staying especially tender and succulent for 2 to 3 months afterward. That's when I am most inclined to roast whole heads of garlic.

Although garlic heads may be roasted whole and naked with no prior treatment, here is a way that maximizes their softness and sweetness. Choose firm, sound heads of garlic. Heat the oven to 350°F. Remove the outer layers of papery skin on the garlic, but leave the cloves intact. Using a paring knife, gently shave the skin from the top ends of the cloves, so just a bit of each clove is exposed. Rub the whole head well with olive oil. Arrange the heads snugly in a baking dish. Take a piece of baking parchment that will fit over the dish, crumple it tightly into a wad, then flatten it out and press it down on top of the garlic. Put a sheet of aluminum foil (shiny side down) over the dish and seal well, crimping the foil around the edges of the dish. The parchment holds in an extra measure of steam and flavor, but if you have no parchment, just use foil. Bake for 30 to 40 minutes, or until the garlic is soft throughout. After your guests have admired the garlic's beauty and symmetry, instruct them to squeeze out the purée from the bottom, as they would a tube of toothpaste. Cut thick slices of warm bread (or toasted or grilled bread), drizzle with olive oil, then squeeze and spread the roasted garlic purée over the bread. Sprinkle with salt. This is a beautiful accompaniment to Roast Chicken (page 346).

Garlic Soup

SERVES 2

This very old European peasant dish is a good use for any day-old bread that's not too sweet; well-textured, chewy, artisan-style bread is ideal. Any of the savory bread recipes in this book (see the chapter beginning on page 129) work well, too.

3 cups water

½ teaspoon salt

pinch of dried sage, thyme, or rosemary

2 thick slices good bread

1 large clove garlic, halved

extra-virgin olive oil

grated Parmesan cheese

freshly ground black pepper

Bring the water to a boil in a medium saucepan with the salt and a pinch of the dried herb of your choice. Toast the bread until the surface is golden brown. Rub the garlic into the rough toasted surfaces of the bread. Put a slice of bread in each of 2 wide soup bowls, and drizzle with extra-virgin olive oil. Pour the boiling-hot herb broth over the bread. Grate Parmesan over the top, and twist that peppermill. A poached egg (see page 101) is very good in this soup. You may also fortify the soup with a handful of cooked Greens (recipe at right).

Greens

SERVES 2 TO 4

By "greens" I mean cooked leafy greens: kale, chard, spinach, collards. . . . Many Americans, other than Southerners, are still unfamiliar with the idea of eating cooked greens (besides spinach) as a vegetable, but they are powerfully nutritious and equally delicious if grown and cooked with care. Although they may be grown year-round, greens are best when they have undergone a frost; cold temperatures stimulate the plant to produce sugars you can taste. In Deep Springs' garden, the greens remain for some time, still producing, long after the tomatoes and other summer crops have been turned under. Once you acquire a taste for greens, you will find that your body craves them when you need an extra boost of vitamins and minerals in cold weather.

Though they must be washed like lettuce, greens are easy to incorporate into all kinds of foods, such as pasta, rice, soups, stir-fries, omelets, and scrambled eggs. Cooking times for greens depend on three factors: the variety, the maturity of the plant, and how the leaves are cut. Mature, large-leaved kale and collard greens will withstand lengthy cooking if cut into large pieces. But those same leaves will become tender much more quickly if cut into fine ribbons first.

Certain greens, such as spinach, are almost always best just wilted or quickly sautéed.

Most cooking greens, such as kale, collards, arugula, mustard greens, and many Asian greens, including choi sum, bok choy, and tatsoi, belong to the huge Brassica family, which also includes cabbage, broccoli, and cauliflower. A second significant greens family includes spinach, chard, and beet tops. Finally, certain lettuces and chicories (radicchio, endive, and escarole), though most familiar raw in salads, are also very good cooked.

My favorite accompaniment to greens is always hot, creamy Polenta (page 404) and maybe a small pork chop.

Here is a method that, in my experience, works for all greens. It's especially suited to the greens varieties listed here, but other types work, too:

¾ to 1 pound (1 large bunch) leafy cooking greens, such as chard, collards, kale, mustard, turnip, or beet greens

2 tablespoons olive oil or bacon fat

½ small onion, finely diced (extra-fine if the greens will not need much cooking time)

about ½ teaspoon salt

1 or more cloves garlic, crushed (optional; or use instead of onion)

black pepper

a few drops fresh lemon juice or red wine vinegar

Separate the leaves of the greens. Immerse the leaves in a clean basin of cool water and swirl gently to thoroughly rinse off dirt. Lift the greens out of the water and heap them into a colander to drain. If your basin is small and the greens were crowded in it, you may have to repeat this process a couple of times until the water is clear. (My grandmother always washed her spinach three times.) Let the greens drain in the colander.

If you are using collard, chard, or kale greens, gently strip the leafy parts off the stems. To easily do this, form an "O" shape with your thumb and forefinger and pull the stem of the leaf through the O, tearing the leaves from the stems. Cut or tear the leaves into bite-size pieces. Using a knife, slice a handful of the most tender stems paper-thin and combine with the leaves—this way, the stems will cook at the same rate as the leaves.

Heat the olive oil in a wide, heavy skillet over medium heat until it shimmers. Throw in the onion with a pinch of salt and sauté quickly until the onion begins to soften, 3 to 4 minutes. Stir in the garlic, if you opt for it, with another pinch of salt. Add the greens—the water still clinging to them will create steam and aid in the cooking. Add ¼ teaspoon salt and stir until the greens are coated with oil and beginning to wilt. A splash of water may be necessary if the pan seems hot and
continued . . .

. . . continued

the greens seem dry—greens should not brown. Continue to cook, stirring frequently, until the greens are tender—this could take anywhere from a few seconds for tender young spinach to 15 minutes for cabbage or kale—to check the doneness, taste a piece. *Do not cover the pan if you are cooking spinach, chard, or beet greens,* as certain compounds in these vegetables, once volatilized, may precipitate back into the pan and dull the color of the greens to an uninspiring olive drab. Add more salt, if necessary, and black pepper to taste. Most varieties of greens benefit from a touch of acidity—vinegar or lemon juice. Serve the greens immediately.

Sautéed Kale and Corn

SERVES 4 TO 6
LARGE QUANTITY RECIPE: SERVES 30 TO 40

This sauté is a great way to get people to eat their kale.

1 tablespoon olive oil
½ cup olive oil

½ small yellow onion, cut into medium dice
6 large yellow onions, cut into medium dice

1 fat clove garlic, crushed
10 fat cloves garlic, crushed

about ¼ teaspoon salt
about 1 tablespoon salt

1 large bunch kale, washed, stemmed, and cut into bite-sized pieces
5 gallons loosely packed washed, stemmed kale, in bite-sized pieces

kernels cut from 2 ears fresh sweet corn
8 cups fresh or frozen sweet corn

¼ teaspoon hot red pepper flakes
2 teaspoons hot red pepper flakes

black pepper

Heat the olive oil over a medium flame in a large, heavy pot. Add the onions and garlic with a little salt, and sauté until the onion is tender, about 5 minutes. Don't let the onion brown. Raise the heat to medium-high and add the kale in two or three batches, each with a pinch of salt, letting each batch wilt before adding another. Add a splash of water if the pan seems too dry—the kale shouldn't brown. When the kale is tender, add the corn, red pepper flakes, additional salt, and black pepper to taste. Heat to bubbling and serve.

Leek and Vegetable Purée Soup

SERVES 4 TO 6

Leeks, highly prized by the French for their haunting flavor and tonic health benefits, are surprisingly good simply steamed, but they really come into their own in soups. The following recipe could be considered a template for using all manner of cool-weather vegetables. A bowl of thick, silky puréed soup, using leeks as the backbone, goes a long way to restore one's vitality in the long winter months.

2 large leeks

about 3 tablespoons butter

½ medium onion, cut into medium dice

about 1 teaspoon salt

4 to 5 medium turnips or 1 large rutabaga (about 1½ pounds), peeled and cut into medium dice

2 carrots, peeled and cut into medium dice

black pepper

pinch of cayenne pepper

½ teaspoon balsamic vinegar or fresh lemon juice, if necessary

continued . . .

. . . continued

First, clean the leeks: cut off any brown or withered parts, and entirely remove the outermost layer. With a knife, carefully trim off the dark green tops of the leek in an upward motion, leaving the white and pale green parts intact. Reserve the dark green tops. The trimmed leek will be pointed like a pencil. Cut the dirty root end off the leek, then cut the leek in half lengthwise. Under cold running water, thoroughly rinse each layer of the leek— dirt and mud might lurk between the layers. Also rinse the reserved dark green tops. Cut the white and pale green leek bottoms into medium dice.

Chop the dark green leek tops coarsely, put in a small saucepan, and cover with water. Bring to a boil to make a simple stock.

Meanwhile, in a large, heavy soup pot over a medium-high flame, melt 1½ table-spoons of the butter. When it is bubbling, throw in the diced leeks and onion with a pinch of salt. Cook, stirring frequently, for about 2 minutes, then add the turnips and carrots with another pinch of salt. Cook all the vegetables, stirring frequently, until they are slightly softened. Pour the leek stock through a strainer over the vegetables, then add enough water to just barely cover the vegetables. Bring the soup to a boil, then reduce to a simmer. Let simmer until all the vegetables are tender, about 10 minutes.

Using a blender, purée the soup in batches, adding a small pat of butter to each batch. *Be careful when blending hot liquids: fill the blender jar only half full, hold the lid in place with a kitchen towel, and start the blender on lower speeds.* Purée until completely smooth and silky. Return the soup to the pot and add salt to taste. Start with ½ teaspoon; it might need more. Carefully add a few twists of black pepper and a pinch of cayenne. If the soup tastes quite sweet and needs a little oomph, add a tiny amount—about ½ teaspoon—balsamic vinegar or lemon juice to balance. Reheat gently, and serve.

Cauliflower, butternut squash, or celery root may all be used in place of, or in addition to, the turnips.

Brothy Vegetable Soup

When a brothy vegetable soup—not a purée, but a soup with chunks of vegetables—is called for, simply follow the recipe above, taking care to cut the vegetables into evenly sized medium dice, and skip the puréeing step. Such a soup may be enriched with chopped cooked Greens (page 232), with Handmade Egg Noodles (page 388), or with Cornmeal-Egg Soup Dumplings (page 398). While this leek-based recipe is most appropriate in the cooler months of the year, Soupe au Pistou (page 260) is a brothy soup made of warm-weather vegetables.

Sautéed Mushrooms

SERVES 2 TO 3

4 ounces white or brown mushrooms

2 teaspoons butter

1 or 2 generous pinches salt

freshly ground black pepper

Sautéed mushrooms are a source of deep, satisfying flavor in many dishes. Mushrooms, it must always be remembered, are a life form as different from plants as you and I are. Thanks to the glutamic acid within their cells, mushrooms enhance the flavors of the foods they accompany. When they are fresh, white or brown mushrooms look clean, with closed gills. If you are using fresh shiitake mushrooms, completely pull off the tough stem of each mushroom before slicing (reserve the stems to enrich chicken or vegetable stock). The following basic technique works for virtually all fresh mushrooms. *If you are consuming wild mushrooms, be certain of the expertise of whoever picked them.* Unless they are very dirty, don't rinse mushrooms in water: they will absorb a lot of the water, making them quite difficult to brown in the pan, and will end up soggy. To slice mushrooms evenly, first cut them in half lengthwise, then arrange the two halves so you can slice them lengthwise at the same time.

Trim off and discard all but ⅛ inch of the mushroom stems, then wipe clean, halve, and slice the mushroom caps thickly. You should have about 2 cups. Melt the butter in a wide skillet over a high flame. When it just begins to brown, throw in the mushrooms with 1 or 2 generous pinches of salt (mushrooms need a good amount of salt). Toss to coat with butter, then let the mushrooms cook, undisturbed, for several seconds. Continue sautéing the mushrooms, stirring and tossing every 20 seconds or so, letting them brown appetizingly. Taste—they are usually cooked after 1 to 2 minutes. Twist a little black pepper over them.

Variations

The Italians add chopped garlic and parsley at the end and cook for a moment more. Thyme is also a very good mushroom herb. For a great *mushroom steak sauce*, add a splash of red wine to the skillet after the mushrooms are cooked, let it reduce for a moment or two until syrupy, then swirl in another pat of butter. Or use white wine for serving with fish or chicken.

NETTLE BROTH

A green forest of stinging nettles grows each summer under the leaky hilltop water tower behind the mechanic's shop at Deep Springs. Climb the steep rocky slope up to the water tower. Using thick leather gloves or tongs and your pocket knife, grab and lop off a large bunch of nettle tops and take them down to the kitchen. Keeping the gloves on, rinse the nettles, chop them coarsely, and put them in a pot. Now take off the gloves.

Cover the nettles with water and add a peeled, chopped carrot and a peeled, chopped onion. Bring to a boil, reduce the heat, and simmer for 20 minutes. Cooking deactivates nettles' sting. Add salt to taste and a good drizzle of olive oil. Strain. This makes a deep, powerfully nutritious, surprisingly meaty-tasting, bright green broth.

The eleventh-century Tibetan ascetic Milarepa lived in a mountain cave for twelve years, eating nothing but nettle broth; his skin and beard were said to be tinted green from this austere but sustaining diet. Younger, more tender spring nettles may be prepared and eaten like any tender green: quickly cooked in olive oil or butter and served as a vegetable, or added to brothy soups, pasta, risotto, or omelets.

Cornmeal-Fried Okra

SERVES 2

If you've never tried okra, a late-summer crop, this easy and delicious method will persuade you of its worth. After this, try the Gumbo on page 175. Summer squash is also excellent prepared this way (see page 254).

> about 12 ounces fresh okra (about 4 cups sliced)
>
> about 2 tablespoons cornmeal
>
> 2 tablespoons vegetable oil and/or bacon fat
>
> salt and freshly ground black pepper

Rinse the okra, cut the caps and tips off, and slice crosswise, about ¼ inch thick. Pay attention as you cut—if a particular okra pod seems tougher under the knife than the rest, throw it out. (You can't detect the tough ones visually.) Toss the okra in a bowl with the cornmeal. Heat the oil or fat in a wide, heavy skillet over medium-high heat and sauté the okra, stirring and tossing gently, until browned and tender, 5 to 7 minutes. Salt and pepper to taste, and serve.

Sweet Onions Cooked in Cream

SERVES 3 TO 4

The onions undergo two distinct cooking processes in this very simple recipe: first, in the liquid cream, the onions simmer and soften. But as the cream's water content evaporates, only the cream's fat remains, and the onions begin to fry.

¼ cup heavy (whipping) cream

3 sweet yellow onions, halved, cored, and thickly sliced lengthwise

salt and freshly ground black pepper

Heat the cream to boiling in a wide skillet over a high flame. Throw in the onions with a couple of pinches of salt and cook, stirring constantly, until the onions wilt and the cream reduces to a thick sauce. Reduce the heat and continue cooking, stirring frequently, letting the onions brown lightly as the liquid evaporates. Add salt and freshly ground pepper to taste.

Red Onion Galette

SERVES 4 TO 6

What is a galette? It's a pie baked free-form on a flat sheet, not in a pie pan. At Deep Springs, we first made these to simultaneously accompany roast beef and serve as a satisfying, meatless main dish for the herbivores. We like them so much that we often serve them as the backbone of a meatless dinner with, for instance, risotto, vegetable sauté, green salad, tomatoes, hard-boiled eggs, and bread, and ice cream for dessert. Leftover galette is delicious, even cold.

This recipe is a little more elaborate than many; to streamline the process, you may make the various elements—the dough for the crust, the onions, and the cheese filling—on the first day, then assemble and bake the galette the next day. The amount of cheese may seem small, but it plays a supporting role, bolstering and deepening the rich flavor of the caramelized onion. You can also try other kinds of soft fresh cheese, including goat cheese.

continued . . .

. . . continued

Sometimes I make two smaller pies rather than one large one. These take a little less time to bake and may be cut into hors d'oeuvre–sized wedges, whereas a piece of the large pie is most appropriately served on a plate with a fork.

CRUST

1 cup all-purpose flour

¼ cup whole-wheat flour

3 tablespoons wheat germ

scant ½ teaspoon salt

6 tablespoons cold butter

about ¼ cup cold apple juice, orange juice, or milk

—

ONION FILLING

1½ tablespoons olive oil

3 large red onions, thinly sliced (about 1¾ pounds; about 8 cups sliced)

¾ teaspoon salt, plus more as needed

¼ teaspoon brown sugar

½ teaspoon red wine vinegar

1 teaspoon balsamic vinegar

freshly ground black pepper

—

CHEESE FILLING

4 ounces cream cheese

pinch of salt

pinch of ground nutmeg

freshly ground black pepper

1 egg, beaten

If you are unfamiliar with making piecrust, see page 443. Mix both kinds of flour, wheat germ, and salt in a medium mixing bowl. Cut the butter into small pieces, and toss with the flour. Using your hands (or a pastry blender), rapidly work the butter into the flour, breaking up the pieces of butter, until the flour is somewhat moistened and there are pea-sized pieces of butter in the mixture. Stir in the cold juice; the mixture should cohere. Squeeze the dough into a ball, and wrap well with plastic wrap. Flatten the wrapped dough into a disc, and refrigerate for 1 to 2 hours, or overnight.

To cook the onions, first heat the olive oil in a wide, heavy skillet over medium-high heat. Pile in the onions with ¾ teaspoon salt and cook, turning and stirring as the onions cook down. When a browned, caramelized residue, called *fond*, forms in the pan, take the pan off the heat for a moment and allow the *fond* to dissolve, stirring it into the onions; this careful caramelization is the key to full, sweet flavor. Return to the heat, let another *fond* form, then stir it into the onions. Repeat a few times. Do not let the mixture burn— watch carefully, stirring often. Cook until the onions are completely tender, darkened in color, and sweet, 30 to 40 minutes. Season the onions with the brown sugar, red wine vinegar, balsamic vinegar, a pinch or two of additional salt, and freshly ground pepper to taste. Let cool in the pan.

To make the cheese filling, in a medium bowl, gently work the cream cheese with the salt, nutmeg, and pepper until smooth. Gradually add half the egg to the cheese, blending until smooth. Reserve the rest of the egg.

When you are ready to assemble and bake the galette, heat the oven to 375°F. On a floured surface with a flour-dusted rolling pin, roll the dough out into a circle. Continue rolling out the dough until it is about 14 inches in diameter, leaving the center somewhat thick, the edges thinner. For a neat final appearance, trim any rough outer edges of the circle.

Place the rolled-out crust on a baking sheet lightly dusted with flour, and lightly brush the inner surface of the dough with some of the reserved egg. Spread the cream cheese mixture into a 6- to 7-inch circle in the center of the crust, leaving about 3 inches of dough around the edge. Spread the onions evenly atop the cream cheese. Fold the crust partway over the filling in 6 even folds, tucking the final fold under the first, making a roughly symmetrical, hexagon-shaped galette. A small window of onion filling will show in the center.

Brush the crust on the top of the galette with the remaining egg. Bake, rotating the sheet once or twice, for 40 minutes to an hour. The crust should be a nice golden brown. Before slicing, let the galette cool on the sheet to room temperature or until just warm—it's fragile when hot.

Parsnip Soup with Toasted Almond Olive Oil

SERVES 4 TO 6

Parsnips, a winter crop, have a pronounced banana-like flavor that can be cloying. When chunked and roasted with other root vegetables, they tend to dominate. This elegant, velvety soup, however, showcases all their best qualities. Your guests will be surprised that it contains no cream.

TOPPING

¼ cup whole almonds, lightly toasted (see page 301) and coarsely chopped

3 tablespoons extra-virgin olive oil

pinch each of salt and black pepper

—

SOUP

about 3 tablespoons butter

5 large parsnips, peeled and cut into 1-inch chunks (about 2 pounds)

1 medium yellow onion, cut into medium dice

3 cloves garlic, crushed

¾ teaspoon salt, plus more as needed

5 to 6 cups vegetable stock

black pepper

continued . . .

. . . continued

To make the topping, in a small bowl stir the toasted, chopped nuts into the 3 tablespoons olive oil with a pinch of salt and pepper.

To make the soup, in a heavy soup pot, melt 1½ tablespoons of the butter over medium-high heat. When it sizzles, throw in the parsnips, onion, and garlic with ¾ teaspoon salt. Stew the vegetables, stirring frequently, until they are beginning to soften, 7 to 8 minutes. Add the stock and bring to a simmer. Simmer until the parsnips are completely soft, about 15 minutes. Purée the soup in batches in a blender, adding a pat of cold butter to each batch as it blends. *Be careful when blending hot liquids: fill the blender jar only half full, hold the lid in place with a kitchen towel, and start the blender on lower speeds.* Blend until completely smooth. Carefully season the soup to taste with salt and pepper. Top each bowl of soup with a spoonful of toasted almond olive oil.

Peanut Soup

SERVES 3 TO 4

This unusual, delicate soup is a specialty of the American South, with hints of Africa and France. If you have a fresh jar of natural peanut butter, before stirring it up, use a little of the oil on top to sauté the vegetables.

1 tablespoon vegetable oil (or peanut oil from the jar of peanut butter)

1 medium leek, white and light green parts only (see page 236), cleaned and cut into medium dice

1 medium carrot, peeled and cut into medium dice

pinch of salt, plus more as needed

4 cups chicken stock

⅔ cup natural peanut butter, well stirred

½ teaspoon honey, or more as needed

½ teaspoon apple cider vinegar, or more as needed

¼ teaspoon Tabasco or other hot sauce, or more as needed

black pepper

Heat the oil in a large saucepan over a medium flame and sauté the leeks and carrots with a pinch of salt until they are softened, 5 to 6 minutes. Add the chicken stock and bring to a boil, letting the soup cook until the leeks have lost their crunch. Whisk in the peanut butter, honey, vinegar, and Tabasco. Blend the soup smooth in a blender. *Be careful when blending hot liquids: fill the blender jar only half full, hold the lid in place with a kitchen towel, and start the blender on lower speeds.* Return the soup to the pan, reheat gently, and add salt and pepper to taste. The salt added will depend on whether the peanut butter is salted or not, and on the saltiness of the chicken stock. If necessary, judiciously add more honey, vinegar, or Tabasco to balance the flavors.

MINTY PEAS

These peas make a good accompaniment to springtime grilled meats (especially lamb) or roast beef (see page 313).

Shell fresh English peas, if it's springtime (or just take a bag of frozen peas out of the freezer), and cook them in a covered pot with a splash of water, a bit of butter, and a mint teabag sitting right on top of the peas. Take out the teabag when you stir the peas, then put it back on top. Cook until the peas are tender. Season with salt and pepper and more butter, if you like. Remove the teabag once it has scented the peas to your liking. For a stronger mint flavor, tear open the teabag and stir the dried mint into the peas.

SNAP PEAS

These springtime treats have a sweet, edible pod. Just rinse a handful in cool water and then pinch the tough ends off, pulling away any tough strings along the edges of the pod. For each big handful of snap peas, put a scant teaspoon of butter, a tablespoon of water, and a pinch of salt in a small covered skillet or omelet pan. Set the pan over high heat. When the butter is melted and bubbling, throw in the peas, tossing to coat. Cook quickly, tossing a few times but otherwise keeping the pan covered, for about 45 seconds, or just until the peas are steaming hot and have lost their raw flavor. Larger, late-season snap peas may require 2 to 3 minutes. They should be pleasantly crisp-tender—taste to check. Serve immediately.

Spring Pasta with Snap Peas and Asparagus

For a lovely springtime pasta, cut the peas in half on the diagonal so they look like little boats. Cut a handful of asparagus into 2-inch lengths. Cut up a few small spring onions. Cook the onions, peas, and asparagus together as described above, then toss them with a serving of cooked Handmade Egg Noodles (page 388) or penne, medium shells, or other similar-sized pasta, a spoonful of the pasta cooking water, a gob of butter, freshly grated Parmesan, and a few good twists of black pepper. Slide onto a warmed plate and grate more Parmesan over.

Roasted Red Peppers

SERVES 8 TO 12

These peppers enhance many things: you may strew them over pork chops, chicken, or skirt steak, or toss a handful into sautéed sweet corn. Peppers are available in supermarkets all year-round, but they are at their most succulent in summer.

6 large, sound, fleshy red bell peppers, or a combination of colors

1 teaspoon olive oil

¼ teaspoon balsamic vinegar

¼ teaspoon salt

¼ teaspoon black pepper

1 sprig fresh basil

Arming yourself with tongs, roast the peppers directly over the gas flame of your stove, or put them on a baking sheet and roast them close to your oven broiler, or char them over a charcoal fire while the fire is still too hot to cook the meat. Whichever heat source you use, allow the peppers to blacken and char evenly on all sides. Watch carefully—do not let them burn so much that the outer skin turns ashy gray. When the peppers are evenly charred, transfer them to a sealable glass or plastic container. Seal the container and let the peppers sweat for 20 to 30 minutes.

When removing the peppers from the container, be careful not to lose any of the juice that has accumulated. Break open the peppers and allow any juice inside to run into the container. Using your hands, remove the skin from the peppers, as well as the stems and seeds. *Do not rinse the peppers in running water*—a few bits of charred skin are part of the charm. Sometimes it helps to wipe your hands with paper towels a couple of times during the process. Cut the pepper flesh into strips and put in a bowl. Pour the reserved liquid through a strainer to catch the seeds—pour it over the peppers, if you like your peppers juicy (I do), or reserve for another use. Season the peppers with very small amounts of olive oil and balsamic vinegar, and the salt and pepper. Pick the leaves off a sprig of basil, cut them into fine ribbons (called *chiffonade*) with a sharp knife, and toss with the peppers.

Scalloped Potatoes

SERVES 6 TO 8

Serve this classic right from its baking dish; a glazed ceramic oval casserole, about 1½ quarts in capacity, is ideal.

2 pounds russet potatoes

1 tablespoon butter

1 cup heavy (whipping) cream

¼ cup milk

1¼ teaspoons salt

freshly ground black pepper

Heat the oven to 400°F. Under cool running water, rinse the potatoes well, scrubbing the skins with a clean cloth. Leave on any smooth, light-colored skin. Peel away any rough or blemished spots. (For an especially classic appearance, peel the potatoes completely.)

Slice the potatoes in even, ¹⁄₁₆-inch slices— this is quick work with a mandoline slicer. If slicing by hand, I find it easiest to cut the potatoes in half lengthwise first. Take your time to produce even slices—any thick pieces might still be raw when the rest of the potatoes are done.

continued...

. . . continued

Rub the tablespoon of butter all over the inside of your baking dish. In a large bowl, thoroughly toss together the potato slices, cream, milk, salt, and pepper to taste. Separate any stuck-together clumps of potatoes—you want all the potato surfaces to get a coating of cream. Dump the potatoes and all liquid into the baking dish and pat the potatoes down to make an even layer, with no pieces sticking up. Cover the potatoes with aluminum foil (shiny side down), taking care not to let the foil touch the potatoes but making sure the foil is crimped around the rim, sealing the dish. Bake for about 40 minutes, or until the potatoes are bubbling around the edges and cooked through. Test by inserting a small knife into the center of the dish—the potatoes should feel completely soft. Remove the foil and bake for another 10 to 15 minutes, or until the top is golden. Let your scalloped potatoes set for about 10 minutes in a warm place before serving.

Variations

A well-executed, golden, bubbly dish of scalloped potatoes seasoned with nothing but cream, salt, and pepper could never be considered dull. Sometimes plainly flavored food is a revelation; your guests will be amazed that anything with so few ingredients could be so delicious. Your skill and technique shine through. Nonetheless, there are infinite possibilities for embellishing scalloped potatoes. Try one or two of the following additions:

1 to 2 teaspoons chopped fresh thyme

1 teaspoon chopped fresh rosemary

about 1 cup sliced sautéed onions

about 1 cup sliced sautéed fennel

about 1 cup sliced sautéed turnips

about ¾ cup Sautéed Mushrooms (page 237)

about ¾ cup grated Gruyère cheese

You may also substitute, for an equal amount of the potatoes, up to 12 ounces of other cool-weather vegetables, thinly sliced: sweet potatoes, butternut or other winter squash, or celery root.

Simple Roasted Potatoes

SERVES 4 TO 6

Potatoes come in myriad shapes, sizes, colors, and degrees of starchiness. For the creamiest mashed potatoes or crispy fries, russets or other "starchy" varieties are always recommended. For this recipe, "waxy" types give the best results: red or white. Yellow potatoes, such as Yukon gold, have a medium level of starch and may be successfully used for any recipe.

1½ pounds red, yellow, or white potatoes

1 teaspoon salt

black pepper

1 tablespoon olive oil

1 teaspoon chopped fresh rosemary (optional)

Heat the oven to 450°F. Scrub the potatoes and trim away any blemishes. Cut into 1-inch chunks. In a large bowl, toss the potatoes with the salt, pepper to taste, and olive oil. Scatter on a parchment-lined or nonstick baking sheet and bake, tossing and redistributing occasionally, for about 30 minutes, until the potatoes are browned and soft. If you like, sprinkle the rosemary over the potatoes, toss, and return to the oven for 2 to 3 minutes more.

Roasted Potatoes, Apples, and Onions

This variation is excellent with pork chops. Replace some of the potato in the recipe above with chunks of tart, firm, flavorful cooking apple. Add a diced onion, too. Omit the rosemary, or not, or use thyme or sage.

Roasted Potatoes and Fennel

These are particularly good with fish, pork, or poultry, and invite a dollop of Aioli (page 427). Omit the rosemary and include 2 large fennel bulbs, trimmed of any brown spots, stalks removed (reserve the fronds), and cut into ½-inch chunks, adding a good extra pinch of salt. Once the potatoes and fennel are tender, scatter them with the coarsely chopped feathery inner green fronds of the fennel. Serve immediately.

Potatoes, Tomatoes, and Pesto

This simple summer dish makes good use of three of the most abundant Deep Springs garden crops: potatoes, tomatoes, and basil. Roast potatoes with olive oil and plenty of salt as described in the master recipe. Cut ripe summer tomatoes into chunks and drain in a colander (save or drink the refreshing, vitamin-rich tomato liquid). Scatter the room-temperature tomatoes over the hot potatoes. Drizzle pesto (see page 260) lightly over everything, serving extra pesto in a dish on the side. Serve immediately.

Potato, Fennel, and Celery Root Gratin

SERVES 4 TO 6

Fennel bulb, sometimes sold in stores as anise, is best in the cooler months of the year. It is much loved in southern France and Italy, where it is called *fenouil* and *finocchio*, respectively. (Incidentally, *finocchio* is Italian slang for a gay man, and was the name of a famous old San Francisco nightclub where the entertainers were all female impersonators.) Looking vaguely like celery, fennel has fat, pale green bulbs; thin, darker, fibrous stalks; and feathery dill-like fronds. Very fresh fennel has a marvelous faint sweetness and a delicate anise scent. I love fennel raw, shaved paper-thin on a mandoline slicer and tossed with enough lemon juice to keep it from turning brown (see page 285). But cooked fennel has its own particular savor, more subtle and far-reaching than celery. I have never put it in a soup or stew and wished I hadn't. Thick slices of fennel may be brushed with olive oil and grilled, or roasted with potatoes in the oven, or browned in butter in a skillet.

Celery root, also known as celeriac, is more versatile in its uses and more subtle and complex in flavor than stalk celery. A common vegetable in northern Europe, it can be cooked like a potato; many potato dishes are enhanced by substituting celery root for some of the potato. Cut raw into fine julienne, it is a good salad ingredient, combined with crisp apples and walnuts in a sophisticated Waldorf, or tossed with herbs and lemon juice (see page 283) to accompany steak.

Fennel and celery root are, in fact, botanical cousins; the Umbelliferae family gives many cuisines around the world a plethora of highly flavored roots, stalks, leaves, flowers, and seeds: angelica, anise seed, caraway seed, carrots, celery, celery root, chervil, cilantro, coriander, cumin, dill, fennel, fennel seed, lovage, parsley, parsley root, parsnip, and many more.

This gratin is wonderful with roast lamb. Serve Apple and Candied Orange Pie (page 448) for dessert.

2 pounds yellow or russet potatoes, peeled and cut into bite-sized chunks

1 large celery root, peeled and cut into bite-sized chunks

2¼ teaspoons salt, plus more as needed

1 scant tablespoon olive oil

1 large sweet onion, cut into medium dice

1 large fennel bulb, trimmed, stalks and fronds removed, cut into medium dice

1½ cups heavy (whipping) cream

¼ teaspoon freshly ground black pepper, plus a little more

Heat the oven to 400°F. Put the potatoes and celery root in a large pot, and cover with water by ½ inch. Add 2 teaspoons of the salt and bring to a boil. Lower the heat to medium and cook until the vegetables are soft, about 10 minutes; the cut edges of the potato should start to look a little rounded, and it should be quite easy to crush a potato cube with the back of a spoon. Drain well in a colander.

Meanwhile, stew the onion and fennel: heat the olive oil in a small, heavy saucepan over a medium-high flame. Add the onion with a pinch of salt and cook, stirring frequently, for 2 to 3 minutes. The onion should not brown—lower the heat if necessary. Add the fennel with a pinch of salt and cook, covered, stirring occasionally, until the onion and fennel are tender, about 10 minutes.

Heat the cream in a small pot on the stove with ¼ teaspoon each salt and black pepper. Butter a large (9-by-13-inch) glass or ceramic baking dish and dump in the drained potatoes and celery root, and the stewed onions and fennel. Toss gently to combine the two mixtures. Pour the heated cream over all, gently pressing the vegetables down into the cream. Bake, uncovered, until brown and bubbly, 30 to 35 minutes. Use a small knife to peer into the center of the gratin: what liquid cream remains (there should be some but not a lot) should be thick. Twist a bit more black pepper on top and let the gratin rest for about 10 minutes in a warm place before serving.

Scallion-Buttermilk Potatoes

SERVES 4 TO 6

These are like mashed potatoes, except with chunky potatoes and bits of scallion, commonly known as green onions. We often make them with Deep Springs–grown potatoes. The bulk of the liquid must be heated; cold liquid will seize up the potatoes' starch and make for a less creamy texture. Though white pepper is traditional in mashed potatoes so they keep their pristine whiteness, I like black pepper too much not to include it.

> 2 pounds yellow or russet potatoes, trimmed but left unpeeled, cut into chunks
>
> 1 tablespoon butter
>
> 1 bunch green onions, trimmed, white and green parts thinly sliced on the diagonal
>
> 2 big pinches salt, plus more as needed
>
> ½ cup half-and-half
>
> ½ cup buttermilk, at room temperature
>
> 1 to 2 tablespoons butter, at room temperature, for finishing
>
> freshly ground black pepper

Put the potatoes in a large pot with just enough water to cover. Bring to a boil over a high flame. Melt 1 tablespoon butter in a small pan over medium-high heat. Add

continued . . .

. . . continued

the green onions with a big pinch of salt, and cook until softened, 1 to 2 minutes. Add the half-and-half and heat until steaming; set aside.

The potatoes are done when a chunk yields easily to gentle pressure with the back of a spoon. Pour off the water completely (this unsalted potato water is excellent for making bread, by the way); add the green onion/half-and-half mixture, buttermilk, butter, and salt and pepper to taste. Stir gently; the potatoes will break up somewhat and emulsify the liquid. If the potatoes seem too liquidy, keep mashing until the mixture thickens. Taste for salt and pepper. Transfer to a warmed serving dish, and serve immediately.

Mashed Potatoes

Use the proportions and methods in the previous recipe, omitting the green onions and peeling the potatoes, if you like. For a perfectly smooth texture, put the potatoes through a ricer or a food mill. If you like a few lumps, mash with a potato masher. Don't whip mashed potatoes for long or the starch could break and the potatoes will be sweaty and gummy. You may boil the potatoes whole—they will take quite a bit longer to cook but will retain, some say, a bit more potato flavor. Waxy potato types, such as red potatoes, do not mash well. You can omit the buttermilk and use all half-and-half, though I love the bit of tang that buttermilk gives. If you are feeling luxurious, use cream in place of the half-and-half or sour cream in place of the buttermilk. Use white pepper if you want a classic appearance. For a delicious, unusual change of pace, use a hefty shot of fragrant extra-virgin olive oil in place of the butter and some of the liquid.

ROASTED RADICCHIO

This cool-weather dish, perfect with any simple meat, doesn't sound—or look—remotely as good as it tastes. Raw radicchio's ("ra-DEEK-ee-yo") brilliant burgundy color fades to an unfortunate dull brown, but the vegetable's characteristic bitterness softens into melting, savory sweetness under the broiler. An average-sized head of radicchio will serve two.

Heat your oven's broiler. Remove any withered leaves from a fat, tight head of radicchio. Trim the discolored surface from the base. Cut the head lengthwise through the base into about 16 wedges. Carefully toss the wedges with a good drizzle of extra-virgin olive oil and a good pinch of salt. Arrange the radicchio in a single layer, flat, on a baking sheet. Put the sheet a couple of inches under the broiler flame and broil for 4 to 5 minutes, or until the radicchio is tender and blackened here and there. Serve immediately.

Sautéed Spinach

SERVES 2 TO 3

Spinach is easy—it's almost always available in markets, it's easy to cook, it's loved even by finicky eaters, and it's good company to many other foods. This simple sauté can be served as is or tossed into pasta, folded into rice, thrown into soup, strewn over pizza, or stirred into curry. I don't recommend using bags of prewashed baby spinach, especially for this recipe—baby spinach cooks down to a surprisingly minuscule volume, and its flavor is not as well developed as the more mature bunched spinach specified.

2 bunches fresh spinach

butter or olive oil

small amount of chopped onion or garlic (optional)

salt

freshly ground black pepper

Cut most of the stems from the spinach, and wash the leaves well in a large basin of water, as you would lettuce—spinach tends to be muddy and gritty. Drain the spinach briefly in a colander. Heat a skillet over medium-high heat, and throw in the spinach to wilt it—the water clinging to the leaves will create sufficient steam. Stir the spinach around for about 30 seconds, until it is all wilted. Turn the clump of spinach out onto a plate and let cool for

continued . . .

. . . continued

a few minutes. When cool enough to handle, with clean hands, gently squeeze some of the excess water out of the spinach. (Sometimes I save this mineral-rich liquid and drink it as a tonic.) Chop the spinach coarsely.

Heat a little butter or olive oil in the skillet over a medium-high flame (you may cook a little chopped onion or garlic in the butter first, if you like). When hot, add the spinach and sauté briefly to concentrate the flavor, just a minute or two. Add salt and pepper to taste and serve immediately.

Butternut Squash Soup with Diced Pear

SERVES 4 TO 6

This cool-weather soup requires going at a big, hard squash with your kitchen knife, but the deeply flavored, velvety result is worth the effort.

GARNISH

1 small, ripe, fragrant pear

3 tablespoons extra-virgin olive oil

pinch each of salt and black pepper

SOUP

1 medium butternut squash
(about 2½ pounds)

4 cups water

1 large onion, cut into medium dice

¼ teaspoon salt, plus more as needed

about 2 tablespoons butter

1 small carrot, peeled and cut into medium dice

freshly ground black pepper

To make the garnish, halve the pear and cut out the core and stem. Don't peel it. Patiently cut the pear into small dice. Put it into a small bowl and add the extra-virgin olive oil. Stir in a pinch each of salt and pepper. Set aside while making the soup.

Wash the squash and pop off the stem. Arming yourself with a large chef's knife, cut the bulbous portion off the bottom of the squash. Cut the meaty top section in half, into two big cylindrical pieces. With your knife, carefully peel all 3 sections of the squash, reserving all the peel. Cut the bulbous bottom section in half and scoop out the seeds, reserving them with the peels. Cut the flesh of the squash into 1-inch chunks.

Put the peel and seeds in a small saucepan. Add the water and bring to a boil over high heat. Add about one-fourth of the onion (including any scraps from chopping it) and ¼ teaspoon salt. Reduce the heat somewhat and let this simple stock boil not too violently for 10 to 15 minutes.

To make the soup, meanwhile, in a large, heavy soup pot, melt a tablespoon of butter over a medium-high flame. Add the remaining onion with a pinch

of salt and cook, stirring frequently, until the pieces of onion are clear around the edges, about 2 minutes. Add the carrots with another pinch of salt and cook for a minute or so more. Reduce the heat to medium and stir in the squash cubes with a big pinch of salt. Continue to cook, stirring frequently, for about 5 minutes as the stock finishes cooking.

Strain the stock into the soup pot—it should just cover the vegetables. If not, bring the required amount of water to a boil and add it. Bring the soup to a lively simmer and cook, stirring occasionally, for 5 more minutes, or until the squash is completely soft. Purée the soup to a uniform smoothness in batches in a blender, dropping a small pat of cold butter into each batch as it blends. *Be careful when blending hot liquids: fill the blender jar only half full, hold the lid in place with a kitchen towel, and start the blender on lower speeds.* Unlike other vegetable purée soups, this one does not need straining—it will be silky smooth. Carefully add salt and pepper to taste.

Gently place spoonfuls of pear and oil into the center of each bowl of hot soup.

BUTTERNUT SQUASH CHIPS

At Deep Springs everyone cheers when butternut squash chips are on the menu.

Peel and seed a butternut squash as described in the previous recipe. Cut the thickest pieces down to long, inch-thick blocks. Using a swivel-bladed vegetable peeler or a mandoline slicer, shave paper-thin strips from the squash (save the thick scraps for another use). In a large, heavy pot, heat 4 to 5 cups of safflower, peanut, or other fry-friendly vegetable oil to 325°F. Fry the strips in batches, stirring gently to submerge the squash as it fries, until crisp but not deeply browned, 2 to 3 minutes. Remove with a skimmer and drain on paper towels or brown paper. *While the chips are still hot,* sprinkle with fine salt, and a little pepper if you like. They will crisp as they cool.

Potato Chips

This technique is also how you make potato chips, if you have a mandoline slicer. Scrubbed, unpeeled russet potatoes work well; red potatoes do not. Feel free to experiment with other types of potato. Most varieties will fry more satisfactorily if you first rinse out their heavier starch in cool running water. Drain and *dry these washed chips very well*, using a salad spinner, before frying them.

Cornmeal-Fried Summer Squash

SERVES 2 TO 3

Like many mothers, mine encountered great success in growing zucchini and other summer squash in her garden. This was our supper many a July night in New Mexico when I was quite young.

> 1 pound assorted summer squash: zucchini, yellow crookneck, pattypan, or other varieties
>
> ¼ teaspoon salt, plus more as needed
>
> 2½ tablespoons yellow cornmeal
>
> 2 tablespoons olive oil, bacon fat, or a combination
>
> black pepper

There are two ways to make this: you can cook large slices of squash over a medium flame, turning them once like steaks, or you can toss smaller bits around in the pan. Some of the cornmeal will fall off the squash while cooking, but it fries up into crispy crumbs in the oil and still tastes delicious. Okra is also excellent prepared in this manner (see page 238).

Wipe the summer squash clean with a kitchen towel, or rinse briefly and towel-dry. (Squash has a tendency to absorb water if rinsed, making the final result mushy.) Cut into ¼-inch slices or ½-inch chunks. In a large bowl, toss the squash with ¼ teaspoon salt and the cornmeal. Heat the oil in a big skillet (a nonstick skillet is ideal) over a medium-high flame, and throw in the squash, as well as the cornmeal in the bottom of the bowl. Cook, tossing occasionally, until the squash is tender and the cornmeal golden. Let the squash cook undisturbed for moments at a time to allow an appealing golden-brown crust to develop. Season with 1 to 2 big pinches of salt, and black pepper to taste.

If you have squash blossoms in your garden that you want to use but don't want to make a big fuss with, chop a couple of them up coarsely and throw them into your fried squash, as you would an herb, in the last minute or so of cooking.

Priscilla's Fried Green Tomatoes

SERVES 4 TO 6

When frost threatens Deep Springs Valley in the early fall, we harvest all the tomatoes and put flats of green tomatoes on every conceivable surface in the Deep Springs Boardinghouse. Many continue to ripen for use in salads, but we are also compelled to make fried green tomatoes. They are never better than when made by Priscilla, a recent Deep Springs chef.

1½ pounds green tomatoes

1 egg

2 tablespoons milk

pinch of brown sugar

½ cup all-purpose flour

½ cup cornmeal

1¼ teaspoons salt

black pepper

pinch of cayenne pepper

2 to 3 tablespoons vegetable oil

2 to 3 tablespoons bacon fat

Slice the tomatoes a little thinner than ¼ inch. Beat the egg, milk, and sugar in a shallow bowl, and combine the flour, cornmeal, salt, black pepper to taste, and cayenne in another shallow bowl. Dip the

continued...

tomatoes in the egg, then dredge them in the flour mixture. Place the tomatoes on a sheet pan in a single layer, not touching. Don't let the prepared tomatoes sit for more than about 20 minutes, or the coating will become soggy.

Heat a wide, heavy skillet over a medium-high flame. Add a tablespoon each of oil and bacon fat. Heat until the surface of the oil shimmers. Carefully lay in about a third of the tomato slices without crowding. Cook until the underside is an appetizing golden brown, 1 to 2 minutes, then flip and cook the other side. Drain on paper towels. Taste a slice, and sprinkle extra salt and pepper over the hot tomatoes if necessary. Drain the used oil from the pan, wipe clean, and add fresh oil and bacon fat to fry the remaining tomatoes. Serve immediately.

Use leftover fried green tomatoes in the next day's ham sandwiches.

Watercress Soup

SERVES 6 TO 8

A small bowl of this very simple, intense green soup alongside a freshly made egg salad sandwich on wheat bread makes a savory, invigorating winter lunch. The soup may also be made with spinach.

¼ cup olive oil

1 small onion, diced

1 carrot, peeled and diced

1 small stalk celery, diced

2 teaspoons salt, plus more as needed

4 cups water

8 to 10 ounces watercress (2 small bunches), washed, largest stems removed, and coarsely chopped

freshly ground black pepper

In a large, heavy soup pot over a medium-high flame, heat the olive oil until fragrant. Throw in the onion, carrot, and celery with a pinch of salt and cook, stirring frequently, until the vegetables are sweetened and beginning to soften. Add the water and bring to a boil. Stir in the watercress, bring back to a boil, and boil for about a minute. Add 2 teaspoons salt and pepper to taste. Transfer the soup to a blender and blend at high speed (in batches, if necessary), until the soup is completely smooth. *Be careful when blending hot liquids: fill the blender jar only half full, hold the lid in place with a kitchen towel, and start the blender on lower speeds.* If it seems very fibrous, pass the soup through a wire-mesh sieve, using the back of a ladle to press through as much liquid and purée as possible. Serve immediately.

ROASTED YAMS

Yams are in season in the fall and winter. Choose orange-fleshed yams (in common usage, *yams* are orange fleshed and *sweet potatoes* are yellow fleshed, but the two are essentially interchangeable; I prefer the color of yams). Scrub well under running water, and bake on a foil-covered baking sheet in a 400°F oven until they are completely soft, about 1 hour. The foil is necessary because yams expel syrup as they cook, which burns onto whatever surface they are baked on. Allow the yams to cool until you can handle them. Peel off the skins, but retain as much of the syrup as possible. Gently fold in butter, salt, and pepper to taste. A little brown sugar or cane syrup can be added, if you want to be especially Southern.

Ratatouille

SERVES 4 TO 6

Ratatouille is a traditional dish of stewed summer vegetables from southern France. Like many Mediterranean summer dishes, it is very good reheated the next day, or simply served at room temperature, like a salad, with a fresh drizzle of olive oil. It is happy company with many simple foods: pork chops, steaks, roasts, chicken, wide noodles, eggs. . . .

There are many methods for making ratatouille. On one end of the spectrum, you could just stew everything together in a big pot with lots of olive oil until the vegetables are all cooked into a mush. On the other end, I have seen fussy recipes in which each vegetable is cooked separately and then blended only at the end. The following recipe is a compromise: the vegetables are initially cooked in a couple of simple, separate processes, then the whole thing is baked together like a casserole. Each vegetable retains something of its own identity, but there is also a lovely blending of the various flavors. Ratatouille is a bit more work than many other vegetable dishes, but it is well worth the effort.

1 globe eggplant (about 1¼ pounds), cut into 1-inch chunks

about ⅓ cup extra-virgin olive oil

1 teaspoon salt, plus more as needed

1 medium yellow onion, cut into 1-inch dice

2 red bell peppers (about 8 ounces), cut into 1-inch dice

1 tablespoon red wine vinegar

3 cloves garlic, crushed

1 to 2 pinches hot red pepper flakes

2 or 3 assorted summer squash (about 1 pound), cut into 1-inch chunks

2 or 3 red ripe tomatoes (about 1½ pounds)

8 to 10 fresh basil leaves, coarsely chopped

1 tablespoon coarsely chopped parsley

3 or 4 oil-cured black olives, pitted and coarsely chopped

freshly ground black pepper

Heat the oven to 450°F. Toss the eggplant in a medium bowl with a good drizzle of the olive oil and ¼ teaspoon of the salt. Scatter the eggplant on an oiled baking sheet and bake until it is well browned on the edges and silky soft, 15 to 20 minutes. Remove from the oven.

While the eggplant is baking, heat 1½ tablespoons olive oil in a large, heavy skillet over a medium-high flame. Add the onions with a pinch of salt and cook for 1 to 2 minutes, stirring constantly, until they begin to soften. Add the bell peppers with ¼ teaspoon of the salt and cook, stirring frequently, for about 5 minutes, until the peppers are soft. The onions and peppers should brown slightly. Transfer the onions and peppers to a 9-by-13-inch baking dish. Let the skillet cool for a moment, then add the red wine vinegar. The vinegar will deglaze all the flavorful brown residue that formed while the onions and peppers were cooking. Taste·— if the vinegary liquid tastes burned and bitter, throw it out. If it tastes good and savory, add it to the peppers and onions.

Wipe the skillet clean and add another 1½ tablespoons of olive oil. When the oil is hot, add the crushed garlic with a pinch of salt. Let the garlic cook for just a few seconds, then add the hot red pepper flakes and the squash with another ¼ teaspoon salt and cook, stirring frequently, just until the squash is soft but not falling apart. Transfer the garlicky squash to the dish with the onions and peppers. (Don't wash the skillet yet; you might need it to reduce the juices when the ratatouille is finished.)

Heat the oven to 375°F. Bring a small pot of water to a boil and plunge the tomatoes in for 15 to 20 seconds, then remove them. The skins should now slip off easily with the aid of a small knife. Cut the peeled tomatoes into 1-inch chunks, and add them, with their juice, to the vegetables in the baking dish. Add a final ¼ teaspoon salt. Add the eggplant (and any accumulated juices) to the dish, *gently* tossing all the vegetables together. Bake for about 30 minutes. Remove from the oven and let cool for about 15 minutes. If the ratatouille is swimming in juice, drain off the juice and reduce it in your skillet, over a medium flame, to a thin, syrupy consistency. Drizzle it back over the vegetables. Gently toss the vegetables with the basil, parsley, olives, and salt and pepper to taste. Serve warm or at room temperature, with a fresh drizzle of olive oil.

Soupe au Pistou

SERVES 6 TO 8

Another southern French summer classic, this soup is full of good things from the summer garden: tomatoes, beans, green beans, squash, sweet corn (quite un-French, but delicious), and basil. *Pistou* is the southern French term for the pesto that tops the soup. I like the deep, satisfying flavor that chicken stock gives this soup, but vegetable stock (see facing page) is fine to use, too.

12 ounces ripe summer tomatoes, different colors if possible

¼ cup olive oil

½ medium onion, finely diced

1 small inner rib celery, finely diced

1 small carrot, peeled and finely diced

3 pinches of salt, or more as needed

handful of fresh green beans, tops and tails cut off, cut into ⅛-inch pieces

8 ounces summer squash, different colors if possible, finely diced

½ cup fresh corn kernels or cooked small pasta

1 cup cooked beans, preferably fresh shell beans (see page 187)

5 cups chicken stock

black pepper

PESTO

2 cloves garlic

about ¼ teaspoon salt

2 tablespoons coarsely chopped walnuts or pine nuts

1 bunch fresh basil (2 cups loosely packed leaves), coarsely chopped

about ⅓ cup extra-virgin olive oil

2 tablespoons freshly grated Parmesan cheese

black pepper

Bring a small pot of water to a boil and plunge the tomatoes in for 15 to 20 seconds, then remove them. The skins should now slip off easily with the aid of a small knife. Halve the peeled tomatoes crosswise, and squeeze out the seeds and pulp into a small bowl. Chop the tomato halves into medium dice and put in another bowl. Using a screen sieve, strain the seeds out of the pulp and add the seedless juicy pulp to the diced tomatoes.

In a large, heavy soup pot, heat the olive oil over medium-high heat. When it is fragrant, add the onion, celery, and carrot with a pinch of salt. Stew these vegetables, stirring frequently, until they are beginning to soften, 3 to 4 minutes. Add the cut green beans with another pinch of salt and cook, stirring, for 1 to 2 minutes more. Add the squash with a pinch of salt and continue to stew the vegetables, stirring, until the squash is just tender, 2 to 3 minutes more. Add the corn, beans, prepared tomatoes, and chicken stock and bring to a boil, then reduce the heat to a simmer. Simmer until the squash is soft but not falling apart. Taste for salt, and add a little pepper.

While the soup is cooking, make the pesto: pound the garlic in a large mortar with a little salt until it is smooth. Pound in the nuts until smooth, then the basil, with a pinch more salt. Adding olive oil as necessary, keep pounding until the basil is reduced to a chunky purée. Add the Parmesan and dilute with enough olive oil to make a runny consistency. Add pepper to taste.

You may also make the pesto in a food processor, but the flavors are subtly truer when the garlic and basil are pounded, rather than cut by whirling knives. Using the food processor, first thoroughly process the garlic, half the oil, the walnuts, and salt to a smooth purée. Next, add the basil (coarsely chopped) and pulse the machine until the basil is mostly incorporated. Add the Parmesan, remaining oil, and pepper to taste, and pulse to a chunky purée.

Ladle the hot soup into bowls, and spoon a generous tablespoon of *pistou* into each bowl. Serve.

Vegetable Stock or Broth

MAKES 12 CUPS

What is the difference between broth and stock? Broth implies a liquid suitable for consuming on its own, whereas stock implies "something out of which other things are made." This is an all-purpose vegetable stock, flavorful enough to be served on its own as a broth. When fresh, it tastes almost as substantial and satisfying as good homemade chicken stock. I often use it for risotto, meatless borscht, and many other vegetable soups. Do not be tempted to use onion skins, carrot tops, or any other vegetable trimmings that should go in the compost. *If it's not something you'd eat yourself, don't put it in your stock!* Always peel carrots, even for this recipe; because carrot skin is often slightly bitter, the end result will taste cleaner. Feed carrot peels to the horses or goats.

2 tablespoons butter or olive oil

1 large yellow onion, halved, peeled, and thickly sliced lengthwise

1 large carrot, peeled and cut into chunks

3 stalks celery plus 1 inner rib of celery with the leaves, thickly sliced

continued . . .

. . . *continued*

½ teaspoon salt, plus more as needed

5 or 6 large white or brown mushrooms, wiped clean, trimmed, halved, and thickly sliced

1 bay leaf

2 sprigs fresh thyme, or ½ teaspoon dried

1 sprig parsley

1 teaspoon whole black peppercorns

10 cups cold water

soy sauce

In a large soup pot, melt the butter over medium-high heat, and add the onion, carrot, celery, and ½ teaspoon salt. Lower the heat slightly and cook for about 5 minutes, uncovered, stirring the vegetables frequently and allowing them to stew and sweeten. Add the mushrooms with a pinch of salt, and stew for 5 minutes more.

Add the bay leaf, thyme, parsley, peppercorns, and water to the pot. Cover, raise the heat to high, and bring the stock to a boil. Reduce the heat and gently boil for 30 minutes. Season with salt and soy sauce until it tastes good—the soy sauce provides depth. Strain the stock through a sieve. Use it or freeze it on the day you make it—its freshness fades if it's kept.

Variations

Stock is infinitely variable, depending on what it will be used for. You can vary the herbs, use wine in place of some of the water, or add small amounts of dried mushrooms. If you save the rinds from chunks of Parmesan cheese, these give excellent flavor to vegetable stock. You may sauté the onions—or the mushrooms—separately until they are deep brown. Or add garlic, stewing it with the vegetables. Clean potato peelings will give the stock a little body and good flavor. You may add other vegetables, such as leeks (including the greens) or the clean peelings and seeds of winter squash in cool weather, or tomatoes or corncobs (after you've cut off the kernels) in warm weather.

Modern Man

Old farmer
down the road
a ways,
wife died
last March,
says he got hisself
a microwave
in May,
says
at sundown
he just totes
a beet
or a potato
big 'uns, no pesticides,
from the west field,
stops to wash
hands,
food,
the day's accumulation
of memories,
pops that beet in,
or potato,
hacks off chunks of
rat cheese,
bread,
cold butter,
and
there,
by gum,
is a dandy
supper.

—*Ann Applegarth*

CHAPTER 8

Salads and Dressings

Refrigeration technology is a recent development in our evolution. Food writers often herald ice cream as refrigeration's greatest gift to mankind, but I'd nominate the ubiquity of fresh, cool, crunchy, healthful salads. However, refrigeration is a double-edged sword: food may *seem* fresh under refrigeration when actually it could be quite old and unfit for consumption. Ironically, widespread refrigeration, coupled with the demands of commerce, means we frequently eat food that is far less fresh than what our forebears consumed, when surely the opposite was intended as refrigeration developed.

In any case, we are fortunate to have fresh, green salads readily available year-round. Salads are a superb medium for inspired cooks to practice their ingenuity. So vast is the field of salad possibilities, it is challenging to exactly define the word "salad." A salad may be composed of leafy greens or only of chopped or shaved vegetables. Salads usually contain a fresh, raw element, but not always. A salad may be cold or hot, a side dish or a main course, rich or lean. Someone once told me his favorite salad was a live oyster with a drop of fresh lemon juice. An acidic element (citrus or vinegar) is the rule for most salads, but a handful of pristine baby lettuces, just picked from the garden, may be so delicate that no dressing is needed beyond a drizzle of olive oil and a whisper of salt. And some relishlike salads contain no oil at all.

GREEN SALAD

To me, green salad occupies the same place that bread and butter did in generations past—it's an everyday thing. Serving it as part of every lunch and dinner at Deep Springs, I always vary the greens, toppings, and dressings. Salad greens are among the easiest vegetables to grow. Throughout the spring and summer we enjoy beautiful, though sometimes weather-damaged, lettuces from the greenhouse and garden. There is a vast spectrum of salad greens, from fragile yellow-green butter lettuce to deep purple-red radicchio, from the easy sweetness and crunch of head lettuce to peppery mustard or succulently bitter endive.

Though bagged, washed, ready-to-use salad greens are a great convenience, whole heads of lettuce that you have cut and washed yourself will taste fresher and more vibrant. For an intriguing salad blend that will surpass, with clear, individual flavors, any bagged store-bought variety, include something from each category below, balancing the various flavor characteristics:

LETTUCE (SWEET)

red- or green-leaf lettuce

romaine lettuce

butter lettuce

oak leaf lettuce

iceberg lettuce (not very nutritious, and usually not good for salads, but see the Blue Cheese Dressing recipe, page 298)

CHICORY FAMILY (BITTER, BUT COMPELLINGLY GOOD ONCE THE TASTE IS ACQUIRED)

radicchio

Belgian endive

escarole

frisée

young dandelion

BRASSICA FAMILY (SPICY AND STRONG)

green and red cabbage

savoy cabbage

arugula

baby mustard greens

tatsoi

mizuna

SPINACH FAMILY (HAS A MINERAL TASTE)

spinach

very young chard

CRESSES (PEPPERY)

watercress

garden cress

curly cress

continued . . .

. . . continued

**HERBS
(AROMATIC; USE SMALL AMOUNTS)**

parsley leaves

chervil fronds

tarragon (chopped)

chives (chopped)

mint leaves

A salad mix of all sweet lettuces stands up well to a creamy dressing, and benefits from the addition of other vegetables, such as shredded carrots, sliced mushrooms, radishes, cucumber, celery, and fennel. Iceberg lettuce, though lacking in the vitamins and minerals so rich in other greens, has an unparalleled crunchiness. It can be cut in a dramatic wedge, generously topped with a creamy dressing, and served with a knife and fork. Although most Mexican restaurants in the United States serve shredded iceberg lettuce alongside their enchiladas, super-nutritious shredded cabbage is more commonly served in Mexico.

Some people have an aversion to the stronger-flavored salad greens, with their bitter or spicy qualities, but the taste for these is readily acquired if they are served at first in small quantities or proportions and tossed with a tasty dressing.

HOW TO WASH SALAD GREENS

1. Clean your sink well and fill with cool water.

2. Immerse the lettuce leaves in the water, swirling them around gently with your hands.

3. Drain the leaves in a colander.

4. Spin dry in a salad spinner (or roll in a large, dry kitchen towel).

5. Chill, if you won't be serving the salad soon.

6. Cut large leaves into bite-size pieces with a sharp knife, or tear them.

   ⁎ Spinach tends to be very dirty; you might need to wash it twice.

   ⁎ Any especially strong-tasting greens may be cut into smaller pieces.

   ⁎ Add herbs when you toss the salad, and don't wash them with the rest of the greens.

DRESSING A GREEN SALAD

Recipes for vinaigrettes and creamy dressings are on pages 295 to 299. Also see the method for Bowl-Dressed Salad on page 272.

A green salad tossed with dressing just before serving is much tastier—and lighter—than one that gets drizzled with dressing on a plate (the usual practice in the Boardinghouse line at Deep Springs). Allow about 2 tablespoons of vinaigrette for a medium green salad. Put the greens and toppings in a large bowl, add the well-stirred dressing, and gently toss until all the dressing is evenly distributed over the greens. If you are serving individual salads, pile the dressed greens high in the center of each plate. If you are serving family style, serve from the bowl, or gently transfer the salad to a large, shallow bowl, piling the salad in the center. Serve tossed salad immediately.

SALAD TOPPINGS

A simple salad of mixed greens is wonderfully satisfying, especially in the context of a multicourse menu containing complexly flavored dishes. But there are endless possibilities for topping your salads: croutons, vegetables, fruit, cheese, nuts, beans, meats. . . . As with any composed dish, however, it's best to keep it simple. One, two, or three harmonious garnishes are usually ample.

CROUTONS (see page 300)

THINLY SLICED VEGETABLES

onion

radish

fennel

mushroom

summer squash

carrot

celery

cucumber

OTHER VEGETABLES

halved cherry tomatoes

chunked large tomatoes

cut corn

lightly cooked broccoli or cauliflower

julienned kohlrabi

BEANS

any type of bean, cooked and cooled in its broth, then well drained

(avoid combining beans with fruit)

NUTS

lightly toasted (see page 301) and then tossed with a few drops of olive oil and a little salt

CHEESE

hard cheeses (such as Parmesan), shaved with a vegetable peeler or grated

medium-hard cheeses (such as Cheddar), cut into small cubes

soft cheeses (such as goat cheese), spread generously on little toasts or crackers

(avoid combining cheese with fish)

FRUIT

thinly sliced or sectioned fresh fruit: apples, stone fruit, pears, Fuyu persimmons, citrus

(fruit is generally good with nuts and cheese, but be careful when combining it with vegetables or meat; certain combinations are better than others. Summer berries are good in salads with a little

continued...

. . . continued

soft, fresh cheese such as goat cheese or ricotta. Avoid combining fruit with beans, egg, or fish.)

———

MEAT/POULTRY

cooked and chilled, trimmed of skin or fat, cut into bite-size chunks or slices

———

FISH

cooked and chilled, gently flaked over the finished salad

(avoid combining fish with cheese or non-citrus fruit)

———

HARD-BOILED EGGS (PAGE 164)

halved or quartered; for the best presentation, arrange over the finished salad, giving each egg a pinch of salt and pepper

(avoid combining egg with fruit)

BOWL-DRESSED SALAD

This is how I usually make salads at home. Once you have made vinaigrettes and other dressings using recipes and have a sense of the right proportions, you may successfully make dressings "to order," right in the salad bowl.

Put your washed greens, vegetables cut just so, croutons, and other toppings into your big, wide salad bowl. Carefully but generously drizzle in olive oil (a cruet allows a thin, even, easily controllable stream of oil), and toss gently. With utmost care, sprinkle in *just enough vinegar* to sparkle the flavor of the greens and oil: toss and taste. Sprinkle salt cautiously, but twist the peppermill more freely. Toss and *taste again*. Toss thoroughly and serve at once.

GREEK SALAD

On sweltering summer days, sometimes there is no better choice for dinner than a big Greek salad. Make a simple vinaigrette with fresh lemon juice, red wine vinegar, extra-virgin olive oil, salt, and pepper. Toss sweet, crunchy lettuces (spinach is very good in Greek salad, and sometimes I throw in a few mint leaves) with a small amount of the vinaigrette. Mound lettuce onto plates, and liberally top each salad with sliced sweet ripe summer tomatoes, sliced cucumber, thinly sliced red onion, coarsely crumbled feta cheese, and whole kalamata olives (or other black Mediterranean olive of your choice— *warn your guests that the olives have pits*). Drizzle a little more dressing over the toppings. Serve with an extra lemon wedge, and hunks of bread to mop up the extra vinaigrette.

Chef's Salad

SERVES 6 ABUNDANTLY

Traveling through Wyoming one rainy spring, I ate in a classic American, pretense-free restaurant and ordered a chef's salad and chicken soup with rice. Though the salad was made with ordinary ingredients—iceberg lettuce and perhaps not the freshest crinkle-cut carrot sticks—it hit the spot, and I quickly introduced my version into the Deep Springs lunch repertoire. The community loved it so much that for a time it became our special-occasion lunch—huge, fresh, colorful trays of chef's salad welcomed Deep Springs trustees, alumni gatherings, visiting scholars, and families for graduation. The particular specified components are classic and familiar to everyone, but you may vary the suggested lettuces, vegetables, toppings, and dressings to suit any circumstance.

In warm weather, serve chef's salad alone with freshly baked bread or biscuits; in cold weather, include a hot vegetable soup as well.

continued . . .

continued...

GREENS

1 small head red-leaf lettuce

1 small head butter lettuce

1 small bunch spinach

1½ cups shredded red cabbage

TOPPINGS

½ small red onion, shaved thin

4 slices turkey breast, cut into bite-size ribbons

4 slices ham, cut into bite-size ribbons

4 slices sharp Cheddar cheese, cut into bite-size ribbons

4 slices provolone cheese, cut into bite-size ribbons

½ English cucumber, sliced into rounds

4 large red radishes, thinly sliced

2 small, tender stalks celery, thinly sliced on the diagonal

½ cup white or brown mushrooms, wiped clean, trimmed, halved, and sliced

1 small carrot, peeled and shaved into strips with a vegetable peeler

1½ cups Croutons (page 300)

24 cherry tomatoes, halved with a serrated knife

4 Hard-Boiled Eggs (page 164), cut into quarters

FOR SERVING

Ranch Dressing (page 297)

Blue Cheese Dressing (page 298)

Lemon Vinaigrette (page 296)

Wash and spin the greens dry, and cut into bite-sized pieces. Chill while preparing the other ingredients. Lay out 6 large plates. In your large salad bowl, toss the greens with a little of the lemon vinaigrette, and mound in the center of the plates. Evenly scatter all the other toppings, in the order listed, on and around the greens, letting things fall as they will, with no fussy arranging. Serve the salads immediately, passing bowls of creamy dressings and lemon vinaigrette, letting your guests drizzle their dressing of choice over their salad.

SPINACH SALAD

Bagged ready-to-use baby spinach, though fresh, is still a processed product; for the most flavorful spinach salad, buy bunches of spinach (preferably with a little dirt still on them). Spinach suffers in hot weather but is otherwise available year-round. Very fresh, well-grown spinach sometimes tastes faintly chocolaty.

Cut off the leafy top half of the bunches, discarding the stems. In plenty of water, carefully wash the leaves and spin dry. (Spinach in my grandmother's day was very dirty—she always washed spinach three times.) If the leaves are large, cut them into bite-size pieces.

Warm spinach salads are as fortifying as they are delectable. The spinach should be at room temperature. Warm the dressing slightly, place it in a large metal bowl, add hot components (such as bacon) and then the spinach, and toss over a very low flame until the spinach just barely begins to soften and wilt. Quickly mound on a plate and serve immediately. Add cheese to warm salads at the end.

Here are three good spinach salads, the first warm, the rest cold:

* Hot bacon, warm soft-boiled egg, Croutons (page 300), slightly warmed mustard vinaigrette (see page 296) or Lemon Vinaigrette (page 296), and chunks of Gruyère cheese

* Lemon juice and zest, freshly grated Parmesan, extra-virgin olive oil, crushed garlic, salt and pepper, and Croutons (page 300)

* Crisp apples, dried Zante currants plumped in red wine, crumbled blue cheese, and sherry vinaigrette (see page 296)

Tracy's Caesar Salad

SERVES 4 TO 6

This is a good, fresh, lemony-garlicky, old-fashioned Caesar salad from my sister Tracy's recipe file.

2 large heads romaine lettuce (about 1½ pounds)

about ½ cup extra-virgin olive oil

2½ cups day-old bread cubes

3 or 4 cloves garlic, finely crushed

¼ teaspoon salt for dressing, plus more as needed

freshly ground black pepper

3 or 4 anchovy fillets, drained and well crushed

¼ cup fresh lemon juice, plus more as needed

1 teaspoon red wine vinegar

1 egg

⅓ cup freshly grated Parmesan cheese, plus at least another ¼ cup for sprinkling

Discard any large, blemished outer leaves of romaine. Wash (see page 270), gently tear by hand into bite-size pieces, and spin dry.

In a wide skillet, heat 1 tablespoon of the oil over a medium-low flame, and add the bread cubes. Sauté, stirring and tossing constantly, until the cubes are golden brown, 7 to 8 minutes. Blend another tablespoon of olive oil with a third of the garlic, and toss this with the croutons. Cook for a minute more. Salt and pepper the croutons, transfer them to a plate, and set aside.

In a small bowl, combine the remaining garlic, anchovy, lemon juice, vinegar, and ¼ teaspoon salt. Put the egg in a small pot of cold water and bring to a boil. Remove from the heat and let the egg sit in the hot water for 3 minutes. Transfer the egg to a bowl of cold water to stop the cooking.

Put the romaine in a very large salad bowl. Drizzle with 3 tablespoons of the oil and toss well. Using a spoon, scoop the warm egg from its shell into the lemon juice mixture, mash well, and add to the salad. Add 2 to 3 tablespoons more oil, croutons, freshly ground pepper to taste, and Parmesan, and toss very well.

Taste a piece of romaine to see if the flavors are balanced; if necessary, add more salt, pepper, Parmesan, or lemon juice. Grate extra Parmesan over each serving. Pile the salad onto large plates and serve immediately.

Creamy Caesar Dressing

This is a more modern method for making Caesar dressing. Put 2 or 3 cloves garlic, 2 anchovy fillets, ¼ cup fresh lemon juice, 1 teaspoon red wine vinegar, ¼ teaspoon salt, and a soft-boiled egg (see page 102) into the jar of a blender. While blending at low speed, slowly drizzle in 6 to 7 tablespoons extra-virgin olive oil, as if you were making mayonnaise (see page 426). Stir in ⅓ cup freshly grated Parmesan and freshly ground black pepper to taste. Taste for salt—the amount required will depend on the saltiness of the anchovies and Parmesan.

Apple and Pear Salad

SERVES 4

There are many apple and pear trees in the Deep Springs orchard; I serve this salad frequently when there is a bumper crop. This autumn recipe uses about 1 pound of fruit but may be multiplied successfully. It is good with Reatha's Macaroni and Cheese (page 153).

1 shallot or ¼ small red onion, sliced lengthwise, paper-thin

juice of ½ lemon

¼ teaspoon salt

1 crisp, flavorful apple

1 ripe, sweet pear

1 small rib celery, split lengthwise and thinly sliced on the diagonal

1 tablespoon extra-virgin olive oil

freshly ground black pepper

In a medium bowl, combine the shallot, lemon juice, and salt, and let sit. Leave the apple and pear unpeeled. Cut 4 big sections of flesh away from each piece of fruit, leaving box-shaped cores. Using a sharp knife and a patient, steady hand,

continued . . .

continued . . .

slice the fruit lengthwise into thin slices.
Toss with the lemon juice mixture.
Add the celery, olive oil, and pepper to
taste, tossing gently to combine. Serve
immediately.

Variations

Vary this salad by replacing the celery
with thinly sliced fennel bulb, or by adding lightly toasted, salted almonds or
walnuts (see page 301) or shredded red
cabbage or radicchio.

Fuji Apple Coleslaw

SERVES 6 TO 8

This is the best coleslaw: the crisp, sweet
Fuji apple provides enough sugar to bring
out the natural sweetness of the cabbage.
Both cabbage and apples are especially
good in the cooler months of the year.
This recipe calls for cutting the apple into
julienne, or fine matchsticks—excellent
knife practice.

½ small red onion, thinly sliced

juice of ½ lemon, plus more as needed

1 teaspoon apple cider vinegar

¼ teaspoon salt, plus more as needed

1 large Fuji apple, peeled, quartered,
and cored

1 small green cabbage, finely shredded

freshly ground black pepper

1 teaspoon celery seed

½ cup mayonnaise, or to taste

In a large bowl, combine the onion with the lemon juice, vinegar, and salt. Using a sharp knife, cut the apple into fine julienne, and toss it with the onion and lemon juice. Add the cabbage, pepper to taste, celery seed, and mayonnaise. Toss well and taste, adding more salt and lemon juice if necessary. Serve right away, or chill for an hour or two, tossing again before serving.

If you'd like to make the coleslaw in advance, lightly salt the shredded cabbage first, let it sit in a bowl for 20 to 30 minutes, and then, taking up the cabbage in handfuls, gently squeeze some of the excess liquid out of the cabbage before tossing it with the other ingredients.

Variations

There are many ways to vary coleslaw. It's great with a vinaigrette dressing instead of mayonnaise. I prefer using plain vegetable oil in such dressings, as strong olive oil tastes out of place on cabbage. My friend Elge makes a brilliant red-cabbage coleslaw sweetened with shredded carrot and flavored with crushed fennel seeds.

ARTICHOKE

Serve a boiled artichoke (see page 213) chilled, with a lemon wedge and a dish of homemade Mayonnaise (page 426) or Aioli (page 427).

ARUGULA SALADS

Once a taste is acquired for arugula, the desire for it becomes quite keen. Arugula salads need only a few additions and enhancements, so delicious is the nutrient-rich arugula itself. Arugula suffers in very hot weather but is otherwise available year-round. Quite often I will dress a handful of arugula with just a squeeze of lemon, a drizzle of olive oil, a pinch of salt, and a half-twist of pepper.

Here are some ideas:

* Sliced fresh oranges, toasted pistachios, Citrus Vinaigrette (page 297)

* Summer tomatoes, Croutons (page 300), shaved Parmesan, mustard vinaigrette (see page 296)

* Shaved pecorino romano cheese, fresh mint leaves, lemon-oil dressing

* Crisp sweet apples, toasted walnuts, Shallot Vinaigrette (page 295)

* Peeled and sliced Fuyu persimmon, toasted pecans, apple cider vinaigrette (see page 296; perfect on the Thanksgiving table!)

* Sliced ripe pears, shaved Parmesan, Lemon Vinaigrette (page 296)

* Sliced fresh plums, dried cherries, toasted almonds, Shallot Vinaigrette (page 295)

ASPARAGUS SALAD

For asparagus to be served cool with a vinaigrette, cook according to the directions on page 216, using just a little olive oil rather than butter. Cool to room temperature, dress, and serve. Very fresh, fat asparagus may be cut into fine matchsticks and served raw. Lemon Vinaigrette (page 296) is a good dressing for either type of salad.

Marinated Beets

SERVES 4 TO 6

Beets are maybe not universally loved, but we beet lovers love beet salads with especial zeal, to which this recipe attests. I almost never prepare beets any other way, and over the years, I've won over many a beet hater—those who insist beets taste like dirt or recall bad childhood experiences with canned or overcooked beets. Well-cooked beets are appealingly sweet and yet, well, earthy tasting. (Of course, they taste particularly good if they are grown in good earth.) To keep the earthiness in check, I always include at least a little orange, and often a fennelly thing as well: shaved fennel (see page 285), or a bit of tarragon or chervil. Somehow, beets taste more broad and substantial than many other vegetables. Grown year-round, they are especially welcome in the fall, winter, and spring.

Serve a pile of these beets atop a green salad, or on a bed of shaved fennel tossed with lemon juice (see page 285). Or topped with a few slices of peeled fresh orange and strewn with crushed toasted walnuts. Or sprinkled with fresh chervil sprigs (or chopped tarragon) and draped with prosciutto. Sliced beets can be layered with rounds of goat cheese, or simmered in beef stew to make Russian Borscht (page 317). Possibilities abound.

If not only red beets but Chioggia (pink striped) beets or golden beets are available, cook, peel, slice, and dress all three varieties separately and keep them in separate bowls until serving time—a salad or composed dish with all three colors (the Chioggia sliced horizontally to show off the bull's-eye pattern) is one of the most spectacularly colorful sights of cool-weather cookery. Although the yellow and Chioggia varieties taste very good, plain old red beets, awash in pigment, are still my favorite.

> 1½ pounds beets (if possible, choose beets of even size)
>
> 2 teaspoons olive oil
>
> ¼ teaspoon salt, plus more as needed
>
> ¼ cup water
>
> ¼ teaspoon finely grated orange zest
>
> 2 tablespoons fresh orange juice
>
> 2 tablespoons red wine vinegar
>
> freshly ground black pepper
>
> 1 tablespoon chopped tarragon, chervil, or wild fennel flowers (optional)

Heat the oven to 400°F. Cut off all but ½ inch of the beet greens and, if fresh and leafy, save for another use (see page 232). Scrub the beets well under running water. Toss them with the olive oil and ¼ teaspoon salt, and arrange them in a baking dish in which they will fit comfortably in

continued...

. . . continued

one layer. Pour ¼ cup water into the dish and cover with aluminum foil (shiny side down), tightly—otherwise the water will evaporate and the beets will burn. Bake for 40 minutes (for golf ball–sized beets), or until the biggest beet offers no resistance when pierced to the center with a small knife. In my experience, large beets might take as long as 1½ hours.

Remove the foil very carefully—the steam can burn your hand. Let the beets cool in the dish for about 20 minutes, then cut off the tops and tails and slip off the skins. Wipe any remaining bits of skin off with your hand—*do not rinse the beets in running water.* Sometimes the skin is stubborn and must be cut off with a paring knife. Slice the beets lengthwise into wedges and place in a medium bowl. Add the orange zest and juice, red wine vinegar, additional salt, and pepper to taste. Toss well, and taste for balanced sweet, acidic, and salt flavors. Toss the beets again in their dressing just before serving.

Carrot-Raisin Salad

SERVES 6 TO 8

This salad updates the old church-potluck classic with citrus and black pepper.

⅓ cup golden raisins or Zante currants

4 cups grated carrots

grated zest and juice of ½ orange

grated zest and juice of ½ lemon

1 teaspoon red wine vinegar

⅔ cup mayonnaise, or to taste, or a blend of yogurt and mayonnaise

¼ teaspoon salt

freshly ground black pepper

Pour boiling water over the raisins in a small bowl. Let plump for about 15 minutes, then drain and cool.

Take handfuls of the grated carrots and gently squeeze out some excess juice (I always drink this). In a medium bowl, combine the drained raisins and carrots with the orange zest and juice, lemon zest and juice, vinegar, mayonnaise, salt, and pepper to taste. Taste: there should be just enough salt and lemon juice to temper the inherent sweetness of the other ingredients. Serve, or chill if serving later.

Celery Root Salad

SERVES 2 TO 3

If you want a light, lunchtime accompaniment for steak in the cold months, try my friend Chef Mona's simple herbed celery root salad. For more information on celery root, see page 248.

 1 medium celery root, scrubbed and peeled

 juice of ½ lemon

 ½ teaspoon canola oil or other vegetable oil

 salt and freshly ground black pepper

 2 to 3 tablespoons chopped fresh dill

 2 to 3 tablespoons chopped fresh parsley

Cut the celery root into fine julienne. Toss in a medium bowl with the lemon juice, canola oil, a pinch of salt, pepper to taste, and the dill and parsley. Serve alongside your favorite steak.

Corn Salad

SERVES 2 TO 4

Cooking corn "locks in" the sweetness, so I prefer to cook it first for salad, rather than just using it raw. I love to eat this alongside a simple piece of Baked Salmon (page 372).

 3 ears cooked corn on the cob (see page 227), chilled

 about 2 tablespoons Lemon Vinaigrette (page 296, substituting lime for the lemon, if you like)

 1 small green jalapeño, seeded and minced

 1 small red jalapeño, outer dark red part only, minced

 ¼ teaspoon salt

 few twists freshly ground black pepper

Cut the corn kernels from the cobs with a knife. Scrape the bare cobs with the back of the knife to extract all the germ and milk. In a medium bowl, toss the corn with the vinaigrette, green and red jalapeño, salt, and pepper. Taste for salt, piquancy, and acidity.

CHAPTER 8: Salads and Dressings — 283

Summer Cucumber Salad

SERVES 2 TO 3

This refreshing, simple salad contains no oil. It's a great opportunity to use the variety of cucumbers that grows each year in the Deep Springs garden (or that you find at your summer farmer's market): lemon cucumbers, Persian cucumbers, English cucumbers, Armenian cucumbers, and so on. Peel only if the skin is tough or bitter; scoop out the seeds only if they are big.

White balsamic vinegar has a singular sweetness that is especially well suited to cucumbers. If you don't have any, just mix a few drops of honey into red wine vinegar.

These cucumbers are excellent company to a spoonful of Marinated Beets, page 281.

1 small clove garlic, finely crushed to a purée

2 teaspoons white balsamic vinegar (or 1¾ teaspoons red wine vinegar mixed with ¼ teaspoon honey)

heaping ¼ teaspoon salt

2 cups bite-size cucumber chunks (from an assortment of cucumbers)

6 basil leaves, coarsely chopped

Mix the garlic, vinegar, and salt together in a medium bowl. Toss in the cucumbers and basil. Serve immediately.

SHAVED FENNEL

Raw shaved fennel, seasoned only with a little lemon juice, is an excellent base for many salads, or served by itself with pork, chicken, or fish. Fennel is best in cool weather; hot weather dulls its flavor and appeal. Try it with a sandwich, instead of chips; it may be successfully eaten with your fingers. Fennel is best freshly cut but will hold in an airtight container or bag, refrigerated, for a few hours. It pairs well with beets, pears, nuts, citrus, and shellfish. For more information on fennel, see page 248.

Fennel bulbs that are flatter tend to have a more pronounced fennel flavor than ones that are more bulbous. Trim the outer layer and dark green stalks from a large bulb of fennel. Reserve a small bunch of fronds from the top, preferably the feathery inner fronds. Using a mandoline slicer, shave the fennel bulb across the grain in paper-thin slices. If you don't have a mandoline, use a knife to first cut the fennel bulb in half lengthwise, then slice crosswise on the diagonal as thinly as possible, being patient but decisive. Chop the reserved fronds coarsely. Toss the fennel and fronds with a squeeze (about ½ teaspoon per fennel bulb) of lemon juice.

Shaved Fennel with Pears and Parmesan

Gently toss a big handful of shaved fennel with 2 sliced sweet, ripe pears (peeled or not), a squeeze of lemon juice, ample shavings of Parmesan, a pinch of salt, a twist of pepper, and a good drizzle of extra-virgin olive oil. Slices of prosciutto are great with this salad.

Fennel, Blood Orange, and Toasted Almond Salad

SERVES 3 TO 4

Blood oranges are a great winter treat. They don't come into their season until January, and they are usually finished by March. They look and taste as if the cells of an ordinary small, tart orange had been injected with the juice of fresh raspberries. This salad is one of the blood orange's nicest manifestations. The unusual marriage of flavors will continue to haunt you long after you have licked the plate clean.

½ cup whole almonds, lightly toasted (see page 301; walnuts are also good)

3 tablespoons extra-virgin olive oil

1 fennel bulb

½ lemon

2 to 3 blood oranges

salt and freshly ground black pepper

When the toasted almonds are cool, chop them haphazardly (with many coarse pieces, but also plenty of fine pieces), then mix them well with the olive oil in a small bowl. Shave the fennel thinly (as described in the previous recipe) and toss with a squeeze of lemon juice in a medium bowl.

Wash the blood oranges in cool water, towel dry, then finely grate the outer colored zest of one of the oranges onto a plate. Using a small, sharp, serrated knife, peel the oranges, cutting all the white pith away from the flesh. Cut the oranges lengthwise in half, then crosswise into thin half-moons, removing any seeds. Collect all the juice as you cut the oranges, mix the juice with the zest on the plate, and then lay the orange slices in the zesty juice.

Gently but thoroughly toss together the shaved fennel, an extra squeeze of lemon, the oranges with all their juice and zest, and the almond-oil mixture, with a couple of good pinches of salt and a twist of pepper. For best results, mound the salad on individual serving plates (or serve family style, heaped on a big platter) and serve immediately.

Gazpacho

SERVES 4

Here is a magnificent version of the famous Andalusian summertime chilled soup. For best results, your tomatoes should be dead-ripe and bursting with flavorful juice.

SOUP BASE

3 pounds sweet, red, ripe tomatoes

1¾ teaspoons salt, or more as needed

freshly ground black pepper

4 teaspoons red wine vinegar, or more as needed

1 teaspoon balsamic vinegar

1 small clove garlic, finely crushed

5 tablespoons extra-virgin olive oil, or more as needed

GARNISHES

½ cup additional chopped tomato

1 tablespoon minced red onion

2 tablespoons chopped cucumber

1 tablespoon minced red or yellow bell pepper

2 to 3 teaspoons minced jalapeño or other hot pepper

½ cup Croutons (page 300), lightly crushed

1 to 2 tablespoons chopped parsley

To make the soup base, cut the tomatoes into chunks, saving all the juice from the cutting area. Using your clean hands, squeeze the tomatoes over a screen sieve set over a glass bowl. Gently rub through as much juice and pulp as possible without excessively frothing the tomatoes. Once all the tomatoes are juiced, carefully skim the froth off the top (I save the froth and the skins for vegetable stock). You should have about 4 cups of juice. Season the juice with 1¾ teaspoons salt, pepper to taste, the red wine vinegar, balsamic vinegar, and garlic. Gently whisk in about 5 tablespoons of extra-virgin olive oil. Taste for balanced acidity, salt, and oil, adjusting as necessary.

Keeping in mind the flavor of the soup base, stir in judicious, restrained amounts of the garnishing ingredients: more chopped tomato, minced red onion, chopped cucumber, minced sweet bell pepper, minced hot pepper, lightly crushed croutons, and chopped parsley. Chill well, taste again for salt, and serve the same day in small bowls.

Variations

Try a *gazpacho californiano*, adding a little fresh, cooked corn and a little cubed avocado, and using cilantro instead of parsley.

continued . . .

. . . continued

If you have yellow and green-ripe tomatoes in addition to red, you can serve a spectacular two-tone presentation. Make two gazpachos: one yellow/green, the other red. Using 2 ladles and a mustering of confidence, simultaneously fill each bowl with both colors of soup. The gazpachos will remain separate in the bowl. For the most striking appearance, use wide, white bowls.

Jícama

SERVES 3 TO 4

Jícama is a big, round, buff-colored tuber, sold year-round in most supermarkets (usually next to the hot chiles) or Latin American markets. It is easy to grow in warm climates. In Asian markets, it is often called "chop suey yam." It has a mild sweetness and a satisfying, crunchy texture. Kids love jícama once they try it. In Mexico, jícama is often served dressed with fresh lime juice, salt, and powdered chile, but I am usually so taken with just the lime and salt that I never get to the chile. As part of a festive table of Mexican dishes, you may mimic the colors of the Mexican flag with red radishes, green lime wedges, and lovely snow-white jícama.

1 small jícama, about 12 ounces

1 juicy lime

about ¼ teaspoon salt

Peel the jícama with a knife—the outer ⅛ inch of skin is tough. Cut out any blemishes. Slice the jícama in ¼-inch-thick slices, then cut the slices to make large matchsticks. Squeeze the lime juice into a medium bowl, add the jícama, and toss with enough salt to balance the sweetness of the jícama and the acidity of the lime; taste small pieces until you get it right.

Kohlrabi-Apple Slaw

SERVES 3 TO 4

A crunchy, elegant slaw, made from an almost-forgotten winter vegetable. Like other members of the cabbage family, kohlrabi tastes sweetest when grown in cool weather. Resist the temptation to use olive oil; it tastes "off" in this salad.

½ large Fuji apple, cut into julienne (matchsticks)

1 large kohlrabi (about 12 ounces), peeled and cut into julienne (matchsticks)

¼ cup finely diced shallot or red onion

juice of ½ lemon

½ teaspoon apple cider vinegar

¼ teaspoon salt

¼ teaspoon celery seed

1 tablespoon canola oil or other vegetable oil

If you are slow at cutting the apple, douse it with a bit of the lemon juice so it doesn't brown. Combine the apple, kohlrabi, shallot, lemon juice, vinegar, salt, celery seed, and oil in a medium bowl. Serve chilled. It will still be good and crisp the next day.

Orange and Date Salad

SERVES 4 TO 6

This salad, based on a recipe from a hundred-year-old American fruit cookbook, is timelessly delicious in the cooler months, served with pork, poultry, or lamb.

8 ounces Medjool dates

2 large navel oranges

⅓ cup Shallot Vinaigrette (page 295), made without the optional garlic

lettuce leaves for serving

Halve the dates, remove the pits, and cut each half lengthwise in two. Wash and dry the oranges, and finely grate the colored outer zest of one of the oranges into the vinaigrette. Using a small, sharp, serrated knife, peel the oranges, removing all the bitter white pith. With the knife, cut each orange section from the membrane. Gently toss the dates, orange sections, and vinaigrette together in a medium bowl. Serve immediately (before the orange throws off too much of its juice), atop lettuce leaves on individual plates or piled in the center of a platter lined with lettuce leaves.

Potato Salad

SERVES 8 TO 10

When freshly made with ample mayonnaise, this is your potato salad dream come true. I first started making it while cooking at a neighborhood deli in Hawaii (a job I loved, after years of more formal restaurant work). One morning, when I hadn't been at the job long, I found myself with little to work with besides a large bunch of dill, a red cabbage, some cucumbers, and a box of russet potatoes. Knowing that the islanders don't fool around with their potato salad—they like lots of hard-boiled eggs and mayonnaise—I decided we couldn't go wrong with a big bowl of it in the deli case, laced with bright-tasting vegetables and tinted an appealing golden yellow with a bit of American mustard. Lo and behold, it was an instant favorite. Fresh cucumber and fresh dill replace the usual pickle, and the cabbage adds crunch and more fresh flavor. Though virtually all potato salad recipes call for waxy-type potatoes instead of russets, here is a case where the texture and starchiness of russets are better suited.

6 eggs

6 large russet potatoes, peeled and cut into ¾-inch chunks

1 tablespoon salt, plus more as needed

1 small red onion, finely diced

2 tablespoons red wine vinegar, or more as needed

¾ cup finely diced celery

1 cup diced seedless cucumber

½ cup chopped green cabbage

½ cup chopped red cabbage

½ cup coarsely chopped fresh dill

¼ cup yellow mustard or other mustard

about 1 cup mayonnaise, or more as needed

½ teaspoon freshly ground black pepper, or more as needed

Hard-boil the eggs according to the directions on page 164. Peel and chop them coarsely. (To chop eggs easily, I press them through the grid of a cooling rack or other wire grid.)

Put the potatoes in a pot and cover them with cold water. Add the 1 tablespoon salt and bring to a boil. Reduce the heat to medium-high and skim off any scum that rises to the surface. (When I must use potatoes that have begun to sprout, I add a bay leaf to the cooking water—it does away with the alkaloidal flavor sprouted potatoes sometimes have.) After 7 or 8 minutes, check the potatoes: when done, the corners and edges will have rounded a little, and a cube will yield easily without melting to a mush when gently crushed with a fork. Drain the potatoes well in a colander for about 5 minutes, then scatter on a tray to cool completely. This method results in potatoes that are dry and ready to absorb moisture and flavor from the dressing. In a small bowl, macerate the diced red onion in the red wine vinegar with a pinch of salt while you prepare the other vegetables.

In a large bowl, mix together the cooled potatoes, eggs, onion-vinegar mixture, celery, cucumber, green and red cabbage, dill, mustard, mayonnaise, and pepper, tasting to make sure the salt, pepper, and vinegar are balanced. Add more mayonnaise if you would like a creamier salad.

This potato salad is best served immediately, when the potatoes still have their freshly cooked texture and the mixture is just slightly cooler than room temperature. If made of sound ingredients (mayonnaise from a newly opened jar, for instance), it will still be perfectly fit to eat after an hour of sitting, covered, at room temperature. Otherwise, it's best to chill it immediately. If you plan on having leftover potato salad, refrigerate the amount you want left over as soon as you make it.

RADISHES

When the weather starts to cool, watch the radishes in your market: when they appear nice and fresh, with few cracks, their greens vibrant, buy a bunch, pull off the greens, pinch off the little roots, wash well, and chill in a shallow bowl with a little water added. Drain off the water and serve in their bowl with a good loaf of bread (a French baguette is ideal), sweet butter, and salt. To eat, dip a radish lightly in the salt and eat bites of radish between bites of generously buttered bread.

Summer Squash Carpaccio

SERVES 2 TO 3

This quick, simple, beautiful salad is best made with very fresh, young (but not "baby") summer squash, in a variety of colors and shapes, such as dark green zucchini, yellow crookneck, and pale green pattypan. See page 330 for a classic beef carpaccio recipe.

2 or 3 very fresh young summer squash

salt and freshly ground black pepper

1 piece of Parmesan or Pecorino Romano cheese (for shaving over the carpaccio)

extra-virgin olive oil

¼ cup chopped, lightly toasted walnuts (optional)

several leaves of fresh mint or basil

Wipe the squash clean with a damp towel, and shave it paper-thin with a mandoline slicer. Arrange the slices, overlapping slightly, on large plates. Sprinkle evenly with salt and pepper. With a vegetable peeler, shave some strips of Parmesan over the squash. Drizzle everything with extra-virgin olive oil. If you like, scatter a handful of chopped, lightly toasted walnuts (see page 301; for excellent flavor, rub the excess skin off the walnuts, and toss them in a drop or two of olive oil and a sprinkling of salt). Arrange the mint leaves into a stack and cut into fine ribbons (*chiffonade*) with a sharp knife. Strew over the carpaccio and serve immediately.

TOMATOES WITH SALT

One of my Deep Springs classmates used to quote his Tennessee grandfather: "Ain't but two things in this world money can't buy—true, true love and homegrown tomatoes." In late summer, the Deep Springs community revels in the garden's inevitably abundant tomato crop. Some students, in fact, taste their first homegrown tomato at Deep Springs. During tomato season, rarely do I serve a meal that does not include a slice or two of tomato with a sprinkling of sea salt. That includes breakfast—tomatoes are very good with eggs, bacon, and toast.

Tomatoes are in season, depending on the climate of your area, from roughly mid-July through October. Ripe summer tomatoes are extraordinarily good with nothing more than salt. Balanced sweet and acid, juicy, and succulent—few other fruits or vegetables possess such dynamics within their skin. There are dozens of varieties, of all shapes, sizes, and colors. Each has its own characteristics and balance. Though an assortment is beautiful to behold, the cultivation, not the variety, determines the goodness of the tomato.

The plant itself needs ample water to grow, but as it fruits, less water is needed. Once the plant sets fruit, some growers allow the roots to find water deep in the soil, letting the soil's surface remain dry.

Such "dry-farmed" tomatoes are excellent, with deeply concentrated flavors and pigments.

As assorted, colorful "heirloom" tomatoes have grown in popularity (and price), commercial growers have profited from such practices as overwatering the tomatoes to increase weight, shipping them long distances, cold-storing them for long periods, and even growing them in hothouses for year-round availability—all deleterious to quality. *The most delicious tomatoes are grown in warm soil, with minimal water, in summer, close by.*

Finally, keep tomatoes at room temperature whenever possible. They should be refrigerated only when you suspect they might go bad before you can use them.

Slice ripe summer tomatoes and arrange them, slightly overlapping, on a plate. Sprinkle evenly with salt. *Tomatoes benefit from rather a lot of salt.* Pepper lightly, if you like. After salt, if you want to enrich this simplest of salads, drizzle with a little extra-virgin olive oil. If you wish, sprinkle with a thoughtfully chosen herb—while coarsely chopped basil is, like olive oil, an old, familiar friend of the tomato, other herbs, such as dill, mint, marjoram, and thyme, are equally persuasive. Serve tomatoes very soon after you salt them; they will throw off liquid—and flavor—as they stand.

continued . . .

. . . continued

Summer Tomato Sandwich

Spread mayonnaise generously on a slice of soft bread. Place thick, juicy slices of summer tomato over the mayonnaise, sprinkling well with salt and a little pepper if you like. Eat over the sink.

Thyme Salt

You may enhance tomatoes—or many other foods—with this lovely green, aromatic salt. Take 4 or 5 fresh sprigs of thyme (marjoram is also good) and tear off the tiny leaf clusters, discarding the tough stems. Pound the thyme in a mortar and pestle with about 3 tablespoons of salt (ideally, coarse sea salt) until the herb is pulverized and the salt is green. If the salt seems to be dissolving in the juice, add a tablespoon more salt to keep it granulated. If there are visible pieces of herb left in the salt, you may strain them out by rubbing the salt through a screen sieve.

Watercress Salad

SERVES 2 TO 3

The bracing, peppery savor of watercress perfectly balances roast beef, steak, and many other rich meat dishes. After something rich and gratifying, such as cheese soufflé, a simple fluff of watercress tossed with just olive oil, lemon juice, salt, and a tiny bit of pepper may be all that is wanted. Watercress is strictly a cool-weather crop; summer temperatures cause it to be overly hot.

Separate a bunch of watercress into large, bite-size sprigs, discarding only the fattest stems. Wash and dry (see page 270). Toss with a drizzle of olive oil, a squeeze of lemon juice, a pinch of salt, and just a little black pepper (watercress is already peppery). Serve immediately, in fluffy mounds on individual plates or mounded high in the middle of a platter.

Shallot Vinaigrette

MAKES ABOUT 1½ CUPS

First, pronunciation: "vinaigrette" has only three syllables, not four; it is pronounced "vin-ay-GRET," not "vin-e-gar-ette." But however you say it, it's a terrifically tasty and versatile salad dressing.

I make this and the lemon vinaigrette that follows constantly at Deep Springs. Both recipes contain a small amount of Dijon mustard. If the oil is added slowly while whisking, the mustard emulsifies the dressing. Even after it has sat for awhile and separated, the dressing will reemulsify when shaken if it was correctly made the first time.

The ratio of oil to vinegar varies. Use the lesser amount of olive oil at first, then taste the vinaigrette by dipping the tip of a lettuce leaf into it. Depending on the flavor of your salad greens and your own taste, you may want a sharper vinaigrette (less oil) or a smoother one (more oil).

1 small shallot, finely minced (or 2 to 3 tablespoons finely diced red onion)

1 small clove garlic, crushed to a purée (optional)

¼ cup red wine vinegar

2 tablespoons balsamic vinegar

¾ teaspoon salt

¼ teaspoon freshly ground black pepper

1 tablespoon Dijon mustard or other type of mustard

½ teaspoon chopped fresh thyme, or ¼ teaspoon dried thyme

¼ cup canola oil or other vegetable oil

½ to ¾ cup extra-virgin olive oil

In a deep bowl, mix the shallot, garlic (if using), red wine and balsamic vinegars, salt, pepper, mustard, and thyme with a whisk or a fork. Let stand for about 15 minutes.

Slowly whisk in the oils, beginning with the canola oil. The technique is similar to that for making a mayonnaise (see page 426): drizzle the canola oil into the bowl in a thin stream while whisking constantly; the mixture should thicken slightly. After adding the canola oil, whisk in the olive oil in a thin stream. Taste for balanced salt and vinegar—it should not be so vinegary that it burns the back of your throat. Add more oil if necessary. *The correct amount of oil can never be specified exactly;* it depends on the flavor of your salad greens, the acidity level of the vinegar, the season, the temperature . . . and your mood. Sometimes you will want a very tart vinaigrette, other times a more oily one. Vinaigrette is best used the day it's made but will taste good for a few days if kept refrigerated (let it come to room temperature if the oil congeals).

continued . . .

. . . continued

Other Vinaigrettes

For a good *tart balsamic vinaigrette*, reverse the amounts of balsamic and red wine vinegar (¼ cup balsamic vinegar, 2 tablespoons red wine vinegar). For a *sweet balsamic vinaigrette*, use all balsamic vinegar. Use a tablespoon more of mustard, and a tablespoon less of vinegar for a *mustard vinaigrette*. Sherry vinegar, apple cider vinegar, and champagne vinegar will yield, respectively, *sherry vinaigrette, apple cider vinaigrette,* and *champagne vinaigrette.*

Lemon Vinaigrette

MAKES ABOUT 1¼ CUPS

This vinaigrette is tasty and bright, with a good lemon color, not from the lemon but from the olive oil. It is excellent tossed with spinach salad with hard-boiled egg, with arugula and other "assertive" greens, or with sweet lettuces (such as romaine) and shaved Parmesan. Good on many cooked vegetables, it is ideal with asparagus or artichokes.

1 small clove garlic, crushed to a purée

finely grated zest of 1 lemon

juice of 2 lemons (about ⅓ cup)

2 tablespoons champagne vinegar, red wine vinegar, or cider vinegar

¾ teaspoon salt

¼ teaspoon white pepper

1 tablespoon Dijon mustard

¼ cup canola oil or other vegetable oil

½ cup extra-virgin olive oil

In a deep bowl, combine the garlic, lemon zest, lemon juice, vinegar, salt, white pepper, and mustard. Slowly whisk in the oils, beginning with the canola oil. The technique is similar to that for making a mayonnaise (see page 426): drizzle the canola oil into the bowl in a thin stream while whisking constantly; the mixture should thicken slightly. After adding the canola oil, whisk in the olive oil in a thin stream. Taste for balanced flavors—if the vinaigrette is too tart, add a little more oil.

Citrus Vinaigrette

Use half lemon juice and half lime juice, and include lime zest and some orange zest in the dressing.

Ranch Dressing

MAKES ABOUT 1 CUP; SERVES 4 TO 5

Delectable when freshly made, this dressing is also still good the next day. For greater speed and convenience, you may omit any or all of the herbs and call it simply "buttermilk dressing." It will still taste good and ranchy.

½ clove garlic

⅛ teaspoon salt, or more as needed

¾ cup mayonnaise

2 tablespoons fresh lime juice, or more as needed

⅓ cup buttermilk

1 heaping tablespoon finely chopped cilantro

1 heaping tablespoon finely chopped parsley

1 heaping tablespoon finely chopped chives

¼ teaspoon black pepper, or more as needed

In a deep bowl, crush the garlic well with ⅛ teaspoon salt. Mix in the mayonnaise, then whisk in the lime juice, buttermilk, herbs, and pepper until smooth. Or shake the ingredients together in a jar. Taste, and adjust the salt, pepper, and lime juice as necessary.

Ranch Dip

Substitute sour cream for the buttermilk.

Blue Cheese Dressing

MAKES ABOUT 3 CUPS; SERVES 10 TO 12

For a treat, heavily drizzle this dressing over a standing-up wedge of iceberg lettuce on a plate, and serve with a knife and fork. For an even more indulgent treat, scatter warm, crispy bite-size chunks of bacon over the top. You could pack up to 8 ounces of blue cheese into this, but at that point you would have a blue cheese dip, not a dressing.

1½ cups mayonnaise

1 cup buttermilk

1 cup crumbled blue cheese (about 6 ounces)

1½ tablespoons apple cider vinegar, or more as needed

¼ teaspoon dry mustard

¼ teaspoon white pepper

In a medium bowl, whisk together, one by one, the mayonnaise, buttermilk, blue cheese, vinegar, dry mustard, and white pepper, or shake together in a jar. Taste for salt and acidity, adding salt and more cider vinegar if needed.

Toasted Cumin–Mint-Yogurt Dressing

MAKES 2 CUPS; SERVES ABOUT 8

Two strong, distinctive flavors—cumin and mint—marry beautifully in this creamy dressing, complementing and tempering one another.

1 tablespoon ground cumin

1 cup yogurt

¾ cup mayonnaise

½ cup buttermilk

¼ cup chopped fresh mint

¼ teaspoon black pepper, or more as needed

½ teaspoon salt

Toast the cumin in a small skillet over a medium-high flame until it releases a nutty fragrance; do not let it scorch. In a medium bowl, combine the cumin, yogurt, mayonnaise, buttermilk, mint, pepper, and salt with a whisk until smooth, or shake together in a jar. Taste and adjust the seasoning as necessary.

Improvised Creamy Dressings

Using the previous three recipes as a rough guide, you may easily improvise a quick creamy dressing. Start by blending mayonnaise with either yogurt or buttermilk—you decide the proportions. Add a bit of vinegar or lemon or lime juice for added tartness, salt for balance, and, always, freshly ground black pepper. Throw in a minced shallot for a creamy shallot dressing; crushed garlic, Parmesan, and olive oil for a Caesar-like dressing; or half a ripe avocado and finely chopped herbs for a Green Goddess–like dressing. Taste and adjust the seasoning as necessary.

Dijon-Yogurt Dressing

MAKES ABOUT 1½ CUPS; SERVES 5 TO 6

A fresh and flavorful creamy salad dressing that happens—imagine!—to contain little or no fat.

1 cup plain yogurt, whole milk or nonfat

3 tablespoons Dijon mustard

1 teaspoon red wine vinegar

¼ teaspoon salt, or more as needed

¼ teaspoon freshly ground black pepper, or more as needed

¼ cup chopped fresh dill
(from 2 to 3 large sprigs)

Mix the yogurt, mustard, vinegar, salt, pepper, and dill in a small bowl—or shake in a jar—and let sit for 30 minutes before serving. Taste for balanced salt and acidity.

CROUTONS

I am inordinately fond of croutons. If I want to add a single element to a simple mixed green salad, I choose croutons. It was a great day when I discovered that one may have a salad of mostly croutons, tossed with the same volume of ripe, juicy tomatoes; a sharp, garlicky vinaigrette; and a handful of greens or herbs.

Different kinds of bread result in different kinds of croutons; most sliced sandwich bread is decidedly sweet and will taste odd in salads. Baguettes or other sturdy-textured, artisan-style breads make good croutons, as do any of the savory breads in this book (see the chapter beginning on page 129).

Heat the oven to 325°F. Cut the crust from a loaf of day-old bread. Tear the loaf into bite-size pieces (or cut into evenly sized cubes). Toss the pieces in plenty of olive oil—about ½ cup for a large loaf of bread—and a little salt. Bake on a rimmed baking sheet, tossing and redistributing every 7 to 8 minutes (even after many years of cooking professionally, I always set a timer for croutons). Be patient and vigilant. Bake just until pale gold and crispy throughout. The moment you take them from the oven, gently toss them in a tablespoon or two more olive oil (this time, use your best extra-virgin) and salt (if necessary) and pepper to taste. When you make tossed salads, toss the croutons with everything else, so the croutons will absorb some of the dressing.

TOASTED NUTS

You may toast nuts at 300°F, 325°F, or 350°F, or even a low 250°F. The lower the temperature, the longer it takes, but the less chance there is of burning them. Scatter raw, shelled nuts on a sheet pan, and put in the oven. At 350°F, check them every 5 minutes or so, tossing and redistributing the nuts on the sheet. At 250°F, check every 10 minutes. As with croutons (see facing page), I always set a timer when toasting nuts. I think all nuts are best toasted until they are a very pale brown; darker brown nuts take on a toasted-grain flavor, and the characteristic fragrance of their variety is lost. Once nuts begin to brown, they quickly burn.

Almonds, loved by everyone when freshly toasted, take about 10 minutes in a 350°F oven and 45 to 50 minutes in a 250°F oven. **Hazelnuts** (also called *filberts*) take about as long as almonds. **Walnuts** take less time, depending on the size of the pieces. Walnuts and hazelnuts have papery, shiny, bitter skin that may be partly rubbed off after they are toasted—take up handfuls and rub lightly, letting the bitter skins fall out. **Pecans** must be watched carefully, as their skins are dark to begin with.

While the nuts are still warm, toss them with a few drops of olive oil—just enough to coat—and a few pinches of fine salt. To make fine salt, grind regular salt to a powder in a mortar, or in a cup with the handle of a wooden spoon. In addition to the salt, a pinch of cayenne is often good, as is black pepper.

CHAPTER 9

Beef, Pork, and Lamb

There is no question: to an omnivorous food lover, red meat is a primary gustatory pleasure. Whether we eat meat or not, our ancestors certainly did. Although eating too much meat causes health problems, meat consumption is nonetheless an inherent component of our evolutionary history.

Living and working at Deep Springs, we are very close to many sources of our food: we grow fruits and vegetables in the garden, orchard, and fields; we obtain eggs from the chickens and milk from the dairy cows; the ranchers maintain small "slaughter herds" of cattle and hogs, and sometimes lambs, goats, and fowl. Deep Springs students, with supervision from the ranch staff, take responsibility for the tough work of slaughtering cattle and other animals. Some Deep Springs community members even bring their young children to slaughters, so the kids will see the source of the meat they enjoy so much. To feed the Deep Springs community of some fifty people, we use about ten head of cattle each year. We always strive to grow more of our own vegetables, but, being a cattle ranch, we have all the good range beef we want. We attempt never to forget how fortunate we are.

Not long ago, the Deep Springs ranch staff maintained an edict that meat had to be served at all three meals each day. But now the community occasionally enjoys a meal with no meat. Nutritional science affirms this middle ground; it is not nutritionally necessary to eat meat every day, or to avoid it entirely. As a chef, I take satisfaction in very gently discouraging extreme eating of any kind. I consider it a small triumph when a self-proclaimed vegetarian enjoys a morsel of meat, or when a die-hard meat-and-potatoes man enjoys a meatless meal.

Marinated Steak

SERVES 6

Really great steak cuts, such as rib-eye or T-bone, to my mind need only salt and pepper, even if I'm just pan-frying them. Tougher, cheaper steaks benefit from a tart marinade. Once, in a Turkish cookbook, I found a recipe for lamb chops marinated in freshly squeezed onion juice and thyme sprigs, a discovery that led to much experimentation (see Carne Asada, page 311). The sharpness of onion juice gives meat a wonderful tenderness and succulence. This recipe gives instructions for pan-frying, but you can grill the steaks over a fire, too.

> 2 large yellow onions
>
> 6 small sirloin steaks (about 6 ounces each), about 1 inch thick
>
> 10 sprigs fresh thyme
>
> salt and black pepper
>
> 2 to 4 teaspoons olive oil
>
> about 6 tablespoons dry red wine or water

Peel the onions, trim off any brown or dry spots, and rinse clean. Grate the onions, using the medium or large holes of a box grater (burn a candle close by to lessen fumes!), or chop them coarsely and then pulverize to a smooth slush in a food processor. Take a large, clean, flour-sack-type cotton kitchen towel (or 2 or 3 layers of cheesecloth) and rinse it well in warm water. Wring the towel out well, then drape it over a large bowl. Dump the onion slush into the towel. Take up the corners of the towel and squeeze out as much liquid from the onion into the bowl as possible. Discard the onion solids left in the towel (or toss them into simmering stock).

Add the steaks and thyme sprigs to the bowl and toss everything together well. Let the steaks marinate at room temperature for about an hour, turning and tossing them a few times.

Heat a wide, heavy skillet over a medium-high flame. Remove the steaks from the onion juice and pick off any bits of thyme. Pat the steaks dry with paper towels. Salt and pepper the steaks well on both sides. Add 1 to 2 teaspoons olive oil to the skillet—just enough to coat the bottom. The moment the oil begins to smoke, lay in 3 of the steaks. Let them sizzle, undisturbed, for about 3 minutes, then flip and cook on the other side for another 3 minutes, or until juices collect on the top side. The steaks should be medium-rare; cook for another 30 seconds for medium. Remove the steaks to a clean, warmed platter, then pour off any excess fat in the skillet. Splash in about 3 tablespoons of wine or water and scrape up the browned bits in the bottom of the skillet. Let the liquid reduce for a few seconds, then pour this scant sauce over the cooked steaks. Wipe out the skillet with a damp paper towel and heat it up again with fresh olive oil; repeat with the remaining 3 steaks.

Steak Fried in Beef Tallow

SERVES 1 TO 2

If you love steak, render a little bit of beef tallow (see the Deep Springs Soap recipe on page 572) and try this method, a favorite of longtime Deep Springs cattleman Geoff Pope. Fat provides a perfectly even and very hot medium in which to cook steak. Any tender cut of steak (T-bone or rib-eye) may be used, but New York steak is ideal. The steak's fat cap emerges ethereally crackly-crisp and golden. Be assured that cooking it this way doesn't mean that more fat gets into the steak than was already there.

Select a 1-inch-thick steak with a little fat on the edges. Pat dry with paper towels. Season well with salt and pepper, pressing the seasoning into the meat. Take care to season the fat on the steak also. Heat about ½ inch of beef tallow in a heavy skillet over a medium-high flame until it is very hot—about 375°F. The fat should sizzle and bubble fiercely when you dip the tip of the steak in it. Using tongs, lay the steak carefully into the fat. For a medium-rare steak, let it cook for about 3 minutes on the first side, then flip carefully and cook on the other side for another 3 minutes, or until juices begin to collect on the top side of the steak. Drain the steak on several layers of paper towels for about 5 seconds on each side. Transfer the steak to a warmed plate or platter and let it rest for 1 minute. Serve.

If you'd like to serve the steak with potatoes, have ready cubes of peeled russet potato that have been boiled in salted water until tender. While the steak is resting, fry these in the hot fat until they are golden brown, about 1 minute. Drain on paper towels, and give them a final sprinkle of salt, some freshly ground pepper, and a tiny bit of finely chopped parsley. Serve alongside the steak.

Flank Steak

SERVES 3 TO 4

Flank steak is not the most tender or expensive cut, but it is excellent if cooked carefully, with a far-reaching, true beef flavor. It must be thinly sliced before serving.

1 small flank steak (about 1¼ pounds), about ½ inch to ¾ inch thick

1 teaspoon salt

1 teaspoon olive oil, plus 1 tablespoon

¼ teaspoon dried thyme

3 pinches cayenne pepper

black pepper

2 tablespoons water or red wine

small pat of butter (optional)

Cut the oval-shaped flank steak into 4 evenly sized pieces. The grain of flank steak is easily discernible—take each piece and make 4 or 5 shallow cuts (1⁄16 to 1⁄8 inch deep) across the grain of each piece. This helps the meat stay flat as it cooks. Pat dry with paper towels. Rub the meat well with the salt, the 1 teaspoon olive oil, thyme, cayenne, and black pepper. Let sit at room temperature for ½ hour, or refrigerate for several hours. Bring the meat back to room temperature before cooking.

Heat a wide, heavy skillet over a medium-high flame—a 12-inch cast-iron skillet is ideal. Swirl the remaining tablespoon of olive oil in the skillet to coat the bottom. When the oil just begins to smoke, lay the steaks in the skillet; they should not crowd or touch each other. Let sizzle for 4 minutes on the first side, then flip and cook on the other side for another 4 minutes, or until juices collect on top. The steaks are best cooked to medium—they will still be pink in the middle. Rare flank steak is a bit tough.

Remove the steaks to a warmed platter to rest. Add about 2 tablespoons water or red wine to the skillet, scraping up the browned bits from the pan with a spatula and letting the liquid reduce to a syrup. As the steaks rest, juice will collect on the platter. Add this to the sauce in the skillet. If you want a richer sauce, swirl in a small pat of cold butter. Slice the rested steaks thinly across the grain, arrange on the platter, and drizzle with the sauce.

Carne Asada

SERVES 2 TO 3 AS AN ENTRÉE, 4 TO
5 AS TACOS

This is my own version of Mexican grilled steak, or carne asada, but the taste is true. There are two steps in marinating the meat: first you rub ground dried chiles and cumin into the meat and let it sit for several hours, then you drench it with freshly made onion-garlic-cilantro juice and let it sit for a couple of hours more before cooking it. This makes superlative tacos (see the variation at the end of the recipe).

Skirt steak is extremely flavorful. Sometimes you can buy it well trimmed of excess fat, but otherwise you will have to perform this operation yourself, using a small knife and some patience.

1 pound (trimmed weight) beef skirt steak, trimmed of excess fat if necessary

2½ teaspoons ground chile or chili powder (see page 193)

½ teaspoon ground cumin

¼ teaspoon black pepper

1 large white or yellow onion, peeled and coarsely chopped

2 or 3 cloves garlic, peeled

several sprigs cilantro, stems and leaves torn into small pieces (optional)

½ teaspoon salt

1 scant tablespoon canola oil or other vegetable oil

Cut the meat into 3 pieces. Mix together the ground chile, cumin, and black pepper, and rub all over the steak. Put the meat in a deep, nonreactive (glass, porcelain, or plastic) bowl. Cover the bowl and marinate the meat, refrigerated, for several hours or overnight.

A few hours before you want to start cooking, put the onion, garlic, and cilantro (if using) in the bowl of a food processor and process to a juicy purée. (Or grate the onions and garlic with a box grater and chop the cilantro fine.) Lay a couple of large squares of cheesecloth or a clean dish towel, dampened and wrung out, over a medium bowl, and dump in the onion purée. Gather up the ends of the cheesecloth and squeeze the onion juice into the bowl. Discard the dry solids left in the cheesecloth. Pour the onion juice over the meat, turning the meat to coat it with juice. Marinate the meat at room temperature for about 1 hour, turning occasionally.

Remove the meat from the marinade, pat dry with paper towels, and season it with salt on both sides, using about ½ teaspoon of salt in all. Set a large, heavy skillet over a medium-high flame. The skillet should be wide enough to accommodate all the pieces of meat without touching. When the skillet is hot, add a scant tablespoon of oil and lay in the steaks—they should sizzle loudly. Cook until well browned on one side, about 4 minutes, then turn and
continued . . .

cook on the other side for another 3 to 4 minutes, until juices begin to collect on top. The total cooking time will be 8 to 10 minutes. The meat should be medium-rare inside; however, if you want to be authentically Mexican, cook it through to well-done. Let the meat rest for about 5 minutes before slicing thinly across the grain.

Tacos de Carne Asada

Often, here in what Frida Kahlo liked to call *Gringolandia*, tacos are crispy deep-fried tortilla shells with a ground beef filling. Although they are delicious, the joys of the simpler soft tacos served in Mexico are also well worth discovering. At its simplest, a taco is a flavorful bit of protein with a sauce, wrapped in one or two warm, soft corn tortillas. There are few things better than a good carne asada taco, found in taquerías and taco trucks in all parts of the United States, wherever there is a large Mexican population. In San Francisco's Mission neighborhood, there are a few taquerías that serve especially tasty *tacos de carne asada*. The gruff men shout behind the counter, the mariachi music blares over the sirens and traffic outside, a drug addict collapses in a corner, but a bite of one of their tacos is like coming home to *Mamá*.

For each taco, heat 2 corn tortillas directly over your stove's flame (or on a hot, ungreased griddle) until they are floppy and steaming, with appealing brown spots here and there. Put them on a plate, stacked together. Pile about ⅓ cup of chopped warm carne asada in the center of the tortillas. Top with a spoonful of salsa (see Fresh Salsa, page 419), and strew with chopped white onions and chopped cilantro. Serve immediately, with the traditional accompaniments: a whole, crisp, red radish and a lime wedge.

To eat, first squeeze lime juice over the taco. Then pick the whole thing up, holding in the meat, and start nibbling at one end. Use plenty of napkins. Tacos are messy; eating them neatly is an acquired skill. The scent of lime oil on your hands enhances the whole experience. Munch the radish.

Roast Beef

SERVES 10 TO 12

Roast beef has become uncommon on American home tables, yet its preparation is absurdly easy, requiring simple attention to timing and little else. I make and serve it all the time at Deep Springs—the hardest part is getting it into the oven early enough so that it roasts to tenderness, unhurried, and rests sufficiently before slicing. There is nothing more satisfyingly elemental. Leftover roast beef is so good in sandwiches or salads that I sometimes make it expressly for those. For a splendid, authentic English dinner, serve hot slices with horseradish cream, Yorkshire pudding, and watercress. In summer, I like to serve fresh Horseradish-Tomato Relish (page 420) with roast beef.

If you are roasting beef for sandwiches, let the cooked roast cool to room temperature, then wrap well and refrigerate overnight. Slice the cold roast as thinly as possible across the grain. Cold roast beef sandwiches are superb with the same accompaniments: horseradish cream and watercress.

The recipe may be halved, using a 3-pound roast.

6-pound, boneless, bottom round or top round beef roast, with fat cap

2 tablespoons salt

1 tablespoon freshly ground black pepper

pinch of celery seed

1 large yellow onion, sliced

6 cloves garlic, peeled and halved

2 bay leaves (or a few sprigs of fresh thyme or rosemary)

FOR SERVING

Yorkshire Pudding (page 314)

Watercress Salad (page 294)

Fresh Horseradish Cream (page 314)

Bring the meat to room temperature. For a 6-pound roast, this will take about 3 hours. (Once it has begun to come to room temperature, don't change your mind and decide to roast it another day!) Heat the oven to 325°F. Pat the roast dry with paper towels, and rub it all over with the salt, pepper, and celery seed. Make a bed in a roasting pan of the sliced onions, halved garlic cloves, and bay leaves. Place the meat on top, fat side up, and place in the oven.

Remove the roast from the oven when an instant-read thermometer inserted in the center registers 125°F for rare, 135°F

continued . . .

. . . continued

for medium-rare, or 140°F for medium. It should take a little over 2½ hours for a 6-pound roast, or about 1 hour for the first pound and 20 minutes for each additional pound. A very rare roast will still feel very springy inside when pressed with a finger; a more thoroughly cooked roast will be firmer. Let the roast rest for 15 to 20 minutes before slicing. (Make Yorkshire pudding with the fat and drippings in the pan while the roast is resting.) Serve hot slices with a fluff of watercress to one side of the meat and very traditional English fresh horseradish cream on the other.

Yorkshire Pudding

Use the batter for Dutch Babies, page 118, omitting the butter. While the beef is resting, raise the oven heat to 450°F and remove the onion, garlic, and bay leaf from the beef roasting pan. Pour out all but 3 to 4 tablespoons of the fat and drippings in the pan. Put the pan back into the hot oven to reheat it, pour the batter in, and bake for 15 minutes. Reduce the oven temperature to 350°F and bake for another 8 to 9 minutes while you slice the beef. Present the Yorkshire pudding dramatically puffed, fresh out of the oven, then cut into wedges and serve immediately.

Fresh Horseradish Cream

4 ounces fresh horseradish, peeled and finely grated

1 cup cold heavy (whipping) cream

¼ teaspoon sugar

½ teaspoon salt

Combine the ingredients in a mixing bowl and whip (using an electric mixer, or by hand with a whisk) until soft peaks form. Taste for balanced salt, sweetness, and sharpness. Serve in a chilled silver dish, if you want to be especially English.

Roast Beef Salad

To serve about 4 people, toss together bite-size slices of roast beef, a little red onion sliced paper-thin, a big ripe tomato cut into chunks, a cup of croutons, and 2 or 3 big handfuls of mixed salad greens with enough mustard vinaigrette (see page 296) to thoroughly moisten all the components. Taste and adjust the seasonings as necessary. Serve immediately.

Roast Lamb

You may successfully roast a leg of lamb by following the directions and timing for roast beef. A boneless leg will be easier to carve than a bone-in one, but the bone contributes flavor and helps the meat cook more evenly, so if possible, ask the butcher to carve the bone free but rewrap and tie the meat around it. You can then easily remove the bone after roasting. Cook to an internal temperature of 135°F for tender, medium-rare meat. Instead of celery seed, flavor the lamb with a restrained amount of chopped fresh rosemary. Include, if you like, a strip or two of orange zest in the bed of onions.

In my student days at Deep Springs, the ranch mechanic kept a flock of lambs. I will never forget the sight—or the delicious smell—of legs of lamb marinating in red wine in large roasting pans on a shelf in the Boardinghouse pantry, to be cooked by the mechanic's wife that evening. Deep Springs lamb has a rich, definitive "lamb-y" flavor that I love. Only lamb imported from Australia or New Zealand has that great gamy flavor—much American-raised lamb is mild to the point of blandness.

No matter how much you have finessed the seasonings, if you are serving roast lamb to older Americans, they are likely to expect a dish of bright green, sweet mint jelly served alongside.

Beef Stew, with Nine Variations

SERVES 6 TO 8

Homemade beef stew is increasingly rare in American kitchens and, therefore, increasingly special. It takes inexpensive ingredients and a bit of work, time, patience, and watchfulness, and yields a result that is incomparably soothing and restoring.

Rarely does a week go by in the Deep Springs kitchen when we don't serve beef stew in some form or another. This one has big, tender chunks of beef, carrots, and potatoes. The vegetables are well cooked but not falling apart. If you were to pare down beef stew to its barest essentials, it would contain little beyond beef, onions, and stock. Feel free, then, to decrease, vary, or omit the supporting ingredients; exact quantities are not as crucial as following the basic steps. The recipe directs you to cook the stew in the oven, as we do at Deep Springs, but you may just as successfully cook it on the stovetop, if you carefully adjust the heat so the stew simmers gently. Or use a slow cooker, if you have one.

continued . . .

. . . continued

2½ pounds beef chuck, not too lean, cut into 1-inch chunks

1½ teaspoons salt, plus more as needed

½ teaspoon coarsely ground black pepper, or more as needed

pinch of ground cloves

about 8 teaspoons canola oil or other vegetable oil

1 cup good-tasting, fruity red wine

3 cups chicken stock, vegetable stock, beef stock, or water

1 bay leaf

¼ teaspoon dried thyme, or 2 sprigs fresh thyme, leaves picked and chopped

one 14-ounce can diced tomatoes

1 large yellow onion, cut into medium dice

3 cloves garlic, crushed

3 medium carrots, peeled and cut on the diagonal into 1-inch chunks

1 long stalk celery, cut into medium dice

12 ounces yellow, red, or white potatoes, unpeeled, trimmed and cut into 1-inch chunks

(OPTIONAL, FOR THICKENING)

¾ cup cold water

⅓ cup all-purpose flour

few drops of red wine vinegar (optional)

¼ cup chopped parsley

Heat the oven to 300°F. To brown the meat, it must first be dry; if it's sitting in juice, transfer it to a plate and pat dry with paper towels. Put a large skillet over a medium-high flame. In a large bowl, toss the beef chunks with 1½ teaspoons salt and the pepper and cloves. Heat about 2 teaspoons of the oil in the skillet and scatter half or a third of the beef evenly in the pan—it should sizzle when you add it. Don't crowd the meat. Let it turn a nice mahogany brown on one side before turning it. Ideally, all sides of the beef chunks should be this rich brown. Transfer the browned meat to a large, heavy stew pot (a pot that can go in the oven as well as on the stovetop). Deglaze the hot skillet with a splash of the wine, scraping up any browned bits with a wooden spoon. Add this flavorful liquid to the pot with the beef. Add more oil and brown the remaining beef in one or two more batches, deglazing the skillet after each batch. As the vegetables will eventually take their turn in the skillet, there is no need to wash it yet.

Add the chicken stock, remaining wine, bay leaf, thyme, and tomatoes to the beef and bring the whole just to a simmer over medium-high heat, skimming off any scum that rises to the surface. Taste the liquid for salt. Cover the pot and put it in the hot oven. After ½ hour, reduce the oven heat to 250°F and let simmer for another hour, or until the beef is still chewy but beginning to become tender. The stew should only simmer—it must never boil hard or the beef will be dry.

In your skillet over a medium flame, warm 2 more teaspoons of oil and gently cook the onion, garlic, carrot, and celery with a pinch of salt, stirring frequently, for 3 to 4 minutes, or until they lose their crunch—do not let the vegetables brown. Put a lid on the skillet when you're not stirring. Add the potatoes with a large pinch of salt and cook, continuing to stir frequently, for another 3 to 4 minutes. Add the vegetables to the pot with the beef, along with a flour slurry for thickening, if desired (see the next paragraph), and continue to simmer until the beef, vegetables, and potatoes are tender, about ½ hour more.

This recipe gives a flavorful broth with plenty of body as it is; still, you may want to thicken the stew, especially if you want to serve it on plates over potatoes, noodles, or rice. In a jar with a tight-fitting lid, vigorously shake together the cold water and flour until the flour is completely dissolved. Stir this mixture into the stew when adding the vegetables, and bring the stew back up to a simmer—the remaining ½ hour of simmering will cook the flour thoroughly. If you have decided to thicken your stew late in the game, just drain the liquid from the stew, thicken it in a separate pot, and return the thickened liquid to the beef and vegetables.

Taste the finished stew for salt and pepper—the salt will depend on the saltiness of the chicken stock, and you may well want a fresh shot of pepper. If you feel that the flavors need brightening, sprinkle in a few drops of red wine vinegar. Beef stew is perhaps even better reheated the next day. In either case, stir in the parsley just before serving. Serve in wide bowls.

Elizabeth's Winter Beef Stew

This variation pays homage to my friend Elizabeth—her beef stew was legendary, and she had a masterful, encyclopedic knowledge of produce and of cooking appropriately to the season. I think of beef stew as cold-weather fare anyway, but you may make it even more warming and hearty by omitting the tomatoes and adding 2 medium turnips, peeled and cut into 1-inch chunks, and 1 medium bunch kale, stemmed (see page 233) and coarsely chopped. Cook these vegetables along with the onion, celery, and carrots. Peeled winter squash, cut into 1-inch chunks, is a good option too, but add it later, in the last 40 minutes of simmering.

Russian Borscht

Longtime Deep Springs cattleman Geoff Pope and his wife, Iris, are big fans of this borscht. Once I overheard Geoff say to Iris, "No, I don't want any dessert—I'm having another bowl of borscht instead." The natural meatiness of beets melds beautifully with beef. Even people who are not fond of beets "straight" often love borscht. Proceed with the master beef stew recipe, omitting the thyme and tomatoes. With the chicken stock and wine, include 1½ cups water; you will probably have to add a little extra salt as well. With the onion, carrot, and celery, include half a small cabbage, cut into bite-sized squares. In the last ½ hour of cooking, add ½ recipe of Marinated Beets (page 281), cut into chunks. The

continued . . .

. . . continued

hint of orange is wonderful with the beef. Accompany with platters of both pickled and fresh cucumbers, good rye bread, and lots of sour cream.

Goulash

Substitute 1 teaspoon caraway seeds for the thyme in the master recipe. Omit the tomatoes. For the oil, substitute fresh lard or bacon fat, and include some chunks of bacon, if you like. With the vegetables, include half a small cabbage, coarsely chopped. Omit the potatoes. Add ¼ cup sweet Hungarian paprika (or a combination of sweet and hot paprika) to the pot before putting it in the oven. Serve over egg noodles (to make your own, see page 388) or Spaetzle (page 397). For a Slovenian-style goulash, serve over hot soft Polenta (page 404). Goulash hails from Hungary, polenta from Italy. Slovenia is nestled between the two. This just might be my favorite version of beef stew.

Carbonnade Flamande

For a version of the famous Belgian dish, proceed with the master recipe, omitting the carrots, celery, tomatoes, and potatoes. Double the amount of onion. For the wine and chicken stock, substitute a smooth-tasting ale (a rich Belgian ale is ideal, preferably made by Trappist monks). Finish with a teaspoon of cider vinegar or malt vinegar. Serve boiled potatoes on the side, tossed with butter and finely chopped parsley, or serve with Herbed Spaetzle (page 397).

Italian Beef Stew

This lighter, brighter stew appeals in hotter weather. Follow the master recipe, using olive oil instead of canola oil. Substitute white wine for the red wine. Double the amount of garlic. With the bay leaf and thyme, include 1 strip of lemon zest and 1 teaspoon chopped fresh rosemary. Omit the potatoes, if you wish. Don't thicken the stew, and finish with a squeeze of fresh lemon juice instead of red wine vinegar.

Boeuf Bourguignonne

For a rather simple version of this French classic, follow the master recipe, substituting bacon fat for the canola oil, and using a whole bottle of good, fruity red wine (merlot, pinot noir, and zinfandel are all good candidates) instead of a combination of red wine and chicken stock. Omit the tomatoes and potatoes and, for an authentic touch, use pearl onions. If you like, add chunks of thick bacon (2 to 3 ounces) that you have slowly browned in a skillet. In the last 15 minutes of cooking, add 8 ounces of fresh mushrooms that have been sliced and sautéed in butter with salt and pepper. Swirl a small pat of cold butter into the stew just before serving. Serve alongside boiled and buttered potatoes.

Mexican Braised Beef (or Goat)

Omit the thyme, carrots, celery, potatoes, and parsley in the master recipe. Double the amounts of cloves, onion, and garlic.

In a small, dry skillet, toast 2 teaspoons ground cumin. When it has released its fragrance, add 1 teaspoon dried oregano. Remove from the heat and add 2 teaspoons sweet paprika. Mix in 2 to 3 tablespoons ground chile or chili powder. Stir this spice mixture, 1 corn tortilla torn into small bits, and 1 square of unsweetened chocolate into the stew before putting it in the oven to simmer. The tortilla and chocolate not only contribute wonderful flavor, but also conspire to slightly thicken the stew. If you like, stir in a little chopped cilantro. Serve with warm corn tortillas.

When we kept milk goats at Deep Springs, an inevitable fate awaited all the young male goats. Should you, too, be lucky enough to have or find fresh goat meat (known in Spanish as *cabrito* or *chivo*), this spicy stew is an ideal use for it.

Lamb Stew

When I arrived at Deep Springs as a student, I had eaten lamb only a couple of times in my life. By the time I left, I had eaten it many different ways, cooked it in almost as many, and taken the opportunity to observe lamb's transition from animal in the field to "quarters" hanging in the walk-in refrigerator to chops and roasts to that warm, satisfied feeling of a good dinner in my belly.

Occasionally we let the lambs get just a bit past lambhood, making their richly gamy flavor even more pronounced. One evening at dinner in the Deep Springs

Boardinghouse, a visiting scholar who had just returned from Mongolia looked down into her bowl of stew and said, "Mutton. I feel like I'm back in Mongolia."

Substitute chunks of lamb shoulder for the beef in the master recipe, use olive oil instead of canola oil, and omit the thyme, carrots, and celery. With the bay leaf, add a bit of rosemary and a strip of orange zest. This makes a lovely, light Mediterranean-style lamb stew, good served with White Bean Gratin with Fennel (page 199).

Shepherd's Pie

For a rich, traditional English shepherd's pie, make a simpler lamb stew, omitting the wine, tomatoes, carrots, and celery from the master recipe, doubling the onions, and adding 2 teaspoons of chopped fresh rosemary with the bay leaf. Thicken well with a flour slurry, as described in the master recipe. Without the liquid from the tomatoes or the wine, the thickening will produce an appropriate gravylike consistency. Season the stew well with salt and pepper, put in a wide casserole dish, and cover with a blanket of hot, fresh Mashed Potatoes (page 250). Bake in a 400°F oven for about half an hour to brown the potatoes.

New Mexico Green Chile Beef Stew

SERVES 4 TO 5

This particular combination of beef, potatoes, and green chile is especially characteristic of southern New Mexico, where I spent some of my growing-up years. Serve in wide bowls, with sour cream and hot corn tortillas (see page 327 for a good way to heat tortillas).

1¾ pounds stew beef (chuck is ideal), cut into 1-inch chunks

½ teaspoon dried oregano, crumbled

1 teaspoon salt, plus more as needed

2 tablespoons all-purpose flour

3 to 4 tablespoons canola oil or other vegetable oil

1 large onion, cut into medium dice

6 cloves garlic, crushed

4 medium yellow, red, or white potatoes, unpeeled, cut into 1-inch chunks

2 cups chicken stock or beef stock

2 cups water

½ to ¾ cup coarsely chopped roasted New Mexico green chiles (see page 423)

¼ teaspoon black pepper

FOR SERVING

sour cream

corn tortillas

Pat the beef dry with paper towels. Combine the oregano, ½ teaspoon of the salt, and the flour in a large bowl, add the beef, and toss together. In a heavy soup pot over a medium-high flame, heat a scant tablespoon of oil. Brown about a third of the beef in the oil, letting the pieces brown well on each side. Remove the browned beef to a large bowl and deglaze the pot with a little water, scraping the browned bits from the bottom of the pot. Add this liquid to the beef. Repeat with the remaining beef in two more batches, adding fresh oil to the pot for each batch. Add a final scant tablespoon of oil to the pot and stew the onion with a pinch of salt. When the onion is partly cooked, add the garlic with another pinch of salt, and cook for a moment more. Add the reserved beef and deglazing liquid, potatoes, stock, water, ½ teaspoon salt, and chiles to the pot, and bring to a simmer. Gently simmer the stew until the beef and potatoes are tender, 1 to 1½ hours. Add the pepper and more salt to taste.

Glazed Meatloaf

SERVES 6 TO 8

Let me assure you that this is the classic juicy and flavorful meatloaf of your dreams, adapted from a great recipe in the pages of *Cook's Illustrated*. Meatloaf is best baked on a rimmed baking sheet, rather than in a loaf pan, so that more of the surface browns appealingly. Wrap leftover meatloaf tightly in plastic wrap, put it between two trays or baking sheets, with a heavy object on top, and refrigerate it, weighted, overnight. It will then slice neatly for sandwiches.

2 teaspoons olive oil

1 large onion, finely diced

2 cloves garlic, peeled and crushed

1¼ teaspoons salt

1 pound lean ground beef

1 pound ground pork

⅓ cup chopped parsley

⅔ cup crushed saltine crackers

⅓ cup plain yogurt or buttermilk

6 ounces fresh mushrooms, wiped clean and grated using a box grater or very finely chopped

2 large eggs, beaten

½ teaspoon dried thyme, or 1 teaspoon fresh thyme or rosemary

½ teaspoon black pepper

1 tablespoon Worcestershire sauce

1 tablespoon Dijon mustard

¼ teaspoon hot sauce

———

GLAZE (IF YOU LOVE GLAZE, DOUBLE THE QUANTITY)

¼ cup bottled "chili" sauce or ketchup

2 tablespoons brown sugar

1 tablespoon cider vinegar

Heat the oven to 350°F. Heat the olive oil over a medium-high flame in a medium-sized skillet, and sauté the onion and garlic with ¼ teaspoon of the salt until the onion is transparent and no longer crunchy, about 5 minutes. Set aside to cool.

In a large bowl, *without smashing, kneading, or otherwise overworking the meat*, lightly but thoroughly combine the meats with the parsley, crushed saltines, yogurt, mushrooms, eggs, thyme, remaining 1 teaspoon salt, pepper, Worcestershire sauce, mustard, hot sauce, and the cooled onions and garlic until amalgamated. If you have used different proportions of the listed ingredients and want to taste the mixture, fry a bite-sized piece in a small skillet until cooked through, and taste.

Line a shallow roasting pan or rimmed baking sheet with aluminum foil (shiny side up), and grease the foil so the meatloaf
continued...

. . . *continued*

won't stick. Pat the meat into a narrow, free-form loaf (about 15 inches long, 4 inches wide, and 2 inches high) in the pan.

To make the glaze, mix the ketchup, brown sugar, and vinegar in a small bowl and spoon the glaze in a stripe down the center of the meatloaf.

Bake the meatloaf for 40 to 45 minutes. Crank up the oven's heat to 500°F and bake for about 15 minutes more to brown the top and set the glaze. Using a small knife, peek at the interior of the meatloaf—no pink should remain. The internal temperature of the meatloaf, taken with an instant-read thermometer, should register 165°F. Let rest for about 10 minutes before slicing.

Italian Meatballs

SERVES 4 TO 6

For years I tended to bake meatballs and wonder how I could make them better. Then I learned to sauté them in olive oil—now that's-a-great-a-meatball! The coarse breadcrumbs are essential to the recipe. A student brought this method to the Deep Springs kitchen from his Italian family.

Structurally, meatballs and meatloaf have much in common: ground meats bound with egg, breadcrumbs, seasonings, and liquid. Once you have successfully followed a recipe, you are well equipped to improvise. Good-quality ground turkey and turkey sausage work well in this recipe, standing in for the beef and pork sausage. If you want to use ground pork rather than pork sausage, season it up with salt, pepper, hot red pepper flakes, and crushed fennel seeds. For a good all-beef meatball, see Mediterranean Meatballs, page 321.

3 to 4 tablespoons olive oil

1 medium yellow onion, finely diced

2 large cloves garlic, minced or crushed

1½ teaspoons salt

¼ teaspoon dried oregano, crumbled

1 cup coarse day-old breadcrumbs (see Note)

⅓ cup buttermilk or plain yogurt, or more as needed

1 pound lean ground beef

1 pound fresh Italian sausage, hot or sweet

2 large eggs

¼ teaspoon black pepper

—

FOR SERVING

cooked rice (see page 398) or pasta (see page 393)

about 4 cups Tomato Sauce (page 416)

3 to 4 tablespoons chopped Italian parsley

freshly grated Parmesan cheese

Heat 1 tablespoon of the olive oil in a small saucepan over a medium flame, and gently cook the onion and garlic with ¼ teaspoon of the salt for about 5 minutes, or until the onion has turned translucent—it should not brown. Stir in the oregano and set aside to cool.

In a large bowl, toss the breadcrumbs with the buttermilk. Add the cooled onion mixture, the beef, the sausage (casings removed), eggs, remaining 1¼ teaspoons salt, and black pepper. Mix with your clean hands, gently breaking up the meats to amalgamate with the other ingredients. *Don't whip or beat or knead the mixture.* Rinse your hands well; you should be able to form 1½-inch balls (handling lightly; it's fine if the meatballs are not perfectly

smooth or perfectly round) with damp hands without the mixture sticking. If the mixture is sticky, add a little more buttermilk.

Heat the oven to 350°F. Heat 2 to 3 table-spoons of olive oil in a wide, heavy skillet over medium-high heat. When the oil is hot but not smoking, put in the meatballs without crowding (it may be necessary to cook them in batches). The meatballs should sizzle merrily upon contact with the oil. When they have nicely browned on the underside, gently turn them with tongs. They should not get crispy-brown—at that point they're overcooked. Drain the meatballs on several thicknesses of paper towels, then arrange them in a shallow roasting pan. Put the pan in the oven for a few moments to finish cooking the meatballs through—no pink should remain.

Serve the meatballs with rice or pasta and, always, tomato sauce. If you are serving individual plates, the rice or pasta should be on the bottom with 3 to 4 meatballs sitting on the rice, tomato sauce spooned over the meatballs, and a scattering of chopped parsley over all. If you are pre-senting the meatballs in a dish to be passed at the table or on a buffet, serve the rice or pasta in a separate dish. Choose a large, wide dish for the meatballs, make a pool of red sauce on the bottom, arrange the

continued...

. . . continued

meatballs over the red sauce, spoon more red sauce over the meatballs (not coating them completely; let bits of the brown meatballs show through), and sprinkle parsley over all. In any case, serve extra sauce and freshly grated Parmesan cheese on the side.

Note: If denizens of the far north are said in popular legend to have a hundred words for snow, how nice it would be if cooks had a hundred words for breadcrumbs. Every dish containing breadcrumbs ideally requires a slightly different type. Not only are there myriad types of bread, but very different kinds of crumbs might come out of a single loaf. The ideal breadcrumbs for this recipe come from 1- or 2-day-old Italian white bread. Cut the crust off with a serrated knife, then tear the bread with your fingers into raisin-sized chunks.

Mediterranean Meatballs

SERVES 3 TO 4
LARGE QUANTITY RECIPE: SERVES 30 TO 40

This tender and flavorful all-beef meatball dish is good in hot weather, with gentle Middle Eastern flavors everyone loves.

3 to 4 tablespoons olive oil
about 1 cup olive oil

1 small yellow onion, finely diced
4 large yellow onions, finely diced

1 to 2 fat cloves garlic, crushed
10 fat cloves garlic, crushed

pinch salt, plus 1 teaspoon
generous pinch salt, plus 3 tablespoons

1¼ pounds lean ground beef
12 pounds lean ground beef

½ cup coarse breadcrumbs
6 cups coarse breadcrumbs

2 tablespoons plus ½ cup plain yogurt
3½ to 4 cups plain yogurt

1 egg
8 eggs

2 pinches of cayenne pepper
1½ teaspoons cayenne pepper

½ teaspoon paprika
1 tablespoon paprika

¼ teaspoon ground cumin
2 teaspoons ground cumin

1 or 2 dashes Tabasco or other hot sauce
½ teaspoon Tabasco or other hot sauce

⅛ teaspoon black pepper
1 teaspoon black pepper

3 to 4 tablespoons chopped fresh mint
2 cups chopped fresh mint

2 tablespoons chopped parsley
1 cup chopped parsley

Heat the oven to 350°F. Heat 1 tablespoon *(¼ cup for large quantity)* of the olive oil in a large skillet and sauté the onion and garlic with a good pinch of salt until tender, about 5 minutes, then let cool. Transfer the onion mixture to a large bowl (don't wash the skillet yet), and add the beef, breadcrumbs, 2 tablespoons *(1½ cups)* of the yogurt, egg*(s)*, cayenne, paprika, cumin, Tabasco, remaining 1 teaspoon *(3 tablespoons)* salt, black pepper, and mint. Using your clean hands, mix everything lightly but thoroughly. *Don't smash the meat or knead the mixture.* Form into 1½-inch balls.

The meatballs can be fried, as described here, or baked, as discussed at the end of the recipe. To fry, heat a few tablespoons of olive oil over a medium flame in the same skillet until the oil shimmers. Arrange the meatballs in the pan without crowding (it may be necessary to cook them in batches), and let them cook, undisturbed, until they are golden brown on the underside. Turn with tongs to brown all sides. If the meatballs are not cooked through, finish them in a 350°F oven, or cover the skillet and continue to cook slowly over a low flame, turning as necessary.

Remove the meatballs to a platter. Pour off most of the oil in the skillet, keeping as much of the juice and browned bits as possible. Add the final ½ cup *(2 to 3 cups)* yogurt to the skillet, and heat through without boiling. Drizzle this sauce over the cooked meatballs, and garnish with parsley.

For an easier cooking method, bake the meatballs instead of frying them: with the oven at 475°F, place the meatballs on a lightly oiled sheet pan, and bake until cooked through, about 12 minutes. Carefully drain off the juices into a medium saucepan, skim off any excess fat, add the yogurt for the sauce, and gently heat through (do not let the sauce boil). Drizzle the sauce over the meatballs and garnish with parsley. You won't get the nice browned flavor the skillet provides, but preparation is far easier, especially for a crowd.

SKILLET
HAMBURGERS

For each person, obtain 6 to 7 ounces of ground chuck, about 80 percent lean. Ideally, the meat has been ground that day with a very sharp, cold grinder. Gently shape the meat into a ¾-inch-thick patty, taking care that you don't rearrange the structure of the meat too much; otherwise the burger will be tough. It's fine if the patty is not perfectly shaped. *The center of the patty should be a bit thinner than the edges*—this prevents the burger from puffing in the middle as it cooks. Over a medium-high flame, heat a heavy skillet for a few minutes. Place the meat in the skillet—it should sizzle on contact—and gently press down. (Don't press the meat at any other point after this; you'll just squeeze out the juices.) Let cook for 4 to 5 minutes, then flip and cook the other side. Amply salt and pepper the cooked side. (Burgers are juiciest, I think, if salted after cooking, not before.) At this point you may put a thin slice of cheese on top. Cook for another 3 to 4 minutes, then transfer the burger to the prepared bun or plate.

Lightly toast the buns—in the same pan if there's room (I like it when the buns get a little greasy). Don't be too stingy with the mayonnaise or too generous with the mustard. Top with red onion sliced paper-thin, leaf lettuce, and ripe tomato sprinkled with salt.

Salting the tomato is as important as seasoning the meat. I remember a good old burger place in Oakland, California, run by an Afghani family. There was nothing remarkable about their ingredients; they used frozen patties, premade buns, and supermarket lettuce and tomatoes. The burgers were good because they were prepared with care; the cooks grilled the burgers and toasted the buns side by side on a gas grill. They cut the iceberg lettuce into ribbons. They were generous with their tasty mayonnaise-based, ketchup-laced sauce. And they salted the tomato on every burger.

For a recipe for homemade hamburger buns, see page 136.

Hamburger en Salade

I like to stack lettuce leaves, sliced tomatoes, and chopped onion—salting and peppering the layers, smearing and daubing them with mayonnaise and maybe a little vinaigrette here and there—on a plate with a burger on top and go at it with a knife and fork, bun forgotten. It is a direct and satisfying answer to the burger craving. Echoing the "diet plate" of many decades ago, a little scoop of cottage cheese is perfect alongside.

Rico's Tacos

SERVES 4 TO 6

A beloved, recurrent, simple dinner in our household, these tacos evoke our childhood in New Mexico. The meat filling is quite plain, inviting a generous topping of spicy salsa. Authentically, the tortillas are briefly sizzled and softened in a shallow pan of hot oil, but I prefer the lighter result when the tortillas are simply heated over a flame.

1 tablespoon canola oil or other vegetable oil

1 medium white or yellow onion, finely diced

1 teaspoon salt, plus more as needed

2 medium yellow potatoes, unpeeled, finely diced

2 pounds lean ground beef

pinch of celery seed

black pepper

FOR SERVING

12 corn tortillas

2 cups salsa, mild or hot (use Fresh Salsa, page 419, or your favorite prepared salsa)

avocado slices (optional)

1 cup natural sour cream, well stirred

Heat the vegetable oil in a heavy skillet over medium-high heat. Add three-quarters of the onion with a pinch of salt and cook, stirring frequently, until the onion begins to soften, about 5 minutes. Set aside the rest of the onion to top the tacos. Add the potato with another pinch of salt and cook, stirring frequently, for about 3 minutes. Add the ground beef and celery seed. Stir to combine the beef, onion, and potato. Reduce the heat to medium, cover the skillet, and let cook, stirring frequently, for about 15 minutes, or until the meat is cooked completely and the potato is soft, releasing starch to thicken the meat juices somewhat. Add 1 teaspoon of salt and pepper to taste, and cook for a moment longer. Taste again—it may need more salt and pepper.

When you are ready to eat, heat corn tortillas directly on the flame of a gas burner (or in a hot, dry skillet) until they get appetizing brown spots. Place a tortilla on the flame or skillet, turn, place another on top, turn both, place another on top of that, turn all three, and so forth, building up the stack and giving each tortilla its moment of direct contact with the heat. The accumulated heat will steam and soften the whole stack.

Put a hot tortilla on a plate (warming the plates is a nice touch), scoop about ⅓ cup of the meat mixture on top, then

continued . . .

. . . continued

top with a bit of diced onion, salsa, avocado (if desired), and a dollop of sour cream. Eat immediately: pick up the filled tortilla and take a bite from one end, holding up the other end with your finger so the filling won't fall out. This dinner is messy, requiring a little skill and plenty of napkins, but it is well worth it.

Steak Tartare

SERVES 6 AS A LIGHT COURSE, 8 TO 10 AS AN
HORS D'OEUVRE

Steak tartare's allure is tantalizingly laced with danger and taboo. Something of a Deep Springs tradition, it is a culinary rite of passage, much like one's first raw oyster: if you are able to eat *that* and love it, you are no longer the picky little kid you once were. What other previously shunned delicacies await?

There is something vitally appealing about raw meat. Chefs are always particularly appreciative of a good raw beef or raw fish dish. I once knew a cook who told me how her mother, on grocery-shopping trips, used to buy a quarter-pound of ground round for the two of them to share, raw, in the car on the way home as a reward for completing the shopping. The mother carried a salt shaker in her purse for the purpose. Raw meat is more easily digested than cooked meat. A knob of steak tartare wrapped in a lettuce leaf is my definition of health food.

All that said, a word to the wise: *eating raw meat is potentially hazardous to your health*. Please don't make this dish unless you are absolutely certain of the freshness and quality of your beef. Honor a good butcher with your steadfast business. I completely trust the quality of our beef at Deep Springs.

Our cows not only eat quantities of nutritious, organically grown hay, but over the course of their lives have access to all manner of wild desert grasses and other green plants, both down in the Valley and up in the White Mountains in summer. Though we always finish the animals on grain, our beef still has a distinctive flavor—the effect, perhaps, of the rugged desert plants.

I first encountered *tartarski biftek* when I was an exchange student in Slovenia, where it was always very finely ground and always served with mayonnaise (on the side, or piped decoratively over the mound of meat) and toast points. I don't see mention of mayonnaise in any American cookbook recipes, but the older ones do specify grinding the meat to a uniform paste. The more contemporary chefly versions of steak tartare always call for hand-chopping the meat fine. I like a compromise: a spreadable paste with a portion of the meat hand-chopped. The seasonings might seem strong, but they are added in flavor-enhancing, not flavor-dominating, quantities. And finally, I briefly sear the piece of meat on all sides to guard against any kind of surface contamination.

TOASTS

1 medium loaf good white bread, thinly sliced

melted butter

SAUCE

½ cup mayonnaise

2 tablespoons extra-virgin olive oil

1 tablespoon fresh lemon juice

pinch of salt

MEAT

1½ pounds beef tenderloin, perfect quality, visible fat trimmed off, well chilled

salt and black pepper

1 tablespoon olive oil

2 high-quality, freshly shelled egg yolks (traditional, but 1 to 2 tablespoons of olive oil may be substituted)

3 anchovies, blotted of excess oil

3 tablespoons minced onion

1 tablespoon finely chopped capers

¼ teaspoon salt

several twists of black pepper

juice of ¼ lemon

1 tablespoon coarsely chopped parsley

10 to 15 small lettuce leaves, washed and spun dry, for serving

To make the toasts, heat the oven to 350°F. Cut the bread into small rectangles the size of dominos, arrange on a baking sheet, brush lightly on one side with melted butter, and toast in the oven until pale golden brown, about 10 minutes. Let the toasts cool on a rack.

continued . . .

. . . continued

To make the sauce, slowly whisk the olive oil into the mayonnaise in a small bowl, then add the lemon juice and salt. Cover and refrigerate.

To prepare the meat, season the beef well with salt and pepper, keeping it well chilled. Over a high flame, heat the olive oil in a heavy, medium-sized skillet until it smokes, and carefully lay the cold beef in the sizzling oil. Cook for about 20 seconds per side, turning until all sides—including the ends—are seared. Put the beef on a plate and stick it in the freezer for about 5 minutes. Remove from the freezer and chop a third of the beef *very finely* by hand with your sharpest knife. Cut the rest into chunks and process in the food processor with the egg yolks (or olive oil) and anchovies until it is reduced to a fine paste. In a medium bowl, combine the beef-egg-anchovy mixture with the chopped beef, onion, capers, salt, pepper, lemon juice, and parsley. Mound the mixture in the center of a platter, surrounded by the little toasts and lettuce leaves, the dish of mayonnaise sauce close by. Serve immediately.

Spread a generous layer of meat on a piece of toast and top with a small blob of mayonnaise sauce. Or wrap a ball of meat and a bit of sauce in a lettuce leaf.

You may also use lamb: once, when chef (and Deep Springs alumnus) David Tanis was visiting, I made a Middle Eastern–inflected lamb tartare, with a little cilantro and cayenne.

Carpaccio

SERVES 6 AS A LIGHT COURSE, 8 TO 10 AS AN HORS D'OEUVRE

Whole slices of raw meat! Simpler and lighter than tartare, and therefore more elegant, yet also more crude (in a good way) and respectful of the integrity of the good product from which it is made: that defines good Italian food.

Carpaccio was conceived in 1950 at the renowned Harry's Bar in Venice, Italy, during a major exhibition of the Renaissance painter Vittore Carpaccio. The deep red of the beef and the white of the mayonnaise sauce is said to echo the painter's famous reds and whites. At Harry's Bar, this still-popular dish is served simply: raw, well-trimmed shell steak, thinly sliced, served with a mayonnaise sauce—no other embellishments. Carpaccio now refers to any thinly sliced food tiled over a plate and sprinkled with seasonings—see Summer Squash Carpaccio, page 292.

Lamb may also be used for carpaccio; instead of the mayonnaise sauce, drizzle with a vinaigrette to which you have added a few pitted, chopped oil-cured black olives.

Please use only *impeccably fresh, high-quality meat* for this recipe (see the Steak Tartare recipe, page 328). Eating raw meat is potentially hazardous to your health.

SAUCE

use the same sauce ingredients and procedure as in Steak Tartare, page 328

———

MEAT

1½ pounds beef tenderloin, perfect quality, trimmed of fat, well chilled

salt and black pepper

1 tablespoon olive oil

———

3 anchovies, blotted of excess oil and finely chopped

3 tablespoons minced green onion

1 tablespoon finely chopped capers

salt and freshly ground black pepper

juice of ¼ lemon

1 tablespoon coarsely chopped parsley

Make the mayonnaise sauce; cover and refrigerate.

To prepare the meat, season the beef well with salt and pepper, keeping it well chilled. Heat the olive oil in a skillet until it smokes, and carefully lay the cold beef in the sizzling oil. Cook for about 20 seconds per side, turning until all sides—including the ends—are seared. Put the beef on a plate and stick it in the freezer for about 20 minutes.

Slice the beef crosswise as thinly as possible, using your sharpest knife. (I find this easier if the cylinder of meat is first halved lengthwise.) Place the slices between two layers of wax paper and gently roll to a translucent thinness, using a rolling pin. This may be done a few hours ahead of serving time.

Peel off one layer of the wax paper, put one slice of the meat facing down on an individual plate, and peel off the top layer of wax paper from the slice. Continue until the center of the plate is attractively "tiled" with meat. Repeat with the remaining plates. Put the mayonnaise sauce in a plastic bag, cut a tiny hole out of the corner, and squirt the mayonnaise in fine threads in a crosshatch pattern over the meat. Don't be too lavish with the mayonnaise. Evenly sprinkle the anchovies, green onions, capers, salt, pepper, lemon juice, and parsley over the meat. Serve immediately; eat with a knife and fork.

Beef Liver with Bacon, Onions, and Mushrooms

SERVES 6

Liver is quite rich and should be served in small portions—3 or 4 ounces. We always serve liver the day after a slaughter at Deep Springs, along with any other organ meats the cook is ambitious enough to prepare ("Organ Meat Festivals" we call such meals). A single beef liver is huge, and far more than the community will eat. With a controversial menu item such as liver, I always include familiar, guaranteed-to-please foods: a big tossed green salad, manicotti with cheese, warm bread, and a dessert such as Chocolate Mayonnaise Cake (page 487).

I love runny egg yolks and bloody meat, mayonnaise oozing out of sandwiches, steak tartare. I love bitter things: chicory lettuces and English marmalade, candied citrus peel. I find there is more good fruitcake in the world than many people think. I love all the "icky" vegetables: Brussels sprouts and beets, turnips, rutabagas, and kale. I love all the strange things in the deli case, even the head-cheese, the olive loaf, and especially the mortadella with chunks of white fat. I love anchovies and capers. I love the fat on roast beef, the skin on roast chicken. I love pickled pigs' feet and fried-tripe tacos.

Nonetheless, as a child, I was a very picky eater indeed. When I was seven or eight, I wouldn't eat much beyond Rice Krispies, peanut butter, hamburgers with ketchup only, and celery. Happily, I soon discovered that you can acquire a taste for just about anything. Why dislike something when you could instead just enjoy it? In Hawaii, I first learned to appreciate the gray, sticky, cold, watery taro root paste known as *poi* only in the context of a whole, traditional island meal, alongside rice, salty pit-cooked pork, and braised cabbage. Until recently, I did not like beef liver, black-eyed peas, dill, or spaghetti squash. But now I like them all. Well, maybe not every day. The following preparation finally won me over to liver.

six 3- or 4-ounce slices of well-trimmed, very fresh beef or calves' liver, about ½ inch thick

milk for soaking

2 to 3 tablespoons butter

1 large yellow onion, thinly sliced with the grain

2 pinches of salt, plus more for seasoning

8 ounces white or brown mushrooms, wiped clean, trimmed, halved, and thickly sliced

3 to 4 thick-cut strips bacon, cut into bite-size squares

black pepper

In a wide, shallow bowl, soak the liver in enough milk to barely cover for 1 hour prior to cooking it. Meanwhile, make the accompaniments. Take a wide skillet and melt a tablespoon of butter over a medium-high flame. Throw in the onion with a big pinch of salt. Sauté, stirring and tossing constantly, allowing the onion to brown. Reduce the heat to medium-low and let the onion continue to brown and caramelize. If a brown, caramelized residue forms on the bottom of the pan, slap the lid on the pan and remove from the heat for a few moments—the steam from the onions will melt this residue back into the onions, making them more tasty and savory. The total cooking time will be about 20 minutes. When the onions are tender and taste good, transfer them to a dish, and keep warm.

Sauté the mushrooms in two batches in butter with a pinch of salt until brown and flavorful (see page 237). Set the mushrooms aside in a bowl.

Rinse out the skillet if necessary, and cook the bacon slowly in the skillet until browned and crispy. Pour the fat into a metal cup, reserving it for cooking the liver. Drain the bacon on paper towels and set aside. You may prepare the mushrooms, bacon, and onion ahead of time, but they should be warm when you start cooking the liver.

Drain the pieces of liver and pat dry with paper towels. Season the liver on both sides with salt and pepper. Wipe out the skillet, and heat 1 tablespoon of bacon fat over medium-high heat until the liver sizzles merrily upon contact. Cook 3 pieces of the liver until brown on one side, turn, and cook until just beginning to brown on the other side. If the liver is about ½ inch thick, this should take 40 to 50 seconds on each side. *Do not overcook.* The liver should still be barely pink in the middle. Remove the liver to a warmed plate or platter. Repeat with the remaining 3 pieces of liver. Spoon the onions over the liver, sprinkle the mushrooms and bacon on top, and serve right away. Now, what wouldn't taste good with onions, bacon, and mushrooms strewn over it?

Pork

Each spring, we buy a few young hogs, fatten them on kitchen scraps from the Deep Springs kitchen throughout the summer, and finish them on windfall apples from the orchard and the mash left over from cider pressing in the fall. The meat is uncommonly sweet and succulent; once we tasted a Deep Springs pork chop side by side with a commercial one, and the Deep Springs chop was unmistakably sweeter and cleaner tasting. Sometimes, an enterprising student will fire up the smoker and treat the grateful community to delicious home-smoked hams, bacon, and sausage.

Pork is an excellent, versatile meat. Three great cuisines of the world—those of China, the American South, and Germany—have fully realized, in completely different ways, the glories of pork cookery. Yet pork also suffers image problems: a couple of major world religions proscribe it, it is saddled with the reputation of being heavy or fatty, and until recently most people drastically overcooked it, fearing trichinosis. It doesn't help that the intelligence of pigs is well documented, or that beloved children's movies feature personable pigs narrowly avoiding slaughter. However, hogs are now bred to be much less fat than they once were, certain cuts of pork are leaner than many other more commonly consumed meats, and the trichina parasite is not only all but eradicated in commercial hogs but is killed at a low 137°F. And children grow up to face their inherited human omnivory.

Lean pork cuts—chops, loin, and tenderloin—are not at their best if simply cooked in a hot pan, like steak. To be tender, they need to be either brined (a brine is a flavored saltwater solution; see page 336) or cooked over gentle heat.

Apple-Marinated Pork Chops

SERVES 3

These pork chops are seasoned with salt and marinated with fresh apple a day ahead. The salt penetrates and tenderizes the meat much as a brine does, and the apple's sugars help the pork brown beautifully in the pan. They are perfect with Roasted Potatoes, Apples, and Onions (page 247).

After the chops are cooked, the apples and onions in which the pork marinated are simmered briefly in apple cider. The onions remain a little crunchy, but if they taste good to you, you may serve them with the chops or use them in another dish: once I tossed the apples and onions into sautéed Swiss chard—the combination was delicious.

3 center-cut pork chops, about 1 inch thick, a little fat left on

1 teaspoon salt

½ teaspoon freshly ground black pepper

½ flavorful apple, unpeeled, thinly sliced

¼ small yellow onion, thinly sliced

1 tablespoon olive oil

1 cup apple cider

Rub the pork chops with the salt and pepper. Place the apple slices over the top and bottom surfaces of each chop, put the chops in a shallow bowl, and scatter the onion over them. Cover tightly with plastic wrap, pressing the wrap down on the surface of the chops, and refrigerate overnight. Set them out at room temperature for about 1 hour before cooking. Remove and reserve the apples and onions. Pat the chops dry with a paper towel.

Heat the olive oil in a wide, heavy skillet over a medium-high flame and brown the chops for about 4 minutes on each side, or just until they feel firm when pressed with a finger. If they don't seem cooked, lower the flame and continue cooking for a few minutes more. They are thoroughly cooked, but still juicy, when they have reached an internal temperature of 150°F. Remove the chops to a clean plate.

Reheat the skillet over a medium-high flame. Pour off any fat left in the skillet. Add the apples and onions and pour in the apple cider. Bring to a boil, scraping the browned, flavorful bits from the bottom of the skillet with a wooden spoon and letting them dissolve into the cider. After everything has boiled for about a minute, strain out the apples and onions. Or, if you prefer, leave them in. Boil until the liquid is reduced to a thin syrup, just a few tablespoons. Pour over the warm chops and serve.

Tender Cured Pork Chops

SERVES 8

The meat fibers in lean cuts of pork often "seize up" and may be very tough if not cooked with care. One way of counteracting this tendency is simply to cook the meat over very gentle heat (see Pork Chops Slow-Cooked in Olive Oil, facing page). Another way is to brine the meat. A brine is not simply a marinade—the salt solution actually penetrates the meat and alters the structure of the protein, curing the meat. Once cured, chops may be cooked on high heat and will remain tender. This brine will also flavor and tenderize chicken (page 347) as well as other cuts of pork, such as a whole boneless loin—allow an extra 24 hours for each extra inch of thickness, for cuts up to 4 inches thick.

In this recipe, the water, salt, sugar, and soy sauce are essential, but the remaining ingredients—the aromatic flavorings—may be varied to suit the occasion. Garlic, fennel, allspice, coriander, thyme, red pepper—any of these could be delicious.

BRINE

6 tablespoons kosher salt (see page 71)

heaping ⅓ cup firmly packed brown sugar

8 cups water

⅓ cup soy sauce

1 small, leafy stalk celery, thinly sliced

1 small carrot, peeled and thinly sliced

½ small yellow onion, thinly sliced

4 large leaves fresh sage, bruised and torn up

several sprigs of parsley, bruised and torn up

3 bay leaves, crushed in your hand

2 teaspoons crushed juniper berries

½ teaspoon crushed black peppercorns

—

8 bone-in pork chops, about ¾ inch thick

about 2 tablespoons canola oil or other vegetable oil

To make the brine, stir the salt and sugar into the water in a large bowl until completely dissolved. Add the soy sauce, celery, carrot, onion, sage, parsley, bay leaves, juniper berries, and peppercorns, then add the pork chops.

Refrigerate the chops in the brine, stirring and redistributing several times, for at least 24 and preferably 36 hours (½-inch pork chops take only 24 hours; 1-inch chops take about 48 hours). Remove the chops from the brine, and pat dry with paper towels.

Heat the oven to 350°F.

Over a medium-high flame, heat about a tablespoon of oil in a wide, heavy skillet. Cook 4 of the chops until well browned on one side, about 4 minutes. Flip and cook on the other side for another 3 to 4 minutes. Repeat with the remaining 4 chops. If necessary, you may finish cooking the chops in the oven once they have been browned on the stovetop. They are best cooked to medium, until the meat is firm and there is only a faint rosy pink next to the bone. These chops may also be grilled, to wonderful effect, over a charcoal fire.

Pork Chops Slow-Cooked in Olive Oil

SERVES 3

These tender pork chops require no chopping or peeling of ingredients and no marinating or brining, making them perfect for a quick weeknight supper. They can be cooking in the pan just minutes after you walk into the kitchen. To keep them tender, you cook them slowly over a low flame. The lower temperature results in less spattery mess than most other pan-cooked meat. Although they don't brown, paprika, balsamic vinegar, and soy sauce provide a good stand-in for browned flavor.

3 center-cut boneless or bone-in pork chops, about 1 inch thick (bone-in chops will need a minute or two more in the pan)

¾ teaspoon salt

½ teaspoon black pepper

2 or 3 pinches of cayenne pepper

1 teaspoon paprika

½ cup olive oil

2 teaspoons balsamic vinegar

2 teaspoons soy sauce

2 teaspoons honey

continued . . .

. . . continued

Rub the chops all over with the salt, black pepper, cayenne, and paprika. Over a low flame, heat the olive oil in a wide, heavy skillet for a minute. Gently lay the pork chops in the warm oil. Raise the heat slightly. Listen carefully: as soon as you hear a low, gentle sizzle, turn the heat down slightly, adjusting it as necessary to maintain this slow sizzle. Let the chops cook in this manner for 6 to 7 minutes on each side—the precise timing depends on the chops' thickness and the intensity of the heat. When done, they should feel firm throughout when pressed with a finger. The interior of the chops will be a juicy, pale pink. Remove the chops to clean plates, blotting excess oil with paper towels.

Pour the oil from the pan into a metal cup or other heatproof container, reserving it for cooking more pork chops or for another use—it's very good for cooking vegetables. Add the balsamic vinegar, soy sauce, and honey to the warm pan, bring to a bubbling boil, and drizzle over the chops.

Pork Tenderloin

SERVES 4 TO 5

When you want lean, tender, succulent meat that requires little advance preparation, you want pork tenderloin. Though the seasonings suggested here are lively and classic, you can vary them to suit your taste. Serve pork tenderloin amid an array of simple vegetable dishes and salads, such as beets with orange, steamed artichokes, watercress, and boiled new potatoes dressed with olive oil.

2 pork tenderloins, each a little over a pound

about 2½ teaspoons olive oil

1 teaspoon salt

¼ teaspoon cayenne pepper

scant ¼ teaspoon black pepper

¼ teaspoon rubbed sage

1 to 2 tablespoons water or wine

Pat the tenderloins dry with a paper towel. Cut each tenderloin crosswise into 2 pieces of equal weight. With a meat pounder, rolling pin, or other heavy object, pound the bulbous-end piece until it is flattened and slightly thinner than the tapered-end piece—this way, the two differently shaped pieces will cook at about the same rate. Rub 1½ teaspoons of the olive oil, salt, cayenne, black pepper, and sage into the meat. Let sit at room temperature for 20 to 30 minutes.

Heat a wide, heavy skillet over a medium flame. Add a teaspoon or so of olive oil to the skillet, and lay the pieces of pork in the oil. Let the meat cook, turning several times, for a total of 15 to 20 minutes, or until the thickest pieces are beginning to feel firm. (The internal temperature should register 150°F on an instant-read thermometer.) Remove the pork to a clean plate and let rest for 5 minutes before slicing on the diagonal, across the grain. The meat will be rosy pink but cooked throughout. Add a couple of tablespoons of water or wine to the skillet and return to the flame, scraping the flavorful brown bits on the bottom of the skillet with a wooden spoon and letting them dissolve into the liquid. Boil until the liquid is reduced to just a spoonful, and pour this scant sauce over the sliced pork.

Cynthia's Garlic-Studded Milk-Braised Pork Loin

SERVES 4 TO 6
LARGE QUANTITY RECIPE: SERVES 12 TO 14

The pork emerges tender, juicy, and milky white in this lovely Italian recipe, taught to me by a terrific chef.

1 boneless pork loin roast, about 2 pounds, with just a little fat left on
1 whole boneless pork loin, about 6 pounds, with just a little fat left on

2 to 3 cloves garlic, cut into matchstick-sized slivers
4 to 6 cloves garlic, cut into matchstick-sized slivers

1 teaspoon salt
1 tablespoon salt

¼ to ½ teaspoon black pepper
1½ teaspoons black pepper

1 tablespoon olive oil
a good glug of olive oil

4 cups whole milk
8 to 12 cups whole milk

2 strips lemon zest, taken with a vegetable peeler
4 strips lemon zest, taken with a vegetable peeler

5 or 6 fresh sage leaves
10 to 12 fresh sage leaves

continued . . .

. . . continued

If you are cooking a whole pork loin, cut it crosswise into three 2-pound pieces. Pat the pork dry with paper towels. Using a small knife, poke holes all over the surface of the meat and insert slivers of garlic, until the garlic is used up. Salt and pepper the meat well on all sides.

Choose a large, heavy pan that will comfortably accommodate the meat. Heat the olive oil in the pan over medium-high heat and brown the pork loin well on all sides (sturdy tongs are a great help here). Pour in the milk, and submerge the lemon zest and sage. Lower the heat to medium. Slowly bring the milk to a low simmer (reduce the heat further, if necessary) and cook the pork, turning several times, just until the meat is cooked through, 30 to 40 minutes. For very good results, if you are patient, you may prolong the cooking further, taking up to an hour over very low heat—in effect slowly poaching the loin in the milk.

When the pork is cooked, it should feel firm when gently squeezed and should register about 145°F in the center with an instant-read thermometer. If the internal temperature is much higher than 145°, the meat might be overcooked and dry. The inside of the meat should still be a faint rose color, but it should be thoroughly opaque, not raw looking. Remove the meat from the liquid and let rest for about 10 minutes. Slice thinly across the grain. Return any unsliced pork to the liquid, and refrigerate it in the liquid when cool.

The gray, milky, curdled liquid left over from cooking the pork looks hideous but tastes savory and delicious. How to serve it without letting anyone see it? One strategy is to hide it underneath the meat, spooning a little into the serving dish or plate before laying down the sliced pork. Or incorporate it into your chosen starch: fold it into cooked rice, toss with cooked pasta, or stir into polenta or mashed potatoes. Finally, be sure your accompaniments are bright and colorful: bright green vegetables, beets, citrus. . . .

My Mother's Polish Sausage Stew

SERVES 3 TO 4

Absolutely simple and restorative, this is one of the best winter-warming suppers. The term "stew" is used loosely here; New Englanders will find this dish similar to their beloved, corned beef–based "boiled dinner." Serve with rye crackers and cucumbers.

1 pound kielbasa (Polish smoked pork/beef sausage), cut into 6 pieces

1 small head green cabbage, cut lengthwise, through the stem, into 6 wedges

10 boiling onions, peeled, or 2 to 3 small onions, peeled and quartered

3 small carrots, peeled and each cut in half

6 small red or yellow potatoes, about golf ball–size, unpeeled

8 cups cold water

1 tablespoon salt, plus more as needed

Throw all the ingredients into a large pot and bring to a boil. Reduce the heat to low and simmer for about 10 minutes. Taste the broth for salt, adding more if necessary. Poke some of the potatoes and other vegetables with a small knife to make certain they are tender. Simmer longer if necessary. Let stand, covered, off the heat for about 5 more minutes. To each guest serve a couple of pieces of sausage and an assortment of vegetables swimming in plenty of broth in a large bowl. Serve with a knife, fork, and spoon.

CHAPTER 10

Chicken and Turkey

I've kept egg-laying chickens at various times and once raised one to eat (it was delicious). I've also raised turkeys, beginning with one in Hawaii. That Thanksgiving, we thanked the turkey, we thanked the universe, and we thanked each other. A few years later, at Deep Springs I enjoyed raising a flock of two dozen Bourbon Red turkeys, letting them have free run of my yard. But alas, tragedy struck, at least from my perspective: half the flock was picked off by some very lucky coyotes in a single night. I found turkey feathers strewn across a field.

I am grateful to know the satisfaction of producing my own food, but it's a lot of work. I am grateful to know, quite intimately, how much energy goes into producing just a little meat. I am also grateful for all those birds, raised from chicks, in all their incarnations: their youth, their life, their corporal selves. We took the lives of these animals and incorporated them into our own.

If you use kosher chicken or turkey, reduce the salt in these recipes to a pinch: kosher poultry is already salted.

Roast Chicken

SERVES 3 TO 4

Once, as a fascinating experiment, I raised a chicken "for the table." Wanting to cook it very simply, I used this method, based on what Paul Bertolli, in *Chez Panisse Cooking,* calls his "tribute to roast chicken." Seasoned like fresh Italian sausage, this chicken has become many people's favorite over the years. At Deep Springs I serve whole chickens family-style—I put the birds on oval platters, garnish with sliced lemons and parsley sprigs, place a carving knife and fork alongside, and put one on each table in the Boardinghouse. In this way, the students gradually learn how to carve a chicken.

If you would like to roast a cut-up chicken or 4 pounds of chicken parts, increase the oven heat to 450°F—the chicken will take only about 30 minutes to cook, and the higher heat will help the skin to crisp in this shorter amount of time.

1 whole chicken, about 4 pounds

1½ teaspoons salt

¾ teaspoon black pepper

1½ teaspoons fennel seed, coarsely crushed

¼ teaspoon red pepper flakes

¼ teaspoon dried thyme

Pull the excess fat out of the cavity and around the neck flap of the chicken. Tie the legs together with a length of butcher twine. Tuck the wings behind the neck. Set the chicken out at room temperature for 1 hour. (Once the chicken has begun to come to room temperature, don't change your mind and decide to cook it another day!)

Heat the oven to 425°F. Mix the salt, pepper, fennel seed, red pepper, and thyme together in a small bowl. Rub the seasoning all over the chicken, inside and out. Rub a greater proportion of seasoning on the breast. Roast the chicken, breast side up, on a rack (or simply on a foil-covered rimmed baking sheet, with the foil's shiny side facing up) for 1 hour, or until an instant-read thermometer inserted in the thickest part of the breast or thigh registers 165°F. Using a small knife, you may peek into the interior of one of the thighs—no pink should remain, nor should any pink-colored juices run out. Let the chicken rest for 10 minutes before carving.

Cumin Roast Chicken

Sometimes I substitute cumin seeds for the fennel, and it's an entirely different bird.

Holiday Roast Chicken

SERVES 3 TO 4

Here, the chicken undergoes a light cure for two days in a brine before being roasted. This festive treatment tenderizes and seasons the meat deliciously down to the bone.

Use the brine recipe for Tender Cured Pork Chops (page 336). The juniper berries in the brine will impart a flavor evocative of wild game—especially appropriate with pork but a bit unusual with chicken; you decide whether or not to include them. Let the chicken—either parts or a whole bird—soak in the brine, completely submerged, for 36 hours.

Remove the chicken, pat dry with paper towels, and put on a rack, *uncovered*, in the refrigerator for several more hours or overnight (this helps the skin dry and emerge crisp after roasting).

Roast the chicken as directed in the previous recipe (omitting the spice rub): for a whole chicken, roast at 425°F for about an hour; for parts, roast at 450°F for about 30 minutes.

Marmalade Chicken

SERVES 3 TO 4

To prepare this delicious chicken, you allow salt and pepper to penetrate into the meat for several hours or overnight but apply the marmalade just before baking. Why not just marinate the chicken in the marmalade, too? Because the concentration of sugar in the marmalade will draw moisture out of the chicken, ultimately resulting in tougher, drier, less flavorful meat. What's more, the marmalade, now diluted, will fail to coat the chicken and will merely pool in the pan. This is very good with Walnut Couscous (page 396).

> 1 large chicken, cut up into 8 pieces
>
> 1 teaspoon salt
>
> few pinches of cayenne pepper
>
> black pepper
>
> 1 large red onion, thinly sliced
>
> ½ cup marmalade, any type (to make your own, see page 434)

Pat the chicken dry with paper towels. Rub with salt, cayenne, and black pepper, putting a slightly larger proportion of the seasoning on the breasts. Let the chicken sit, covered and refrigerated, for several hours or overnight.

continued...

... *continued*

Heat the oven to 350°F. Line a large, rimmed baking sheet with aluminum foil (shiny side up), and scatter with the sliced onions. In a big bowl, toss the chicken with the marmalade and place, skin side up, on the sheet, evenly spaced, tucking the onions underneath the chicken. Scrape all the remaining marmalade from the bowl onto the top surfaces of the largest pieces of chicken. Bake for an hour. Let the pan rest at a slight tilt for about 10 minutes so the juice pools. Transfer the chicken (and the onions, if you like) to a warmed platter or plates. Carefully pour off the liquid into a cup, then spoon off and discard the clear fat from the top. Use the remaining flavorful brown sweet-salty juice as a sauce.

Sautéed Chicken Breast

SERVES 2 TO 3

Here is a thorough run-down on how to sauté a chicken breast. It's elegant, quick, easy, reliable, and universally loved and appreciated.

Much effort is made in this recipe to cook the skin to an appealing brown crispiness. However, if you choose to use skinless breasts, they too can emerge from the pan savory and juicy, provided you don't overcook them. Once you get the hang of cooking chicken breasts this way, you can infinitely vary the flavors by including in the seasoning, or in the sauce, judicious amounts of lemon zest, fresh herbs, cayenne, ground chile, cumin, fennel seed, or other aromatic ingredients.

A single chicken breast half might weigh 8 ounces or more; accompanied by potatoes or rice, a vegetable, and salad, it is ample—sometimes too much—for a serving. But these chicken breasts are also good served cold in their sauce, thinly sliced, so do not be afraid of having extra.

1 boneless, skin-on whole chicken breast or 2 boneless, skin-on breast halves

¾ teaspoon salt, plus a pinch

several twists of black pepper

2 teaspoons olive oil

2 tablespoons dry white wine or chicken stock

1 tablespoon cold butter

1 teaspoon fresh lemon juice

A whole, boneless chicken breast is heart shaped; remove the tough seam down the middle and you have two teardrop-shaped chicken breast halves, each with a tapering "tenderloin"—a small, separate strip of meat loosely attached to the underside. I usually pull these tenderloins off and cook them alongside the breasts. Using a small, sharp knife, trim off any excess fat, tendon, or bit of bone. Trim out the tough little tendon in the center of the rounded end of each breast. Put the chicken breasts in a plastic bag. Using the smooth side of a meat pounder or other heavy object, gently pound the rounded, fatter end of each breast half until it is the same thickness—about ¾ inch—as the pointed, thinner end.

Pat the skin surface of the chicken dry with a paper towel, and season the chicken all over with the ¾ teaspoon salt and the pepper.

Set a wide, heavy skillet over a medium flame. Let the pan heat for about 2 minutes. Raise the heat to medium-high, and add the olive oil. When the oil just begins to smoke, place the chicken breasts in the pan, skin side down (first stretch and smooth the skin so as much of its surface as possible contacts the pan). You should hear an excited sizzle: this, to me, is one of the happiest sounds in cooking. The sputtering grease vapor will leave a mess on your stove—a spatter screen helps. Cook the breast halves on the skin side for 4 to 5 minutes, or until the skin has crisped to a nice mahogany brown.

Turn and cook the skinless side for 2 to 3 minutes, or until the breast is just cooked through (if the breast is thicker than ¾ inch, it might take more time). The texture of the breast, when pressed with a finger, will have progressed from squishy to just springy. Transfer the chicken, skin side up, to a warmed plate while you make a pan sauce.

Pour off any fat in the pan. Add the wine or stock—it will boil up furiously. With a spatula or a wooden spoon, scrape the browned bits from the bottom of the pan—they will dissolve into the sauce. This brown flavor residue is called the *fond*, most conveniently translated as "flavor base." When the wine has reduced by half, swirl the tablespoon of cold butter into the sauce, off the heat. Squeeze lemon juice—1 to 2 teaspoons—into the sauce and add a pinch of salt. Pour over the chicken breasts and serve immediately.

Cayenne-Rubbed Chicken with Potatoes and Garlic

SERVES 3 TO 4

This roast chicken is a simple, frequent, and much-loved dinner in our household, always served with a salad or a simply prepared green vegetable. The cayenne pepper (extremely healthful, by the way) is present but not overpowering. If dark meat is preferred, leg-thigh portions are equally good prepared this way.

2 teaspoons salt

2 teaspoons paprika

½ teaspoon cayenne pepper

½ teaspoon black pepper

1 tablespoon olive oil

3 medium yellow, red, or white potatoes, cut lengthwise into quarters, then crosswise into ¼-inch slices

about 15 cloves garlic or more, unpeeled

2½ pounds bone-in, skin-on chicken breast halves, about 3 large or 4 medium, excess fat trimmed off

Heat the oven to 450°F. In a small bowl, combine the salt, paprika, cayenne, and black pepper. Divide this mixture in half. Put the olive oil in a large bowl. Add the potatoes, unpeeled garlic cloves, and half of the seasoning mixture, tossing well to coat. Dump into a shallow baking dish and press down to make an even layer. Rub the remaining seasoning mixture all over the chicken breasts, including the underside. Arrange the chicken breasts atop the potatoes. Bake for about 25 minutes if the chicken breasts are large, for a bit less time if they are smaller. The breasts should feel firm all the way through when pressed with a finger—they should register about 150°F at their thickest point.

Remove the chicken to a plate. Give the potatoes and garlic a gentle stir, and return to the oven to finish cooking, 5 to 8 minutes more. If there is a lot of fat at the bottom of the baking dish, let the dish rest for a few minutes at a slight tilt so the fat pools to one side; scoop the potatoes from the other side. (Save this flavorful fat for sautéing vegetables.) Serve a chicken breast and some potatoes and garlic to each person, letting them squeeze the roasted garlic over everything.

Crispy Pan-Fried Chicken

SERVES 2 TO 3

This recipe uses the classic three-step breading process, in which you dredge the seasoned chicken first in flour, then in egg, then in breadcrumbs. The coating adheres well, can be done hours ahead of time, and emerges from the pan irresistibly golden and crispy. Certain varieties of mild white fish, such as snapper or cod, are also good treated this way. Whether served with chicken or fish, Meyer Lemon–Olive Relish (page 428) is a superb accompaniment.

Homemade breadcrumbs will lend their own character to the finished product, but be assured that packaged Japanese breadcrumbs, called panko, are made exactly for this purpose and will produce an incomparably light and crispy coating. Finally, for a rich, luxurious flavor, use clarified butter instead of vegetable oil to fry the chicken.

2 boneless, skinless chicken breast halves

1 clove garlic, crushed

1 or 2 pinches of dried thyme

½ teaspoon salt

black pepper

BREADING (APPROXIMATE AMOUNTS)

⅓ cup all-purpose flour

1 egg

1 teaspoon Dijon mustard

1 cup dry breadcrumbs (use Japanese panko for best results)

canola oil or other vegetable oil or clarified butter (see page 63) for frying

Trim any fat or gristle from the chicken breast. Gently pull away the "tenderloin"—the tapered strip of meat—from underneath each breast. Put the chicken breasts in a plastic bag, and with a meat pounder or other heavy object, gently pound the breasts to an even ½-inch thickness. Cut each breast in half lengthwise. Pat the breasts and tenderloins dry with paper towels, and season with the crushed garlic, a pinch or two of dried thyme, the salt, and pepper to taste.

To bread the chicken, sprinkle the flour over a wide plate. Beat the egg with the mustard in a wide, shallow bowl. Spread the breadcrumbs over another wide plate. Dredge the chicken in the flour, then dip it in the egg, coating all sides, then in the breadcrumbs. Lay the pieces of breaded chicken on a rack set atop a baking sheet and let rest for about 20 minutes. This "sets" the breading, allowing the crumbs and flour to thoroughly hydrate, for fewer spatters while frying.

continued . . .

. . . continued

In a wide, heavy skillet or sauté pan, heat about ¼ inch of vegetable oil or clarified butter over a medium-high flame. To test whether the oil is hot enough, throw in a breadcrumb: if it sizzles excitedly right away and browns after 15 to 20 seconds, the oil is ready. Gently lay the chicken in the pan. If your pan is on the small side, cook the chicken breasts in batches. Crowding the chicken in the pan cools down the oil too much, allowing it to saturate the coating. Let the chicken fry on one side until golden brown. Check the underside after about 30 seconds—if it has browned too quickly, just turn the chicken, lower the heat, and continue to turn the chicken a few times during cooking. It should take about 2 minutes on each side to cook the chicken through, 4 to 5 minutes in all. You may cut into a piece of the chicken to make sure it is cooked through. Drain briefly on paper towels and serve immediately.

Tarragon-Roasted Chicken with Tomatoes

SERVES 6

This is a superb way to prepare light or dark meat. Serve with bread to soak up the flavorful tomato-chicken juices. In the cooler seasons, Roma tomatoes, ripened on a windowsill, are fine. Once, to celebrate the last day of a semester at Deep Springs, we accompanied this chicken with Stuffed Artichokes (page 214) and Wild Mushroom Risotto (page 403)—a great menu.

6 large, bone-in, skin-on chicken breast halves or 1 whole chicken, cut into parts

2 teaspoons salt

2 tablespoons olive oil

½ teaspoon freshly ground black pepper, plus more for seasoning tomatoes

3 tablespoons coarsely chopped fresh tarragon, plus an extra sprig for garnish

1 teaspoon finely grated lemon zest

1 pound red, ripe tomatoes

In a large dish, rub the chicken breasts all over with 1½ teaspoons of the salt, olive oil, pepper, 2 tablespoons of the tarragon, and lemon zest. Cover the chicken with plastic wrap, and leave it to marinate at room temperature for 30 minutes, or refrigerate overnight. If refrigerated, set the chicken out at room temperature for about 1 hour before serving.

Heat the oven to 450°F. Lightly oil a large, shallow roasting pan. Arrange the breasts in the pan, pat the skin dry with paper towels, and roast for 25 to 30 minutes, or just until firm and no longer pink in the middle. An instant-read thermometer inserted into the middle of the thickest part should register 165°F. The skin should be golden and crispy. Remove the chicken to a warmed serving platter.

While the chicken is roasting, cut the tops out of the tomatoes and cut them into quarters. As soon as the chicken is out of the roasting pan, drain off the fat that has accumulated in the pan, and return the pan to the hot oven. After it has heated for a moment or two, throw in the tomatoes with the remaining ½ teaspoon salt, pepper to taste, and the remaining tablespoon of tarragon, and gently toss the tomatoes

in the hot pan drippings, scraping up any brown bits on the bottom of the pan. The tomatoes will release juice. After a couple of minutes, when the tomatoes are barely warmed through, distribute them evenly over the chicken and pour some of the juice over all. Garnish with a sprig of tarragon. Make sure everyone gets some of the flavorful juices in serving.

Variations

If you prefer, substitute 1 to 2 tablespoons of fresh thyme leaves or ½ cup chopped fresh basil for the tarragon. Both, like tarragon, are good with chicken and tomatoes.

Chicken Cooked Under a Brick

SERVES 4

This is an elegant treatment for the good old chicken leg, as festive as a sautéed chicken breast but cheaper and more laborious. It's luxuriously boneless, with browned, crispy skin and deeply flavored meat. The aluminum foil–wrapped brick is not heated, but its weight helps the meat to cook rapidly, the fat to render, and the skin to crisp. Serve with Parmesan polenta and vegetables of the season.

Deep Springs students like this flavorful chicken, but they love the name. Once, a student baked some sourdough bread that utterly failed to rise, so the Student Cooks were inspired to make "Chicken cooked under Michael's bread."

"Chicken leg" denotes the entire leg: the drumstick and the thigh, still attached to one another. One large chicken leg is enough for a serving. You may also use thighs, allowing two per serving; see the variation at the end of the recipe for skinless thighs. Perhaps you have the good fortune to know a butcher who will expertly bone the chicken legs but keep the skin on for you. More probably, you will have to bone the legs yourself.

EQUIPMENT

2 standard-sized, clean bricks (they should fit into your skillet)

—

4 whole chicken legs, skin on (for skinless thighs, see the variation below)

1½ teaspoons salt

1 medium clove garlic, finely crushed

1 teaspoon fresh thyme leaves, or ½ teaspoon dried thyme

freshly ground black pepper

¼ teaspoon hot red pepper flakes

1 teaspoon olive oil, plus more for sautéing

Wrap the bricks in 2 layers of aluminum foil, shiny side facing out. Make sure there is a clean, seamless side to each one.

Bone, but don't skin, the chicken legs. *Warning: This procedure offers many opportunities for poking and cutting oneself—be very careful; always point the knife toward the surface of the cutting board, not your fingers!* Put the leg on a clean cutting board, skin side down. First, visually and with your fingers, locate the bones, then make a cut along their length with a boning knife or small, sharp knife. Keep making shallow cuts along the bone and around the joint until the bone is separated from the meat, trying to avoid piercing the skin. It's fine if the meat is not too neat-looking—rips or shreds will be hidden in the cooking. Repeat with the remaining legs. Season the chicken with the salt, garlic, thyme, black pepper to taste, red pepper flakes, and 1 teaspoon olive oil. Let marinate, covered, for an hour, turning the pieces a few times.

Heat a large, heavy skillet over a medium flame for several minutes. Lightly brush the clean side of each brick with olive oil, and drizzle a little oil into the skillet. Pat the skin side of the chicken dry with paper towels. Lay 2 of the legs, skin side down, in the hot skillet (they should sizzle happily), and place the 2 bricks on top, weighting the chicken down. When the skin is golden brown and crisp, after about 2 minutes, they are ready to turn. Cook on the other side, *without the brick,* for about 2 more minutes. Cook the remaining 2 pieces of chicken in the same manner. Serve immediately, while the skin is still crisp.

Bacon-Wrapped Chicken Cooked Under a Brick

In a hurry, and have only boneless, skinless chicken thighs available? Just replace the crispy fat of chicken skin with the crispy fat of bacon. Using 6 boneless, skinless thighs and a lighter hand with the salt, carefully wrap a thin strip of bacon (cheaper bacon is usually thinner) around each marinated, seasoned thigh, and cook as directed in the master recipe. The bacon will render its fat and become crisp during the cooking.

Herbed Braised Chicken, with Five Variations

SERVES 3 TO 4

To braise meat means to cook it slowly in a small amount of flavorful liquid. Often, meat to be braised is first browned on the stovetop, but in this easier method, the chicken skin browns and crisps in the heat of the oven while the meat beneath slowly cooks to a melting tenderness. Most people who think they don't like dark meat find they love it prepared this way. This recipe (and all variations) may be prepared a day ahead and then popped back into the oven on serving day to heat through and recrisp the skin. If you wish to use boneless, skinless chicken thighs, the result will be more of a stew than a proper braise but will still be good. Use about 8 boneless, skinless thighs, and submerge the meat completely in the liquid before putting it into the oven.

4 whole chicken legs or 6 large bone-in, skin-on chicken thighs, about 2¼ pounds total

1½ teaspoons plus a pinch of salt

freshly ground black pepper

continued...

. . . *continued*

2 teaspoons chopped fresh thyme,
or ½ teaspoon dried thyme

2 teaspoons chopped fresh sage,
or ¼ teaspoon dried sage

1½ teaspoons chopped fresh rosemary,
or ½ teaspoon dried rosemary

1 tablespoon olive oil

1 yellow onion, sliced

2 carrots, peeled, split lengthwise, and
sliced on the diagonal

1 stalk celery, split lengthwise and
sliced on the diagonal

2 to 3 cloves garlic, crushed

½ cup dry white wine

about 2 cups chicken stock

1 bay leaf

2 tablespoons chopped parsley

FOR SERVING (CHOOSE ONE)

Rice (page 398)

Handmade Egg Noodles (page 388)

Polenta (page 404)

Spaetzle (page 397)

Scallion-Buttermilk Potatoes (page 249)

Heat the oven to 350°F. Pat the chicken dry with paper towels. Trim off any excess fatty skin around the thigh, if you like. Season with 1½ teaspoons salt and black pepper to taste. Rub the thyme, sage, and rosemary all over the chicken; if using dried herbs, crumble them first in your hand. Let the chicken sit at room temperature while preparing the vegetables.

Heat the olive oil in a large saucepan over medium-high heat. Throw in the onion, carrot, celery, and garlic with a good pinch of salt. Cook the vegetables briefly, stirring frequently, until they begin to go limp, about 3 minutes. Transfer to a 9-by-13-inch baking dish or other dish in which the chicken pieces will fit without crowding. Arrange the seasoned, herbed chicken over the vegetables.

In the same saucepan, bring the wine and stock to a boil with the bay leaf, and pour into the dish (don't pour it directly over the chicken, or you'll rinse off the herbs and seasoning) until the chicken is halfway covered with the liquid. Put the dish in the oven, uncovered. Let the chicken bake for about 30 minutes, then turn the oven temperature down to 300°F. It shouldn't boil hard or the end result could be dry (chicken, however, is more forgiving in this respect than beef). Let the chicken simmer until it is very tender, almost falling off the bone, 50 minutes to 1 hour more. Even after the chicken has cooked through, it still needs further simmering to become tender. Don't baste the chicken, or the skin won't be crisp. Serve soon after it emerges from the oven, while the skin is crisp.

Carefully pour off the pan juices into a deep bowl, let settle for a moment, then spoon the fat—the clear layer—off the top. Serve the chicken in wide bowls over rice, polenta, noodles, spaetzle, or potatoes, with plenty of the flavorful broth spooned around and parsley sprinkled on top. The vegetables will have given much of their flavor to the broth and chicken. Serve them, or not—they are still tasty, in a homely way.

Braised Chicken with Fennel

Select a large fennel bulb with feathery fronds attached. Separate the bulb from the young fronds. Omit the herbs from the master recipe, adding instead a strip of lemon zest, a pinch of hot red pepper flakes, and ½ teaspoon crushed fennel seeds. Quarter the fennel bulb and braise it alongside the chicken, serving a quarter to each person. Garnish the finished dish with the coarsely chopped fennel fronds.

Chicken Paprikash

Follow the master recipe, omitting the herbs, carrots, and celery. Use red or white wine. When seasoning the chicken, include a teaspoon of sweet Hungarian paprika. Include 2 to 3 *tablespoons* of paprika with the onions. Whisk together some of the defatted liquid with enough sour cream to make a slightly thick, rich sauce. Serve the chicken, onions, and sauce over the starch of your choice, garnished with chopped parsley or dill.

Braised Chicken in Red Wine with Mushrooms

This variation is in the spirit of the French classic, *coq au vin*. Omit the sage and rosemary from the master recipe. Instead of white wine and chicken stock, use a full bottle of good-tasting, fruity red wine.

Marinate the chicken in the wine overnight, draining it well (reserve the wine) and patting it dry before seasoning with the salt, pepper, and thyme. Cut 4 ounces of thick bacon crosswise into ½-inch strips. Slowly brown the bacon in the skillet. Remove and reserve the cooked bacon, and cook the vegetables in the rendered fat. Transfer the vegetables to the baking dish, add the chicken and reserved wine, and braise as directed in the master recipe. While the chicken is braising, sauté 6 to 8 ounces sliced mushrooms in butter until golden brown (see page 237). Add the bacon and mushrooms to the braise in the last 15 minutes of cooking. Serve with boiled buttered potatoes, and spoon plenty of the dark, flavorful sauce over it.

If you have dried wild mushrooms, you may use them in this dish, in place of or in addition to the fresh mushrooms: reconstitute them in some of the wine and braise them with the chicken. Depending on their texture and flavor after cooking, you may or may not want to serve them with the chicken. Once my friend Elge and I made a startlingly good *coq au vin* using dried lobster mushrooms, pinot noir, pearl onions, and a strip of orange zest.

Chicken with Tomatoes and Olives

Substitute a 14-ounce can of diced tomatoes (in juice) for the chicken stock in the master recipe. Use red or white wine. Scatter ½ cup of flavorful oil-cured black

continued...

. . . continued

olives or whole green olives over the vegetables after transferring them to the baking dish. Serve each person 3 to 4 braised olives along with the chicken. Polenta (page 404) enriched with Parmesan is an ideal accompaniment.

Chicken Curry

Follow the master recipe, omitting the celery, wine, and all herbs. Double the amount of garlic, and include with the garlic and onion 2 ounces (about the size of your big toe) of fresh ginger, minced, a teaspoon each of ground cumin and coriander, and 2 tablespoons curry powder (a recipe for homemade curry powder is at right). Cook the vegetables in ghee (see page 63) or butter or vegetable oil. Serve over basmati rice. If you like, lavishly sprinkle the finished dish with coarsely chopped cilantro.

CURRY POWDER

You may make your own curry powder if you have a coffee grinder designated for spices. Whether authentic or not, this medium-spicy blend is flavorful and well balanced.

- 2 teaspoons coriander seed
- 2 teaspoons cumin seed
- 1 teaspoon fennel seed
- 1 teaspoon brown mustard seed
- ½ teaspoon white peppercorns
- 7 cloves
- 2 teaspoons hot red pepper flakes
- ½ teaspoon ground cinnamon
- 1 teaspoon ground turmeric

Grind the whole spices to the finest powder in your grinder, then stir in the cinnamon and turmeric. This makes a little over 3 tablespoons; store the extra in the freezer.

Chicken and Dumplings

SERVES 6 TO 8

When I serve this at Deep Springs, many students ask, "So, what exactly is a dumpling?" Dumplings, bits of dough simmered in broth or water, are the great-grandmother of pasta. They are an all-but-extinguished art in American cooking; the appeal of the simple, savory softness of a dumpling has been forgotten in our al dente age. Matzoh Ball Soup (page 362), fluffy matzoh dumplings served in rich chicken broth, is to my mind the greatest dumpling dish in the world. Chicken and dumplings—tender, thick dumplings in a hearty, simple chicken stew—is matzoh ball soup's country cousin. These herb-flecked dumplings are tender yet have textural character at the same time. They are cooked separately in water for a lighter, more digestible, cleaner-tasting result than if they were cooked directly in the broth.

CHICKEN STEW

1 whole chicken, about 3½ pounds, with giblets

2 cups chicken stock (page 364)

5 cups water

2¾ teaspoons salt, or more as needed

1 bay leaf

¼ teaspoon dried thyme, or several sprigs fresh thyme

2 inner celery ribs with leaves

½ large yellow onion, thickly sliced

¼ teaspoon hot red pepper flakes

pinch of dried sage, or 1 to 2 fresh sage leaves

1 teaspoon butter

1 large carrot, peeled and cut into chunks on the diagonal

1½ large yellow onions, cut into medium dice

2 stalks celery, cut on the diagonal into thin slices

6 tablespoons all-purpose flour

1 cup cold water

freshly ground black pepper

DUMPLINGS

¼ bunch flat-leaf parsley

⅓ cup pale, tender inner celery leaves

1½ cups all-purpose flour

1 teaspoon baking powder

scant ¼ teaspoon baking soda

¾ teaspoon salt

3 tablespoons cold butter

1 jumbo-sized egg, or 1½ regular eggs

3 tablespoons buttermilk

continued . . .

. . . continued

To make the stew, remove as much excess fat as possible from the neck area and from the main cavity of the chicken. Using kitchen scissors, trim away the fatty parts of the skin around both openings. If there are giblets, remove the skin from the neck. Put the whole chicken, neck, giblets, chicken stock, water, and 2½ teaspoons of the salt in a large stockpot (the liquid will almost, but not quite, cover the chicken). Bring to a boil over high heat, then immediately reduce the heat to a simmer.

As the chicken begins to boil, skim off any scum that collects on the surface. Once the chicken and broth have settled down to a simmer (with small bubbles appearing not too rapidly here and there on the surface of the liquid), skim any remaining scum and add the bay leaf, thyme, celery, onion, pepper flakes, and sage. Cook for 30 minutes from the time the chicken reaches a simmer, turning the chicken in the broth three or four times. Remove from the heat, cover the pot, and let sit for 5 minutes. With 2 large, sturdy spatulas or spoons, carefully remove the chicken to a deep platter to cool. If there is a visible slick of fat on the surface of the broth, skim off some, but not all, of it with a wide spoon. Keep the broth hot.

Meanwhile, cook the vegetables. In a large saucepan big enough to hold the finished stew (a 4-quart pan is ideal), melt the teaspoon of butter over a medium-high flame. Throw in the carrot, onion, and celery with the remaining ¼ teaspoon salt. Cook the vegetables, stirring frequently but otherwise keeping the pan covered, until they are translucent, about 5 minutes. Pour the hot chicken stock through a wire-mesh strainer over the vegetables, and bring to a simmer. (Don't wash the stockpot yet; it will be used to cook the dumplings.)

Vigorously shake the flour and water together for a full minute in a jar with a tight-fitting lid. Quickly whisk this slurry into the hot vegetables and broth, and simmer until the liquid is thickened and the vegetables are tender, 10 to 15 minutes. Add pepper and taste for seasoning, adding salt if necessary. Keep warm.

Once the chicken is cool enough to handle, remove and discard the skin and tear the meat off the bones, discarding any remaining visible fat. Cut the meat into large bite-size chunks, and reserve in a bowl.

To make the dumplings, chop the parsley and celery leaves together finely. Reserve half these herbs for garnishing the finished stew. In a medium bowl, sift together the flour, baking powder, baking soda, and salt. Slice the butter into the dry ingredients, then work the mixture with your fingertips until the butter is evenly dispersed throughout the mixture and the visible pieces of butter are quite small—lentil sized.

Whisk the egg, buttermilk, and remaining chopped herbs together in a small bowl, then drizzle this mixture over the dry ingredients and mix just until the dry ingredients are mostly moistened—there should be streaks of dry flour here and there. Cover the surface of the dough with plastic wrap and let rest at room temperature for 10 minutes. Put a gallon of water on to boil while you roll and cut the dumplings.

For best results, work the dough only as much as specified in the following instructions; overworking the dough could result in tough, chewy dumplings. Dust a clean, dry countertop with flour. Turn the rested dough onto the countertop (the dough will appear very raggedy at this point), dust your hands with flour, and gently pat it out to a rough square, about 8 by 8 inches, turning and lightly dusting with flour as necessary to prevent sticking. Fold the square of dough in thirds, as you would fold a letter. Pat this folded dough out the long way until it is doubled in length, forming a long rectangle. Moisten the top surface of the dough lightly with water. Roll it up to form a long, thick rope. Cut this in half. Gently roll each piece on the countertop with your hands until it is doubled in length. With a sharp knife dipped (and redipped, as necessary) in flour, cut into ¼-inch-thick rounds, and arrange the dumplings in a single layer on a floured baking sheet.

Finally, cook the dumplings. Add a tablespoon of salt to the boiling water and gently drop in all the dumplings, stirring them around gently. They are cooked 1 to 2 minutes after they rise to the surface (rinse one in cold water and taste; if it still seems raw, let the dumplings cook for a minute longer). Gently lift them out with a wire skimmer or a slotted spoon and transfer them to the hot chicken stew. Add the reserved chicken and the reserved chopped herbs to the stew, and serve in wide bowls.

Matzoh Ball Soup

SERVES 8 TO 10; MAKES ABOUT
30 MATZOH BALLS

Here you have the king of chicken soups, with fluffy dumplings reposing in a luxurious, golden, rich chicken broth.

RICH CHICKEN BROTH

1 large roasting chicken, about
4½ pounds, kosher if preferred

1 medium onion, sliced

1 medium carrot, peeled

1 stalk celery

4 sprigs parsley

8 black peppercorns

1 bay leaf

a 3-inch piece of lemongrass (optional)

2 teaspoons salt

MATZOH BALLS

¼ cup rendered chicken fat, at room temperature

4 large eggs, separated, at room temperature

1 cup matzoh meal

2 teaspoons salt

¼ cup chicken stock, at room temperature

2 to 3 tablespoons chopped parsley

To make the broth, heat the oven to 450°F. Rinse the chicken well and pat dry with paper towels. Remove and reserve the large fat pockets from the main cavity and the excess fat from around the neck flap. Using kitchen shears, snip the fat into small pieces. Put the fat in a small saucepan with about ¼ cup water and cook over medium heat until the water has boiled away (the bubbling sound will give way to a sizzling sound). Pour off the liquid fat through a mesh strainer to use in the matzoh balls—you should have at least ¼ cup.

Meanwhile, roast the chicken, unseasoned, in a roasting pan until the skin is deep brown and crispy, about 45 minutes. Put the chicken and any juice that has accumulated in the pan in a large stockpot, cover by 3 inches with cold water, and bring to a boil over high heat, skimming off any scum that rises to the surface.

As soon as the broth reaches a boil, reduce the heat to low and add the onion, carrot, celery, parsley sprigs, peppercorns, bay leaf, lemongrass, if desired (quite untraditional but subtly delicious), and salt to the pot. Adjust the heat as necessary to maintain a simmer—if the broth boils hard, the fat will emulsify into the liquid and the broth will be cloudy and not as clean-tasting. Gently simmer broth for 1 hour, breaking up the chicken and stirring from time to time. Strain the broth through a mesh strainer, allow the fat to rise to the surface, and skim much, but not all, of it off with a spoon. Stir the broth and taste for salt—it may need several pinches more—the taste should be rich and deep and very good. The meat of the chicken is quite overcooked by this point; most of its flavor and value have been given over to the broth.

To make the matzoh balls, combine the chicken fat and egg yolks in a large bowl. Stir in the matzoh meal, salt, and stock. In a perfectly clean, separate bowl, beat the egg whites with clean beaters until soft peaks form. Fold a third of the whites into the matzoh meal mixture to lighten it, then gently fold in the remaining egg whites, just until the mixture is uniform. Chill, covered, for 1 hour.

Wet your hands and lightly form 30 balls about 1 inch in diameter, placing them on an oiled plate. Bring a gallon of water to a boil in a wide 8-quart pot. Add 1½ tablespoons salt—the water should taste lightly salty. Slide the matzoh balls into the boiling water, all at once. Bring up to a simmer. Cover the pot and simmer gently for about 20 minutes. Remove the matzoh balls to warmed bowls with a slotted spoon.

Bring the chicken stock to a boil. Place 3 hot matzoh balls in each bowl, cover with hot chicken broth, sprinkle with a bit of chopped parsley, and serve.

Gin Chicken Liver Pâté

SERVES 4 TO 6 AS AN HORS D'OEUVRE

This pâté is adapted from a recipe by Elizabeth David, one of my favorite cookbook authors. (Strictly speaking, it is not pâté, but "chicken liver spread" just doesn't sound good, and "gin chicken livers," as Elizabeth David calls this recipe, brings to mind a dish of whole livers.) Whenever you ply your guests with wine, beer, or especially cocktails, it is wise to serve munchy food that is high in fat— the fat helps the alcohol metabolize more slowly in the body. Otherwise, if your drink is strong, your empty-stomached guests may pass out before you've had a chance to serve dinner. This simple liver spread, served with crackers or bread, will work splendidly. A dish of olives complements it well.

4 ounces (weighed after trimming) very fresh chicken livers, trimmed of veins and fat

6 tablespoons unsalted butter, at room temperature

1 pinch salt, plus ¾ teaspoon

3 tablespoons gin

a few twists of black pepper

continued ...

. . . continued

FOR SERVING

crackers (see page 143 to 144) or toasts

olives or pickled fruit (see page 436)

In a medium-sized skillet over a medium-high flame, sauté the livers in 1 tablespoon of the butter with a good pinch of salt until brown on the outside and still a little pink on the inside, about 2 minutes. Remove from the heat and transfer the livers to the jar of a blender. Let the pan cool for a moment. Pour the gin into the hot pan to deglaze, using a wooden spoon to scrape up the browned bits and letting them dissolve into the gin. Blend the livers, gin, remaining 5 tablespoons butter, ¾ teaspoon salt, and pepper until completely smooth. Pack into a small, deep glass or china bowl, cover, and chill. Serve thickly spread on crackers or toasts and accompany with olives. It is also very good with pickled fruit.

Chicken Stock

MAKES ABOUT 12 CUPS

This basic chicken stock is a perfect base for soups, stews, or risotto. The chicken leg meat is sacrificed; when it emerges from the stockpot it has given its flavor to the stock and is not especially tasty.

1 whole chicken, including gizzard, heart, and neck (liver gives a strong flavor; you may include it or not)

12 cups cold water

1 medium onion, coarsely chopped

1 medium carrot, peeled and coarsely chopped

1 stalk celery, cut into a few pieces

1 sprig thyme

1 bay leaf

1 teaspoon peppercorns

½ teaspoon crushed fennel seed

1 teaspoon salt

Using a boning knife or other narrow, sharp knife, cut out the 2 breast halves from the chicken and reserve for another use (such as Sautéed Chicken Breasts, page 348). Make a few gashes in the meaty parts of the chicken, to better release the flavor. Remove any chunks of fat around the cavity and neck. Put the chicken and giblets in a stockpot with the water and bring just to a boil. Immediately reduce the heat to medium. With a wide spoon, skim off the scum (as well as some, but not all, of the fat) that rises to the surface. You might need to do this a few times—the scum consists partly of impurities, and the stock will taste better if it is removed.

When the liquid is well skimmed, add the onion, carrot, celery, thyme, bay leaf, peppercorns, fennel seed, and salt. Raise the heat to quickly return the liquid to a boil, then immediately reduce to a lively simmer, with bubbles here and there in the pot. Don't let the stock boil hard. Covering the pot helps hold in the heat, but leave the lid slightly ajar. Let the stock simmer, skimming at times and stirring once or twice, for about an hour, then strain it through a fine-mesh sieve. Cool to room temperature, stirring occasionally, and refrigerate until needed.

Stock from Leftover Roast Chicken

A cooked chicken carcass, with most of the leg meat as well as the breast meat gone, will yield less flavor than a fresh chicken with much of the meat left on. Follow the recipe above, using 6 cups of water instead of 12.

Turkey Stock

A 12-pound turkey is more or less the equivalent of four 3-pound chickens. Multiply either of the recipes above accordingly to make some good turkey stock.

Apple- and Rosemary-Scented Roast Turkey

SERVES 8 TO 10 WITH LEFTOVERS

And here is how we prepare the Thanksgiving turkeys at Deep Springs, using apples from the orchard. Some of the apples are scattered in the main cavity, but most are stuffed into the neck cavity, providing moisture and aroma for the breast meat. The apples scent the bird while it roasts but are not necessarily meant to be eaten.

12-pound fresh turkey (natural, not flavor enhanced)

¼ cup apple cider vinegar

¼ cup salt, plus more for seasoning apples

2 tablespoons freshly ground black pepper, plus more for seasoning apples

1½ pounds flavorful cooking apples

4 sprigs rosemary

PAN GRAVY

1 cup water

⅔ cup all-purpose flour

3 cups chicken stock or giblet broth, cooled

continued . . .

. . . continued

salt and black pepper

chopped cooked giblets (optional)

¼ cup applejack (American apple brandy; optional)

If possible, *season the turkey 2 days in advance* (on Tuesday of Thanksgiving week). First, remove any excess fat from just inside the main cavity of the turkey and from inside the neck flap. Soak a paper towel in the cider vinegar and rub the turkey all over with it. Mix the salt and pepper in a small bowl and rub it evenly all over the turkey, inside and out. Put a greater proportion of salt and pepper on the breast. Cover and refrigerate the seasoned turkey for 2 days, turning it over a couple of times.

If you will be using the turkey giblets to enrich the gravy, cook them shortly after bringing the turkey home; they will keep better cooked than raw. I usually throw away the liver unless I knew the turkey when it was alive. Simmer the giblets in water to cover in a small saucepan until tender. When tender, drain, reserving the stock, and remove as much meat as possible from the neck, then chop the neck meat and the rest of the giblets finely. Store the stock and chopped giblets separately in the refrigerator until you make the gravy.

Set the turkey out at room temperature for about 3 hours before roasting. This will help it cook more evenly. (Once it's coming to room temperature, don't change your mind and decide to roast it another day!)

Heat the oven to 375°F. Choose a sturdy roasting pan of the proper size: it shouldn't be so small that the turkey has to be crammed in, nor so large that the juices cook away and burn in the heat of the oven. Tuck the wings behind the neck of the turkey and put the turkey in the pan, breast side up. Quarter, core, and slice the apples, and toss them with a little salt and pepper. Stuff most of the apples, along with 2 of the rosemary sprigs, into the neck flap. Scatter the remaining apples and rosemary into the main cavity. Roast the turkey, uncovered, for about 2 hours.

When an instant-read thermometer inserted into the thickest part of the thigh registers 160°F, the turkey is done. Alternately, you may peek into the interior of a thigh with a small knife—no pink should remain. Put the turkey in a warm place to rest for 10 minutes, then turn it *breast side down,* remove to a serving platter, and allow it to rest for another 10 minutes before turning it breast side up and carving.

To make the gravy, while the turkey is resting, pour all the juices from the roasting pan into a deep bowl. Carefully spoon off the fat (the clear layer) from the top. In a jar with a tight-fitting lid, shake the water and flour together vigorously for a full minute, until no flour lumps remain. Pour this slurry into the roasting pan, along with the chicken stock and the defatted juices, set the pan on medium-high heat, and bring to a boil, stirring and scraping the browned bits off the bottom of the pan with a wooden spoon, until thick. There should be no floury taste. Season the gravy with salt and pepper, and add the cooked giblets, if you have them. If you like, splash in a little applejack.

Turkey with Roasted Grapes

I like to serve this turkey in summer, or at times of the year other than Thanksgiving. Roast a turkey as described, substituting thyme for the rosemary, and sherry vinegar for the cider vinegar. Instead of apples, stuff the neck cavity with stemmed red seedless grapes. Instead of serving gravy, accompany the finished turkey with clusters of roasted red grapes. Heat the oven to 500°F. Separate a large bunch of red grapes into serving-sized clusters. Lay the clusters on an oiled baking sheet, and drizzle with olive oil. Lightly salt and pepper the grapes, and roast in the hot oven for about 7 minutes, or until the grapes are crackly. Serve warm or at room temperature with the turkey. Accompany with rice (the pilaf on page 400 is very good) and a big green salad garnished with toasted nuts.

Fish and Shellfish

Welcome to one of the briefest chapters in the book. Fish, rarely served at landlocked Deep Springs, is among the only truly wild foods we still eat regularly. Occasionally, a student will catch a trout in one of Deep Springs' reservoirs—these taste astonishingly sweet and fresh. On rarer occasions, a Deep Springs community member, returning from a trip to California's coast, will drive triumphantly into the Valley with much fanfare, bearing a fresh whole wild salmon or a chest full of just-caught shellfish, and everyone will gratefully feast.

If you obtain very fresh fish and don't overcook it, you are virtually guaranteed to make a delicious meal, even with the plainest cooking methods and seasonings. If you feel inexperienced, know that your nose is not; it's always a good idea to insist on smelling any fish you wish to buy. Fresh fish smells clean and briny, not fishy—you will know.

CLAY'S BROILED TROUT

At home, "catching" trout in a market, I'm never tempted by the boneless trout; bones add flavor, character, and juiciness to the delicate flesh. Allow a one-pound whole trout for each person.

Preheat your oven's broiler. Pat the fish dry with paper towels. Lightly prick the skin here and there with the tip of a knife. Generously salt and pepper the fish inside and out, put it in an oiled, shallow pan, and stick it under the broiler, a few inches from the flame. Broil for less than 5 minutes on each side, until the skin on each side is a nice bronze color. When the flesh of the fish is opaque throughout, it's done.

If you have just caught, gutted, and stream-cleaned your trout in the wild, say, somewhere in the Sierra Nevada, do as my brother Clay, an avid fisherman, does: wrap the salt-and-peppered trout in aluminum foil (shiny side facing in), seal well, and cook it, turning occasionally, for about 5 minutes on the roaring flames of your campfire. Excellent.

Baked Salmon

SERVES 1

The only key to cooking fish (presupposing, of course, that the fish is impeccably fresh) is not overcooking it. While pan-frying or grilling will produce an appealing brown, crusty exterior, sometimes you want to cook it in the simplest way possible. Baking is the most transparent method: the natural flavor of the fish is all that's there, with no supports or embellishments, no chef's ego. A good method for a beginner, baking makes it easy to observe the fish while it cooks. Served with an appropriate flavorful sauce or accompaniment (see the following list), baked fish shows how honest, clean, and delicious something very simple can be.

Wild Pacific salmon comes into season in late spring, continuing through the summer. Halibut, a variety of white-fleshed fish popular on the West Coast of the United States, is also very good simply baked, and enjoys a longer season.

5- or 6-ounce portion freshest wild salmon fillet, skinless (see Note)

olive oil

about ¼ teaspoon salt

Heat the oven to 400°F. Rub the salmon all over with olive oil and salt. Put on a foil- or parchment-lined baking sheet and stick the sheet in the oven. Depending on the thickness of the fish, it will cook in 9 to 10 minutes. You may peek into the interior of the fish with a small knife: it should flake easily but still be very moist and retain a faint translucency. Some people like their salmon a little rarer; others prefer it a bit more well-done.

Note: In late spring, when salmon season begins, the flesh is leaner and benefits from cooking with the skin on. Later in the season, in the heat of summer, the flesh is fattier and may be successfully baked without the skin. If you bake the salmon with the skin, remove the skin after cooking (it peels right off), flip the fish over, and serve skin side down on the plate. Salmon skin, seared in a nonstick pan in a bit of oil over high heat, is delicious, but skin cooked at the low temperature called for here will be flabby and unappealing to most diners.

FOR SERVING (CHOOSE ONE)

lemon wedges and a sprinkle of fresh herbs; dill is classic and especially good

Marinated Beets (page 281) and Aioli (page 427) thinned with a little water and lemon juice

Corn Salad (page 283)

Meyer Lemon–Olive Relish (page 428) and Simple Roasted Potatoes (page 247)

sweet ripe tomatoes tossed with salt and fresh dill, with boiled red potatoes and drizzles of sour cream

hot bacon and curly endive salad with Shallot Vinaigrette (page 295)

a salad of freshly cooked summer green beans and tomatoes, with balsamic vinaigrette (see page 296)

summer vegetables and Pesto (page 260)

Pickled Summer Vegetables (page 429) and slices of avocado

Snap Peas (page 244) and basil

shell bean and corn succotash (see page 218)

Other Simple Methods

Season the fish well with salt several hours in advance, bring a cup or two of dry, flavorful wine to a gentle simmer, and poach the fish in the wine—just drop the seasoned fish into the hot wine and let it sit on the lowest flame until the fish is just

continued...

... *continued*

barely cooked through. Include sprigs of herbs—whatever is appropriate—in the wine while poaching, if you wish.

Or, bake a larger fillet of salmon, skin on, rubbed with olive oil and salt, skin side up, in a 200°F oven for 45 minutes to an hour, until the flesh is creamy and barely opaque throughout. Remove the skin and serve the fish in rough chunks with Shaved Fennel (page 285), Watercress Salad (page 294), and lemon wedges.

Gravlax

SERVES 4

This splendid hors d'oeuvre is at once simple and sophisticated.

4-ounce portion freshest wild salmon fillet, skin on

2 heaping teaspoons kosher salt

½ teaspoon brown sugar

3 or 4 cracked peppercorns

3 or 4 crushed juniper berries

2 or 3 sprigs fresh dill

FOR SERVING

sliced cucumbers

sour cream

chopped fresh dill

tomatoes

rye crispbread

Season the salmon generously all over with the kosher salt. Sprinkle with the brown sugar, peppercorns, and juniper berries. Bruise the fresh dill and press it into the flesh of the fish. Wrap with a layer of cheesecloth, then with several layers of paper towels (to absorb liquid), and finally with plastic wrap. Put the wrapped fish between two plates, and place a weight over the top plate. Refrigerate, weighted, for 4 days.

Unwrap and remove the dill and large chunks of pepper or juniper. Slice the salmon *very thinly* with a sharp knife. The skin helps the flesh keep its shape during slicing, but it is not good to eat in this form. Serve the sliced gravlax arranged on a platter, alongside sliced cucumber, a dish of sour cream, chopped fresh dill, tomatoes, and caraway-studded rye crispbread.

Pan-Fried Sole

SERVES 2

This delicate, simple dish is quite similar to the French classic, *sole meunière*. An ode to butter, the recipe uses both clarified and brown butter.

8 to 10 ounces sole fillets

½ teaspoon salt

⅓ cup flour

about 4 tablespoons clarified butter (see page 63) for sautéing

2 tablespoons butter

¼ lemon

Pat the fish dry with paper towels, and season with salt. Sprinkle the flour onto a plate, and dredge the fish in the flour, shaking off the excess. Over a medium-high flame, heat a heavy skillet of ample size to accommodate the pieces of fish without crowding: it may be necessary to cook the fish in two batches. Add enough vegetable oil or clarified butter to generously coat the bottom of the skillet. When the oil is *very* hot and beginning to smoke, lay the fish in the pan, without crowding it (cook in batches if necessary). Cook until golden brown on one side, 1 to 2 minutes, then gently flip with a wide spatula (being careful not to spatter yourself with oil) and cook the other side for about a minute

continued...

. . . continued

more. The timing will, of course, depend on the thickness of the fish—the inside of the thickest part of the fish should be opaque and should flake easily. Lift the fish onto a warmed plate, browner side up. Pour out the butter and use fresh clarified butter if you are cooking the fish in batches.

When all the fish is cooked, pour off the butter and return the skillet to a high flame. Melt the 2 tablespoons butter in the skillet. Watch the butter—when it turns a fragrant hazelnut brown, squeeze in a little fresh lemon juice. Drizzle the lemony browned butter over the fish. Serve immediately.

Sole Stuffed with Leeks

SERVES 3

This is a simple, clean-tasting, elegant, old-fashioned dish. The delicate flavors are best appreciated with a simple accompaniment, such as white rice, or alone in a meal of a few courses. For instance, start with Handmade Egg Noodles (page 388) tossed with butter, herbs, and Sautéed Mushrooms (page 237); then serve this stuffed sole all by itself; then serve a green salad with sliced oranges and Citrus Vinaigrette (page 297). For most occasions, I like this sole unadorned with any sauce besides the pan juices. But on occasions when a sumptuous sauce is appropriate, try Lemon Butter Sauce (page 425).

about 6 thin sole fillets
(about 1¼ pounds)

1 teaspoon salt

2 large or 3 medium leeks

about 3 tablespoons butter

Trim the sole so the pieces are roughly of even size, reserving the trimmings. Chop the trimmings finely with a sharp knife.

Sprinkle the fillets with ¼ teaspoon of the salt, and keep both the fillets and the chopped fish cold.

Cut out any discolored, shriveled, or browned parts of the leeks. Cut away all the darker-green top parts, keeping them separate from the white and pale-green bottom portions. Rinse a handful of the longest dark-green leek tops (discard the rest or save for stock), chop coarsely, and arrange over the bottom of an 8-by-8-inch baking pan. These provide moisture and deepen the leek flavor.

Trim the dirty root end off the white and pale-green bottom part of the leeks, then halve lengthwise. Under cool running water, rinse the leeks, making sure all the outer layers get thoroughly rinsed—they easily trap sand and dirt. Drain, then cut the leeks into small dice.

Heat the oven to 350°F. Melt a tablespoon of the butter in a small saucepan over medium heat. Add the diced leeks with ½ teaspoon salt and stew, stirring frequently but otherwise keeping the pan covered, until tender, 7 to 10 minutes. If the leeks seem dry, add teaspoonfuls of water as necessary—the leeks shouldn't brown. Remove from the heat. You should have about 1 cup of tender, cooked leeks.

Remove the sole fillets from the refrigerator. Have toothpicks on hand. Stir the chopped fish into the leeks quickly with another ¼ teaspoon salt. Spread the leek-fish mixture evenly over the fillets, roll the fillets up, starting with the thicker end, and secure each roll with a toothpick. Place the rolls toothpick side down on the bed of leek tops in the baking pan. Put a thin slice of butter atop each roll. Bake for about 20 minutes, or until the fish is cooked through.

Using a wide spatula, carefully transfer 2 rolls to each person's plate, then slide out the toothpicks. Some juice will have accumulated in the baking pan; spoon it over the fish.

PAN-FRIED COD
OR SNAPPER

If you have cod or snapper (or other thick-filleted, mild white fish) and would like to pan-fry it with a golden, crispy bread-crumb coating, use the Crispy Pan-Fried Chicken recipe on page 351. A pound of fish will serve about 3 people. Serve with lemon wedges and Fuji Apple Coleslaw (page 278).

Fried Catfish

SERVES 4 TO 6

Catfish suffers from a somewhat lowbrow reputation, but these delicate, golden, cornmeal-dusted fillets will please the most discriminating palates.

1 cup white or yellow cornmeal

2½ teaspoons salt

¼ teaspoon cayenne pepper

¼ teaspoon paprika

¼ teaspoon black pepper

about 6 cups safflower oil, peanut oil, or other vegetable oil appropriate for deep-frying

1¾ pounds thin catfish fillets

In a big, wide bowl, mix the cornmeal, salt, cayenne, paprika, and black pepper. Heat the oil in a deep, heavy pot to 350°F. Dredge the catfish fillets thoroughly in the seasoned cornmeal, then drop them, 4 or 5 at a time, in the hot oil. As soon as they float in the oil, they're done. Lift out with a wire skimmer and drain on brown paper bags or paper towels. Serve immediately, with Skillet Cornbread (page 116), Tabasco sauce, and lemon wedges.

SEARED TUNA

Obtain steaks (5 to 6 ounces for each person) of very fresh tuna, about 1 inch thick. Pat dry with paper towels, and season well with a big pinch of salt on each side of each steak. Heat a tablespoon of olive oil or vegetable oil in a heavy skillet over a medium-high flame until very hot. When the oil smokes, gently lay the tuna steaks in the skillet (be careful not to spatter yourself with oil). Let the steaks cook for about 1 minute on one side, then carefully flip with a wide spatula and cook on the other side for about 50 seconds more. Remove to a warmed plate, browner side up. The tuna steaks will be very, very rare, but warm, inside.

For medium-rare tuna, leave the steaks in the pan but take the pan off the heat. Let them continue to cook for about 20 more seconds on each side. Want well-done fish? Choose another fish variety—fresh tuna becomes dry and stringy when seared to well-done.

Grind a good shot of fresh pepper over the fish, sprinkle with a pinch more salt, drizzle with a little extra-virgin olive oil, and serve immediately, with simple salads and vegetables. Aioli (page 427), thinned to sauciness with a little water, is always a great accompaniment.

MUSSELS

Fresh mussels are a good and relatively inexpensive delicacy. Though available year-round, they are best in the cooler months of the year. Most of the mussels sold in the United States these days are sustainably farmed in the cold Atlantic waters off Prince Edward Island in Canada. When buying them, make sure they are quite fresh and alive; they should smell briny, not fishy, and if there are a lot of cracked or open mussels, it is perhaps best to wait until your fish market gets a fresh shipment.

Mussels lend themselves to almost any flavor combination you could imagine. Use the three recipes on the next page as a guide and introduction, but do not feel bound by them. I have had exquisite mussels with Asian and Latin American flavors, with red wine instead of white, with beer, with sausage or bacon, with a plethora of herbs, or with almost no adornments at all. Mussels are traditionally served with bread to soak up the flavorful juices; you may toast the bread, if you like, and rub it with olive oil and a cut clove of garlic. All three recipes below are good served in wide bowls over linguine or other thin, long pasta. Serve with knife, fork, and spoon, and plenty of napkins. Accompany with a big, cheerful green salad, full of vegetables and croutons.

Moules Marinière de Bretagne

This is a traditional recipe from the windswept coast of Brittany, in northwestern France.

Allow 25 to 30 fresh mussels per person. They should smell fresh, like the ocean. Wash well in cold water. Discard any that are cracked or broken, and any open mussels that do not close when agitated. Pull out any bits of rough "beard" that are sticking out of the shells. For each serving, have ready a good pat of butter, about ¼ cup finely chopped shallot or onion, ¼ cup dry white wine, ¼ cup heavy cream, a big tablespoon of chopped parsley, and a thick slice or two of fresh bread.

Over a high flame, melt the butter in a big pot (with a tight-fitting lid) that will accommodate the entire pile of mussels. When the butter sizzles and foams, add the shallot and sauté for a moment. Add the mussels, and flip them around to coat with the butter and shallot, letting them cook for about a minute. Splash in the wine and cream, and immediately cover the pot. Steam the mussels, shaking the pot frequently, just until the mussels open, 1 to 2 minutes. Divide the mussels into serving bowls, pour the precious liquid over each serving, sprinkle with parsley, and serve immediately, with bread to soak up the liquid. Serve with small forks, and put a big empty bowl on the table for the shells.

The deliciousness of the winy-creamy-briny liquid cannot be underestimated. A fishmonger once told me, "I have a great recipe for mussels: I steam them with olive oil, garlic, and white wine, then I throw out the mussels and just drink the liquid."

Mussels with Leeks and Orange Zest

For a sprightly, fresh, natural marriage of flavors, use olive oil instead of butter, diced leeks instead of onion, and all white wine, no cream. When you splash in the wine, throw in about ¼ teaspoon of finely grated orange zest for each serving.

Mussels with Spicy Tomato Sauce

Cook the mussels as described, using olive oil instead of butter, minced garlic instead of onion, and a thin, flavorful tomato sauce (see Fresh Summer Tomato Sauce, page 418) instead of wine and cream. Throw in a good pinch of hot red pepper flakes a moment before you add the mussels. For extra richness, brown a little crumbled hot Italian sausage in the pot first.

OYSTERS ON THE HALF-SHELL

Oysters should be impeccably fresh, and taken from clean, cold waters. Scrub oysters well under cold running water. Shucking oysters quickly and easily requires practice. Take an oyster knife and hold the oyster, its more rounded side down, folded in a thick kitchen towel. With determination, insert the knife into the "hinge" at the pointed part of the shell, and wiggle it from side to side. Once that tendon is severed, the top shell should loosen. Remove the top shell, cutting loose the place on it where the oyster attaches. Still using the knife, loosen the oyster from its bottom shell, but *keep it in the shell, retaining as much of the liquid in the shell as possible.* Place the opened oyster on a bed of crushed ice. When all the oysters are opened, serve them on the ice.

When you eat an oyster, smell it first: it should smell briny and fresh. This is not only a safeguard against ingesting a bad oyster, but a great part of the pleasure. Spoon a little sauce over, or not, and slurp the oyster and all liquid from the shell. Chew.

Some people prefer their oysters completely unadorned, with perhaps just a wedge of lemon. Some prefer fresh lime, accompanied by amber Mexican beer. Others favor the following strong, traditional French accompaniment.

Mignonette Sauce

For every dozen oysters, macerate a tablespoon of minced shallot in a mixture of 2 tablespoons red wine and 2 tablespoons red wine vinegar. Add a pinch of salt and a healthy pinch of cracked black pepper. Let the flavors develop while you open the oysters. Some dip their oysters in the sauce, while others drizzle a few drops of sauce over each oyster.

Boiled Shrimp

SERVES 2 TO 3

This is the most delightfully direct shrimp experience. Technically, these peel-and-eat shrimp are poached, not boiled; gentler heat keeps the shrimp tender. Cooking shrimp in their shells retains more of their integrity; the shell imparts a deeper flavor to the meat and keeps the meat moist. Even if I intend to serve the shrimp peeled, I still cook them in their shells and peel them when they are cool. This method works for medium or large shrimp; medium shrimp have a better meat-to-shell ratio.

1 gallon water

⅓ cup salt

1 bay leaf

¾ teaspoon hot red pepper flakes

¾ teaspoon whole allspice

¾ teaspoon black peppercorns

1½ pounds medium or large shell-on shrimp

—

FOR SERVING

melted butter

lemon wedges

In a large pot over a high flame, bring a gallon of water to a boil. Add the salt, bay leaf, red pepper flakes, allspice, and black peppercorns and let boil for 1 minute. With the water at a furious boil, throw in the shrimp, give the pot a stir, slap on the lid, and let the water return almost to a boil. When the shrimp begin to float and the water is beginning to bubble again, the shrimp are cooked. Quickly rinse, peel, and taste a shrimp to make sure they are cooked to your liking—leave them in the water for another minute if necessary. Drain and serve immediately; peel-and-eat, with melted butter, lemon wedges, and plenty of napkins.

The heat contained in a gallon of boiling water is sufficient to cook 1½ pounds of shrimp. If you have more shrimp, adjust the water and seasonings accordingly.

If you want to serve your shrimp chilled, spread them on a baking sheet after draining so they cool quickly. When they have cooled to room temperature, immediately put them in the refrigerator. Peel when they are well chilled. If they are to be picked up with the fingers, leave the tails on. Chilled shrimp are superb in a salad with avocado cubes and Lemon Vinaigrette (page 296). Aioli (page 427), thinned with a little water, is a good but rich sauce for chilled shrimp. Meyer Lemon–Olive Relish (page 428), all the components especially finely chopped, is also successful. But if American tradition is your bent, try the following flavorful, basic cocktail sauce.

Cocktail Sauce

½ cup ketchup (or bottled "chili sauce")

½ cup very finely diced fresh tomato

¼ teaspoon Tabasco sauce or other
hot sauce

2½ teaspoons fresh squeezed lemon juice

⅛ teaspoon salt

good twist of black pepper

1 teaspoon vodka (optional)

1 tablespoon finely grated fresh horseradish

Mix everything in a small bowl and let sit
for about 30 minutes at room temperature
before serving.

CHAPTER 12

Pasta, Dumplings, Rice, and Stuffing

This chapter tackles what might be called the "bones" of cooking. Carbohydrate-rich grains (wheat, rice, corn) and dough products form the backbone of every traditional cuisine. Meat and vegetables lend themselves to the simplest of treatments, but rice, pasta, dumplings, and other starch dishes often require technique and skill. While roast beef or baked salmon may be superb provided the cook has merely taken them out of the oven at the right moment, the excellence of a dish of homemade noodles sauced with cream depends on a whole succession of judgments and decisions by the cook.

Potato dishes are in the hot vegetables chapter (beginning on page 207), and other starchy dishes are found in the Great Lunches chapter (beginning on page 149). Keep in mind, too, that beans (pages 184 to 204) are rich in starch and may deliciously accompany meat, fish, and vegetable dishes in place of rice, pasta, or potatoes.

Handmade Egg Noodles with Cream

SERVES 4 TO 6

Fresh pasta takes *practice* to make well. This recipe aims to describe the process clearly, but ultimately, the only guarantor of success will be your own tactile experience. Mastering fresh pasta will teach you about the properties of gluten (the protein in wheat responsible for its elasticity), imparting an excellent "dough sense" that carries over to bread and pastry baking.

I always use a stainless-steel, hand-crank pasta roller device from Italy to make fresh pasta. Many Italian purists think the metal devices are rubbish, and that rolling out your dough on a wooden countertop with a wooden rolling pin is the only way to proceed, but I am neither Italian nor a purist. If you want to roll these out with a rolling pin, by all means try—it is possible, but it takes work, patience, and space.

If you go to the trouble of making fresh pasta, you don't want a complex sauce to overwhelm it. These wide noodles are wonderful underneath braised chicken (see page 355) or beef stew (see page 315). But I think I like them best on their own, just with cream. Since this is an extremely simple (which is different from "easy") recipe, you'll get great results if the ingredients are of good quality. At Deep Springs we are lucky to have good farm-fresh eggs to make the noodles and our astonishingly thick, aromatic farmhouse cream to sauce the noodles. It's that simple: no cheese, no onion, no garlic, no parsley . . . just cream, a little butter, salt, and pepper.

EQUIPMENT

hand-crank pasta roller

pizza cutter

NOODLES

1¾ cups all-purpose flour, preferably unbleached

½ teaspoon olive oil

2 large eggs

1 egg yolk

1 to 2 teaspoons water (only if necessary)

semolina flour for dusting (if unavailable, use all-purpose flour)

SAUCE

1¼ cups heavy (whipping) cream

¼ teaspoon salt, plus more as needed

2 tablespoons butter

freshly ground black pepper

To make the noodles, before beginning to mix, bear in mind that pasta dough is much denser and more resilient than bread dough. In a sturdy mixer fitted with the paddle attachment, using its slowest speed, or by hand in a medium bowl using a wooden spoon, mix the flour and olive oil together for a moment, then add the eggs and yolk. The mixture will at first appear dry and crumbly. Keep mixing until it becomes more uniform. If it still seems too dry, add just enough water— a few drops at a time—for the dough to begin to cohere. You should need no more than a teaspoon or, if your flour is especially dry or your eggs small, two. The dough should not be so wet that it comes together in a ball by itself in the mixer, only moist enough that when you take a handful of the crumbles and squeeze they stick together readily. If there's too much water, the noodles will be sticky and flabby. Don't overwork the dough—it will make the pasta tough. Wrap the dough well in plastic wrap and let it rest at room temperature for 1 to 2 hours.

Divide the dough into 4 pieces, each slightly bigger than a golf ball. Keep the pieces you aren't using well wrapped. Take a piece of the dough and flatten it with your hand. If it seems sticky, dust it well with semolina flour. Using a hand-crank pasta machine, roll the dough first through the thickest setting. You will have an oval-shaped piece of dough. Fold this in thirds to make a square-shaped piece of dough, and run it through the rollers again at the thickest setting. Roll the dough through successively thinner settings until it is about as thick as 4 or

5 sheets of paper. Some cooks like to roll out each ball of dough partway and then let them rest, well covered, before rolling them through the thinnest setting. If your dough is soft and would rather stick than not, keep it well coated with flour at all times and hope for the best. If your dough is hard, has lots of white streaks, and tends to crumble and break, try misting it lightly with water before reflouring and rerolling. If your dough is elastic but firm, with a silky suppleness to it, and if it rolls out easily with only a slight crack here and there, you have made perfect pasta dough.

Before cutting all the noodles, make a test batch: take a sharp pizza cutter (or a knife) and cut a few inch-wide crosswise strips, slightly on the diagonal, from your sheet of pasta. Boil up a small pot of salted water and cook these noodles for 20 to 30 seconds. Drain the noodles well and turn them out onto a plate. If they fall completely flat, tear easily, and seem insubstantial, the dough has been rolled too thin—this can be remedied somewhat by reducing the boiling time. If they look thick and sturdy and taste tough and chewy, the dough is too thick—roll it thinner. If the noodles stand up nicely on the plate and taste good, with just the right balance of tenderness and firmness, they are just right. Proceed with rolling the other 3 pieces of dough, keeping any dough you're not handling at the moment covered with plastic wrap so it doesn't dry out. Cut all the noodles into 1-inch-wide
continued . . .

. . . continued

strips with your pizza cutter, as described previously. Toss them with extra semolina flour and place them in loose clumps on a floured tray or baking sheet. Don't pile them heavily on top of each other. Keep the noodles on this tray, covered with a dish towel or with plastic wrap, refrigerated, until just before cooking/serving time.

To make the sauce and cook the noodles, pour the cream into a wide skillet, add the salt, and set over a low flame to warm. Bring a large pot of water (about 1½ gallons) to a furious boil. Add enough salt to the water so that it tastes lightly salty, and throw in the noodles all at once. Gently stir them around in the pot. Once the water returns to a boil, the noodles should take only about a minute to cook—to test, taste one. Drain well (don't rinse), and transfer the noodles to the skillet with the warmed cream, adding the butter, cut into small pieces, and salt and pepper to taste. Raise the flame to medium-high, and toss gently to coat. Taste for salt. Divide the pasta and sauce among wide, shallow bowls. Twist a little more black pepper over each, and serve immediately.

Ricotta Ravioli with Sage Brown Butter

MAKES ABOUT 50 RAVIOLI; SERVES 4 TO 6

Once you have made the noodles in the previous recipe a few times, try these classic, simple ravioli. But when you have less time, use small wonton wrappers, sold refrigerated in many grocery stores.

EQUIPMENT

hand-crank pasta roller

pizza cutter

water mister

———

PASTA

1 recipe dough for Handmade Egg Noodles (page 388)

———

FILLING

1½ cups whole-milk ricotta cheese

¼ teaspoon salt

few twists of black pepper

pinch of cayenne pepper

scant ¼ teaspoon ground nutmeg

1 tablespoon extra-virgin olive oil

———

6 tablespoons unsalted butter

6 to 8 fresh sage leaves, coarsely chopped

freshly ground black pepper

Parmesan cheese for grating

While the pasta dough is resting, spread the ricotta in a rectangle about ¼ inch thick directly on a clean, white, dry dish towel. Wrap the towel gently around the cheese and let the towel absorb excess moisture from the cheese for about 30 minutes.

Roll out the pasta into sheets a little thinner than described in the egg noodles recipe, keeping it well covered at all times. Ideally, the sheets should be about 4 inches wide, resulting in 2-inch ravioli— no trimming necessary.

To make the filling, unwrap the ricotta and transfer it to a medium bowl. Season well with the salt, black pepper, a little cayenne, a few good scrapings of nutmeg, and a tablespoon of good olive oil. Taste— it should be rich and well seasoned.

Have ready a clean water mister filled with water.

Cut the pasta sheets into manageable lengths. Using one sheet at a time, place teaspoonfuls of ricotta filling 2 inches apart, off-center, along the sheet of pasta.

Mist the pasta sheet lightly with water, then fold it over lengthwise, enclosing the filling. Carefully and systematically press out any air pockets, pressing firmly to fuse the pasta together. Using a pizza cutter, cut the ravioli apart. Trim if necessary. Transfer the ravioli to a sheet pan well dusted with semolina flour.

When all the ravioli are made, bring a large pot of water to a boil. Salt the water generously, and gently throw in half the ravioli. Let the ravioli cook for 40 to 45 seconds after the water returns to a boil, gently stirring the pot from time to time. Don't fret if a couple of them break. Rinse one in cold water and taste—it might need more cooking time to become tender. Scoop the ravioli out with a wire skimmer, drain briefly, then turn out into a buttered serving dish. Save some of the pasta-cooking water in case it's needed for the sauce.

To make the sauce, in a skillet, melt 3 tablespoons of the butter on high heat. When the butter turns golden brown and smells nutty, throw in half the sage—it will sizzle. Tip the ravioli into the skillet, toss gently, then slide them back into the dish. Repeat with the remaining ravioli, butter, and sage. If the ravioli seem in need of a little moisture, add a spoonful or two of the pasta-cooking water. Lightly grind black pepper and grate a little Parmesan over the ravioli, and serve immediately.

Manicotti

MAKES ABOUT 16 CREPES; SERVES 4 TO 6

In this recipe, sheets of "pasta" are cooked like crepes, filled with seasoned ricotta, and baked with a simple tomato sauce.

CREPES

3 eggs

1 egg yolk

2 cups water

½ teaspoon salt

1½ tablespoons olive oil, plus more for cooking

1¼ cups all-purpose flour

FILLING

1½ cups whole-milk ricotta cheese

1 egg

1 teaspoon olive oil

pinch of salt

pinch of black pepper

pinch of ground nutmeg

SAUCE (OR USE FRESH SUMMER TOMATO SAUCE, PAGE 418)

1 tablespoon olive oil

1 large shallot, minced

1 clove garlic, crushed

pinch of hot red pepper flakes

one 28-ounce can diced tomatoes in juice

2 sprigs fresh basil

salt and freshly ground black pepper

freshly grated Parmesan cheese for serving

To make the crepes, whisk the eggs, yolk, water, salt, and olive oil together in a medium bowl. Whisk in the flour, then let the batter rest for at least 1 hour before making the crepes.

Heat a small omelet pan (nonstick is ideal) over a medium-high flame. Brush a scant film of olive oil in the pan, then pour in 3 tablespoons of the batter. I find it easiest to use a ¼-cup measure, filling it three-fourths full. Scoop the batter from the bottom of the bowl. Swirl the pan so the batter evenly covers the bottom, and cook until the top of the crepe has lost its glossiness. Flip and cook on the other side for a few seconds, until the crepe puffs, then flip it onto a plate. This takes skill—the recipe makes enough to allow for a few mess-ups. Don't let the crepes brown. Continue cooking the crepes until the batter is used up, stacking the crepes atop one another.

To make the filling, mix the ricotta, egg, olive oil, salt, pepper, and nutmeg together in a medium bowl. Have the filling at room temperature when you assemble the manicotti.

For the sauce, heat the olive oil over medium heat in a medium-sized, heavy, nonreactive pot until fragrant. Quickly cook the shallot, garlic, and pepper flakes in the oil, then add the tomatoes and basil. Bring to a simmer and simmer for 10 minutes. Let cool for a few minutes, then purée the sauce in a blender. *Be careful when blending hot liquids: fill the blender jar only half full, hold the lid in place with a kitchen towel, and start the blender on lower speeds.* Pass the blended sauce through a screen sieve, pressing as much liquid and pulp through as possible, using the back of a ladle. Discard the solids left in the sieve. Taste the sauce for salt and pepper.

Heat the oven to 350°F. Spread some warm tomato sauce in the bottom of a wide, shallow casserole dish. Spread about 1½ tablespoons of ricotta filling across a crepe. Roll the crepe up cigar-style, and place in the casserole. Repeat, lining up the crepes snugly in the pan, until the crepes and filling are used up. Drizzle the remaining sauce evenly over the manicotti, cover, and bake for about 30 minutes. Allow to rest for 5 minutes before serving. Serve topped generously with freshly grated Parmesan cheese.

PASTA COOKERY

The preceding recipes address fresh pasta preparations; the following ones concern packaged, "dry" pasta: spaghetti, linguine, penne, and many other forms.

Deep Springers consume great quantities of pasta; beginning Student Cooks and experienced chefs alike rely on "spaghetti and meat sauce" for its ease of preparation, just as our mothers did. Everyone knows how to boil dry pasta; it is one of the most basic cooking operations. But here are a few pointers: for every pound of pasta, bring *3 to 4 quarts of water* to a boil. When the water reaches a *full, rolling boil*, add *a tablespoon of salt* for every 4 quarts of water—the water should taste lightly salted. Throw in the pasta all at once, and *stir frequently* as the water returns to a boil; this prevents the pieces of pasta from sticking to one another or to the bottom. For cooking times, use the times specified on the package as a guideline, from 3 to 4 minutes for angel hair pasta to 8 to 10 minutes for penne. Taste a piece of the pasta toward the end of the cooking time: it should be neither raw and hard in the center nor completely soft and yielding throughout. The center should be just firm but cooked through (if you want an old-fashioned American pasta dish, overcook the pasta).

continued . . .

. . . *continued*

Drain the pasta in a colander, *retaining a bit of the cooking water in a cup;* this water is frequently necessary to adjust the consistency of the sauce. Do not rinse the cooked pasta in running water.

For tomato sauce recipes, see pages 416 to 418.

For best results, toss the pasta with sauce immediately and serve immediately. If it is necessary to serve the plain cooked pasta and the sauce separately, toss the pasta with a bit of olive oil first. Most pastas are enhanced with a sprinkling of freshly grated Parmesan cheese over each serving.

Garlic Bread

American, not Italian, tradition dictates serving garlic bread with pasta. Here is perhaps the simplest one: drizzle thick slices of well-textured bread with olive oil, sprinkle lightly with salt and pepper, and toast until golden. Immediately rub the toasted surfaces of the bread lightly with a clove of freshly peeled raw garlic, rubbing the garlic into the pores of the bread. For a light garlic flavor, rub lightly. Drizzle with a little more olive oil and serve immediately.

Toasted Pasta with Garlic

SERVES 6 TO 8

This treatment transforms dry linguine or spaghetti into a new species of pasta, especially inviting in cool weather.

1 pound dry spaghetti or linguine

1 tablespoon olive oil

salt

4 to 6 cloves garlic, crushed

2 tablespoons butter

1 tablespoon extra-virgin olive oil

½ cup chopped parsley

½ cup freshly grated Parmesan cheese, plus more for sprinkling

black pepper

Heat the oven to 300°F. Line up the uncooked pasta on a sheet pan. Drizzle the oil over it and work the pasta around until evenly coated. Spread the pasta out in an even layer. Bake until the pasta is toasted to a deep golden brown, 15 to 20 minutes. Once it begins to change color, it burns quickly, so keep checking it. While the pasta is toasting, put a gallon of water on to boil.

When the water comes to a boil, salt it until it tastes lightly salty, and boil the pasta just until cooked in the center. This will take several minutes longer than cooking untoasted pasta. Being sure to retain 2 or 3 ladlefuls of the cooking water, drain the pasta. Return it to the pot with a ladleful of pasta-cooking water and the garlic, butter, extra-virgin olive oil, parsley, and Parmesan, quickly and thoroughly tossing everything together. Taste for salt and moisture, adding a bit more hot cooking water, olive oil, or butter, if necessary. Sprinkle with a little more Parmesan and black pepper, and serve immediately.

Variations

You may add up to 3 cups of cooked cool-weather vegetables to this pasta, such as sautéed chopped greens (see page 232), stir-fried carrot slivers, or steam-sautéed broccoli and cauliflower (see page 219). Or toss in pitted, oil-cured black olives, thinly sliced fennel sautéed in olive oil, the chopped inner fennel fronds, and a squeeze of lemon.

Wide Noodles with Broccolini, Feta, Lemon, and Pine Nuts

SERVES 2 TO 3

This pasta contains a simple, bright, healthy balance of flavors. Broccolini is a long-stemmed cross of kale and broccoli, sometimes marketed as "asparagus broccoli." In the Deep Springs broccoli patch, the gardeners harvest the little shoots that the plant continues to put out after the large heads are cut—this recipe is a perfect use for those.

You could make this with Handmade Egg Noodles (page 388), but it's also well suited to dried egg noodles, often sold packaged in serving-sized nests. This good pasta product lacks the long shelf life of more common durum wheat pastas (such as spaghetti or macaroni), so make sure what you're using is fresh. If the pasta seems brittle, it might be old.

continued . . .

. . . continued

⅓ cup pine nuts

3 to 4 ounces feta cheese

1 bunch broccolini

salt

about 6 ounces dry wide egg noodles (2 servings)

½ teaspoon grated lemon zest

pinch of hot red pepper flakes

2 teaspoons olive oil

few twists of black pepper

Set a big pot of water on the stove to boil. Toast the pine nuts in a small skillet over a medium flame, tossing frequently, until they are pale gold, 6 to 7 minutes. Transfer to a small plate to cool. Crumble the feta onto a small plate. Trim the broccolini if necessary, and cut each one in half lengthwise.

When the water boils, salt it until it tastes lightly salty, and boil the pasta. Near the end of cooking, throw the broccolini into the water with the pasta. When both the broccolini and pasta are just tender, drain, retaining just a sheen of the cooking water, then toss in a large bowl with the pine nuts, lemon zest, red pepper flakes, a teaspoon of the olive oil, and pepper to taste. Add half the feta cheese, toss again, and serve, topping the pasta with the remaining feta cheese and drizzling with the remaining teaspoon of olive oil.

Walnut Couscous

SERVES 4 TO 5

Couscous is a traditional Moroccan wheat product, somewhat like tiny bits of pasta. Traditional recipes, using regular couscous, specify a lengthy steaming and fluffing process, but this very simple method works well using whole-wheat couscous and tastes delightful with Marmalade Chicken (page 347).

1 cup water

½ teaspoon salt, plus a pinch

1 tablespoon butter

1 cup whole-wheat couscous

½ cup walnut halves, lightly toasted (see page 301) and finely chopped

1 teaspoon olive oil

black pepper

Bring the water, ½ teaspoon salt, and butter to a boil in a small saucepan. Stir in the couscous, remove from the heat, and cover the pan. Let sit for 5 minutes or longer, keeping the pan in a warm place.

Toss the toasted, chopped walnuts in a small bowl with the olive oil, a pinch of salt, and a twist of black pepper. Just before serving, fluff the couscous with a fork and toss in the walnuts.

Spaetzle

SERVES 6 TO 8

Spaetzle are little pastalike boiled dumplings, traditionally served with meat, Sautéed Mushrooms (page 237), and other wintry food. Perhaps you have seen spaetzle makers: a small hopper, holding the batter, moves back and forth over graterlike holes, releasing the spaetzle into the boiling water. Lacking a spaetzle maker, you need a vessel with widely spaced perforations (holes about ¼ inch in diameter, ¾ inch apart) and a scraper to extrude the batter through the perforations and into the boiling water below. In the Deep Springs kitchen, I use a shallow, perforated "hotel" pan set over a deeper hotel pan containing the water, and a metal dough scraper. In home kitchens, some improvisation and experimentation will be necessary.

2¼ cups all-purpose flour (up to ⅓ cup can be replaced with whole-wheat flour)

½ teaspoon salt

1¼ cups milk or water

1 egg

3 egg yolks

1 tablespoon butter, plus more as needed

Whisk together the flour and salt in a medium bowl. In small bowl, whisk the milk, egg, and yolks together. Whisk the milk mixture into the flour mixture just until uniform. Let the batter stand for 30 minutes before cooking the spaetzle.

While the batter is resting, bring a large, wide pot of water to a boil. Have a wide, buttered dish ready to receive the hot spaetzle. Add the tablespoon of butter to the water and enough salt to make the water taste lightly salty. Reduce the heat to medium-high if the water is boiling violently. Take up about one-fourth of the batter, transfer it to the hopper of your spaetzle maker, and extrude the batter through the holes into the boiling water. After the water returns to a boil, let the spaetzle cook for about 30 seconds. Scoop them out with a wire skimmer or a slotted spoon, drain briefly, and toss into the buttered dish. Repeat with the remaining batter in three more batches. Toss with a bit more butter (use brown butter, see page 220, if you like) and serve.

If you won't be serving the spaetzle immediately, toss with a little butter and let them cool in the dish. Once cool, they may be put in a container and refrigerated. Reheat in a steamer or, for a richer taste, brown them in butter.

Herbed Spaetzle

You may flavor spaetzle with 2 tablespoons of any one or a combination of the following fresh herbs, finely chopped, added to the batter, or to the butter at the end: thyme, parsley, sage, savory, chives, dill, or rosemary.

Cornmeal-Egg Soup Dumplings

SERVES 2 TO 3

These quick, simple, noodlelike dumplings will enrich virtually any brothy soup or stew. Possibilities include any of the braised chicken recipes (see page 355) made with extra broth, the chicken stew base for Chicken and Dumplings (page 359), Soupe au Pistou (page 260), or Brothy Vegetable Soup (page 236).

2 eggs

¼ cup cornmeal

about 4 teaspoons olive oil

1 tablespoon white wine or orange juice

¼ teaspoon salt

In a medium bowl, whisk together the eggs, cornmeal, 2 teaspoons of the olive oil, wine, and salt into a batter. Heat a little olive oil in a small (preferably non-stick) skillet over a medium-high flame. Cook the batter in three or four batches; the result will be like crepes or thin omelets. Cook about 20 seconds on one side, then flip and cook the other side just until solid—the crepes shouldn't brown. As they are done, turn them onto a cutting board. When all the batter is cooked, cut the crepes into 1-inch squares and stir the dumplings into your pot of soup.

Rice

SERVES 4 TO 5

LARGE QUANTITY RECIPE: SERVES 30 TO 40

When you want to serve plain rice, there are a few options for cooking it: on the stovetop in a good, heavy, heat-conducting pot; in a rice cooker; or in a tightly covered pan in the oven. I often find the oven method convenient, whether in the Deep Springs kitchen or at home. Whatever the method, I always use the following ratios: 1 part white rice to 1⅔ parts water, or 1 part brown rice to 2¼ parts water. For brown rice, the cooking time will be *about 50 percent longer*. This plain, pilaf-style recipe is best when a highly flavored, sauced dish, such as one of the braised chicken recipes, is to be served over it.

For Asian-style "steamed" rice, simply omit the oil and salt (and the sautéing).

1 tablespoon butter or olive oil
4 tablespoons butter or ¼ cup olive oil

1 cup uncooked white or brown rice
8 cups uncooked white or brown rice

1⅔ cups water
(for brown rice: 2¼ cups water)
13⅓ cups water
(for brown rice: 18 cups water)

¼ teaspoon salt
1 tablespoon salt

OVEN METHOD:

Heat the oven to 400°F. On the stove-top, melt the butter in a medium *(large)*, oven-safe saucepan. Add the dry rice and sauté, stirring constantly, until very hot, 2 to 3 minutes. Add the water and salt, stir once, and bring to a boil. Cover the pan tightly with aluminum foil (shiny side facing in) and put in the oven. Bake for 20 to 30 minutes (50 minutes to 1 hour for brown rice). Check for done-ness, using a fork; the liquid should be completely absorbed and the rice should be evenly tender; re-cover with foil and return to the oven if necessary. Fluff the rice with a fork and serve.

STOVETOP METHOD:

In a medium *(large)*, heavy, heat-conduct-ing pot with a well-fitting lid, melt the butter over medium-high heat. Add the rice and stir to coat the grains. Sauté for 2 to 3 minutes, stirring constantly. Add the water and salt, stir once, and bring to a boil. Turn the heat down to medium-low, maintaining a lively simmer. Cover the pot and let the rice cook, undisturbed, for about 20 minutes (40 minutes for brown rice), or until the water is absorbed. It's best not to peek at the rice until it's done; to tell if the water is absorbed, tilt the pan slightly. If you hear a hissing, boiling sound, there is still unabsorbed water in the pan, and the rice needs more time. If there is no sound, all the water is absorbed and the rice is ready. Fluff the rice with a fork and serve.

RICE COOKER METHOD:

Sauté the rice in the butter in a skillet as described, then transfer it to the rice cooker, adding the water and salt. Turn on the cooker—it will shut off automatically when the rice is done. Fluff the rice with a fork and serve.

PASTA COOKING METHOD:

If you have an unusual variety of rice and are uncertain of its rice-to-water cooking ratio, simply cook the rice in a pot of boil-ing salted water, like pasta. Watch the rice carefully as it boils, tasting it frequently. When it is as tender as you like, immedi-ately drain it and spread the rice on a tray or plate to stop the cooking. Toss with a little butter or oil. Once it has cooled to warm, put it in a serving dish. Rice cooked this way reheats well.

Variations

If you want to enrich the rice or make it more of a dish in itself, sharing equal weight in your menu with other foods, there are many, many possibilities for deepening its flavor. Here are just a few:

* more butter or extra-virgin olive oil, and salt and pepper (gently tossed in at the end, using a fork)

* chicken stock or other stock instead of the water

* chopped onion (sautéed in the butter at the beginning, before adding the rice)

continued . . .

. . . *continued*

* saffron (crushed and whisked with a little lemon juice and added at the beginning with the water)

* chopped fresh herbs (gently folded in at the end, using a fork)

* citrus (juice and grated zest, gently folded in at the end, using a fork; a little extra salt will be needed)

* Indian spices (whole mustard seed, coriander seed, cloves, cardamom pods, bay leaf, cinnamon stick, all heated in ghee [see page 63] in the beginning, to release their scent, before adding the rice [basmati rice, of course], then ground turmeric added with the water)

Brown, White, and Wild Rice Pilaf with Mirepoix

SERVES 6 TO 8

Once you have experienced the simple rice-cooking procedures in the previous recipe, try this more complex recipe: three different rices, all requiring different cooking times, are initially cooked separately, then allowed to finish cooking together with the classic trio of aromatic vegetables known as *mirepoix*. The result is more than the sum of its parts. To ensure correct timing, be sure the vegetables are cut and ready before beginning.

½ cup uncooked wild rice

1½ teaspoons salt, or more as needed

4¾ cups water

6 tablespoons butter

1 cup uncooked brown rice

2 bay leaves

1 large yellow onion, cut into medium dice

2 carrots, peeled and cut into medium dice

1 large stalk celery, cut into medium dice

1 cup uncooked long-grain white rice

black pepper

In a small saucepan, bring the wild rice, ¼ teaspoon of the salt, and 1 cup of the water to a boil. Cover the pan, remove from the heat, and set aside; do not drain the rice.

In a large, heavy saucepan, heat 2 tablespoons of the butter over medium-high heat. When it sizzles, throw in the brown rice with another ¼ teaspoon salt. Sauté the brown rice in the butter, stirring constantly, until the rice begins to smell nutty. Add 2¼ cups water, the wild rice and the water it cooked in, and the bay leaves. Bring to a boil, reduce the heat to a simmer, and let the rice cook for about 15 minutes, covered, while you prepare the white rice and the vegetables.

As soon as the wild–brown rice mixture settles to a simmer, heat the remaining 4 tablespoons butter in a large saucepan over medium-high heat. Add the onion, carrot, and celery with the remaining teaspoon of salt and stew, stirring frequently, until they begin to soften, about 3 minutes. Add the white rice to the vegetables and sauté for 3 to 4 minutes more. Add the vegetable–white rice mixture and the remaining 1½ cups water to the saucepan containing the brown and wild rice. Stir briefly to combine, raise the heat to bring to a boil again, then reduce the heat to maintain a simmer. Cover the pan and let the rice simmer gently until all the liquid is absorbed, 15 to 20 minutes more. To

check for doneness without removing the lid, tilt the pan slightly and listen for a sizzling sound; if there is no sound, the liquid has all been absorbed. Sprinkle a bit of fresh pepper over the rice, taste for salt (if salt has been added at the various stages as specified, it probably won't need any more), and correct if necessary, fluffing the rice gently with a fork; if you stir it, it could become mushy. Remove the bay leaves and serve immediately.

Risotto

serves 6 to 8

Risotto [ree-SO-toe], quintessentially Italian, is a specific, easy technique for cooking a particular kind of rice. The result—tender grains cloaked in a flavorful, velvety sauce—is unlike any other rice dish in the world. Virtually all risotto recipes call for stock, most often chicken stock. In a pinch, some cooks just use water, building up the flavor with extra onion and garlic. But if you use good homemade chicken stock in this recipe or any of the variations, you will not be disappointed. A plain risotto made with good Italian Parmesan, butter, and homemade chicken stock is a culinary touchstone. Serve risotto immediately, or the rice becomes mushy and the surrounding sauce becomes too thick.

8 cups chicken stock

4 tablespoons cold butter

1 large yellow onion, finely diced (ideally, the onion bits should be similar in size to the grains of rice)

2 pinches of salt, plus more as needed

2 cups uncooked Arborio rice or other Italian risotto rice

1 cup dry white wine

about ⅓ cup freshly grated Parmesan cheese, plus more for topping

freshly ground black pepper

Fill a large stockpot with the chicken stock and bring to a boil. Keep it at a simmer while you are making the risotto.

In a large, heavy saucepot, melt 2 tablespoons of the butter over medium heat. Add the onion with a large pinch of salt and sauté until it just loses its crunch, about 4 minutes. Throw in the rice with another good pinch of salt and cook for about 1 minute, stirring well, lightly sautéing the rice in the onions and butter. Add the wine and stir, enjoying the wonderful aroma, until it is absorbed. Add the stock, 1 to 2 ladlefuls at a time, to your pot of rice, *keeping the rice very moist, a thin film of stock over the surface of the rice, and stirring from the bottom frequently*. Keep stirring and adding stock as necessary. When finished, after about 20 minutes, the risotto should be almost pourable in consistency, each grain of rice cooked through and soft (taste to find out), but not split out from too much liquid. Depending on the size and shape of your pan—a wider pan will permit more evaporation—and the absorbency of your rice, you will probably use up all the broth.

At the moment the risotto is done, add the cheese and stir in the remaining 2 tablespoons cold butter. Carefully salt and pepper to taste. Serve immediately, with extra Parmesan grated over the top.

Saffron Risotto

Crush a generous pinch of saffron threads to a powder in a mortar and pestle. Add a tablespoon of lemon juice and mix well. Add this mixture to the risotto when you start adding the stock, rinsing out the last bit of saffron from the mortar with some of the stock.

Wild Mushroom Risotto

Soak about ½ ounce of dried porcini mushrooms for 30 minutes in 2 cups of the hot chicken stock. Drain the mushrooms and squeeze dry, reserving all the liquid. Chop the mushrooms finely and add to the pot before adding the wine. Use the strained soaking liquid in the risotto. Substitute ½ cup heavy cream for the Parmesan (cream's simple richness allows the complex mushroom flavor to shine through). Garnish with a little chopped parsley. If you are fortunate enough to find fresh porcini mushrooms or other fresh wild mushrooms (see page 237), chop them coarsely, sauté them in butter with a little salt, pepper, and garlic, and add to the risotto at the end.

Butternut Squash Risotto

Halve 1 small butternut squash or other sweet winter squash, scoop out the seeds (you may infuse the simmering stock with the seeds, straining them out before adding the stock to the risotto), and bake in a 350°F oven until the flesh is soft, about 1 hour. Scoop out the flesh and add to the risotto in the last 10 minutes of cooking. The squash purée will dissolve into the risotto, turning it a beautiful orange. Add a little chopped fresh sage at the beginning, and garnish with whole sage leaves briefly sizzled in butter. This risotto is good with roast chicken, roast pork, or ham.

Black Truffle Risotto

Perhaps, in fall or winter, at your produce market or specialty food store, you spot fresh black truffles from the Périgord region of France, nestled in cups of Arborio rice. You decide to buy a small one—for such a small, unassuming object, it is quite expensive. Here is what to do with it once you are back home in your kitchen. Prepare a basic recipe of risotto, using the rice in which the truffle was packed. With a small knife, peel the truffle thinly. Save the peelings and infuse the simmering chicken stock with them. Carefully cut the truffle into fine julienne. At the moment the risotto is finished, stir in the truffle. Keeping the truffle's pungent flavor clear and uncluttered, omit the Parmesan and enrich the finished risotto with a shot of heavy cream. Serve immediately, and take in the extraordinary aroma.

continued...

. . . continued

One winter, when a Deep Springs' biology professor offered a mycology class, I made black truffle risotto with a golf ball–sized $20 truffle I bought on a trip to San Francisco. The chocolaty, pheromoney scent of the truffle filled the Boardinghouse. Virtually no one in the community had ever tasted or smelled a truffle before.

Polenta

SERVES 4 TO 6

Polenta is still unfamiliar to many Americans, though "cornmeal mush" will ring a bell for Southerners. Of northern Italian origin, polenta is a creamy, savory porridge made from coarse yellow cornmeal, enriched with butter and Parmesan cheese, or that same porridge poured into a shallow buttered pan, allowed to cool and firm up, then cut into squares and grilled or sometimes fried. Polenta is quite easy to cook, considering how good it is, with none of the timing particulars of rice or pasta.

I love freshly made creamy polenta with beef stew, especially Goulash (page 318), or with garlicky cooked Greens (page 232). Sautéed Mushrooms (page 237) are especially succulent atop polenta. Other choices are Roasted Red Peppers (page 244), Roast Chicken (page 346), Herbed Braised Chicken (page 355), or any preparation of pork (see pages 335 to 339). In summer, add a cupful of freshly cut corn kernels to the pot of polenta in the last 5 minutes of cooking.

Or pour the hot polenta into a buttered shallow dish, let cool to room temperature, then cover and refrigerate for several hours. Cut the polenta into squares or triangles and layer with Tomato Sauce (page 416) and cheese, and bake like lasagna.

Without the Parmesan and black pepper, made perhaps with milk in place of some of the water, polenta is very good for breakfast.

5 cups water

1 cup polenta or coarse cornmeal

1 teaspoon salt, or more as needed

3 to 4 tablespoons butter

½ cup freshly grated Parmesan cheese

¼ teaspoon black pepper, or more as needed

pinch of cayenne pepper

Bring the water to a boil in a heavy 2-quart saucepot. Slowly whisk in the polenta, and keep whisking as the mixture comes back up to a boil. When it reaches a boil, allow it to cook for about a minute, whisking a few times, until it begins to thicken. Turn down the heat to medium-low, and cover the pot. Switch from your whisk to a wooden spoon, and let the polenta cook, stirring frequently (being sure to run the spoon over the bottom of the pot as you stir, to make sure nothing is sticking), for 30 minutes. *Be careful when stirring—the thick, boiling-hot porridge can spatter and burn your arm.*

When the porridge is nice and thick and the individual grains are tender, it's done. Stir in the salt, butter, Parmesan, black pepper, and cayenne and let cook for a moment more. Taste (carefully; it's very hot), and adjust the seasoning if necessary. The polenta may be held on the lowest heat, or in a double boiler over hot water, for another 30 minutes. Polenta continues to thicken as it sits.

Fried Polenta

This is rich! Grits (page 86) may be prepared in the same way, for a rich Southern breakfast. Make a recipe of Polenta, pouring it onto a buttered baking sheet and allowing it to cool and harden. Cut into squares or triangles. Into ½ cup of flour stir ½ teaspoon salt, and a pinch each of black pepper and cayenne. Dredge the polenta squares in the seasoned flour. Into a wide, heavy skillet, pour about ¼ inch of vegetable oil. Heat over a medium-high flame until the oil shimmers. Fry squares of polenta, a few at a time, until crispy and brown. Drain briefly on paper towels and serve immediately.

Southern Spoon Bread

SERVES 4 TO 6

Should you be able to find stone-ground, whole-grist cornmeal, this is an excellent use for it.

3 cups milk

1¼ cups cornmeal (stone-ground and whole-grain, if available)

3 eggs

2 tablespoons butter, at room temperature

1 teaspoon salt

1 teaspoon baking powder

2 pinches of cayenne pepper

In a medium-size, heavy saucepan over medium-high heat, bring the milk to a boil. Watch carefully—milk readily boils over. Stir in the cornmeal, and continue stirring. When the cornmeal thickens, reduce the heat to low, continuing to stir until very thick. Remove from the flame and let cool, stirring occasionally, until you can comfortably hold your hand on the bottom of the pot.

Heat the oven to 375°F while the mixture is cooling. Butter an 8-by-8-inch baking dish. Add the eggs, butter, salt, baking powder, and cayenne to the cooled cornmeal mixture. Beat for several minutes with a wooden spoon, then scrape into the baking dish. Bake for 30 minutes, or until lightly puffed and set. Serve from the dish, using a large spoon.

Variations

You may add grated cheese—stir a little into the batter, and sprinkle more generously over the top halfway through baking. You may also add some freshly cooked corn kernels, and a little Green Chile Relish (page 423) or minced jalapeño.

Quinoa

SERVES 3 TO 4

This delicate grain has sustained the Incas of Peru and other Andean peoples for millennia. Besides having a unique, herbal flavor, it is very high in protein and minerals.

1 cup quinoa

2 cups water

½ teaspoon salt

2 teaspoons butter

Put the quinoa in a screen sieve and rinse well under cold running water—this removes the bitter saponin that coats and preserves the grain. Put the quinoa, water, salt, and butter in a heavy, heat-conducting pot with a well-fitting lid and bring to a boil. Reduce the heat to medium, maintaining a lively simmer. Cover the pot and let the quinoa cook undisturbed for about 20 minutes, or until all the water is absorbed.

You may also cook quinoa in the oven or in a rice cooker—see the basic Rice recipe, page 398.

Clio's Stuffing

SERVES 6 TO 8

Occasionally, I love participating in live theater; once, I appeared in Tina Howe's *One Shoe Off*, a culinary comedy about a zany dinner party. The character Clio, a young actress, pigs out on stuffing in the second act. She moans, "I can't stop eating this stuffing!" I made this recipe for our production of the play (I also played Clio's husband), and my "wife" loved it so much she didn't need to act.

Stuffing is best baked in a dish, not inside the turkey. Turkey cooks more evenly when the main cavity is empty—by the time the stuffing in a stuffed turkey reaches a safe internal temperature, the turkey itself will be irredeemably overcooked.

Any bread that's not too sour (such as sourdough) or too sweet (such as sliced supermarket sandwich bread) makes great stuffing; the bread recipes in this book are ideal. I prefer bread that contains a good proportion of whole-wheat flour. You may use a blend of cornbread and regular bread (my usual practice

continued . . .

. . . continued

for Deep Springs Thanksgivings), or use all cornbread—in that case, since cornbread is rich, use less butter to cook the onions and celery. There is no need to toast cornbread along with the vegetables—just crumble it coarsely and gently combine with the other stuffing ingredients. An all-cornbread stuffing is so Southern that it's usually called "dressing." You may include the giblets from the turkey, simmered until tender and chopped finely, if you opt not to use them in the gravy.

½ cup butter (1 stick)

4 or 5 stalks celery, cut into large dice, plus some leaves, coarsely chopped

1 fat yellow onion, cut into large dice

1 teaspoon salt, plus a pinch or more as needed

1 tablespoon finely chopped fresh sage, or 2 teaspoons dry rubbed sage

1 large loaf wheat bread, cut into cubes

¾ teaspoon freshly ground black pepper

about ¾ cup milk, heated, or turkey broth

Heat the oven to 375°F. Melt the butter over medium-high heat in a large, heavy skillet. When it sizzles, throw in the celery, celery leaves, and onion with ½ teaspoon of the salt. Cook, stirring frequently, until the celery and onion are soft. Add the sage with a pinch of salt and cook for a minute more. Add the bread cubes, stirring gently to incorporate everything. Continue to cook, letting the bread lightly toast in the skillet. Season with ½ teaspoon more salt and the black pepper. Taste—if the bread is on the sweet side, it might need more salt.

Moisten the stuffing with about ¾ cup hot milk or turkey broth—it should be neither sopping wet nor dry. Taste for salt and pepper again. Arrange the stuffing in a buttered baking dish and bake until lightly browned on top. "What *is* it about this stuffing?" Clio asks.

Mushroom-Barley Stuffing

Sautéed Mushrooms (page 237) are excellent in stuffing. A cooked grain, such as pearl barley or farro (semi-pearled spelt berries; cook either one like brown rice, see page 398), is also a good addition.

Stuffed Winter Squash

A whole winter squash stuffed with this stuffing is very good, and not just for vegetarians. Stuffable varieties include turban, acorn, dumpling, red kuri, kabocha pumpkin, and table pumpkin.

Heat the oven to 350°F. Carefully cut out the top of your squash around the stem, as though you were going to make a jack-o'-lantern, scoop out the seeds, rub the inner cavity with a little olive oil and salt, then gently pack in the hot stuffing, just after you've added the milk or stock. Replace the top, put the squash on a foil-lined baking sheet, and bake for 1½ to 2 hours, depending on the size of the squash, or until the squash is soft to the touch. Use the foil to carefully transfer the squash to a serving platter. To serve, remove the top and scoop from the inside, getting some of the squash's flesh along with the stuffing.

CHAPTER 13

Sauces
and
Relishes

Often, you don't need a sauce; the food itself is delicious enough, flavorful and juicy enough, to stand alone, simple and unadorned. Much good food sauces itself. The rich, flavorful skin on roast chicken "behaves" like a sauce, its fatty, salty qualities enhancing the flavor of the meat. However, a sauce clearly expresses the cook's thoughtfulness and attention. A sauce might bring all the elements of a meal together or, in fact, might be the whole point of the meal (see Aioli, page 427).

Sauce recipes appear throughout this book, not just in this chapter. Frequently, the sauce is an integral part of a recipe; meat is often drizzled with its own pan juices, perhaps enriched with a little wine or butter. When a separate sauce is specific to a particular recipe, it is found next to that recipe: Fresh Horseradish Cream follows Roast Beef (page 313), brown butter is part of the Brussels sprouts recipe (page 220), lemon butter is included with the Artichokes (page 213), and a few of the soup recipes include their own specific garnishing sauce or relish. Versatile vinaigrettes and creamy dressings are found in the Salads and Dressings chapter (beginning on page 265).

Each of the sauces or relishes in this chapter has numerous applications. Marmalade and quince jam are good on toast, of course, but marmalade also makes a great glaze for chicken (see page 347), and quince jam enhances poultry or pork. And though I put good store-bought mayonnaise to everyday use, homemade mayonnaise and aioli are cornerstones of skillful cooking.

continued . . .

Dad's Steak Sauce

SERVES 2

Based on recollections vague and various, I've reconstructed a sauce my father made some forty years ago. It's extremely simple and quick to put together, melting into and magnifying the honest flavor of simple salted-and-peppered steaks. The garlic remains subtle, true to an era when garlic was permitted in American cooking but treated with caution, as if too much could cause harm, whereas fully crushing the garlic and letting it remain in the sauce will deliver a more powerful, modern punch. Pork chops, chicken breasts, burgers, and other simple meats may also be enhanced by this sauce.

1 small clove garlic

2 teaspoons Worcestershire sauce

2 teaspoons honey

¼ teaspoon soy sauce

¼ teaspoon cider vinegar

2 or 3 drops Tabasco or other hot sauce

pinch of salt

1 tablespoon cold butter

Lightly smash the garlic clove so it stays all in one piece. Put the garlic in a small skillet with the Worcestershire sauce, honey, soy sauce, vinegar, Tabasco, and salt. Bring just to a bubbling boil over a high flame, then remove from the heat. Let sit for 1 minute, then remove and discard the garlic. Add the cold butter. Swirl the pan, slowly melting the butter into the warm sauce. Return the pan to the lowest flame if there is not enough residual heat to melt the butter. Once the butter is all melted, whisk the sauce, if necessary, to remove any lumps or flecks of butter, and pour into a small serving dish. Keep the sauce slightly warm, and serve over warm steaks.

Tomato Sauce

MAKES ABOUT 4 CUPS; SERVES 4 TO 6
LARGE QUANTITY RECIPE: MAKES ABOUT
2½ GALLONS; SERVES 40 TO 50

This simple tomato sauce is quick, charged with garlic, and not too sweet. It glows with Italian red-pepper-flake warmth. Neither too thick nor too watery, it is a staple of my cooking at Deep Springs, suited to many purposes. It will keep, covered, in the refrigerator for several days before the garlic starts to taste tired. It also freezes well.

Generally speaking, canned tomatoes are a pure, sound, and consistent product; not bred for shipping or shelf life, tomatoes grown for canning are usually full-flavored, fully ripened, and processed soon after harvesting. Garden-fresh, ripe summer tomatoes occupy, to my mind, a completely separate category of ingredient. I have to have a lot of summer home-grown garden tomatoes before I think of making them into sauce, and then I use the simple Fresh Summer Tomato Sauce recipe on page 418.

2 tablespoons olive oil
½ cup olive oil

2 or more large cloves garlic, finely crushed
2 to 3 entire heads of garlic, cloves peeled and finely crushed

¼ teaspoon dried oregano, crumbled
1 tablespoon dried oregano, crumbled

¼ teaspoon hot red pepper flakes, or more to taste
2 teaspoons hot red pepper flakes, or more to taste

⅓ cup dry red wine
1½ cups dry red wine

one 28-ounce can diced tomatoes in juice
two #10 cans (each 6 pounds 6 ounces) diced tomatoes in juice or, for thicker sauce, one #10 can each diced tomatoes and tomato purée

one 15-ounce can tomato sauce
one #10 can (6 pounds 6 ounces) tomato sauce

black pepper

¼ cup coarsely chopped fresh basil or ½ teaspoon sweet-smelling dried basil or dried marjoram
1½ cups coarsely chopped fresh basil 2 tablespoons dried basil

salt, if needed

Have the ingredients prepared, measured, and ready—they all go into the pot in rapid succession. Heat the olive oil in a large, heavy saucepot over medium-high heat until it shimmers. Stir the garlic into the oil with a wooden spoon, and cook until the sizzling bits of garlic turn from a translucent yellow to an opaque ivory color. It will release an explosion of aroma.

Do not let the garlic brown. Immediately add the oregano and red pepper flakes, then the wine. Let boil for a moment, then add the diced tomatoes with their juice. Do not add the can of tomato sauce yet. Stirring occasionally, bring to a boil, then reduce the heat to a lively simmer and cook until the sauce is reduced a little, about 10 minutes. Stir in the can of tomato sauce, black pepper to taste, and basil. Heat through and taste, adding salt if necessary (the canned tomatoes usually contain enough).

Thick Tomato Sauce

Instead of a large can of diced tomatoes, use a smaller, 15-ounce can, and include a 15-ounce can of tomato purée, adding it with the tomato sauce. *(For large quantities, use a #10 can of diced tomatoes, a #10 can of tomato sauce, and a #10 can of tomato purée [6 pounds 6 ounces each].)* This formula works well on pizza.

Tomato Sauce with Meat

MAKES ABOUT 6 CUPS; SERVES 6 TO 8

Ground beef tomato sauces have their place, but you'll love this one with ground pork. Italian sausage is the flavor inspiration, but real sausage is too fatty.

1 pound ground pork

½ teaspoon crushed fennel seeds

¼ teaspoon hot red pepper flakes

¼ teaspoon salt

¼ teaspoon black pepper

1 recipe Tomato Sauce, small-quantity version (facing page)

Before you begin making the tomato sauce, cook the pork: heat a wide skillet over medium heat. Put the meat in the skillet, gently breaking it up as it cooks. The heat should not be so high that the meat browns. When about half the meat still has its pink color, evenly sprinkle the fennel seed, red pepper flakes, salt, and pepper over it. Continue cooking until the pork is cooked through and well flavored, breaking it up into small chunks. (If there is a lot of fat, drain it off.)

Prepare the tomato sauce, stirring the pork in—juice and all—when adding the diced tomatoes.

Fresh Summer Tomato Sauce

MAKES 3 TO 4 CUPS; SERVES 5 TO 6

Extremely simple, this sauce, though thin, is full of flavor. Instead of basil, you may add sprigs of fresh marjoram. As St. Ignatius might have said, *Add marjoram, Dei gloriam.*

2 pounds fresh, ripe, sweet summer tomatoes, trimmed of any bad spots and cut into large chunks

1 small onion, thinly sliced

2 sprigs fresh basil or marjoram

2 tablespoons olive oil

1 teaspoon salt, or more as needed

freshly ground black pepper

Heat the oven to 350°F. In a 9-by-13-inch or other wide, shallow baking dish, toss together the tomatoes, onion, basil, olive oil, salt, and pepper to taste. Bake in the oven, uncovered, for about 1½ hours, or until everything is bubbly and there are little browned bits of tomato and onion on the surface. Strain through a screen sieve into a large bowl. Using the back of a ladle, force as much of the tomato pulp as possible through the sieve and into the bowl, until the contents remaining in the sieve are quite dry. Scrape the pulp clinging to the outside surface of the sieve into the bowl. A hand-crank food mill also works well. Stir the sauce and taste for salt and pepper.

Fresh Salsa

MAKES ABOUT 4 CUPS

To dice a tomato, use a serrated knife; I prefer the long blade of a bread knife. For a mild salsa, use only the outside of the jalapeño or serrano chile, not any of the inside, light-colored pith. For a hotter salsa, include some of the pith. Beware, when working with hot chiles, of getting the chile's volatile capsaicin oils on your hands. Just washing your hands with soap doesn't get it all off—as you'll find if you rub your eyes or other sensitive areas. The trick is to first rub your hands well with a spoonful of *vegetable oil.* The oil will dissolve the capsaicin. Then wash the oil off with soap.

Once, in a mischievous mood, making this salsa in the usual way in the Deep Springs kitchen, I noticed the big pile of jalapeño pith and seeds to be discarded. Instead of throwing them into the compost, I ground up this searingly hot material in the food processor, added a little of my prepared salsa so it looked right, and labeled it: "Warning: Extremely HOT Salsa! Eat at Your Own Risk!" Inevitably, and much to my amusement, the students ended up having a salsa-eating contest, complete with painful repercussions vividly reported the following day.

3 to 4 large, red, ripe tomatoes (about 1½ pounds), finely diced (about 4 cups)

½ small white or yellow onion, finely diced (about ⅓ cup)

1 jalapeño or serrano chile, seeded and very finely minced (use more for extra heat)

½ cup coarsely chopped cilantro

1 small clove garlic, well crushed

juice of ½ lime, or more if needed

1 teaspoon salt, or more if needed

Combine all ingredients in a medium bowl. Taste for acidity, heat, and salt, adjusting as necessary.

Guacamole

Mash about 6 large, perfectly ripe avocados with 1 cup of the salsa, plus the juice of another lime, another ½ teaspoon salt, 3 to 4 dashes of hot sauce, and (here's the secret) a small pinch of crumbled dried oregano. Don't mash the avocados too thoroughly—a little chunkiness is good. Taste for balanced salt and acidity. Serve with corn tortilla chips.

Mediterranean Avocado Dip

For a surprisingly delicious change, add ½ cup of coarsely chopped fresh mint to guacamole, and serve with oven-crisped triangles of wheat flatbread.

continued...

. . . continued

Horseradish-Tomato Relish

This light and sparkling salsa turns roast beef into a summer dish. It is also good with pot roast, pork chops, leg of lamb, and baked salmon. Omit the jalapeño and cilantro from the master salsa recipe. Use lemon juice instead of lime. Finely grate a generous amount of fresh horseradish—about half a cupful—into the salsa. Add a good twist of black pepper.

New Mexico Red Chile Sauce

MAKES ABOUT 4½ CUPS

The people of New Mexico cultivate a vibrant, distinct cuisine. The two fundamental sauces, the starting points for many traditional dishes, are red and green chile sauce. Red chile is almost always dried, while green chile is almost always fresh (or frozen or canned). Chiles not harvested green are allowed to stay on the plant a little longer. Once they redden, they are picked and dried. Though they are the same fruit from the same plant, red and green chile are very different in character and flavor. Chicken usually goes with green chile, while red meats are most often served with red chile, but sometimes you'll find the opposite. Sometimes the green is hotter, sometimes it's the red. Often, it depends on your mood: the official New Mexico State Question, asked many times a day in restaurants all over the state, is "Red or green?"

Here is a beautiful, authentic, deeply flavored red chile sauce from my Aunt Mary Nell's recipe file—she was a great New Mexico cook. (The word *chile*, with an "e" at the end, refers to the vegetable, whereas *chili*, with an "i" at the end, refers to the stew made from chiles. See page 48.) New Mexico chile is medium-hot, with a marvelous complex flavor. For Thanksgiving, many New Mexico families serve this sauce in addition to gravy. This naturally results in day-after-Thanksgiving turkey enchiladas.

Although I usually make this sauce (and the following green chile sauce) for enchiladas (pages 171 to 174), they have many other uses. Both are superb drizzled over eggs; stirred into beans to make a simple chili; as a medium for braising chicken or beef (see pages 355 or 315); or served alongside Skillet Cornbread (page 116), Polenta (page 404), Southern Spoon Bread (page 406), or any other dish containing corn. Try a plate of whole-wheat pasta tossed with garlic, sweet corn, sautéed summer squash, and cilantro and topped with either red or green chile sauce.

¾ to 1 cup pure ground New Mexico red chile (see Note)

2 cups water

2 cups chicken stock

6 tablespoons lard or vegetable oil

¼ cup all-purpose flour

4 cloves garlic, crushed

1½ teaspoons salt, or more as needed

⅛ teaspoon black pepper

Blend the chile, water, and stock in a medium saucepan. Bring to a boil, remove from the heat, and let sit for 20 minutes.

In a small skillet over medium heat, melt the lard, blend in the flour and garlic, and cook this roux just until it turns from a pasty white color to a pale beige. Let it cool for a few minutes, then whisk it into the chile mixture. Add the salt, bring to a simmer, and cook the sauce for about 10 minutes. Add the black pepper—it may seem redundant to put pepper in chile sauce, but it brings the flavors into focus. Taste, adding more salt if necessary.

Note: Instead of ground chile, you may use 14 to 16 whole dried chiles: rinse briefly in cold water if they are dusty; remove the stems, seeds, and pale veins; and tear the chiles into 1-inch pieces. Put in a saucepan with the water and stock and bring to a boil. Remove from the heat and let sit for 20 minutes, then transfer to the jar of a blender. Quickly pulse the mixture several times—do not purée. Strain through a screen sieve. Using the back of a ladle, press as much flavorful chile pulp through the sieve as possible, then discard the skins. This more laborious method results in a very smooth sauce that is easier on some people's stomachs. Finish the sauce with the roux made from the lard, flour, garlic, salt, and pepper, as described.

New Mexico Green Chile Sauce

MAKES ABOUT 4 CUPS

See the description of chile sauces at the beginning of the recipe on page 420. Green chiles must be roasted and carefully peeled before using. Many New Mexicans buy and roast bushels of fresh green chiles in late summer during harvest, freezing them whole in zipper-lock bags, 6 to 8 chiles to a bag.

This recipe, also from my Aunt Mary Nell, makes enough sauce for Green Chile Enchiladas (page 172). Canned diced green chiles are fine to use, but be sure to pick out any bits of chile skin—these become apparent as you're stirring the sauce. If you have real, fresh, fire-roasted New Mexico green chiles that you've peeled and cleaned yourself, the resulting sauce will be very, very good indeed.

6 tablespoons lard or vegetable oil

¼ cup all-purpose flour

4 cloves garlic, crushed

½ cup finely diced onion

1 cup water

1 cup chicken stock

1½ cups roasted, peeled, seeded, and chopped New Mexico green chile (from about 8 fresh New Mexico green chiles; see instructions in the Green Chile Relish recipe, facing page)

1 teaspoon salt, or more as needed

⅛ teaspoon black pepper

In a medium-sized, heavy saucepan over medium heat, melt the lard, blend in the flour, and cook this roux just until it turns from a pasty white color to pale beige. Add the garlic and onions and cook for about a minute more, then remove from the heat and let cool for about 5 minutes. Add the water, stock, chiles, and salt, bring to a simmer, and cook gently for about 15 minutes. Add the black pepper, bringing the flavors into focus. Taste, seasoning with more salt if needed.

Green Chile Relish

MAKES ABOUT 1 CUP; SERVES 4 TO 6

This simple mixture of chile, garlic, and salt is the most direct green chile experience, though in New Mexico they don't call it "relish"—it's just "green chile." It is addictively good in many things: in Southwestern and Mexican dishes, to be sure, but also mixed into mayonnaise for sandwiches, swirled into corn soup (see page 229) or Corn Chowder (page 159), or stirred into a small carton of sour cream for an extraordinary dip for tortilla chips. Add a spoonful to Blue Cheese Dressing (page 298) or cornbread batter (see page 116).

To echo the distinctive heat, flavor, and complexity of fresh New Mexico green chiles, try roasting a blend of three more commonly available green chile varieties: a few mild Anaheims, a few zippier pasilla chiles (larger and darker green), and a couple of small, hot serrano chiles.

Roasting chiles is similar to roasting peppers (see page 244). Arming yourself with tongs, roast 6 to 8 large chiles directly over the gas flame of your stove, or put them on a sheet pan and roast them close to your oven broiler, or, most deliciously, char them over a hot charcoal fire. Whichever heat source you use, allow the chiles to blacken and char evenly on all sides, but always watch them carefully. Do not let them burn so much that the outer skin turns ashy gray. When they are evenly charred, put them in a sealable glass or plastic container with a dampened paper towel. Seal the container shut and let the chiles sweat for 20 to 30 minutes.

Remove the chiles from the container, being careful not to lose any of the juice that has accumulated. Break open the chiles and allow any juice inside to run into the container. Using your hands, remove the skin, stems, and most of the seeds. Do not rinse the chiles in running water—a few bits of charred skin are part of the charm, as well as a few seeds. Sometimes it helps to wipe your hands with paper towels a couple of times during the process. Put the peeled, seeded chiles on a cutting surface, and save the flavorful juice for another use, or for stirring into the finished relish if you would like a wetter consistency.

Chop the chiles finely with a good pinch of salt and a well-crushed clove or two of garlic. Put the relish into a bowl and serve. It will keep, refrigerated, for a few days.

LIME-PICKLED RED ONIONS

These crisp, refreshing onions are good company to rich Mexican meat dishes (see Mexican Braised Beef, page 319), tacos, beans, avocados, and enchiladas.

Slice red onions thinly and soak in enough fresh lime juice to just cover them. Cover and let macerate in the refrigerator for several hours. The onions will turn bright pink. Bring to room temperature to serve.

YOGURT-SHALLOT SAUCE

Need a great-tasting, quick, not-too-rich, versatile sauce? This yogurt sauce is very good on fish, chicken, ground meat dishes, vegetables, or grains, or tossed with freshly boiled potatoes for an excellent, simple potato salad.

Start with plain, whole-milk yogurt. Stir in salt and pepper to taste, and a small, minced shallot for every cup of yogurt. (Sometimes I grate the shallot—quick and effective, but fumy.)

Lemon Butter Sauce

SERVES 6

When a rich, warm butter sauce is wanted for lean, white fish, this is it. Though not traditional, it is also a superb sauce for Asparagus Pasta (page 216). The more sophisticated classic French *beurre blanc* is made with champagne vinegar in the reduction instead of lemon juice, and no zest. For a *beurre rouge*, use a fruity, bright-tasting red wine and red wine vinegar.

1 shallot, minced

¼ cup dry white wine

finely grated zest and juice of 1 lemon (about ¼ cup fresh lemon juice)

1 cup cold unsalted butter (2 sticks), cut into 1-tablespoon pieces

¼ teaspoon salt, or more if needed

Put the shallot, wine, 3 tablespoons lemon juice, and half of the lemon zest in a small, nonreactive saucepan. Bring to a boil over high heat, and boil until the liquid is reduced to about 2 tablespoons. Reduce the heat to low. Whisk the cold butter into the warm liquid, 1 or 2 tablespoons at a time. Let each addition of butter incorporate before adding the next. The butter will emulsify into a creamy, rich sauce. Add ¼ teaspoon salt and taste—the richness of the butter should be balanced by the tartness of the lemon. Add more salt if the sauce is bland or too tart, more lemon juice if sharpness is needed. For a more potent lemon flavor, add the rest of the lemon zest.

Variations

Add a tablespoon or so of finely chopped herbs, or a tablespoon of crushed dry green peppercorns.

Mayonnaise

MAKES ABOUT 2 CUPS

This is a flavorful whole-egg mayonnaise. The eggs are lightly soft-boiled, then "pickled" with generous amounts of mustard, vinegar, and salt before the oil is added. It will keep, refrigerated, for about 2 weeks.

> 2 eggs
>
> 2 teaspoons mustard of choice: yellow, Dijon, coarse, or brown
>
> 1½ tablespoons red wine vinegar
>
> ¾ teaspoon salt
>
> 2 or 3 dashes Tabasco or other hot sauce
>
> 1½ cups safflower oil, canola oil, or other light oil

Lightly soft-boil the eggs. Put the uncracked eggs in a small pan of cold water, bring to a boil, remove from the heat, and let stand, covered, for exactly 2 minutes. Pour off the hot water and rinse the eggs in cold water. Let them stand in cold water for 2 to 3 minutes. Using a small spoon, gently break the eggs and scoop the white and yolk into the jar of a blender. Add the mustard, vinegar, salt, and hot sauce.

Cover the blender and blend the egg mixture on the lowest setting for about 10 seconds. For the mayonnaise to emulsify properly, begin adding the oil to the egg in a very thin stream. After a third of the oil has been added, increase the speed of the blender to medium and add the rest of the oil in a thin stream. If the mayonnaise gets so thick that the oil just pools at the top, transfer the mayonnaise to a bowl, and incorporate the rest of the oil gradually with a whisk until the mayonnaise is smooth. Spoon the mayonnaise into a clean jar and chill to thicken before using.

Garlic Mayonnaise

Traditional aioli (see recipe on facing page) is always handmade, with garlic pounded to a smooth purée and slowly "mounted" with olive oil, but this lighter homage to aioli will not disappoint garlic lovers. To the master mayonnaise recipe, add 1 or 2 well-crushed garlic cloves to the blender with the eggs, and use olive oil for ½ cup of the oil, adding it after the light oil. If you want a thinner consistency, stir in a few drops of water.

Mustard Mayonnaise

Mix Dijon mustard and mayonnaise in any proportion. Mustard is virtually fat-free, while mayonnaise is almost all fat; mustard is spiky and sharp, mayonnaise is billowy and enveloping. Strike the appropriate balance. This combination is good with vegetables, hot or cold fish, hot or cold meat, burgers. . . .

Aioli

MAKES ABOUT 2 ½ CUPS

Aioli is wonderful with any simple, savory food. For a traditional southern French meal, serve a generous bowl of aioli surrounded by an array of cooked and raw vegetables, boiled potatoes, and simply cooked fish or shellfish. You may use the Garlic Mayonnaise variation on the facing page with very good results, but here is a more authentic, unctuous aioli, made in a mixer (or with electric beaters). The tireless will enjoy making it by hand with a whisk. When I demonstrated the preparation of aioli to a cooking class at Deep Springs, it was such a hit that several of the students whipped up their own big batch and threw an aioli party in the Boardinghouse kitchen late that night!

2 large cloves garlic

¾ teaspoon salt, plus more as needed

3 egg yolks

2 teaspoons Dijon mustard

2 teaspoons red wine vinegar

2 cups extra-virgin olive oil

¼ cup water

juice of ½ lemon

Cut the cloves of garlic in half lengthwise. If there is a large, greenish sprout in the center of the cloves, remove it; it tastes bitter and harsh. Crush the garlic finely in a mortar with a pinch of salt until it's completely smooth, or use the back edge of a knife. Put the garlic, yolks, mustard, vinegar, and ¾ teaspoon salt in the bowl of an electric mixer, and mix well with the whisk attachment. Drizzle 1 cup of the oil into the garlic mixture in a very thin stream while the mixer is running.

The mixture will lighten in color and thicken. Mix in the water to loosen the mixture. Reduce the speed of the mixer, and drizzle in the remaining 1 cup olive oil in a thin stream. Mix in the lemon juice. Taste for seasoning.

If you want to serve the aioli with something rich, like Baked Salmon (page 372), or fried food, thin it with a little more water and lemon juice.

Toasted Walnut Olive Oil

SERVES 4 TO 5

This nut-infused oil enhances summer green beans, summer squash, beets, winter squash, broccoli, cauliflower, and many other vegetables. It may be used to make a vinaigrette (see page 295) or as the basis for Salsa Verde (facing page). Almonds, pecans, pine nuts, or hazelnuts may be treated the same way.

⅓ cup walnuts, toasted (see page 301) and very finely chopped

⅓ cup extra-virgin olive oil

pinch of salt

pinch of freshly ground black pepper

Stir everything together in a small bowl. Let sit at room temperature.

Meyer Lemon–Olive Relish

MAKES ABOUT 1 CUP; SERVES 2 TO 3

Meyer lemons, ubiquitous in parts of China, have a complex floral fragrance and sweeter juice than regular lemons. The soft, aromatic peel can be eaten as well—it is sweet, not bitter like that of other citrus. This fresh, green lemony sauce is well suited to the Crispy Pan-Fried Chicken on page 351. It's also superb drizzled over a plate of baked mild white fish, new potatoes, and artichoke hearts.

1 Meyer lemon or 1 regular lemon

1 large shallot, finely diced

1 tablespoon red wine vinegar

pinch of salt, plus more as needed

1 teaspoon capers, chopped

1 bunch parsley, very finely chopped (about ¾ cup)

½ cup extra-virgin olive oil, or more if needed

¼ cup pitted green olives, coarsely chopped

freshly ground black pepper

If using a Meyer lemon, remove about three-fourths of the peel with a sharp paring knife—the outer zest as well as the white pith. Cut the peel into fine dice and put it into a medium bowl. If using a regular lemon, finely grate the zest into a medium bowl. Put the shallot in the bowl, and squeeze the lemon juice over the peel and shallot. Add the vinegar and a generous pinch of salt. Let sit for about 10 minutes. Add the capers, parsley, oil, olives, and salt and pepper to taste.

To retain the bright, fresh flavor of the parsley, this sauce must be served soon after it's mixed. If necessary, you may make the different components of the sauce in advance: the lemon, shallot, vinegar, and salt in one bowl, and the capers, parsley, oil, and olives in another. Combine just before serving, with pepper and more salt, if needed, to taste. Or just assemble the sauce as directed, but don't stir it until serving time.

Salsa Verde

Omit the lemon peel and olives and add 2 finely chopped anchovy fillets for the classic Italian *salsa verde*, traditionally used to accompany roast pork. It is also good on other red meats.

Dill Salsa Verde

Substitute fresh dill for half the parsley. This sauce is particularly good for drizzling over a plate of baked fish with boiled potatoes and carrots.

Pickled Summer Vegetables

MAKES ABOUT 8 CUPS

These sprightly, colorful vegetables are irresistible. Try Baked Salmon (page 372) topped with avocado slices, with a big spoonful of these vegetables—and a little of their juice—strewn over and around. Or chop them up and mix into tuna, egg, or potato salad.

BRINE

1½ cups red wine vinegar

3½ cups water

½ cup kosher salt

1¼ cups sugar

1 teaspoon whole black peppercorns

2 bay leaves

6 whole cloves

½ teaspoon mustard seed

½ teaspoon allspice berries (about 10)

¼ teaspoon hot red pepper flakes

———

continued . . .

. . . continued

VEGETABLES

1 medium carrot, peeled and cut on the diagonal into ⅛-inch slices

1 green zucchini, cut in half lengthwise, then cut on the diagonal into ¼-inch slices

1 yellow zucchini, cut in half lengthwise, then cut on the diagonal into ¼-inch slices

1 fennel bulb, trimmed and cut into ¼-inch slices

4 ounces green beans, tops and tails cut off, cut on the diagonal into thirds

4 ounces yellow wax beans, tops and tails cut off, cut on the diagonal into thirds

1 small red onion, cut into ¼-inch slices

1 bunch red radishes, trimmed and cut into quarters

1 small cucumber, halved and cut on the diagonal into ¼-inch slices

To make the brine, bring the vinegar, water, salt, sugar, and spices to a boil in an enameled or stainless-steel pot (the vinegar will adversely react with other metals). Boil for 1 minute.

Drop the carrots into the brine, cooking just until tender-crisp (20 to 30 seconds after the brine returns to a boil) and removing with a slotted spoon to a heat-proof glass or plastic container (you may use 2 quart-size canning jars). Repeat with the remaining vegetables, one variety at a time, in the order given.

To prepare the vegetables, cut as specified, they should each take about 30 seconds to cook. The beans might require more time (taste to tell), and the cucumber should cook for only about 10 seconds. Between batches of vegetables, remove the pan from the heat if necessary to keep the brine from become overly concentrated. When the vegetables are all cooked, boil the brine for 30 seconds longer, then pour it over the vegetables. Let cool to room temperature, then refrigerate. They are ready to eat the following day and will stay fresh tasting for several days.

Pickled Winter Vegetables

Use the following combination of vegetables in the colder months:

2 medium carrots, peeled and cut on the diagonal into ⅛-inch slices

1 fennel bulb, trimmed and cut into ¼-inch slices

1 small red onion, cut into ¼-inch slices

1 small head cauliflower, cut into ¼-inch-thick florets

1 bunch red radishes, trimmed and cut into quarters

Blond Barbecue Sauce

MAKES 1⅓ CUPS SAUCE; SERVES 6 TO 8

This sweet, spicy sauce is easy to throw together with kitchen staples and makes a wonderful glaze for pork or lamb ribs (or chicken). Just salt the ribs, slather with sauce, and roast on a baking sheet at 350°F, basting occasionally with the sauce, until the meat is tender and the glaze is golden brown.

½ cup honey

¼ cup Dijon mustard

¾ cup apricot preserves

3 tablespoons red wine vinegar

1 tablespoon salt

½ teaspoon black pepper

¼ teaspoon cayenne pepper

Combine everything in a pan and heat, stirring, until bubbling and the preserves are dissolved.

OVEN APPLESAUCE

Some years, the Deep Springs orchard produces an extraordinary bumper crop of peaches, pears, and, most of all, apples. Other years, a late freak snowstorm will demolish all the blossoms, and there will be no fruit. Once, during a bumper year, longtime Deep Springs farmer (and fellow alumnus) Andy Jennings walked into the Boardinghouse kitchen bearing an armload of apples—an assortment of the orchard's finest. We cut into each one, tasting their various sweet, crunchy qualities—some were harder, some were denser, some were tarter, and one was spicy, with a hint, almost, of cayenne.

Any kitchen besieged with apples, as mine was that year, should have this easy recipe in its arsenal. This applesauce is perfect to accompany pork chops, or potato pancakes, or both at the same time, or to be eaten all by itself.

Core Golden Delicious, McIntosh, Gravenstein, or other sweet-tart apples, cut them into big chunks, and put them in a baking dish, crowding them slightly. Dot with a little butter and sprinkle with a small pinch of salt. Cover the dish tightly with aluminum foil (shiny side facing in) and bake at 400°F until the apples are *continued...*

. . . continued

completely soft, 30 to 40 minutes. Remove the foil and gently stir the applesauce to a medium chunky consistency. Scrape into a storage container, let cool, and chill. The applesauce's full flavor often does not develop until the following day.

You may peel the apples, but the peel contributes a deeper apple flavor—the large pieces of peel are easily picked out once the applesauce has cooled. Don't be alarmed if some apple varieties turn pink when cooked into applesauce. Quince, apple's old relative, has aromatic, astringent, yellow-white flesh that turns anywhere from pale pink to wine-dark crimson through long cooking (see page 437).

Cranberry Sauce

MAKES ABOUT 2½ CUPS; SERVES 10 TO 12

For some people, the full glory of cranberry sauce is realized not at Thanksgiving dinner but the following day, in the requisite cold turkey sandwich, thickly overlaying—not mixed into—the mayonnaise.

one 12-ounce bag fresh cranberries

¾ cup sugar, or more as needed

⅛ teaspoon salt

½ teaspoon finely grated tangerine or orange zest

Rinse the cranberries in a colander, discarding any soft ones. Drain thoroughly and put in a medium-sized, heavy saucepan. Add the sugar, salt, and zest and heat on a medium-high flame, stirring frequently. When the cranberry sauce begins to boil, reduce the flame to medium, and cook for 8 minutes more, stirring frequently. Taste for sweetness— I like it quite tart; add more sugar to taste. Cover and remove from the flame. Let sit, covered, for 10 minutes. Stir again and transfer the sauce to a medium bowl. Cool, cover, and refrigerate. Bring to room temperature before serving.

Cranberry Relish

This is the classic uncooked relish; many people like both kinds for Thanksgiving. Make it the Tuesday of Thanksgiving week, as it needs a full 2 days to mellow. Use the same ingredients as in the master recipe, but for the citrus element, use 1 whole small orange or 2 tangerines. Rinse the cranberries and discard any soft ones. Drain thoroughly. Rinse the orange, cut into quarters, and remove the core and seeds. Pulse the cranberries, sugar, salt, and orange quarters—peel and all—to a coarse purée in a food processor, or put through a meat grinder. Cover well and chill for 48 hours before using. After 24 hours, taste the relish—if you think it needs to be sweeter, stir in a tablespoon or two of additional sugar. Bring to room temperature before serving.

Marmalade

MAKES ABOUT 8 CUPS (4 PINTS)

Marmalade on hot buttered toast, with tea, is one of Britain's gifts to the world. But marmalade has other uses—it makes a superb glaze for chicken (see page 347), and it lifts the peanut butter sandwich into a whole new realm.

Make marmalade in January or February, when citrus fruits are at their peak. You may use a single variety of citrus if you like—the Seville orange, an old sour and seedy orange variety, makes extraordinary (and authentically British) marmalade. This method discards some, but not all, of the bitter white pith of the citrus fruit, allowing the fruit's friendlier flavors a clearer voice. The ginger and tea could be considered optional but highly recommended—these additions beautifully enhance the strong citrus flavors.

3 pounds mixed citrus fruit: half sweet varieties (oranges, mandarins, kumquats), half sour/bitter varieties (lemons, sour oranges, limes, grapefruit)

1 ounce (a 2- to 3-inch piece) fresh ginger, peeled and finely grated

3 cups water

3 Earl Grey teabags

about 5 cups sugar

Wash the citrus in cool water and towel dry. Remove all colored outer zest of all the thick-rinded fruit with a vegetable peeler (kumquats, Meyer lemons, and small mandarins or tangerines need only to have their seeds removed but may otherwise be used whole). Patiently cut this zest into small, confetti-like strips with a sharp knife. Using a serrated knife, cut off and discard most, but not all, of the bitter white pith from the fruit. Chop the flesh of the fruit coarsely, removing any seeds. *Save all of the juice.*

Mix the citrus zest, citrus flesh, citrus juice, ginger, and water together in a large, heavy, nonreactive (stainless-steel or enamel) pot, and bring to a boil. Skim off most of the scum that forms on the surface. Reduce the heat slightly and let boil, stirring frequently and making sure nothing sticks to the bottom of the pot, for about 20 minutes, or until the bits of zest are tender (taste to find out). Add the teabags, remove from the heat, and let the tea steep for 5 minutes. Remove the teabags and immediately add the sugar to fix the fresh tea flavor, stirring to dissolve. The amount of sugar depends on your own taste and on the tartness of the fruit; fruit that is more sour and bitter will need more.

Briskly simmer the marmalade, stirring frequently and continuing to skim off most of the scum that forms on the surface, until it is thick enough to form a gel when a small spoonful is put on a cold plate and cooled for a few minutes in the refrigerator.

Pour the hot marmalade into sterilized jars, cap with sterilized caps, let cool to room temperature, then store in the refrigerator.

Pickled Plums

MAKES 4 QUARTS

There was always a cut-glass bowl of pickled peaches at Thanksgiving when I was growing up. They were from a can but were different from regular canned peaches—they were whole, with their pit, and the syrup had a whiff of vinegar and spice to cut the sweetness. My first year away from home, cooking Thanksgiving dinner in the Boardinghouse kitchen my first year as a Student Cook at Deep Springs, I found a recipe for those peaches and made it using plums instead, a tradition I continue to this day.

Recently, I found a recipe for pickled peaches, handwritten, in my grandmother Nell's big recipe box. These are wonderful with turkey or ham. The treatment also lends itself to many other types of fruit (see the following list), and the syrup curiously enhances Baked Custard (page 504).

Sweet, firm-fleshed French or Italian-style "prune" plums, arriving in the market in late summer, are excellent in this recipe. Tarter, earlier, more delicate varieties of plum might fall apart in the pickling but are still delicious.

continued . . .

. . . continued

2 cups apple cider vinegar

4 cups sugar

2 cinnamon sticks

1½ teaspoons whole cloves

¾ cup water

4 quarts fresh small plums or other fruit (see list at right), washed

Bring the vinegar, sugar, cinnamon sticks, cloves, and water to a boil in a large, heavy pot and boil for 5 minutes. Remove and set aside the cinnamon sticks and cloves. Poach the plums in the syrup in batches. When the syrup returns to a boil after the fruit has been added, let boil for about 30 seconds, longer for larger plums. Using a slotted spoon, gently remove the fruit to sterilized glass jars or any heatproof glass or plastic container.

When all the plums are poached, return the whole spices to the syrup, boil for a minute more, then pour the syrup and spices over the fruit. When cool, refrigerate. The fruit will be ready to eat the next day, but it is best after a week or two.

Other Pickled Fruit

The following fruit may be pickled in the same way:

* cherries (whole; particularly good accompanying Gin Chicken Liver Pâté, page 363)

* apricots (whole)

* peaches or nectarines (whole if small, halved or quartered if large)

* figs (halved; add a few slices of lemon to the liquid along with the spices)

* Asian pears (thick slices; add a piece of peeled fresh ginger to the liquid along with the spices)

* Bosc pears (thick slices; add a piece of peeled fresh ginger to the liquid along with the spices)

Quince Jam

MAKES ABOUT 2½ CUPS

The full promise of quince, a very old ancestor of apples and pears, is revealed only through long and careful cooking. This Greek-style jam is good on buttered toast or biscuits, or stirred into yogurt, or with cream cheese (or other, sharper cheese) on crackers, but it's particularly good with rich meats such as pork, duck, turkey, or lamb.

Another way to use quince is to slice a peeled, seeded quince into paper-thin slices and combine it with apples for Apple, Ginger, and Walnut Crisp (page 470) or Apple Pie (page 447).

1 large, fragrant quince
(enough to yield 3 cups diced)

10 whole cloves

2 strips lemon zest

juice of ½ lemon

⅓ cup sugar

⅔ cup honey

2 pinches of salt

Rinse the quince and peel carefully with a vegetable peeler or sharp paring knife—quinces have strangely hard flesh, and the knife can skip and jag. Save a few large strips of peel to deepen the flavor of the jam. Cut the quince lengthwise into quarters, then cut each quarter crosswise in half. Cut out the seeds and the tough, pale flesh around the seeds. Cut the quince into small dice. Put in a medium-sized, heavy, nonreactive saucepan with the reserved strips of quince peel and the cloves, lemon zest and juice, sugar, honey, and salt. Bring to a simmer over medium heat, stirring occasionally. Lower the heat and simmer very slowly for about ½ hour—the quince will turn a lovely red-pink color.

Cool the jam slightly and pick out and discard the quince peels, lemon zest, and most of the cloves. Pack into a sterilized jar, cool, and refrigerate.

CHAPTER 14

Pies and Fruit Desserts

Pie, like jazz or Shaker furniture, is a time-honored, uniquely American craft, a definitive statement of generosity and skill. No European-style tart contains as much fruit as an American pie. It is a fundamental part of our national traditional meal, Thanksgiving. In Bishop, California (Deep Springs' closest big town), the Labor Day Tri-County Fair always features a homemade pie contest judged by a plain-spoken, grandmotherly expert in front of a live audience. It's a rare and beautiful sight: more than a hundred freshly baked pies, each one unique, lined up on picnic tables. One year, the Deep Springs gardener (wife of the Deep Springs farmer) won the grand prize, a 4-day ocean cruise for two, with her lemony white peach pie, using peaches from a pampered tree in the Deep Springs orchard.

At Deep Springs Thanksgivings, with many visitors, we sometimes make and consume forty or more pies. Some years, I collect the community's several school-age children and instruct them to quickly bring all the pies out onto the freshly cleared serving table in the dining room. At this much-anticipated moment, the drama heightened by playing Wagner's "Ride of the Valkyries" or Orff's *Carmina Burana* loudly on the Boardinghouse stereo, the room always erupts into applause.

The first part of this chapter aims to demystify the piemaker's craft, with recipes for many fruit pies (and a few nonfruit ones). The second part offers fruit desserts simpler than pie: irresistible crisps, puddings, cakes, and cobblers, and fruit served in its solitary glory or minimally adorned.

continued . . .

Butter Piecrust

MAKES ONE 10-INCH DOUBLE-CRUST PIE
SHELL OR TWO 10-INCH SINGLE-CRUST
PIE SHELLS

Finishing up my college degree after Deep Springs, I spent much time learning how to make good pies with my friend Elge (raised on an apple and cherry farm in rural upstate New York, she knew her pie). We fantasized about opening a pie bakery in New York City. Producing light, flaky piecrust is tricky—its reputation for being difficult is somewhat justified. However, once you get a feel for it and understand the reasons behind the various steps, there is no reason to fear making piecrust.

Piecrust owes its character to the fat it contains, and from how the fat is incorporated. Many prevailing recipes call for vegetable shortening, a highly processed substance that is quickly falling out of favor in American kitchens. It gives a good, flaky texture, thanks to its high melting point, but it is difficult to digest and has no flavor whatsoever. Many recipes calling for shortening also call for a little butter, to remedy the blandness.

Vegetable oil piecrust (see page 446) has a loyal following. The dough is quite easy to mix and roll—good for beginners, or for when you just don't have the fortitude to make a traditional flaky crust. For single-crust pies, an oil crust is perfectly

fine. But its texture will be sandy, rather than flaky, as it is chunks of solid fat layered in the dough that create flakes.

Pork lard, for which shortening was originally developed as a substitute, makes superlative piecrust (see page 446), especially for apple and pear pies. Like shortening, it has a high melting point. Its flavor is neutral, but it nonetheless gives pies a rich, rounded character. But many people today are afraid or unwilling to eat lard piecrust, and virtually all store-bought lard is full of preservatives.

I believe all-butter crusts are the best compromise. They are delicate, tender, flavorful, and every bit as flaky as shortening or lard crusts. A bite of butter piecrust tastes delicious all by itself.

What is the best way to incorporate your chosen fat into the dry flour? Although many recipes specify using two knives or a pastry blender, I find that I have the most direct control over the process when I use my hands. The recipes also say that the fat should be "cut in until the mixture resembles coarse meal or crumbs." I always wonder: What kind of crumbs? What kind of meal? How coarse?

These questions are important, because when flour comes into contact with water and is then worked, it develops springy, elastic, tough strands of wheat protein called gluten. With yeast bread, you want maximum gluten formation—that's why

continued . . .

. . . continued

you knead bread dough. With cookies or cake, you want very little gluten, which is why you typically mix such doughs or batters "only until combined." With piecrust you want enough developed gluten in the structure to create flakes but not so much that the dough becomes tough. In this recipe, some of the butter becomes fine enough in the mixing process to moisten all the flour, but there are also pea-sized chunks of butter in the finished dough. When the piecrust is rolled out, the chunks flatten. In the heat of the oven, these tiny disks of fat in the dough melt, creating a flaky structure.

Then there is the question of liquid. The amount of liquid can never be exactly specified, as the moisture content of flour and fat varies. Most recipes call for ice water but warn that adding too much will make for a tough crust. My grandmother, brilliantly, always used freshly squeezed orange juice, which provides a touch of acidity that inhibits excessive gluten formation. Elaine Teel, the wife of the longtime Deep Springs mechanic, uses 7-Up. I have used nonfat milk and lemonade. Once I considered using beer. It seems that when you use some kind of slightly acidic liquid, you can make a crust that is easy to roll but still tender and flaky. Orange juice also gives a bit of extra sweetness and contributes a rich, golden color. It will not impart a discernible orange flavor to your piecrust.

The last important point: a *glass pie plate* ensures a golden-brown bottom crust. Ten-inch glass plates seem to have become the standard, so that is the size specified for all these recipes. For single-crust pies, I use a regular 10-inch pie plate—one that holds 5 cups of water all the way up to the rim before it starts to overflow. For double-crust fruit pies, I use a slightly deeper 10-inch pie plate—one that holds 7 cups of water before it starts to overflow.

This recipe makes a generous amount of dough, enough for one double-crust pie or two single-crust pies. After trimming your finished crust, you will have a handful of dough left over. Squeeze this into a ball, roll it out into a rectangle, sprinkle it well with cinnamon sugar, roll it up like a jelly roll, and slice into ¼-inch-thick pinwheels. Bake them on a greased baking sheet while baking your pie, for 10 to 15 minutes. Cook's treat.

2¾ cups all-purpose flour

1 teaspoon salt

¼ teaspoon sugar

1 cup (2 sticks) plus 1 tablespoon cold unsalted butter

6 to 8 tablespoons cold orange juice, ideally freshly squeezed

Combine the flour, salt, and sugar in a large bowl. Slice the cold butter into the dry mixture, tossing to coat the slices. Using your hands, rapidly work in the butter, breaking up large chunks of butter and smearing clumps of the mixture between your palms until the visible chunks of butter are pea-sized. To keep the texture of the crust light and flaky, do this quickly—don't let the mixture warm up from the heat of your hands. As the flour is moistened by the butter, it will darken slightly in color, turning from cream white to pale ivory.

Sprinkle in the orange juice and, using a fork, lightly toss and combine just until the mixture coheres. *Do not overmix.* If the mixture seems dry, sprinkle in a bit more orange juice, but do not add so much that the dough becomes sticky.

Divide the dough into 2 balls of equal size. Wrap each tightly in plastic wrap and press each wrapped ball into a disc. Let the dough rest in the refrigerator for at least 1 hour (this lets the gluten relax), then unwrap it and roll it out on a floured surface with a floured rolling pin, flipping it frequently so it doesn't stick, to a large circle about ⅛ inch thick. When rolling the dough, apply outward, not downward pressure. Rolling piecrust takes practice. Fold the circle gently in quarters, lay it in a 10-inch glass pie plate, and unfold. Gently press the crust into the pie plate so

there are no air pockets. Patch any holes or tears with bits of excess dough, lightly moistened with water.

If your crust is for apple pie or another double-crust fruit pie, roll out the second (top) crust, and reserve it between 2 sheets of plastic wrap. Proceed as directed in the recipe.

If your crust is for a single-crust pie, trim off all but an inch of overhanging crust. Fold the crust in toward the rim, and crimp the edge of the crust in an attractive, even scallop pattern. This is not merely a decorative touch; the structure of this fluted edge helps keep the crust from sliding down off the rim. For single-crust pies, freeze the crust for at least an hour before proceeding—this discourages the crust from shrinking during baking. (This step may also benefit double-crust pies, though it is not as crucial.) Now you have a pie shell ready for filling and baking.

To *pre-bake* or *blind-bake* your single crust (as for lemon meringue or cream pies), remove the crust from the freezer and heat the oven to 325°F. Gently press a sheet of aluminum foil over the inner surface of the piecrust, shiny side down. Fill the foil with about 4 cups of dry beans to weight the crust as it bakes. Bake the crust, checking frequently, until it is an even, pale gold color from the fluted rim *continued . . .*

. . . continued

to the bottom, 30 to 35 minutes. Carefully remove the beans and foil and return the crust to the oven for 8 to 10 minutes more, to crisp the inner surface of the crust. Cool completely—the pie shell is now ready to be filled.

Lard Piecrust

Use the preceding method and ingredients, substituting ¾ cup (6 ounces) of cold lard for the butter. A little more liquid might be needed. To render your own lard, obtain some fresh pork kidney fat and use the instructions for rendering beef tallow in the Deep Springs Soap recipe on page 572. One Deep Springs Thanksgiving, in the piecrust for some of the pies, we used home-rendered lard from a student's rural Wisconsin family.

Vegetable Oil Piecrust

This doesn't need the prolonged resting periods that a butter crust demands. For a single crust, mix ½ teaspoon salt and 6 tablespoons canola or other vegetable oil into 1⅔ cups all-purpose flour (part whole wheat is good here) until smooth. With a fork, mix in 2½ tablespoons orange juice or other sweet-tart liquid (see the introduction to the master recipe). Mix just until blended—6 or 7 strokes. The dough will at first seem gooey and far too wet, but soon the flour will absorb the liquid. Pack it into a ball, wrap with plastic wrap or wax paper, and refrigerate for about 30 minutes. Roll out between two sheets of wax paper.

Vegetable Oil–Butter Piecrust

This hybrid recipe is not quite as flaky as an all-butter crust but is certainly easier and quicker, and still very good. Mix 1 teaspoon salt, 6 tablespoons canola oil, and 6 tablespoons softened butter into 2¾ cups all-purpose flour (part whole wheat is good here) until uniformly crumbly (there will be bits of butter in the mix). With a fork, mix in 5 tablespoons orange juice or other sweet-tart liquid (see the introduction to the master recipe). Mix just until blended. Divide the dough into 2 balls of equal size, wrap well with plastic wrap, press the dough into discs, and refrigerate for about 30 minutes. Roll out each crust between two sheets of wax paper.

Apple Pie

SERVES 6 TO 8

The best apple pies are made during apple-harvesting season. Certain apple varieties are ready for harvest in late summer, while others continue through the fall. Granny Smith and Golden Delicious are both good, commonly available cooking apples. Other excellent regional varieties include Gravenstein, Sierra Beauty, McIntosh, Winesap, Arkansas Black, and Pippin. If you are going to the trouble of making a pie by hand, in-season fruit is essential. Once I made an apple pie in July, with heavily waxed Granny Smith apples from a supermarket. Those apples had been in cold storage for most of the year by that point. They cooked down to a very scant, lackluster brown sludge. What was I thinking? That time of year, I should have made berry or peach pie.

Apple pies should be generously filled. The apples cook down and the top crust buckles beautifully. I like a tart pie and use the lesser amount of sugar; you may add more if you like. I like the subtle flavor profile of the spices listed; you may change the amounts or the combination to suit your taste.

Despite the time-honored pie-with-ice-cream tradition, I've always thought the coldness and extreme sweetness of ice cream compete with the subtle goodness of a homemade pie. I suggest serving your pie simply, with lightly sweetened whipped cream flavored with vanilla (1 cup heavy cream, 1 tablespoon sugar, ¼ teaspoon vanilla extract).

Butter Piecrust (page 443), rolled out for a double-crust pie

7 or 8 large, tart cooking apples, peeled, cored, and sliced ¼ inch thick (for 7 or 8 cups sliced apples)

grated zest and juice of ½ lemon

1 tablespoon all-purpose flour, or as needed

⅓ to ½ cup firmly packed brown sugar

¾ teaspoon ground cinnamon

¼ teaspoon ground nutmeg

¼ teaspoon ground allspice

1 to 2 teaspoons finely grated fresh ginger, or ¼ teaspoon ground ginger

pinch of salt

1 egg, separated

1 tablespoon butter, cut into small pieces

1 tablespoon milk

1 tablespoon granulated (white) sugar

Heat the oven to 425°F. Have the unbaked pie shell ready. As you slice the apples, toss them with the lemon juice in a large bowl to sharpen the flavor and prevent them from browning. Judge the juiciness of the apples—very juicy apples will need about ½ tablespoon more flour than specified; dry, greenish apples will need about

continued . . .

½ tablespoon less flour. Toss the apples with the lemon zest, flour, brown sugar, dry spices, grated ginger, and salt until thoroughly combined. Taste the apples, adding more sugar if they are very tart.

Before filling the pie shell, lightly beat the egg white and brush the entire inside surface of the pie shell with it, making sure to apply a good coat around the rim. This will help keep the bottom crust from getting soggy and will also "glue" the top and bottom crusts together at the edge.

Dump the apples into the prepared pie shell, arranging them in an even layer and slightly mounding them in the center. Dot the apples with the butter and gently drape the top crust over the apples, pressing around the rim to fuse the top and bottom crusts. Using a knife or kitchen shears, cut away the excess crust around the rim, leaving about 1 inch of overhang. Fold the overhanging crust in toward the rim and crimp, pinching the folded edge of the crust in an attractive, even scallop pattern. This is not merely a decorative touch; the structure of this fluted edge helps keep the crust in place.

Make an egg wash: thoroughly mix the egg yolk and milk together in a small bowl. Brush the top and rim of the pie with the egg wash, sprinkle the top with the sugar, and cut 3 vents in the center of the top crust.

Bake in the center of the oven for 15 minutes, then turn down the oven temperature to 325°F. Bake for 40 minutes longer, or until the apples are thoroughly cooked. Test by inserting a small knife into a vent; the apples should offer no resistance when pierced. The bottom of the pie should be golden—this is why you use a glass pie plate. Rotate the pie once or twice during baking. Let the pie cool on a rack for a couple of hours at least, until room temperature or barely warm—the juices will continue to thicken as the pie cools.

Apple and Candied Orange Pie

A friend says the oranges in this pie turn the apples into peaches. Navel oranges have firm flesh that holds together well in this treatment. Rinse an orange well, and take several strips of zest (using a vegetable peeler) from the top and bottom of the orange—from its "polar regions," if you will. Cut 6 thinnish (less than ¼ inch thick) crosswise slices from the orange's "equatorial region," carefully removing any seeds. Cover the slices with 1½ cups water in a small saucepan, add the strips of zest, and squeeze in all the juice from the ends. Bring to a boil, reduce the heat, and simmer, stirring very gently from time to time, for about 20 minutes, or until the orange rind can be easily pierced with the tip of a knife. Add 1 cup granulated (white) sugar to the saucepan, and simmer for 30 minutes more. Carefully drain the 6 orange slices and layer them among the apples in the master recipe. No need to include the grated lemon zest the recipe calls for. Reserve the orange-flavored syrup for another use. This pie is a great conclusion to a winter holiday lamb dinner; for a festive occasion, add a little splash of cognac to the whipped cream.

Apple and Candied Lemon Pie

Proceed as directed for Apple and Candied Orange Pie, using a large, fragrant lemon.

Apple and Quince Pie

Peel and core a quince, slice it paper-thin, and add it to the apples. This addition will deepen, hauntingly, the flavor of the apples.

Bacon-Apple Pie

This pie is the crowning glory of an old-fashioned ranch breakfast, when you want to pull out all the stops. Omit the butter, lemon zest, and salt from the filling ingredients in the master recipe. Cut 5 to 6 ounces of bacon (4 to 5 thick strips) into small dice. Fry slowly in a small skillet until a good deal of the fat is rendered out and the bacon is beginning to crisp. Drain on a paper towel, then toss the bacon with the apples and proceed with the remainder of the recipe.

Pear Pie

This is one of my favorite pies. Ripen 7 Bosc pears on your kitchen table for several days, until their brown skin takes on a golden hue and a matte finish. Peel, core, and slice the pears ½ inch thick—they should be juicy and sweet. Following

the master recipe, use the grated zest of ½ lemon, all of the lemon's juice, a mere pinch of cinnamon, and only a teaspoon of grated ginger; no other spices are necessary to augment the flavor of the pears. Use about ⅓ cup of brown sugar. Use 1½ tablespoons of flour. Remember to add a pinch of salt and to dot the filling with butter before putting on the top crust. A crust made with a small portion of whole-wheat flour is especially good with pears.

Blackberry or Blueberry Pie

Following the master recipe, use 6 cups berries for the filling. Use about 3 tablespoons of quick-cooking tapioca (this gives a cleaner flavor; cornstarch is the next best option) rather than flour to thicken the fruit juices. Use about ½ cup white sugar instead of the brown sugar. For blackberries, add a tablespoon of merlot wine to the filling, if you like. Omit the spices, using only the lemon (use lime instead of lemon in blueberry pie). Remember to add a pinch of salt to the filling and to dot it with butter before putting on the top crust.

Peach, Nectarine, Apricot, or Plum Pie

Following the master recipe, use 5 to 6 cups pitted fruit, cut into large chunks. Use about 3 tablespoons of quick-cooking tapioca (this gives a cleaner flavor; cornstarch is the next best option) rather than flour to thicken the fruit juices. Use white, rather than brown, sugar—at least ¾ cup

continued...

. . . continued

if the fruit is tart (apricots, in particular, "tarten" as they cook). Use lemon, but go easy on the spices; fresh ginger is lovely with stone fruit. Remember to add a pinch of salt to the filling and to dot with butter before putting on the top crust. For an excellent plum pie, use sweet Italian-style prune plums, thicken with tapioca, and flavor with the same spices as for apple pie. All pies made of stone fruit have their silkiest texture the day they're baked.

Diana's Cherry Pie

My sister Diana makes this in the early summer in Oregon, using sour cherries from the tree in her yard, pitting them with a paper clip. Following the master recipe, use 6 cups pitted sour cherries (also known as "pie cherries"), about ¾ cup white sugar, and ½ teaspoon almond extract. Omit the lemon and spices. Use about 3 tablespoons quick-cooking tapioca (this gives a cleaner flavor; cornstarch is the next best option) rather than flour to thicken the fruit juices. Create a lattice top crust, so the color of the cherries shows through. Remember to add a pinch of salt to the filling and to dot with butter before putting on the top crust.

Rhubarb Pie

Following the master recipe, use about 5½ cups sliced, unpeeled red rhubarb, at least ¾ cup white sugar instead of the brown sugar, no lemon, and fewer spices— perhaps only ½ teaspoon cinnamon. Use about 2½ tablespoons quick-cooking tapioca (this gives a cleaner flavor; cornstarch is the next best option) rather than flour to thicken the fruit juices. Remember to add a pinch of salt to the filling and to dot with butter before putting on the top crust. Include strawberries if you must; rhubarb alone is more beguiling.

Lemon Meringue Pie

SERVES 6 TO 8

Meringue topped virtually any sort of pie in our grandmothers' day. Today, lemon meringue is the sole survivor of this tradition—the lightness of meringue marries beautifully with a tart lemon filling. Many recipes for meringue call for a hefty dose of sugar, giving the whites good stability but making the pie quite sweet for my taste. Here, a layer of dry white breadcrumbs (undetectable in the finished pie) absorbs excess moisture from the tender, lightly sweet meringue.

The tart lemon curd is also good by itself, on French toast with berries, spread onto biscuits or scones, or between the layers of a cake. Replacing a couple of tablespoons of the lemon juice with fresh lime juice will curiously pique the lemon flavor without announcing its own presence.

For best results, whip the egg whites for the meringue at the same time the lemon filling goes on the heat. The filling should be piping hot to help the bottom of the meringue set.

½ recipe (single crust) Butter Piecrust (page 443), blind-baked

---

FILLING

6 egg yolks (save the whites for the meringue; see Note)

2 whole eggs

¾ cup sugar

1 tablespoon finely grated lemon zest (from about 3 lemons)

¾ cup plus 2 tablespoons fresh lemon juice (from 4 to 5 lemons)

⅛ teaspoon salt

2 tablespoons butter, cut into small pieces

MERINGUE

6 egg whites, at room temperature

¼ cup sugar

⅛ teaspoon fresh lemon juice

pinch of salt

¼ teaspoon vanilla extract

¼ cup panko crumbs or other dry, white breadcrumbs

Heat the oven to 350°F, and have the baked piecrust ready.

continued . . .

. . . continued

To make the filling, in a medium bowl, thoroughly whisk together the egg yolks, whole eggs, and sugar until completely uniform. In a medium-sized, heavy saucepan, combine the egg mixture with the lemon zest, lemon juice, and salt. Add the butter, and set the pot over low heat. (If possible, start whipping the egg whites for the meringue now; see the next paragraph.) Gently heat the mixture, whisking frequently, to 170°F, or until hot and thick. For stirring, alternate between a wooden spoon (to scrape the thickened mixture from the bottom of the pot) and a whisk (to dissolve lumps). Once the mixture starts heating up, make the meringue.

To make the meringue, in a perfectly clean metal or glass bowl, using an electric mixer, beat the egg whites. When they begin to foam, add the sugar, lemon juice, salt, and vanilla. Beat until soft peaks form, then beat just a moment more, until the meringue is between the soft-peak and stiff-peak stages. Let the meringue sit while you finish cooking the filling.

As soon as the lemon filling is ready, spoon it into the crust and smooth the top. Scatter the panko crumbs evenly over the filling—this layer will absorb excess moisture from the meringue (a common problem with lemon meringue pie).

Spoon the meringue in globs all over the lemon filling, gently spreading it all the way to the crust, sealing in the lemon filling completely. Swirl the meringue in big swirls, creating peaks and valleys. Don't fuss over it too much. Bake in the oven until the meringue is thoroughly golden on top, 15 to 20 minutes. Let the pie cool completely, about 2 hours, and serve at room temperature. Serve this pie just as it is—no accompaniment or final garnish is necessary.

Note: When separating eggs, be careful with any whites intended for beating: even a tiny speck of egg yolk or grease will prevent them from beating properly.

Lemon Cream Pie

Make the lemon curd filling as described in the master recipe, but don't put it in the pie shell yet. Chill it thoroughly in a bowl. Whip up a pint (2 cups) of heavy cream with 3 tablespoons sugar and ½ teaspoon vanilla extract. Fold half the cream into the lemon curd filling, and spread this in the pie shell. Top with the remaining whipped cream, and chill well—at least 4 hours, so the lemon flavor permeates the cream.

Chocolate Cream Pie

SERVES 8

This delectable, old-fashioned pie has offered succor to many a homesick Deep Springs student.

½ recipe (single crust) Butter Piecrust (page 443), blind-baked

---

FILLING

1¼ cups firmly packed brown sugar

3 tablespoons cornstarch

½ teaspoon salt

½ cup plus 1 tablespoon unsweetened cocoa powder

3 cups whole milk

3 egg yolks

2 tablespoons butter

1½ teaspoons vanilla extract

TOPPING

1 cup heavy (whipping) cream

1½ tablespoons granulated (white) sugar

¼ teaspoon vanilla extract

dark chocolate for shaving over the top

Have the baked piecrust ready.

To make the filling, in a medium-sized, heavy saucepan, mix the brown sugar, cornstarch, salt, and cocoa powder. Gradually stir in the milk. Over medium heat, bring the mixture to a boil, whisking frequently. Beat the egg yolks in a bowl, whisk in some of the warm chocolate mixture, then whisk the yolks into the remaining chocolate mixture in the pan. Slowly bring back to a gentle boil and cook for 1 minute, stirring frequently. For stirring, alternate between a wooden spoon (to scrape the thickened mixture from the bottom of the pot) and a whisk (to dissolve lumps). Remove from the heat and add the butter and vanilla. Let cool for about 10 minutes, then pour into the baked pie shell. Let cool completely, then chill.

To make the topping, whip the cream with the sugar and vanilla, using an electric mixer, until almost stiff but still supple. Spread the cream over the pie, not too fussily but completely covering the chocolate filling. Make swirls and peaks and valleys. Using a vegetable peeler, generously shave dark chocolate shavings all over the surface of the cream.

Custard Cream Pie

SERVES 8

This old-fashioned pie celebrates the simple goodness of eggs, cream, butter, and milk.

½ recipe (single crust) Butter Piecrust (page 443), blind-baked

---

FILLING

⅔ cup sugar

¼ cup cornstarch

⅛ teaspoon salt

4 large egg yolks

2½ cups whole milk

3 tablespoons cold butter, cut into 3 or 4 pieces

2 teaspoons vanilla extract

TOPPING

1 cup heavy (whipping) cream

1½ tablespoons granulated (white) sugar

¼ teaspoon vanilla extract

Have the baked piecrust ready.

To make the filling, sift the sugar, cornstarch, and salt together. In a medium-sized, heavy saucepan, beat the egg yolks until smooth, then add the milk and beat together until uniform. Pour in the sugar mixture, and stir to dissolve. Put the pan over medium heat and slowly bring to a simmer, stirring very frequently. For stirring, alternate between a wooden spoon (to scrape the thickened mixture from the bottom of the pot) and a whisk (to dissolve lumps). As soon as the mixture begins to bubble gently, reduce the flame to low. Cook for a minute, stirring constantly, then remove from the heat. Stir in the butter slowly, one piece at a time, then add the vanilla. Pour the hot custard into the baked pie shell. Let cool to room temperature, then chill.

To make the topping, whip the cream with the sugar and vanilla, using an electric mixer, until almost stiff but still supple. Spread the cream over the pie, not too fussily but completely covering the filling. Make swirls and peaks and valleys.

Banana Cream Pie

Slice and layer 2 to 3 large, perfectly ripe bananas (they should have a few brown speckles and no green at the stem) with the hot custard filling. Shave bittersweet chocolate over the whipped cream topping.

Banana Pudding

For a good old-fashioned banana pudding, layer sliced bananas, Vanilla Wafers (page 544), and the master recipe's hot custard filling in a tall glass bowl or trifle dish. Chill overnight, then top with whipped cream.

Pumpkin Pie

SERVES 6 TO 8

Large jack-o'-lantern pumpkins are bred for size, not flavor. For pumpkin pie, use small pumpkins bred for sweet, flavorful meat. The Japanese kabocha pumpkin, squat and heavy, with a dark green outer rind, is excellent for pumpkin pie. The sweet, velvety, dense flesh does not need the final drying step, and it mashes beautifully into a stringless purée. Other types of hard winter squash make good pies—the difference between pumpkin and squash is quite subtle—you may still call it pumpkin pie.

For a breakfast version of this pie, reduce the sugar to about ½ cup, and use some whole-wheat flour and a little wheat germ in the crust.

½ recipe Butter Piecrust (page 443), rolled out for a single-crust pie

1 small sugar pumpkin or other sweet-fleshed winter squash, enough to yield 2 cups purée, or one 15-ounce can pumpkin

1 teaspoon ground cinnamon

¼ teaspoon ground cloves

¼ teaspoon ground allspice

2 teaspoons finely grated fresh ginger (or ¼ teaspoon ground ginger)

¾ cup firmly packed brown sugar

3 eggs

¼ teaspoon salt

1½ cups evaporated milk (one 12-ounce can)

barely sweetened whipped cream flavored with vanilla extract, for serving

Have the unbaked pie shell ready.

Heat the oven to 375°F. Cut the pumpkin in half, remove the seeds and stringy material, and put cut side down on a foil-covered baking sheet. Bake until the flesh is completely soft, about 45 minutes, depending on the thickness of the flesh. If the flesh is juicy (this depends on the variety), it needs to be dried out slightly. Scoop the flesh from the shells into a wide skillet or sauté pan. Put the pan over high heat, and quickly evaporate off the excess water, stirring and scraping the bottom constantly. Let the pumpkin purée cool to room temperature, and measure out 2 cups.

Heat the oven to 400°F. In a medium bowl, mix the spices and sugar with the pumpkin, beating well to break up any pumpkin lumps. Beat in the eggs, then the salt and milk, whisking until uniform. Pour into the unbaked shell.

Bake for 10 minutes, lower the oven temperature to 300°F, and bake until the filling is set but still slightly jiggly in the center and the crust is golden on the bottom, about an hour more. Let cool to room temperature and serve with barely sweetened vanilla-flavored whipped cream.

Sweet Potato Pie

SERVES 6 TO 8

This makes an outstanding Thanksgiving pie—although it resembles pumpkin pie, the flavoring is quite different. Accompany with barely sweetened, vanilla-flavored whipped cream, laced with a spoonful of bourbon, if you wish.

½ recipe Butter Piecrust (page 443), rolled out for a single-crust pie

about 3 orange-fleshed sweet potatoes or yams, enough to yield 2 cups

½ cup firmly packed brown sugar

2 eggs, lightly beaten

¼ teaspoon salt

1¼ cups half-and-half

1 tablespoon finely grated fresh ginger, or ½ teaspoon ground ginger

¼ teaspoon ground nutmeg

¼ cup bourbon

½ teaspoon vanilla extract

Have the unbaked pie shell ready.

Heat the oven to 400°F and roast the sweet potatoes whole on a foil-covered sheet until they are completely soft. Let cool until you can handle them, remove the skin, mash well, and measure out 2 cups.

In a medium bowl, combine the sweet potatoes with the brown sugar, beating well to break up any lumps. Beat in the eggs, salt, half-and-half, ginger, nutmeg, bourbon, and vanilla. Pour into the pie shell, and bake for 10 minutes. Lower the oven temperature to 325°F and continue baking until the filling is set, 45 minutes to an hour. The filling will be slightly puffed around the edges and firm in the center. Serve slightly warm or at room temperature.

Pecan Pie

SERVES 8 TO 10

Here is a wonderful, old-fashioned version of this classic, rich Southern pie. If you dare, make the crust with lard (see page 446) or better yet, with the extra bit of beef tallow you happen to have left over from soapmaking (see page 572).

Cane syrup or *golden syrup* provides a deeper, truer sweetness than the more ubiquitous corn syrup. Cane syrup is found in the American South, and many variations of it (such as golden syrup) are common in Canada, England, and much of northern Europe.

Cutting the pecans in half lengthwise is a chore, but they look more attractive than if they were simply chopped, and the finished pie will slice more neatly.

½ recipe Butter Piecrust (page 443), made, if you like, with lard or beef tallow, rolled out for a single-crust pie

4 eggs, at room temperature

1 cup cane syrup or golden syrup

¾ cup sugar

¼ cup butter, melted

2 teaspoons vanilla extract

¼ teaspoon salt

1½ cups pecan halves (about 5 ounces), each halved lengthwise

continued . . .

. . . continued

Heat the oven to 425°F. Have the unbaked pie shell ready. Beat the eggs slightly in a medium bowl. Add the syrup, sugar, butter, vanilla, and salt. Stir in the pecans and pour into the pie shell.

Bake for 15 minutes, then reduce the oven temperature to 350°F. Bake for another 30 to 35 minutes, until the filling is set—a silver knife, inserted near the center, should come out clean, with only a buttery film.

Rhubarb Custard Pie

SERVES 6 TO 8

This excellent pie will convince even those who are dubious about rhubarb. Though traditionally baked with a lattice top crust, I like it in just a single crust—the red rhubarb forms a beautiful mosaic-like pattern. A Deep Springs student's aunt sent me this recipe after the family visited and cooked with us in the Boardinghouse kitchen. "Tom," she wrote on the back of the recipe card, "this pie is awesome."

Butter Piecrust (page 443), rolled out for a single- or double-crust pie

1¼ cups sugar

¼ cup all-purpose flour

¾ teaspoon ground nutmeg

⅛ teaspoon salt

3 eggs, lightly beaten (my friend Elge likes to add an extra yolk)

¼ teaspoon vanilla extract

1½ pounds red rhubarb, cut diagonally into thin slices (4 cups)

1 tablespoon butter, melted

Have the unbaked pie shell ready. Heat the oven to 425°F. Blend the sugar, flour, nutmeg, and salt together in a medium bowl. Add the eggs, vanilla, rhubarb, and butter, and stir to combine. Pour into the pie shell. Add a top crust (see the Apple Pie recipe, page 447, for instructions), or top with a lattice crust, if you like.

Bake for 15 minutes, then reduce the oven temperature to 325°F. Bake for 40 to 45 minutes longer, or until the filling is set, the rhubarb is tender, and the crust is browned on the top and bottom. If the pie's top is browning too much, lay a sheet of aluminum foil over the top, shiny side up. Let cool completely, or until just warm, and serve plain or with whipped cream.

Jam Pie

SERVES 6 TO 8

My mother still talks about a delicious pie her frugal mother once made during the World War II years, using up odd bits of jam and jelly from several jars.

½ recipe Butter Piecrust (page 443), rolled out for a single-crust pie

3 eggs, at room temperature

1⅓ cups sour cream

3 tablespoons butter, melted

1⅓ cups great-tasting, tart jam

1 teaspoon vanilla extract, or a combination of vanilla and almond extracts

4 teaspoons sugar

¼ teaspoon salt

4 teaspoons cornstarch

Have the unbaked pie shell ready. Heat the oven to 350°F. In a medium bowl, lightly beat the eggs, then mix in the sour cream, butter, jam, and vanilla until the mixture is uniform. Whisk together the sugar, salt, and cornstarch in a small bowl until no lumps remain, and blend thoroughly into the jam mixture. Pour into the pie shell and bake for 30 minutes. Turn down the oven temperature to 325°F and bake for another 15 to 20 minutes, until the jam filling is puffed around the edges and just barely set in the center. Let cool completely.

Maple Syrup Pie

SERVES 8 TO 10

I prefer dark grade-B maple syrup, with subtle but deliciously bitter notes, to the lighter varieties. For several years at Deep Springs we mail-ordered giant tins of this syrup from Maine. This unusual pie is excellent served with fresh fruit and whipped cream.

½ recipe Butter Piecrust (page 443), rolled out for a single-crust pie

2 eggs

1 egg yolk

3 tablespoons all-purpose flour

1 teaspoon salt

2 cups dark maple syrup

1 cup heavy (whipping) cream

1½ teaspoons apple cider vinegar

Have the unbaked pie shell ready. Heat the oven to 425°F. Beat the eggs and yolk together briefly in a medium bowl. Add the flour and salt, beating well. Add the syrup, cream, and vinegar. Pour into the pie shell and bake for 10 minutes. Reduce the oven temperature to 325°F, then bake for 40 minutes more, or until the filling is slightly puffed and bubbly. Let the pie continue to set up and cool completely— 2 or 3 hours—before slicing.

Aunt Lela's Buttermilk Pie

SERVES 8 TO 10

This pie is very rich; do not serve it with whipped cream or any other accompaniment, just good, strong coffee. My Great Aunt Lela brewed her coffee strong by pouring it back through the grounds— only twice for herself, but three times for company.

I entered this pie in the Professional Baked Goods division at the Tri-County Fair in Bishop (Deep Springs' nearest town)—it won Best in Show.

½ recipe Butter Piecrust (page 443), rolled out for a single-crust pie

¼ cup all-purpose flour

1¾ cups sugar

½ teaspoon salt

½ cup butter (1 stick), melted

3 large eggs, at room temperature

½ cup buttermilk

1 teaspoon vanilla extract

1 teaspoon lemon extract

nutmeg for sprinkling on top

Have the unbaked pie shell ready. Heat the oven to 325°F. Mix the flour, sugar, and salt in a medium bowl. Add the melted butter and beat (the mixture will be stiff). Add the eggs, one at a time, then add the buttermilk and extracts. Pour into the pie shell, sprinkle the top evenly with nutmeg, and bake for about 40 minutes, or until set. Let the pie cool completely on a rack—at least 2 hours—before serving at room temperature.

Cheesecake

SERVES 12 TO 16

Structurally speaking, cheesecake is a kind of pie; before springform pans were ubiquitous, people baked their cheesecakes in pie plates and often called them "cheese pie." Here is a classic recipe for this beloved American dessert. It's easy to put together, but keep in mind that it requires a good deal of time. The baking and cooling period takes 4 hours, and *it must be baked at least one day before you serve it.* It's even better 48 hours after baking, when the cheese flavor reaches its zenith.

While this cheesecake tastes glorious simply served plain, the glazed fruit is delicious and pretty. Don't be tempted to garnish rich and creamy cheesecake with rich and creamy whipped cream, as chain restaurants often do—one does not enhance the other.

CRUST

1 cup fine graham cracker crumbs

2 tablespoons sugar

3 tablespoons butter, melted

continued . . .

. . . continued

FILLING

2½ pounds cream cheese (five 8-ounce packages), at room temperature

1⅔ cups sugar

2 tablespoons all-purpose flour

¼ teaspoon salt

6 eggs

½ cup heavy (whipping) cream

1 teaspoon vanilla extract

2 tablespoons fresh lemon juice

½ teaspoon finely grated lemon zest

GLAZED FRUIT TOPPING (OPTIONAL)

¾ cup fruit jelly, jam, or preserves, corresponding to the type of fresh fruit you are using

2 tablespoons water

2 to 3 cups fresh fruit: sweet or sour cherries (pitted), berries, plums (cut into chunks), nectarines or peaches (cut into chunks)

Heat the oven to 350°F.

To make the crust, blend the graham cracker crumbs, sugar, and melted butter together. Lightly butter a 10-inch spring-form pan, and press the crust mixture evenly on the bottom of the pan. Bake the crust for about 10 minutes. Set aside to cool while you mix the filling. Leave the oven set at 350°F.

To make the filling, be sure the cream cheese is at room temperature—set the packages out on your kitchen counter for at least an hour before you mix the filling. In a large bowl, gently stir up the cream cheese with a few strokes of a wooden spoon. Sift together the sugar, flour, and salt and blend into the cream cheese thoroughly. Using a wire whisk or the low setting of an electric mixer, gently beat until the mixture is perfectly free of lumps. Do not violently beat the mixture, or the cheese could turn grainy. Add the eggs one at a time, incorporating each egg thoroughly into the batter before adding the next. Add the cream, vanilla, lemon juice, and lemon zest. Pour into the crust.

Put the cheesecake into the oven and bake for 10 minutes. Lower the oven temperature to 225°F and bake for 1½ to 2 hours, or until the cheesecake is no longer jiggly in the center and is pulling away from the sides of the pan. Leaving the cheesecake in the oven, turn off the oven (do not open the oven door) and let it rest in the oven for another hour. Cool on a rack for yet another hour, then wrap and refrigerate overnight (2 days is even better). For the best flavor and texture, let the cheesecake come to room temperature before serving.

To make the glazed fruit topping (if using), melt the jelly with the water in a medium saucepan, just until the jelly is melted. The fruit may be prepared ahead of time, but combine it with the glaze shortly before serving. Toss the fresh fruit with the glaze, immediately pile the fruit on the cheesecake, and serve.

Gingersnap Crust

When the mother of one of my Deep Springs classmates visited the Valley to teach an informal pottery class, she made gingersnap-crusted cheesecake for us all. Instead of graham crackers, use a generous cup of finely crushed Gingersnaps (page 539), and since gingersnaps are decidedly sweeter than graham crackers, use only 2 teaspoons sugar rather than 2 tablespoons.

APPLES AND ORANGES

Serve crisp, flavorful apples and juicy oranges together as a very simple winter dessert. Satsumas and other small, sweet, seedless, easy-to-peel mandarin oranges come into season in December—these are ideal.

Bring the whole fruit to the table in a bowl, then slice the apples with a small knife, arranging the slices on a plate. Peel the oranges, twisting the peel over the apples—the citrus oil from the peel will agreeably flavor the apples. A few sweet, gooey Medjool dates are most welcome here, too.

MELON WITH ROSEWATER

This summer dessert is as refreshing as it is simple.

Procure an array of sweet, ripe summer melons, different varieties and colors, if possible: red and yellow watermelon (with seeds; seedless watermelon varieties are not as flavorful), cantaloupe, green- and orange-fleshed honeydew. . . . Cut the melon into large, attractive chunks, rind removed or not. Cover and chill. Sprinkle the melon lightly with rosewater and serve.

Orange Bread Pudding

SERVES 4 TO 6

If you find the usual cinnamon- and vanilla-flavored bread pudding dull, try this more sprightly one, made with fresh citrus and almond extract.

1 tablespoon butter

4 cups white bread cubes

2¼ cups whole milk

finely grated zest of 2 medium oranges (about 1 tablespoon)

juice of 2 medium oranges (½ cup)

4 eggs

1 tablespoon fresh lemon juice

⅓ cup sugar

¼ teaspoon salt

1 teaspoon almond extract

⅓ cup dried fruit, such as golden raisins, cherries, prunes, or cranberries

Heat the oven to 325°F. In a large skillet over medium heat, melt the butter and add the bread cubes. Stir the bread around until it is lightly toasted, about 10 minutes. Add the milk (it will boil up) and the orange zest. Remove from the heat.

In an 8-by-8-inch baking dish, gently beat together the orange juice, eggs, lemon juice, sugar, salt, and almond extract. Slowly stir in the milk-bread mixture and the dried fruit. Bake for about 40 minutes, or until a knife inserted near the center comes out clean. This is good served warm, at room temperature, or chilled.

Ginger Peach Crisp

SERVES 6 TO 8

LARGE QUANTITY RECIPE: SERVES 30 TO 40

Rather than topping it with ice cream or whipped cream, I love to serve fruit crisp piping hot in a bowl with fresh, cold, unsweetened, unwhipped heavy cream poured over it.

8 cups pitted sliced fresh peaches
2 gallons pitted sliced fresh peaches

3 to 4 tablespoons granulated (white) sugar
1¼ cups granulated (white) sugar

juice of ¼ lemon—more if using white peaches
juice of 1 lemon

1 tablespoon finely grated fresh ginger, or more to taste
¼ cup finely grated fresh ginger

pinch of salt
¼ teaspoon salt

2 tablespoons quick-cooking tapioca or all-purpose flour
½ cup quick-cooking tapioca or all-purpose flour

continued...

. . . continued

TOPPING

1½ cups all-purpose flour (up to ½ cup
may be whole wheat)

*6 cups all-purpose flour (up to 2 cups
may be whole wheat)*

½ cup rolled oats

2 cups rolled oats

½ cup firmly packed brown sugar

2 cups firmly packed brown sugar

2 tablespoons granulated (white) sugar

½ cup granulated (white) sugar

⅛ teaspoon salt

½ teaspoon salt

12 tablespoons salted butter (1½ sticks),
at room temperature

*3 cups salted butter (1½ pounds,
6 sticks), at room temperature*

whipped cream or plain, unwhipped
heavy cream, for serving

Heat the oven to 350°F. Combine the
peaches, sugar, lemon juice, ginger, salt,
and tapioca in a large bowl. Taste—the
topping is cookie-sweet, so the fruit
mixture should be tart. For a bolder
flavor, add more ginger. Dump the
peaches into a 9-by-13-inch pan. *(For
large quantity, divide peaches between
2 shallow "hotel" pans.)*

To make the topping, combine the flour,
oats, brown and granulated sugars, and
salt in a large bowl, then work in the softened butter until the mixture is crumbly
and there is no dry flour left. Sprinkle the
topping evenly over the peaches. Do not
pat the topping down—the pebbly appearance is much of the charm. Bake for 40 to
50 minutes, or until the topping is golden
brown and thick fruit juices are bubbling
up from below. Serve warm with whipped
cream or plain, unwhipped heavy cream.

Stone Fruit with Almond Sugar

SERVES 6 TO 8

This is one of the simplest, lightest, and most satisfying ways to serve summer stone fruits—nectarines, peaches, and plums. Feel free to experiment with other varieties of fruit and other kinds of extract.

2 to 3 pounds ripe, flavorful stone fruit: nectarines, peaches, cherries, apricots, and plums

½ cup sugar

½ teaspoon almond extract

Cut large peaches and nectarines in quarters, removing the pit. Leave smaller fruit whole and unpitted. Combine the sugar and extract in a small bowl until the mixture is uniform. Serve a few pieces of fruit piled on a plate with a small heap of sugar alongside, so diners can dip their fruit in the sugar.

Poached Pears with Chocolate Sauce

SERVES 6

Pears and chocolate? It's an almost magical combination. Serve this dessert as is, or with a few Almond Cookies (page 532). Add a scoop of vanilla ice cream and you have the French classic *poires belle Hélène*.

PEARS

1 lemon

1¼ cups sugar

1 cup dry white wine

2 cups water

½ vanilla bean, split lengthwise, or 2 teaspoons vanilla extract

6 ripe, fragrant Bartlett pears

CHOCOLATE SAUCE

2 cups water

⅓ cup light corn syrup

1½ cups unsweetened cocoa powder

1 cup granulated (white) sugar

pinch of salt

⅔ cup bittersweet chocolate chips

continued . . .

. . . continued

To poach the pears, first wash the lemon well. Using a vegetable peeler, remove the zest from the lemon in long strips and put it in a large, heavy saucepan. Add the juice of the lemon, sugar, wine, water, and vanilla bean. Bring to a simmer over medium-low heat, stirring occasionally to dissolve the sugar. Using a small, sharp knife, peel the pears, *reserving the peels.* Cut the pears in half and remove the core, keeping the pear halves intact. Put the peels and the pears in the warm poaching liquid. The peels will deepen the pear flavor. Raise the heat to medium, and bring to a simmer. Poach the pears, stirring gently, until the pears are soft and well heated all the way through, about 10 minutes. Let the pears cool to room temperature in the liquid, then refrigerate overnight in the liquid.

To make the chocolate sauce, heat the water and corn syrup together in a medium-sized, heavy saucepan. Combine the cocoa powder and sugar in a bowl, working out any lumps in the cocoa, and add to the pan, whisking well. Bring to a boil, whisking frequently. Remove from the heat and add the salt and chocolate chips, whisking to dissolve the chocolate. Keep warm, or rewarm in a double boiler before serving.

Carefully remove the chilled pear halves from the liquid, and put in attractive individual glass bowls. (Strain the flavorful pear liquid and reserve for another use.)

Spoon about ⅓ cup of warm chocolate sauce around, rather than over, the pears—make sure some of the bare pear's cheek shows through the dark sauce. Serve immediately, while the pear is cool and the sauce is hot. The sauce reheats well; there will be a little left over.

Warm Pears with Chocolate Ice Cream

SERVES 3 TO 4

Here is a pear-and-chocolate dessert that is quicker and simpler than the preceding recipe.

2 ripe, sweet, good-smelling pears

2 tablespoons butter

2 tablespoons sugar

pinch of salt

2 teaspoons fresh lemon juice

¼ teaspoon vanilla extract

1½ pints premium chocolate ice cream, scooped into chilled bowls

Peel, core, and cut the pears into ½-inch slices. Melt the butter in a heavy skillet over medium-high heat. When it bubbles, add the pears, sugar, and salt. Cook until the pears are softened. Add a little lemon juice to balance the sweetness, and add the vanilla. Spoon the warm pears and juice around and alongside scoops of chocolate ice cream, and serve immediately.

These pears are also good with chocolate-almond ice cream or mint chocolate chip ice cream.

Pear, Ginger, and Lemon Crisp

SERVES 6 TO 8

I made this crisp for the Deep Springs community on my visit to interview for the chef's job, and included the recipe in the earliest version of this book. The students, after leaving Deep Springs, reported back to me that they had become very popular potluck party guests on the strength of this recipe.

FILLING

2½ pounds just-ripe, flavorful pears

juice and zest of 1 lemon

2 to 3 tablespoons finely grated fresh ginger

3 tablespoons sugar

1 tablespoon all-purpose flour

pinch of salt

TOPPING

¾ cup sliced almonds, lightly toasted (see page 301) and chopped medium fine

¾ cup plus 1 tablespoon all-purpose flour

¼ cup rolled oats

⅓ cup firmly packed brown sugar

2 tablespoons granulated (white) sugar

½ cup salted butter (1 stick), at room temperature

continued...

. . . continued

> whipped cream or plain, unwhipped heavy cream, for serving

Heat the oven to 350°F.

To make the filling, peel, core, and cut the pears into ½-inch slices. Toss with the lemon juice and zest, ginger, sugar, flour, and salt in a 9-by-13-inch baking dish and arrange in an even layer.

To make the topping, combine the toasted, chopped almonds with the flour, oats, and brown and granulated sugars, then work in the softened butter until the mixture is crumbly and there is no dry flour left. Sprinkle the topping evenly over the pears. Do not pat the topping down—the pebbly appearance is much of the charm.

Bake for 40 to 50 minutes, or until the topping is browned and the fruit syrup is bubbling up around the edges. The pears should be completely soft, offering no resistance to a small knife poked through in the center. Let the crisp cool slightly, and serve in shallow bowls with whipped cream, or simply with cold, unwhipped, unflavored heavy cream (my favorite).

Apple, Ginger, and Walnut Crisp

Substitute apples and walnuts for the pears and almonds.

Other Fruit Crisps

Take a cue from the array of fruit pie recipes (beginning with Apple Pie, page 447), and create the crisp of your choice: rhubarb crisp, cherry crisp with almonds in the topping, winy berry crisps . . . all may be known and loved.

PERSIMMONS

Persimmons come into season in the fall and early winter. They are sweet—very low in acid, with a lush, nutty, pumpkinlike flavor. There are two principal varieties: the teardrop-shaped Hachiya must be slowly ripened after picking until the flesh is completely soft, while the smaller, flatter Fuyu needs only minimal ripening. Usually, both varieties are seedless. Persimmons are still considered an oddity by most Americans, but are well worth getting to know.

Ripen a Fuyu persimmon until just beyond crisp but still firm. Peel, and slice crosswise to reveal a star pattern in the fruit's core. Arrange on a plate. They are perfect on the Thanksgiving table accompanied by a few lightly toasted pecans.

Ripen a Hachiya persimmon on a windowsill, stem side down, until it is deeply translucent and completely soft. It could take weeks. Serve chilled or at room temperature. The texture is slippery, like pudding. On a small glass dessert plate, slice the persimmon lengthwise down to the stem, at right angles, to make 4 quarters. Open out the quarters on the plate to make a flower, and serve with a spoon.

Plum Crumb Cake

SERVES 8

In this summer recipe, fresh, tart-sweet plums are embedded in a simple, almond-scented cake batter.

  about 2 pounds fresh plums

  2 cups sugar

  3 cups sifted all-purpose flour

  1 cup cold butter (2 sticks), cut into thin slices

  ¼ teaspoon salt

  ½ teaspoon baking powder

  ½ teaspoon baking soda

  2 eggs, beaten

  1 cup buttermilk

  1 teaspoon almond extract

  whipped cream for serving (optional)

Using a small, sharp knife, halve and remove the pits from the plums to yield about 4 cups of plum halves. If the plums are large, cut them in quarters.

Heat the oven to 350°F. Butter and flour a 9-by-13-inch baking dish. In a large bowl, mix the sugar and flour. With your hands, rapidly work the butter into the mixture,

continued...

until the mixture is somewhat moistened and only small pieces of butter are visible.

Reserve 1 firmly packed cup of this mixture for the topping. Mix the salt, baking powder, and baking soda into the remainder.

Combine the eggs, buttermilk, and almond extract in a medium bowl. Add to the flour mixture and fold together both mixtures *just until smooth*. Scrape into the prepared baking dish. Sprinkle a third of the reserved topping evenly over the top. Place the plum halves, cut sides up, over the batter. Sprinkle the remaining crumb mixture over the plums. Bake just until a toothpick inserted in the center comes out clean, 45 to 50 minutes. Let cool for at least 15 minutes, allowing the cake to absorb the plum juices, before cutting into squares. Top warm slices with barely sweetened whipped cream, if you like.

Serve this cake the day it's baked—by the next day, the plums' moisture will make the cake soggy.

RHUBARB

This is the simplest, most direct way to experience rhubarb. Scandinavians find this familiar and comforting.

Just wash your rhubarb; don't peel it. Slice it thick, and throw it in a saucepan with a pat of butter, a few drops of water, a pinch of salt, a bit of grated orange zest if you like, and as much sugar as it takes to make the juices taste good but still tart. Heat to a gentle bubble and cook for a few minutes, stirring gently from time to time, until the rhubarb is juicy and tender. Serve warm in a bowl with a little cold cream, sour cream, or a scoop of vanilla ice cream.

My Mother's Strawberry Shortcake

SERVES 4 TO 6 (OR 2 TO 3 FOR DINNER)

Every spring when I was little, when strawberries were at their peak, my mother would purchase an entire 10-pound lug of strawberries. She didn't make jam or anything with them—we would just eat our fill of fresh berries all week long. But on the evening she brought the berries home, we would have nothing but strawberry shortcake for dinner, served in big, shallow, blue-and-white china bowls that belonged to my grandmother.

1 pound fresh strawberries in season, hulled and thickly sliced

2 to 3 tablespoons sugar

fresh lemon juice, if necessary

___

SHORTCAKES

1 recipe dough for Biscuits, page 113, with 1 tablespoon sugar added

2 to 3 teaspoons sugar for sprinkling over the tops

___

1½ cups heavy (whipping) cream, well chilled

1 heaping tablespoon sugar (optional)

¼ teaspoon vanilla extract (optional)

butter, at room temperature, for spreading

Heat the oven to 425°F. Toss the strawberries with the sugar in a medium-sized glass or stainless-steel bowl. Taste, a few drops of fresh lemon juice can do wonders if your strawberries are tired. Cover with plastic wrap and let sit at room temperature while you make the shortcakes.

To make the shortcakes, cut 4 to 6 large biscuits from the biscuit dough. Sprinkle each with ½ teaspoon sugar. Bake until golden brown, 8 to 10 minutes.

Barely whip the cream—it should be only slightly thickened, still pourable. If you like, add the sugar and vanilla; I prefer the cream unflavored.

Have everything ready to assemble when the biscuits emerge from the oven. Let the biscuits rest on the baking sheet for a few moments, then transfer them to shallow china soup bowls. Carefully split the biscuits apart, setting the tops gently to the side. Spread a little softened butter on each biscuit, spoon a generous amount of room-temperature strawberries over each hot biscuit, then spoon the cold cream over the mound of strawberries. Place the biscuit tops back over everything. Serve immediately, with knife, fork, and spoon.

Canned-Fruit Cobbler

SERVES 4 TO 6

My grandmother made this cobbler with canned pears, but it's good with peaches or pineapple, too. It is also a great use for a pint jar of home-canned fruit in light syrup.

  ½ cup butter (1 stick)

  ⅔ cup sugar

  ¾ cup all-purpose flour

  1 teaspoon baking powder

  ¾ teaspoon salt

  ⅛ teaspoon ground mace or nutmeg

  ¾ cup milk

  one 14-ounce can fruit in light syrup: pears, peaches, or pineapple

Heat the oven to 350°F. Melt the butter in the oven in a 9-by-13-inch baking dish. Sift the sugar, flour, baking powder, salt, and mace together in a medium bowl. Whisk the milk into the batter, just until uniform.

Pour the fruit, syrup and all, into the melted butter, distributing the pieces of fruit evenly over the bottom of the pan. Pour the batter over the fruit. *Don't stir.* Bake for 20 to 25 minutes, until the top is pale golden brown. Let the cobbler set up for about 5 minutes before serving.

NUTS FROM THE SHELL

In the fall, the new crop of tree nuts arrives in the market, typically almonds, walnuts, pecans, and hazelnuts. Whole nuts in their shell are a traditional Christmastime treat.

When my mother and her sisters were young, every year for Christmas their dad gave them each a big tin of perfect, unbroken pecan halves he'd shelled himself. Cracking nuts is a developed skill, the object being to apply just enough pressure to crack the shell without damaging the nutmeat.

You may wonder, with shelled nuts readily available, why go to the trouble of cracking them yourself? A nut's shell, as any squirrel will tell you, is nature's best way of preserving a nut, better than any refrigerator or plastic wrapping. Nuts right out of the shell have a full, complex sweetness. You rediscover their character and flavor. With a little cheese or fruit, they can be a delightful, participatory hors d'oeuvre or dessert.

The Strawberry

A man walking across a field suddenly
encounters a ferocious, hungry tiger.
The man flees, and the tiger chases him.
Coming to a cliff, the man grasps a wild
vine and swings over the edge. The tiger
sniffs at him from above. Terrified, the
man looks down and sees another tiger,
pacing and growling below. At that
moment, two mice, one white and one
black, begin to gnaw away at the vine,
bit by bit. The man notices a big, ripe,
luscious red strawberry growing on the
cliffside nearby. Grasping the vine in
one hand, he plucks the strawberry with
the other. How sweet it tastes!

—*Traditional Buddhist story*

CHAPTER 15

Cakes

When my mother was a girl, she'd sometimes arrive home from school to find a large homemade birthday cake on the counter, complete with frosting and candles. Knowing that all the family birthdays were months away, she'd ask, "Whose birthday is it?" "Well, it's someone's birthday somewhere in the world!" my grandmother would say, brightly. After supper, she would serve the cake with the lights dimmed, the candles lit, and the whole family singing "Happy Birthday, Dear Someone."

My criterion for a good cake is simple: it should taste good enough to be thoroughly enjoyed without frosting. You'll find a good recipe for cream cheese frosting accompanying the carrot cake, but there are no standard buttercream-type frosting recipes in this book. When a cake accompaniment is needed, I usually serve a dollop of lightly sweetened, vanilla-flavored whipped cream (1 cup cream, 1 tablespoon sugar, and ¼ teaspoon vanilla extract, whipped just to soft peaks)—it allows the flavors, richness, and light texture of the cake to shine through. For birthday cakes and other special occasions when a frosted cake is called for, I use whipped cream to frost the cake (see Whipped Cream Cake, page 486, and Big Pink Cake, page 496).

Another cake recipe suitable for dessert is Banana Bread (page 124).

Please see the information on flour, page 68, and on buttermilk, baking powder, and baking soda, page 106.

Baking a cake from scratch has the reputation of being difficult, but there are only a few things to bear in mind:

* *Pay attention to the temperature of your ingredients, especially the eggs and butter.* Cake batter should be room temperature when it goes into the oven; it bakes more evenly than a chilled batter. Eggs should always be at room temperature (warm cold eggs for a few minutes in hot tap water). Butter should be pliable but still firm enough to trap tiny air bubbles when whipped—a bit cooler than room temperature.

* *Don't overmix the batter.* Mix just until the batter is uniform; overmixing activates the gluten in the flour, resulting in rubbery, tough cake.

continued . . .

. . . continued

* *Don't slam the oven door at any point during baking.* Until the cake is cooked through, its structure is delicate. Any jostling could deflate the tiny bubbles of air that give the cake its light texture.

* *Don't overbake or underbake your cake.* Remove it from the oven when a toothpick inserted in the center just comes out clean, with maybe a few crumbs clinging, but no raw batter. If over-baked, the cake will be dry. If the cake is underbaked, with a patch of wet batter in the center, it can't be put back in the oven to finish baking—it will dry out.

* *Cool cakes on a rack.* Let your cake sit in the pan, on a rack, for about 10 minutes after taking it out of the oven, then remove it from the pan and let it cool completely on the rack. This allows heat and steam to readily escape, preventing sogginess and making for the best, lightest texture.

Goose Egg Pound Cake

MAKES 1 LARGE CAKE; SERVES 8 TO 10

While many modern pound cake recipes call for sour cream, buttermilk, or some such dairy product, and leavening such as baking powder, this one contains little besides the classic four ingredients: eggs, butter, sugar, and flour. It has no leavening other than the air whipped into the butter and eggs. The rosewater adds a subtle aroma and just a bit of moisture. A little honey is included for two reasons: to deepen the sweetness and to retain moisture. It is a beautifully dense, tender, creamy-tasting cake with a delectable brown outer crust.

The flavorings may be varied to suit your taste. The honey and rosewater are my additions, but I also love citrus zest, almond extract, and mace. The presence of lemon extract, a favorite Southern ingredient, and perhaps its unique "cold-oven" baking method, bespeak its Texas pedigree. My mother says, "This was my favorite cake to bake in Houston in the summer. I could pop it in the oven and then leave the house while it baked!"

One late-summer day, a particularly grumpy and nasty-tempered goose (more correctly, a gander) appeared in Deep Springs Valley under still-unexplained circumstances. In the face of Christmas roast goose jokes, Deep Springs rancher/cattlewoman/animal rescuer Iris Pope named him Louis, gave him the run of the apple orchard, and, from friends in town, fetched a lovely, sweet-tempered Edith of a goose for this Archie of a gander. He is still nasty but more tractable. She radiates in his presence. Iris named her Babette, and we use her eggs in baking. They seem to produce a subtly richer result than hens' eggs in egg-heavy preparations such as this pound cake. But don't wait to get goose eggs to make this cake—you may use 5 hens' eggs instead.

1 cup unsalted butter (2 sticks), at cool room temperature

1⅔ cups sugar

1 teaspoon vanilla extract

1 teaspoon lemon extract

1 tablespoon rosewater, or just plain water

2 tablespoons honey

¼ teaspoon salt

2 or 3 goose eggs or 5 regular large hens' eggs, at warm room temperature (about 1¼ cups)

1 cup sifted cake flour, sifted again after measuring (if you don't have cake flour, use another cup of all-purpose flour)

1 cup sifted all-purpose flour, sifted again after measuring

Don't preheat the oven. Butter and dust with flour 1 large tube pan or 2 loaf pans, tapping the pan to remove excess flour.

Using an electric mixer, cream the butter and sugar together well, until the mixture is cohesive, lightened in color, and fluffy. Beat in the vanilla and lemon extracts, rosewater, honey, and salt. Using a rubber spatula or a wooden spoon, alternately fold in the eggs and the flours by hand in three or four additions, blending in each addition *only partway* before adding the next. Once all the eggs and flour are added, gently blend the batter just until uniform—do not overmix. Scrape the batter into the prepared pan, spread evenly, and put into the cold oven. Turn on the oven to 300°F and bake for 1 hour, or until a toothpick inserted in the center comes out clean. Let cool in the pan for 15 minutes, then turn the cake out onto a rack. Enjoy warm or cooled.

Goose Egg Pound Cake Cinnamon Toast

Twenty of us enjoyed these little toasts with vanilla ice cream on New Year's Eve, 1999, after a dinner of saffron risotto, spicy roast chicken, beet and carrot salad, chickpea salad with lemon and parsley, and rich dinner bread, before an appropriately amazing fireworks display. The cake contained Babette the goose's eggs and butter from the Deep Springs Dairy.

Heat the oven to 400°F. Mix about 2 teaspoons ground cinnamon into ¼ cup sugar. Generously butter thin slices of day-old pound cake, sprinkle heavily with cinnamon sugar, and toast on a baking sheet in the oven until the sugar is melted and the cake is crisp and golden brown on the bottom. Serve like a cookie with vanilla ice cream.

Chocolate Pound Cake

MAKES 1 LARGE CAKE; SERVES 8 TO 12

Seek out Dutch-processed cocoa powder (darker than the regular variety) and bittersweet chocolate chips to make this cake, and chocolate lovers will be in your thrall.

1 cup unsalted butter (2 sticks), at cool room temperature

1⅔ cups sugar

1½ teaspoons vanilla extract (almond extract is also very good)

1 tablespoon water

2 tablespoons honey

¼ teaspoon salt

¾ cup chocolate chips

1⅓ cups sifted all-purpose flour

⅔ cup unsweetened cocoa powder

5 large eggs, at warm room temperature (about 1¼ cups)

Don't preheat the oven. Thoroughly butter 2 loaf pans or 1 large tube pan. Mix together a small amount of cocoa powder and flour, and dust the pan with this mixture, tapping the pan to remove the excess.

Using an electric mixer, cream the butter and sugar together well, until lightened in color and fluffy. Reduce the speed of the mixer and add the vanilla, water, honey, salt, and chocolate chips. Sift the flour and cocoa powder together. Using a rubber spatula or a wooden spoon, add the cocoa mixture to the butter mixture by hand alternately with the eggs, in three or four additions, *partially* blending in each addition before adding the next. Once all the eggs and flour are added, gently blend the batter by hand just until uniform—do not overmix. Scrape the batter into the prepared pans, spread evenly, and put into the cold oven. Turn on the oven to 300°F and bake for 1 hour, or until a toothpick inserted in the center comes out clean. Let cool in the pan for 15 minutes, then turn the cake out onto a rack to cool completely.

Carrot Cake

MAKES ONE 9-INCH CAKE; SERVES 6 TO 8

This was the cake I always relied on early in my professional cooking days. It's *the* classic American cake, appropriate for any occasion, from rustic picnics to elegant weddings. I love the delicate, moist crumb that results when the carrots and nuts are very fine. Like all the cakes in this book, it is perfectly good eaten plain. But as much as I love unfrosted cakes, I'd be the last to deny that cream cheese frosting is perfect with carrot cake.

If you want a double-layer carrot cake, double the cake and frosting recipes.

1 cup walnuts (about 3¼ ounces), lightly toasted (see page 301)

1 cup sifted all-purpose flour

1 teaspoon baking soda

1 teaspoon baking powder

½ teaspoon ground cinnamon

½ teaspoon salt

⅔ cup canola or other vegetable oil

¾ cup firmly packed brown sugar

2 eggs, at room temperature, lightly beaten

1 teaspoon vanilla extract

1¾ cups grated carrots, grated on the small holes of the grater

CREAM CHEESE FROSTING (OPTIONAL)

8 ounces cold cream cheese

finely grated zest and juice of ½ lemon

1 teaspoon vanilla extract

1½ cups sifted powdered sugar

Heat the oven to 325°F. Butter a 9-inch round cake pan or springform pan. To ensure that the cake doesn't stick to the pan, cut a circle of parchment and place it in the bottom of the pan. Butter the parchment and dust the pan well with flour, tapping out the excess.

With your hands, lightly rub some of the excess papery brown skin off the toasted walnuts. Chop the walnuts very fine with a sharp knife, or quickly pulse them in a food processor to a fine meal.

In a medium bowl, whisk together the flour, baking soda, baking powder, cinnamon, and salt, then whisk in the walnuts. In a large bowl, whisk the oil, brown sugar, eggs, vanilla, and carrots together, then fold the dry mixture into the wet mixture with the whisk, just until the mixture is uniform. Scrape into the prepared pan, smooth the top, and bake for about 30 minutes, or until a toothpick inserted in the center of the cake comes out clean. Let cool for 10 minutes in the pan, then turn out onto a plate. Peel off the parchment, and invert the cake onto

continued . . .

. . . continued

a rack to cool completely. Enjoy plain, or frost with the frosting. Make sure the cake is completely cool before applying frosting.

To make the frosting (if using), gently and patiently stir the cold cream cheese by hand together with the lemon juice, zest, and vanilla in a medium bowl. *Don't overbeat the cream cheese*, or the texture might become grainy. Add the sugar in three or four parts, blending each addition partway before adding the next. Blend until smooth, and then spread on your completely cooled carrot cake.

Whipped Cream Cake

MAKES ONE 12-INCH CAKE; SERVES 6 TO 8

Rather than butter in the batter, this simple, old-fashioned cake starts with a bowl of whipped cream. It's delicious warm, topped with—what else?—more whipped cream.

1¼ cups well-chilled heavy (whipping) cream

1 cup sugar

2 eggs, warmed in hot tap water

1 teaspoon vanilla extract

1¾ cups sifted all-purpose flour or cake flour

2 teaspoons baking powder

½ teaspoon salt

TOPPING

1 cup well-chilled heavy (whipping) cream

1 tablespoon sugar

¼ teaspoon vanilla extract

Heat the oven to 350°F. Butter a 12-inch springform pan or two 9-inch round cake pans. To ensure that the cake doesn't stick to the pan, cut a circle of parchment paper and place it in the bottom of the pan. Butter the parchment and dust the pan with flour. Or, more simply, you may bake the cake as a sheet cake, in a buttered 9-by-13-inch pan.

Using an electric mixer, whip the cold cream in a large bowl with half the sugar until soft peaks form, then whip in the eggs and vanilla, then the remaining sugar. Sift together the flour, baking powder, and salt, and gently fold into the cream mixture, just until the batter is uniform. Scrape the batter into the prepared pan, smoothing the top. Bake for 25 to 30 minutes, or until a toothpick inserted in the center comes out clean. Let cool for about 10 minutes in the pan, then turn it out onto a plate. Peel off the parchment, and invert the cake onto another plate (if serving warm) or onto a rack to cool completely. If you have baked the cake in a 9-by-13-inch pan, leave it in the pan.

To make the topping, whip the cream with the sugar and vanilla until soft peaks form. On each person's plate, top slices of warm cake with dollops of cold whipped cream. Or cool the cake completely and frost with the whipped cream, beaten until it holds its shape, then refrigerate until serving time. If you have baked the cake in two 9-inch pans, stack the layers with a good layer of whipped cream between them. Serve alone or with fresh fruit.

Blueberry Whipped Cream Cake

Cool and frost the cake as described. Just before serving, stud the cake's entire surface with a pint of fresh blueberries. Place them randomly, or create a design. Put the largest berries on the top and the smallest ones on the sides.

Chocolate Mayonnaise Cake

MAKES TWO 9-INCH CAKES; SERVES 10 TO 12

When I first tried this, as I mixed in the mayonnaise, I had my doubts. I was amazed to discover what a good, tender cake it was. It's as easy as making a cake-mix cake, but if you use dark or Dutch-processed cocoa powder (see page 65), the result is superb. You don't need to tell all your secrets; you may just call it chocolate cake.

When I first served this cake at Deep Springs, I announced that it contained a secret ingredient and joked that whoever guessed it first would get a kiss from beloved professor Ross Peterson. Absolutely no one in the community could guess what it was, until the visiting girlfriend of a student suddenly remembered that she had once made a mayonnaise cake in a home economics class. "Mayonnaise!" she blurted out. Everyone in the dining room howled with laughter, and I will never forget the slapstick image, post-kiss, of the grinning Ross, his wife, the student's girlfriend, and the student, all four of them red-faced, finally sitting down to enjoy the rest of their cake.

continued . . .

3 cups all-purpose flour

1½ cups granulated (white) sugar

¾ cup unsweetened cocoa powder

1 tablespoon baking powder

¾ teaspoon baking soda

1½ cups hot strong coffee

1½ cups mayonnaise

2 teaspoons vanilla extract

1 tablespoon finely grated orange zest (optional)

powdered sugar for dusting (optional)

whipped cream for serving (optional)

Heat the oven to 350°F. Butter two 9-inch round cake pans. To ensure that this delicate cake is easily removed from the pans, lining the pans with parchment is recommended. Cut circles of parchment to fit the bottoms of the pans. Butter the pans thoroughly, then put the parchment in the bottom and butter the parchment. Mix together a little cocoa powder with an equal amount of flour, and dust the lined pans with this mixture, tapping the pans to release the excess. Lacking parchment, just thoroughly grease the pans—especially the bottoms—and dust them well. You may also simply bake the cake in a buttered 9-by-13-inch pan as a sheet cake.

Sift the flour, sugar, cocoa powder, baking powder, and baking soda together in a medium bowl. In a large bowl, whisk together the coffee, mayonnaise, vanilla, and orange zest (if using). Add the dry ingredients and mix just until uniform. Scrape into the prepared pans and bake just until a toothpick inserted in the center comes out clean, about 25 minutes. Let cool for 10 minutes before turning the cakes out onto plates. Peel off the parchment, then invert the cakes onto a rack. If you have used a 9-by-13-inch pan, leave the cake in the pan. Cool completely and dust with powdered sugar in a sieve, if you like, tapping the sieve over the cake. Or, you may serve it with whipped cream—in that case, the powdered sugar isn't necessary.

Pinky's Jewish Apple Cake

MAKES 1 LARGE CAKE; SERVES 10 TO 12

This autumn gem comes from my friend Elge's mom—the family operates an apple farm in rural upstate New York. The brown sugar and orange juice concentrate give the cake a golden-yellow color that warms the soul on chilly days.

1 cup granulated (white) sugar

1 cup firmly packed brown sugar

1 cup canola or other vegetable oil

⅓ cup orange juice concentrate (undiluted)

4 eggs, at room temperature

2 teaspoons vanilla extract

3 cups sifted all-purpose flour

1 tablespoon baking powder

¾ teaspoon salt

APPLE FILLING

1 tablespoon ground cinnamon

⅓ cup granulated (white) sugar

5 or 6 tart, flavorful apples, peeled and sliced ⅛ inch thick (about 6 cups sliced)

Heat the oven to 350°F. Thoroughly grease a large tube pan and dust with flour, tapping out the excess. Using an electric mixer, beat the granulated and brown sugars, oil, and orange juice concentrate together. Add the eggs, one at a time, beating for a full minute after the addition of each one. Add the vanilla. Sift together the flour, baking powder, and salt, and gently fold the dry ingredients into the egg mixture, just until the batter is uniform.

To make the filling, combine the cinnamon and sugar in a small bowl. Gently pour just enough batter into the prepared tube pan to cover the bottom. Add half the apples. Just drop the apples in—don't rearrange or flatten them. Sprinkle evenly with half of the cinnamon-sugar mixture. Pour half the remaining batter over the apples, then repeat with the remaining apples and cinnamon sugar, ending with the remaining batter.

Bake the cake for half an hour, then lower the oven temperature to 325°F and bake for 40 minutes more. When done, the top of the cake, lightly pressed with a finger, will spring back. The toothpick test is not reliable for this recipe, because of the apple filling. Let the cake cool for 10 minutes before removing it from the pan. It's extraordinary while still warm. Wrap the remainder well after it's completely cool. It will still be delicious and moist the next day.

Elge's Three-Ginger Gingerbread

MAKES 1 LARGE CAKE; SERVES 10 TO 12

Ginger is always welcome after a rich meal—it aids in digestion. This dense, intense cake contains three different forms of ginger: fresh, powdered, and candied. Though great the day it's made, there is a subtle blending and smoothing of flavors after it sits for a day.

3 cups sifted all-purpose flour

1 teaspoon baking soda

1 teaspoon baking powder

1 tablespoon ground cinnamon

1½ teaspoons ground cloves

2 teaspoons ground ginger

¾ teaspoon salt

1½ cups granulated (white) sugar

1 cup canola oil or other vegetable oil

1 cup molasses

½ cup water

2 large eggs, at room temperature, beaten

2 tablespoons finely grated fresh ginger

½ cup chopped candied ginger

powdered sugar for dusting (optional)

LEMON CREAM (OPTIONAL)

1 large, juicy, fragrant lemon, or 1½ small lemons

3 tablespoons granulated (white) sugar

2 cups well-chilled heavy (whipping) cream

Heat the oven to 350°F. Butter a 12-inch springform pan. To ensure that the cake doesn't stick to the pan, cut a circle of parchment and place it in the pan's bottom. Butter and flour the parchment and dust the pan with flour, tapping out the excess. You may also bake the cake in a buttered 9-by-13-inch pan.

Whisk the flour, baking soda, baking powder, cinnamon, cloves, ground ginger, and salt together in a medium bowl. In a large bowl, whisk together the sugar, oil, molasses, water, eggs, fresh ginger, and candied ginger. Add the dry ingredients to the wet, and gently fold together with a whisk just until thoroughly combined. Scrape into the prepared pan. Bake just until a toothpick inserted in the center comes out clean, about 45 minutes. Let the cake cool in the pan for about 10 minutes, then turn out onto a plate. Peel off the parchment, and invert the cake onto a rack to cool completely. If you've used a 9-by-13-inch pan, leave the cake in the pan. Wrap well and age for 1 day before serving.

Dust the top with powdered sugar through a sieve, or leave plain. Serve with hot tea as an afternoon restorative, or serve as a dessert with the lemon cream.

To make the lemon cream (if using), into the bowl in which you intend to whip the cream, finely grate the zest of the lemon. With the back of a wooden spoon, mash the lemon zest with the sugar. Add the cream and whip it until soft peaks form. Fold in the juice from the lemon, and serve immediately.

Fresh Ginger Cake

MAKES 1 LARGE CAKE; SERVES 10 TO 12

Another excellent ginger cake, based on a famous recipe by my old Chez Panisse friend David Lebovitz. It must be aged a day before serving—as with the preceding recipe, the ginger-molasses flavor doesn't reach its full bloom until the next day.

4 ounces fresh ginger, peeled and thinly sliced before weighing

1 cup canola or other vegetable oil

1 cup sugar

1 cup molasses

1 cup hot strong coffee

2 eggs, at room temperature, beaten

¼ teaspoon vanilla extract

2½ cups sifted all-purpose flour

½ teaspoon baking soda

1 teaspoon baking powder

¼ teaspoon salt

¼ teaspoon ground cinnamon

¼ teaspoon black pepper

Heat the oven to 350°F. Butter a 12-inch springform pan. To ensure that the cake doesn't stick to the pan, cut a circle of

continued . . .

. . . continued

parchment and place it in the pan's bottom. Butter the parchment and dust the pan with flour, tapping out the excess.

In a blender or food processor, blend the ginger and oil with the sugar until the ginger is completely pulverized into the mix—there should be no chunks. Reduce the speed of the blender, and pour in the molasses, coffee, eggs, and vanilla. Pulse just until blended. Sift the dry ingredients into a large bowl and add the wet ingredients, carefully mixing just until the batter is uniform.

Scrape the batter into the prepared pan. Bake just until a toothpick inserted in the center comes out clean, about 40 minutes. Let the cake cool in the pan for about 20 minutes, then turn it out onto a plate. Peel off the parchment, and invert the cake onto a rack to cool completely. Wrap well and let age for 1 day before serving. It will stay moist and delicious for 3 days.

For a great topping for this cake, David suggests lemon curd lightened with whipped cream. Take a cup or two of the filling for Lemon Meringue Pie (page 451), let it chill, then fold it into an equal amount of barely sweetened whipped cream. Chill the mixture for a few hours to let the lemon flavor intensify.

Currant Cake

MAKES TWO 9-INCH CAKES; SERVES 10 TO 12

Toasted, ground walnuts add richness and depth to this elegant cake.

> 1 cup walnuts (about 3¼ ounces), lightly toasted (see page 301)
>
> 1 cup dried Zante currants
>
> 1 cup dry white wine
>
> ¾ cup unsalted butter (1½ sticks), at room temperature
>
> 1⅓ cups firmly packed brown sugar
>
> 3 large eggs, at room temperature
>
> 1 teaspoon vanilla extract
>
> 1⅓ cups sifted all-purpose flour
>
> 1½ teaspoons baking powder
>
> ½ teaspoon baking soda
>
> ¼ teaspoon salt
>
> 1 cup buttermilk
>
> powdered sugar for dusting (optional)

Heat the oven to 350°F. Butter two 9-inch round cake pans, or a 9-by-13-inch rectangular pan. To ensure that the cake doesn't stick to the pans, cut circles of parchment to fit the bottoms of the pans. Butter the parchment and dust the pan with flour.

Take handfuls of the toasted walnuts and rub lightly to release excess papery brown skin. Chop the walnuts fine, or pulse to a fine meal in a food processor. Don't over-grind or you will have walnut butter.

Combine the currants and the white wine in a small saucepan and heat until the wine steams. Remove from the heat and let the currants steep and plump in the wine for about 20 minutes, then drain them. Reserve the currant-sweetened wine for another use. (Use it for part of the water in Focaccia, page 137. Or baste roasting pork with it.)

Using an electric mixer, cream the butter well, then add the sugar and beat on high speed for about 3 minutes. Add the eggs, one at a time, beating each one in thoroughly before adding the next. Add the vanilla. Sift the flour, baking powder, baking soda, and salt together and blend in the ground walnuts. Gently fold this dry mixture into the butter mixture in three parts, alternating with the butter-milk. At the end, just before the batter is completely uniform, fold in the currants.

Scrape the batter into the prepared pans and bake for about 20 minutes, or until a toothpick inserted in the center comes out clean. Let the cakes cool in the pans for about 10 minutes, then turn them out onto a plate. Peel off the parchment, and invert them onto a rack to cool completely. If you've used a 9-by-13-inch pan, leave the cake in the pan. If you like, dust with powdered sugar before serving.

Prune Cake

MAKES 1 LARGE CAKE; SERVES 8 TO 10

Good old prunes—I always like to have them around. They are less sweet and more complexly flavored than raisins. You can add cut-up prunes to oatmeal or cereal or coffeecake batter (even salads!); you can simmer them in Constant Comment tea; you can cut a small hole and stuff them with sweetened, orange-flavored cream cheese and maybe a toasted almond to mimic the pit; or you can make this old-fashioned, moist cake, which you could call "plum cake" if you think "prune cake" would make your guests wrinkle their noses. For the holidays, serve with whipped cream, dressed up with a tablespoon or two of brandy or cognac.

1½ cups pitted prunes

1 cup prune juice (orange juice may be substituted)

3 large eggs, at room temperature

1 cup canola oil or other vegetable oil

1 teaspoon ground cinnamon

½ teaspoon ground nutmeg

2 tablespoons unsweetened cocoa powder

1 teaspoon vanilla extract

¾ teaspoon salt

continued...

. . . *continued*

1½ cups sugar

2 cups sifted all-purpose flour

½ teaspoon baking soda

½ teaspoon baking powder

1 cup walnuts (about 3¼ ounces), lightly toasted (see page 301) and excess papery skin rubbed off (optional)

sweetened whipped cream, with or without a little brandy stirred in, for serving (optional)

Heat the oven to 350°F. Butter a 12-inch springform pan or a 9-by-13-inch pan. If you are using a springform pan, cut a circle of parchment and place it in the bottom of the pan, to ensure that the cake doesn't stick. Butter the parchment. Dust the pan with flour and tap out the excess.

Using kitchen scissors, snip the prunes into quarters. Put them in the jar of your blender, and add the prune juice, eggs, oil, cinnamon, nutmeg, cocoa powder, vanilla, and salt. Blend on a lower speed for about 30 seconds, then raise the speed and slowly add the sugar while the motor is running. If this seems to be too much for your blender, transfer the mixture to a bowl and whisk in the sugar by hand.

Sift together the flour, baking soda, and baking powder into a large bowl. Gently fold the prune mixture into the flour mixture with a whisk, being sure to sweep the bottom and all sides of the bowl. When the mixtures are mostly combined, sprinkle in the toasted walnuts, if using (I like to leave them whole), and continue to fold the batter with the whisk just until it is uniform. Scrape the batter into the prepared pan and bake just until a toothpick inserted in the center comes out clean, 35 to 40 minutes.

Let the cake rest in the pan for 10 minutes before turning it out onto a plate. Peel off the parchment, then invert the cake onto a rack. If you've used a 9-by-13-inch pan, leave it in the pan. Let cool completely, then cut into small squares or wedges with a sharp knife. Serve unadorned or with brandy-laced whipped cream.

Milk and Honey Cake

MAKES TWO 9-INCH CAKES; SERVES 10 TO 12

Deep Springs maintains beehives and produces honey redolent of desert wildflowers. This suave, easy cake sings honey. It's perfect with toasted nuts and fresh fruit.

2½ cups all-purpose flour

1½ teaspoons baking powder

½ teaspoon salt

½ teaspoon white pepper

1¼ cups honey

1 cup canola or other vegetable oil

¾ cup milk, heated

2 eggs, at room temperature

½ teaspoon vanilla extract

GLAZE

2 tablespoons milk

2 tablespoons honey

Heat the oven to 350°F. Butter two 9-inch round cake pans or a 9-by-13-inch pan. If you use round pans, cut circles of parchment and place them in the bottoms of the pans, to ensure that the cake doesn't stick. Butter the parchment. Dust the pans with flour and tap out the excess.

Sift together the flour, baking powder, salt, and white pepper. Whisk the honey, oil, hot milk, eggs, and vanilla in a large bowl until uniform; the eggs will emulsify the mixture. Gently fold the dry mixture into the wet mixture just until blended. Scrape into the prepared pan and bake for about 25 minutes, or until a toothpick inserted in the center comes out clean. Let cool for 10 minutes in the pan, then remove the cake from the pan. Peel off the parchment, and invert the cake onto a rack. If you've used a 9-by-13-inch pan, leave the cake in the pan.

To make the glaze, stir the milk and honey together in a small bowl until the honey is dissolved. Using a spoon, drizzle and spread the glaze all over the warm cake, especially around the edge. Let the cake absorb each application of glaze before applying the next, using the entire amount of glaze. Cool the cake completely on a rack. Wrap well; it will be just as good the next day.

Honey–Olive Oil Cake
A rich, intriguing, very Mediterranean flavor results when you use extra-virgin olive oil in place of the canola oil. Accompany with toasted walnuts and a scatter of jewel-like fresh pomegranate seeds.

Big Pink Cake

MAKES 1 LARGE CAKE; SERVES 10 TO 12

For some occasions, nothing but a Big Pink Cake will do. A Deep Springs favorite for years, this raspberry whipped cream layer cake is as dramatically impressive as it is delicious. The buttermilk cake base, a gem adapted from a recent edition of *The Joy of Cooking*, is also terrific plain.

2 ⅓ cups sifted all-purpose flour or cake flour

1½ teaspoons baking powder

½ teaspoon baking soda

pinch of salt

¾ cup salted butter (1½ sticks), at room temperature

1⅓ cups sugar

3 large eggs, at room temperature

1 teaspoon vanilla extract

1 tablespoon finely grated lemon zest

1 cup buttermilk

RASPBERRY WHIPPED CREAM

8 ounces frozen raspberries (or fresh, in season)

¼ cup sugar

3 cups heavy (whipping) cream

3 drops lemon extract

¼ teaspoon vanilla extract

multicolored nonpareil sprinkles for decoration (optional)

Heat the oven to 350°F. Thoroughly butter two 9-inch round cake pans. To ensure that the cake doesn't stick, cut circles of parchment and place them in the bottoms of the pans. Butter the parchment, and dust the pans well with flour, tapping out the excess.

Sift the flour, baking powder, baking soda, and salt together. Using an electric mixer, beat the butter until creamy, then gradually add the sugar and beat thoroughly until light, about 3 minutes. Add the eggs, one at a time, then the vanilla and lemon zest. To this liquid mixture alternately fold in half the dry ingredients, then half the buttermilk, repeating with the remaining dry ingredients and buttermilk. Mix just until blended. The batter tastes excellent.

Scrape the batter into the prepared cake pans, spreading it evenly. Bake in the center of the oven, rotating if necessary, until the cake feels springy to the touch and a toothpick inserted in the center of the cake comes out clean, 20 to 25 minutes. Let the cakes cool in the pans for about 10 minutes.

Run a small knife around the edges to loosen the cakes, then invert them onto plates. Peel off the parchment, flip the cakes onto a rack, and let cool completely. If you want many layers of cake and whipped cream, you may slice the cakes evenly across, using a long, sharp knife, so you have 4 thin rounds. I usually don't bother.

To make the raspberry whipped cream, in a small, nonreactive saucepan over low heat, gently thaw the berries for a few moments, then raise the heat, add the sugar, and bring the berries to a simmer. If using fresh berries, simply mash the berries and sugar together and heat. Set a screen sieve over a bowl, and dump the berries and juice into the sieve. Using the bottom of a ladle or the back of a large spoon, press as much pulp from the berries as possible. Discard the dry, seedy solids left in the sieve. Cool the berry purée in the refrigerator.

In a large bowl, mix the cream with the berry purée and the lemon and vanilla extracts and whip until the cream holds its shape. Place a cake round, bottom side up, on a nice-looking plate. If the cake seems in danger of sliding around on the plate, anchor it with a small dab of whipped cream. Cover the top with a thick layer of whipped cream. Place the other round atop the first, and cover the top and sides with more whipped cream. Slather the excess whipped cream over the sides and top of the cake—it should look rather free and easy, not fussed over. The cake will keep in fine condition, refrigerated, for several hours. If you wish, shortly before serving, toss small handfuls of multi-colored nonpareil sprinkles on the sides and top of the cake.

CHAPTER 16

Gooey Desserts

In this chapter you will find some of the most gratifying, indulgent, comforting dessert recipes in the book. Pies and cakes reveal the skill of the cook, crisps and cobblers showcase good seasonal fruit, cookies deliver big flavor in portable little bites, but the elemental bowl-and-spoon desserts in this chapter—custard, ice cream, sherbet, pudding, even Jell-O—often elicit a long, closed-eyed sigh, down to the last spoonful.

Chocolate Pudding

SERVES 6 TO 8

This makes a deep, dark chocolate pudding. The skin that forms on the top as it cools is some people's favorite part. If you're one of those people, choose a wide, shallow bowl for the pudding, to allow more surface area for skin to form. Serve alone or with whipped cream.

¾ cup sugar

3 tablespoons cornstarch

¼ teaspoon salt

½ cup unsweetened cocoa powder

3 cups whole milk

3 egg yolks

1 ounce (1 square) unsweetened chocolate

¾ teaspoon vanilla extract

In a medium-sized, heavy saucepan, mix the sugar, cornstarch, salt, and cocoa powder until there are no lumps. Gradually stir in the milk. Over medium-low heat, slowly heat the mixture, whisking frequently, until it steams and thickens slightly.

Beat the egg yolks in a small bowl, whisk in a few spoonfuls of the warm chocolate mixture, then whisk the yolk mixture into the remaining chocolate mixture in the pan. Bring to a gentle simmer and cook for 1 minute. Remove the pan from the heat and add the chocolate and vanilla. Stir to melt the chocolate. Let cool for about 10 minutes, then pour into a bowl. Let cool completely, then chill.

Peach Leaf Custard Sauce

MAKES ABOUT 2 ¼ CUPS; SERVES 4 TO 5

Several peach trees thrive in the Deep Springs orchard. Their leaves lend a delicate almond flavor to this "pouring custard." It is excellent served warm over a wedge of plain cake, generously topped with sliced, lightly sugared peaches and plums.

20 fresh, unsprayed peach leaves, washed

2 cups milk

4 egg yolks

¼ cup sugar

⅛ teaspoon salt

Heat the milk with the peach leaves in a medium-sized, heavy saucepan over a low flame until the leaves release an almond scent into the milk. Strain the milk, squeezing the leaves gently. Put the milk in a double boiler over, not in, boiling water, and heat. In a small bowl, beat the yolks, sugar, and salt together. Whisk a few spoonfuls of the hot milk into the yolks to temper them, then whisk the yolks into the hot milk. Cook in the double boiler, whisking frequently, until thickened. Let stand, off the heat, whisking frequently, for about 5 minutes.

Vanilla Bean Crème Brûlée

SERVES 8

I've always thought of crème brûlée as a modern dessert, but I found this recipe on yellowed paper, written in my grandmother's inimitable backhand script, in her old box of recipes. It is the use of the blowtorch, I think, that makes this recipe so perennially appealing to Deep Springs students.

½ vanilla bean

3 cups heavy (whipping) cream

6 tablespoons sugar, plus about ½ cup

pinch of salt

6 egg yolks

Heat the oven to 350°F. With a small knife, split the vanilla bean lengthwise. Pour the heavy cream into a small, heavy saucepan. Scrape the fine seed paste from the vanilla bean into the cream, and put the bean pod into the cream also. Add the 6 tablespoons sugar and salt, and gently warm the cream over medium heat, stirring frequently, until the sugar is dissolved. *continued...*

. . . continued

In a medium bowl, whisk the egg yolks. Slowly whisk a couple of spoonfuls of the hot cream into the yolks, then whisk the yolks into the rest of the cream in the saucepan. Strain the custard through a screen sieve into a pitcher. Pour the custard into 8 wide, individual custard dishes (4- or 5-ounce capacity; wide dishes mean there is more top surface area for the brûlée crust). Place the dishes in a deep baking pan, place the pan in the center of the preheated oven, and then carefully pour boiling water into the baking pan, being careful not to splash water into the custard. Pour in enough water to come halfway up the sides of the custard dishes. Gently close the oven and bake for 30 to 40 minutes, or until the custards are just set, still jiggly in the center.

Carefully remove the custards from the pan and set on a wire rack to cool—you may bake and refrigerate the custards, covered, well ahead of serving time. Before applying the remaining sugar and serving, bring the custards to room temperature.

To serve, evenly sprinkle about 1 tablespoon of sugar over the surface of each custard. Using a propane blowtorch, burn the sugar until it is a deep mahogany brown, moving the flame of the torch over the sugar until it beads, bubbles, and finally caramelizes. For best results, let the sugar get quite dark. Let the sugar cool and harden for a moment or two, then serve immediately.

Don't have a blowtorch? Here is my grandmother's alternative:

Turn on your oven's broiler. Sieve 1½ tablespoons brown sugar onto a buttered baking sheet. Spread the sugar out with a spoon into a circle, about ⅛ inch thick. Do 4 of these at a time. Put in the oven, turn the oven to broil, and *watch very carefully.* When the sugar is melted and has run together, let cool for a minute, test with a spatula, lift quickly onto wax paper, and let cool until hardened. Repeat with the other 4. Place a disc of hardened sugar onto each custard and serve immediately.

Baked Custard

SERVES 3 TO 4

Here is a glimpse into the past from my grandmother's recipe file: the simplest baked custard imaginable, crème brûlée's good country ancestor. Serve it unadorned at those times when you want something gloriously plain. It's also good with maple syrup, melted jam or jelly, or the syrup from pickled fruit (see page 436).

2 cups whole milk

⅓ cup sugar

pinch of salt

3 eggs, lightly beaten

¾ teaspoon vanilla extract

Heat the oven to 325°F. Scald the milk by heating it in a medium-sized, heavy saucepan over a medium-high flame, stirring frequently, until steaming. Remove from the heat, add the sugar and salt, and stir until dissolved. Slowly whisk about ½ cup of the hot milk into the eggs in a small bowl, then slowly whisk the eggs into the pan of hot milk. Add the vanilla. Pour (straining through a sieve if you like, to remove tough bits of egg) into a 4-cup loaf pan or other medium-sized baking dish, and set the dish in a larger pan. Place the whole thing in the center of the preheated oven, then carefully pour boiling water into the larger pan, being careful not to splash water into the custard. Pour in enough water to come halfway up the side of the custard dish. Gently close the oven and bake for 20 to 30 minutes, just until a knife inserted in the center comes out clean. The custard will still be slightly jiggly in the center. Remove from the water bath and let cool for a few minutes before serving warm. The custard is also good cold; cool to room temperature before putting it in the refrigerator.

Colostrum Custard

To ensure healthy calves, cows (and other mammals) produce a special milk called colostrum, pale yellow in color and especially high in protein, when calves are born. Deep Springs' dairy cows, by their nature, produce more colostrum than their calves are able to drink. Most of the excess is collected and frozen, reserved for the struggling calves of Deep Springs' main cattle herd, typically born in winter. When those who work closely with the calves can be persuaded to part with a precious gallon of colostrum milk, the community is treated to this rare delicacy. The yellow milk tastes very rich and slightly thick, as if eggs were already whisked in. When you heat it, it firms up exactly like egg custard. Proceed as directed in the master recipe, using colostrum milk and omitting the eggs and the milk-scalding step: just whisk sugar into the milk until dissolved, stir in the vanilla, and bake in a water bath.

Gooseberry Fool

SERVES 4

Fool was a term of endearment hundreds of years ago. This traditional English way of preparing tart fruit is very simple and very good. This recipe reflects my preference for a tart fool; adjust the sugar to your taste. Serve in wineglasses or other tall goblets.

2 cups gooseberries

2 tablespoons water

pinch of salt

3 to 4 tablespoons sugar

1 cup heavy (whipping) cream

¼ teaspoon vanilla extract

Pinch off the tough little stem ends from the gooseberries. Put the berries in a small, heavy, nonreactive saucepan with the water, salt, and 2 tablespoons of the sugar. Heat over a high flame, stirring constantly, until the berries have broken down to a purée and the sugar is dissolved. Let cool to room temperature, then chill thoroughly. Taste the gooseberries for sweetness and add another tablespoon of sugar, if you like.

Using an electric mixer, whip the cream with the vanilla and remaining 1 table-spoon sugar until soft peaks form. Fold in the gooseberry purée somewhat imperfectly—it's fine if there are streaks of purée. Spoon into goblets, chill, and serve.

Other Fruit Fools

Plums, huckleberries, rhubarb, raspberries, other berries—any fruit with a strong flavor and a pronounced tartness is an excellent candidate for making into a fool. For well-pigmented fruit, fold only three-fourths of the purée into the cream, then layer the cream with the remaining purée in the glass.

Vanilla Ice Cream

MAKES ABOUT 1 QUART

This is just a bit leaner than most recipes for vanilla ice cream, and so feels more satisfyingly cold on the tongue. A bit of cornstarch keeps it creamy, while an imperceptible touch of honey haunts the sweetness.

½ cup sugar

1 tablespoon cornstarch

3¼ cups half-and-half

1 tablespoon honey

pinch of salt

4 egg yolks

1½ teaspoons vanilla extract

Mix the sugar and cornstarch together in a medium-sized, heavy pot until there are no visible lumps. Pour in the half-and-half, and add the honey and salt. Slowly bring to a simmer over medium-low heat, stirring frequently, until foamy on top and steaming. Whisk the egg yolks in a small bowl. *Very slowly* whisk in about 1 cup of the hot half-and-half mixture, then slowly whisk this mixture back into the pot of hot half-and-half. Cook for 1 to 2 minutes more over medium-low heat, stirring frequently, until steaming hot and slightly thickened. Remove from the heat and let cool, continuing to stir frequently for about 5 minutes. Let cool to room temperature. Stir in the vanilla and chill thoroughly, preferably overnight. Freeze the mixture in your ice cream maker according to the manufacturer's instructions. Serve immediately, while still soft and creamy, or pack the ice cream into a container, put it in the freezer, and let it freeze hard.

Hard-frozen ice cream tastes best when allowed to "temper" slightly; it should be served a few degrees above freezing. If you are serving ice cream for dessert, move the container of ice cream from the freezer to the refrigerator just as you are sitting down to begin dinner. By dessert time, the ice cream should be perfectly tempered.

Coffee Ice Cream

This requires 3 or 4 shots of fresh espresso. As soon as the espresso is made, *stir in a heaping tablespoon of the recipe's sugar to fix the fresh-brewed flavor.* Let cool to room temperature. For the ice cream base, use only 3 cups half-and-half and only 1 teaspoon vanilla, and add the cooled espresso when adding the vanilla. This ice cream is delightful with Chocolate Sauce (page 467) or with fine chunks of bittersweet chocolate folded in when the ice cream is finished churning.

continued . . .

. . . continued

Strawberry Ice Cream

Crush fresh, perfectly ripe, red-all-the-way-through strawberries (enough to yield 1¼ juicy cups) with 2 tablespoons of sugar until the sugar is completely dissolved (don't crush the fruit to a smooth purée; some chunks should remain). Add a few drops of lemon juice and chill well. For the ice cream base, use only 3 cups half-and-half, 2 egg yolks, and 1 teaspoon vanilla. As soon as the ice cream is solid in the ice cream maker, fold in the strawberries.

Peach Ice Cream

Crush enough perfectly ripe, peeled, sweet summer peaches with 2 tablespoons of sugar to yield 1¼ cups (don't crush the fruit to a smooth purée; some chunks should remain). Add a few drops of lemon juice. Chill the peaches well. For the ice cream base, use only 3 cups of half-and-half and 2 egg yolks. Once the ice cream is solid in the ice cream maker, fold in the crushed peaches. A little almond extract is particularly good with peaches or any other stone fruit.

Lemon Ice Cream

MAKES ABOUT 1 QUART

This ice cream, so lemony it's almost sherbet, goes superbly with Gingersnaps, page 539, but is good enough to be served on its own. I can't imagine a dinner that wouldn't be well concluded with a small dish of lemon ice cream.

1 tablespoon finely grated lemon zest

½ cup plus 1 tablespoon fresh lemon juice (from 4 to 5 lemons)

1 cup sugar

3 large eggs

2 cups half-and-half

½ teaspoon vanilla extract

In a medium-sized, heavy, nonreactive saucepan, whisk together the lemon zest, lemon juice, sugar, eggs, 1 cup of the half-and-half, and vanilla. Cook over medium heat, stirring constantly and going over the entire bottom of the pan with your spoon, until the mixture just comes to a simmer. Remove from the heat, stir for a moment longer, cover, and let sit for about 5 minutes. Stir again and strain the custard through a fine sieve into a bowl, pressing hard on the zest to extract as much of its flavor as possible. Chill, covered with plastic wrap pressed on the surface, until completely cold. Whisk in the remaining cup of half-and-half and freeze the mixture in your ice cream maker according to the manufacturer's instructions. Serve immediately, while still soft and creamy, or pack the ice cream into a container, put it in the freezer, and let it freeze hard. If frozen hard, allow the ice cream to "temper" in the refrigerator for about an hour before serving.

Blackberry Ice Cream

MAKES ABOUT 1 QUART

On a hot, midsummer's day, find a wild blackberry bush on a sunny hillside. The ripe, sweet berries are purple-black and slightly dull, not shiny; they are often hidden among the foliage, hanging like tiny clusters of grapes. A ripe berry will easily separate from the stem—if you have to pull it off with any force, it isn't ripe yet. However, for this intensely flavored ice cream, adapted from a recipe in Lindsey Shere's *Chez Panisse Desserts*, a few underripe ones will keep the flavor bright.

Of course, raspberries or any other tart-sweet berry would be very good treated this way. If your berries taste a little tired, a teaspoon of rosewater will enhance their flavor considerably—blackberries, raspberries, and roses are all in the same botanical family.

> 3 cups ripe, juicy wild blackberries
>
> ⅔ cup sugar
>
> 2 cups heavy (whipping) cream
>
> pinch of salt
>
> ¼ teaspoon vanilla extract
>
> *continued . . .*

. . . continued

Blend the blackberries to a purée in a blender. Pass the purée through a sieve to remove the seeds, pressing it through the mesh of the sieve using the back of a ladle.

Heat the sugar and 1 cup of the cream in a heavy saucepan until the sugar dissolves. Add the blackberry purée, the remaining cup of cream, salt, and vanilla. Chill thoroughly and freeze in your ice cream maker according to the manufacturer's instructions. Serve immediately, while still soft and creamy, or pack the ice cream into a container, put it in the freezer, and let it freeze hard. If frozen hard, allow the ice cream to "temper" in the refrigerator for about an hour before serving. Serve this ice cream alone, or alongside a scoop of Lemon Ice Cream (page 508).

Pear Sherbet

MAKES ABOUT 1 QUART

This refreshing sherbet is pure essence of pear. Make it when pears are at their best, in fall and early winter. I love Bartlett pears—they are fragrant and yellow when ripe, and widely available in their season (September through December), but Comice, French Butter, and slightly overripe, nutty Boscs are worth trying, too.

Pear sherbet needs little accompaniment: perhaps an almond cookie, some biscotti, or, for very special occasions, a scant scattering of painstakingly collected fresh rosemary flowers.

> 3 pounds ripe Bartlett pears, in season
>
> ¼ cup water
>
> ¾ cup sugar
>
> pinch of salt
>
> 2 teaspoons fresh lemon juice

Peel and core the pears, and cut into ½-inch chunks. Heat the pears, water, sugar, and salt in a medium-sized, heavy, nonreactive pot until the mixture is bubbling and the pears are heated through. Purée in a blender or food processor. Let the purée cool to room temperature, add the lemon juice, and chill thoroughly in the refrigerator. Freeze in your ice cream maker according to the manufacturer's instructions. Serve immediately, while still soft and creamy, or pack the sherbet into a container, put it in the freezer, and let it freeze hard. If frozen hard, allow the sherbet to "temper" in the refrigerator for about an hour before serving.

Pear and Black Pepper Sherbet

Using a fine-mesh wire strainer and a regular-mesh strainer, sift freshly ground black pepper into three grinds: fine, medium, and coarse. Stir 1 teaspoon of the medium-grind pepper into the purée in the master recipe when you are ready to freeze it. In place of the lemon juice, use white balsamic vinegar, if you like. This sherbet is wonderfully refreshing in the middle of a long dinner of small courses, should you be so ambitious. Serve with a couple of toasted, salted pecans or almonds.

Snow Ice Cream

SERVES 2 TO 3

Every other winter or so, enough snow falls in and around Deep Springs Valley to close the mountain passes, and the community is stranded for a few days. This recipe is a very good exercise in seizing such a moment. Snow varies like any natural product—some snow will immediately go slushy in the bowl; other snow will stay resolutely fluffy.

1 egg yolk

½ teaspoon vanilla extract

1 tablespoon brandy

¼ cup heavy (whipping) cream

¼ cup sugar

about 8 cups perfectly clean, freshly fallen snow

In a small saucepan, whisk together the egg yolk, vanilla, brandy, heavy cream, and sugar, in that order, to make a custardy syrup. Heat gently, stirring frequently, until the mixture is hot and the sugar dissolved. Let cool to room temperature, then chill until cold.

Minutes before you want to serve the ice cream, take a large mixing bowl, a clean
continued . . .

. . . continued

thing to scoop snow with, the custard-syrup, and a wire whisk outside with you. Collect the snow in the bowl, drizzle the cold custard-syrup over it, and gently mix with the whisk to combine—there should still be lumps of snow. Bring the snow ice cream in and consume immediately. People should be waiting by the door, spoons in hand.

Maple Snow Ice Cream

This is quicker and no less delicious.

> ¼ teaspoon vanilla extract
>
> 1 tablespoon bourbon
>
> ¼ cup dark maple syrup
>
> ¼ cup heavy (whipping) cream

Whisk the ingredients together and chill thoroughly. Mix with snow as directed in the master recipe.

Of course, anything sweet and liquid poured over fresh snow could be a delightful dessert.

GELATIN

In classic, old-fashioned French and English cookery, there are recipes for gelatin desserts that involve simmering fresh veal bones for hours, laboriously clarifying the resulting stock, flavoring it with fruit, and setting it in ice to gel. These are the ancestors of the now-ubiquitous packaged gelatin, known to most Americans as Jell-O. Savory gelatin preparations, called aspic, were once common but are now quite rare.

Decades ago, American housewives put all kinds of things in sweet gelatin: not only fruit and dairy products but vegetables, nuts, and sometimes even ham and turkey, calling such concoctions "salad," to be served with the meal. Such traditions continue in some circles, but at the behest of nutritionists, purveyors of packaged gelatin are now careful to emphasize that their product is a dessert. Despite its toylike colors and equally garish flavors, very few of us truly dislike Jell-O. We ate it as children, and we appreciate its cool, light qualities as adults.

For a treat, make a gelatin dessert from scratch, not from veal bones, but using unflavored powdered gelatin and clear, freshly extracted fruit juice. Sweeten with a restrained hand; fortify, if you like, with some appropriate wine, liqueur, or spirit; jewel with fresh fruit; and call it gelée (zhay-LAY).

For any type of gelatin dessert, I prefer a soft texture. When using unsweetened gelatin to make a gelée, I usually use a ratio of 1 envelope (or 2¼ teaspoons) to 2¼ cups clear fruit juice. Tart fruit juice will provide the liveliest flavor when lightly sweetened—sharpen with a squeeze of fresh lemon or lime if your juice is naturally quite sweet. First, put about ¼ cup of the juice (cold or room temperature) in a small dish. Sprinkle the gelatin evenly over the surface of the liquid—the gelatin will rapidly absorb much of the juice. Heat another portion of juice (about 1 cup) in a small saucepan until hot and steaming, and stir in the gelatin mixture, *dissolving the gelatin completely*. Remove from the heat and stir in the remaining amount (about 1 more cup) of juice. A little wine or liqueur may be included in the volume of liquid. Sweeten lightly to taste while the mixture is still warm.

To serve gelée elegantly, first make the gelée base and chill it to set. Cut the accompanying fresh fruit close to serving time. Layer spoonfuls of gelée with cut fruit in wineglasses or other tall, clear glasses. Top, or not, with whipped cream.

When using packaged, sweetened gelatin, for every 2 cups of water called for, I always add about ¼ cup extra. This more delicate, melting texture means the gelatin can't be successfully unmolded—it must be served out with a big spoon. If you would like to make your gelatin in a mold, very lightly oil the mold first, and follow the standard ratio specified on the package. When the gelatin has stiffened, set the mold in a basin of warm water for a few seconds, then turn the gelatin out onto a serving plate. As many learn in college, vodka or other booze can replace some of the water. When using canned fruit with gelatin, always drain it first. Don't use the liquid from the fruit in place of the water for the gelatin—it will cloud the gelatin and make it too sweet. *If fresh pineapple is used, it needs to be simmered first to destroy an enzyme that would otherwise dissolve the gelatin's protein and prevent it from setting.* The same is true for fresh figs, fresh ginger, guava, kiwi, and papaya.

Here are some great combinations of packaged, sweetened gelatin with fruit.

If you are in an experimental mood, let your imagination—or old cookbooks—be your guide:

* strawberry gelatin with sliced bananas

* cherry gelatin with peeled peaches, apricots, plums, or nectarines

* cherry gelatin with canned fruit cocktail

* raspberry gelatin with canned pears

* lemon or lime gelatin with pineapple

continued ...

* lemon or orange gelatin with crushed pineapple and grated carrots ("Golden Glow Salad"—very 1930s!)

Here are some ideas for elegant gelées:

* sparkling apple cider gelée with Poached Pears (page 467)

* summer berry–red wine gelée with whipped cream and fresh berries

* pomegranate and red wine gelée with fresh oranges

* lemon-mint gelée with fresh strawberries

And here is a sampling of preparations made with packaged gelatin:

Tangy Lemon Sour Cream Gelatin

In a small saucepan, bring to a boil 1 cup water with the finely grated zest of 1 large lemon, and remove from the heat. Completely dissolve a 3-ounce package of lemon-flavored gelatin in the water. Add the juice of the lemon and ¼ cup cold water. Let cool for 5 minutes. Whisk ½ cup sour cream and ½ cup buttermilk together in a medium bowl until smooth. Whisk in about ¼ cup of the gelatin mixture, then whisk in the rest of the gelatin mixture. Chill until set.

Lime Yum

This is an updated version of something I loved when I was very little. In a medium bowl, using an electric mixer, whip 1 cup heavy cream with ¼ teaspoon vanilla extract until soft peaks form. Fold in 1 cup (one 8-ounce can) drained unsweetened crushed pineapple, one 3-ounce package lime-flavored gelatin (dry, not mixed with water), 1 cup (one 8-ounce carton) sour cream, and the finely grated zest and juice of 1 small lime. Chill thoroughly. The texture is creamier the first day, but the flavor is better the next.

Creamy Orange Gelatin

In a small saucepan, bring to a boil ¾ cup water with the finely grated zest of 1 large orange, and remove from the heat. Completely dissolve a 3-ounce package of orange-flavored gelatin in the water. Gradually add the gelatin to an 8-ounce package of softened cream cheese in a medium bowl, whisking out any lumps. Add the juice of the orange and 1 tablespoon of fresh lemon juice. Chill until set.

Ginger Ale–Lemon-Pear Gelatin

My grandmother believed in the healing powers of gelatin—when anyone was sick, she'd say, "Oh, I'll make you some nice

Jell-O." I discovered this sweet concoction in her old recipe box, written in her left-leaning handwriting (I use a sharp ginger beer instead of ginger ale, and add the grated zest and juice of a big juicy lemon):

"1 quart gingerale, 2 packages lemon jello, 1 large can pears, drained & diced. Heat ½ the gingerale, add jello, stir till jello all dissolved. Add pears & remaining gingerale. Chill well or overnight. Serve with whipped cream tinted pale pink and flavored with ½ teaspoon almond extract."

Carol's Fresh Fruit Gelatin

SERVES 4 TO 6

This delicious recipe, relatively low in sugar, is excellent get-well comfort food. When I brought a big bowl of it to my neighbor Carol when she was ill, she loved it so much that she asked for the recipe. She was surprised to learn that it was made with fruit juice and unflavored gelatin. "I never thought of making jello out of anything but Jell-O," she wrote in her thank-you note. "This opens up a whole new vista!" The fruit may be varied; any fruit that tends to brown (such as pears) must first be poached in the juice.

2 cups good apple juice

2 fresh, ripe pears, peeled and sliced

1 envelope (2½ teaspoons) unflavored gelatin

2 tablespoons of your favorite tart fruit jelly

finely grated zest and juice of 1 lemon

1 to 2 tablespoons sugar

1½ cups red seedless grapes, halved (or use the small grapes called Zante or "champagne" grapes)

1½ cups fresh seedless tangerine sections

continued . . .

. . . continued

Bring 1 cup of the apple juice to a boil in a small saucepan. Add half the pear slices, and bring to a boil again. Let boil for 20 seconds, stirring gently, to cook the pears through. Using a slotted spoon, remove the pears to a large glass bowl. Repeat with the remaining pears.

Put a few tablespoons of the remaining apple juice in a small bowl. Sprinkle the gelatin over the juice—it will absorb the juice.

Add the jelly to the hot pear-infused juice in the saucepan. Put the pan back over a low flame, stirring to thoroughly melt the jelly. Add the lemon zest, lemon juice, and sugar. Stir the gelatin mixture into the hot, sweetened juice until the gelatin is thoroughly dissolved. Add the remaining apple juice.

Put the grapes and tangerine sections into the bowl with the pears. Pour the juice mixture over the fruit. Chill for several hours or overnight, until set.

Almond Cream

SERVES 4 TO 6

This creamy dessert, sometimes called Russian cream, is perhaps gelatin's most sophisticated manifestation, quite similar to Italian *panna cotta*. When choosing sour cream, look for brands made simply from cultured cream—no thickeners or stabilizers. You can successfully tame the luxurious richness by substituting good, plain yogurt for some or all of the sour cream. This is always served with fresh fruit—it goes especially well in the fall with the nutty, pumpkiny flavor of persimmons.

1½ teaspoons gelatin (not a full envelope)

3 tablespoons water

1 cup heavy (whipping) cream

½ cup sugar

1 cup natural sour cream (no thickeners or stabilizers)

½ teaspoon vanilla extract

½ teaspoon almond extract

¼ teaspoon lemon extract

FOR SERVING

Fuyu persimmons (see page 471) or other fresh seasonal fruit, peeled and cut attractively

Sprinkle the gelatin over the water in a small bowl. Mix the cream and sugar in a small saucepan. Set over a low flame and heat, stirring almost constantly, until the sugar is dissolved. Add the gelatin mixture, whisking until the gelatin is completely dissolved. Let cool for about 30 minutes, or until room temperature. Put the sour cream in a large bowl and whisk it smooth. Whisk the gelatin mixture into the sour cream until smooth, then stir in the flavorings. Pour into a glass bowl, and chill until set. To serve, using a wide spoon, spoon the cream carefully into glass dessert bowls, and spoon a few pieces of peeled Fuyu persimmon alongside. Other fruits are good, too: pears in the fall, sweet oranges in winter, strawberries in spring, berries or stone fruit in summer.

CHAPTER 17

Cookies and Candy

C ookies are an emblem of American hospitality and nurturing. I prefer them between meals, as a snack with a cup of coffee or tea. Deep Springs students disagree; chocolate chip cookies are made and served for dessert at Deep Springs more frequently than any other sweet.

All these cookies are easy to make; most may simply be mixed, dropped by spoonfuls onto a greased sheet, and baked right away. Most recipes call for butter that is at room temperature. If you have only cold butter, just slice thinly and spread the slices out in a single layer in your mixing bowl. The butter will quickly soften.

The most important moment in cookie making is taking the cookies out of the oven at just the right time—*always watch cookies carefully while they're baking*. Lining your baking sheet with a lightly greased sheet of parchment paper ensures the cookies' easy removal.

An often-overlooked step in cookie baking is removing the baked cookies from the hot sheet to a rack to cool. This allows steam to escape more readily, so the cookies will have their best texture, whether crispy or chewy. Once completely cooled, the cookies can be arranged and stacked on a platter.

continued . . .

. . . continued

Chocolate– Chocolate Chip Cookies

MAKES ABOUT 3 DOZEN 2-INCH COOKIES

I made these on my first night as the chef at Deep Springs.

   2 cups well-sifted all-purpose flour

   ½ cup unsweetened cocoa powder

   ¾ teaspoon baking powder

   ¾ teaspoon salt

   1 cup butter (2 sticks), at room temperature

   1 cup plus 2 tablespoons firmly packed brown sugar

   3 large eggs

   2 teaspoons vanilla extract

   1 teaspoon almond extract

   2½ cups semisweet or bittersweet chocolate chips

Heat the oven to 350°F. Lightly grease 2 baking sheets. In a medium bowl, sift together the flour, cocoa powder, baking powder, and salt. Using an electric mixer, cream the butter and sugar well, then beat in the eggs and extracts. Mix in the dry ingredients and chocolate chips until the dough is uniform. Drop heaping tablespoons of dough 2 inches apart on the baking sheets. Bake just until the tops are no longer shiny, 10 to 12 minutes. Let the cookies rest on the baking sheets out of the oven for a moment, then transfer to a rack to cool. When cooled completely, store in an airtight container.

Chocolate–White Chocolate Chip Cookies

Use white chocolate chips instead of semi-sweet in the master recipe. To get the full color effect, reserve a handful of the white chips and place them randomly over the tops of the cookies before baking.

Mexican Chocolate–Chocolate Chip Cookies

Here, cinnamon and almonds evoke authentic Mexican hot chocolate. Follow the master recipe, adding 2 teaspoons ground cinnamon to the dry ingredients and 1½ cups (6 to 7 ounces) lightly toasted almonds (see page 301), coarsely chopped, with the chips.

Chocolate-Peanut Cookies

Follow the master recipe, omitting the almond extract, reducing the salt to ½ teaspoon, and adding 1½ cups of salted peanuts (red-skin or Spanish are my favorite) along with the chips.

Dark Chocolate Wafers

When an elegant, simple chocolate cookie is called for, try this variation. Proceed with the master recipe, using bittersweet chocolate chips. In a double boiler (or in a 250°F oven), slowly melt the chocolate chips, stirring occasionally
continued...

. . . *continued*

until completely smooth. Let the melted chocolate cool to warm room temperature, then mix it into the creamed butter and sugar. Continue to mix the dough and bake the cookies as usual, watching carefully while baking. This method makes good small cookies (teaspoon-sized drops of dough).

Ella's Chocolate Chip Cookies

MAKES ABOUT 2½ DOZEN LARGE COOKIES

LARGE QUANTITY RECIPE: MAKES ABOUT 5 DOZEN LARGE COOKIES

Ella and Pete Rock (the latter a novelist, professor, and Deep Springs alumnus) often make these cookies. Ella advises, "This recipe also makes good oatmeal cookies, substituting raisins for the chips, and adding a tablespoon of cinnamon to the dry ingredients. The dough freezes well and, in fact, tastes great straight out of the freezer with a carton of ice cream."

1 cup butter (2 sticks), at room temperature
2 cups butter (1 pound or 4 sticks), at room temperature

¾ cup granulated (white) sugar
1½ cups granulated (white) sugar

1 cup firmly packed brown sugar
2 cups firmly packed brown sugar

2 large eggs
4 large eggs

1½ teaspoons vanilla extract
1 tablespoon vanilla extract

1 to 1½ cups coarsely chopped walnuts (3 to 5 ounces; optional)
2 to 3 cups coarsely chopped walnuts (6 to 10 ounces; optional)

2 cups semisweet or bittersweet chocolate chips
4 cups semisweet or bittersweet chocolate chips

2 cups sifted all-purpose flour
4 cups sifted all-purpose flour

2½ cups rolled oats, ground to a fine meal in a food processor or blender
5 cups rolled oats, ground to a fine meal in a food processor or blender

¼ teaspoon salt
½ teaspoon salt

2 teaspoons baking powder
4 teaspoons baking powder

Heat the oven to 375°F. Using an electric mixer, cream the butter, granulated sugar, and brown sugar. Add the eggs and vanilla and blend until uniform. Mix in the nuts, if you're using them, and chocolate chips. In a very large bowl, combine the flour, ground oats, salt, and baking powder. Add the wet mixture to the dry and fold together until you have a uniform dough. Roll into golf ball–sized balls and bake on ungreased baking sheets until light brown all over, about 15 minutes. Let the cookies rest on the baking sheets out of the oven for a moment, then transfer to a rack to cool. When cooled completely, store in an airtight container.

Chocolate Chip–Hazelnut Shortbread Bars

MAKES SIXTEEN 2-INCH BARS

A student once asked me, "What exactly is 'shortbread,' and where does that name come from?" Shortbread is a traditional cookie of Scotland, containing only flour, sugar, and plenty of butter, but no leavening or liquid ingredients. When flour is mixed with water, as with bread dough, the flour's gluten, or protein, forms long, resilient strands that account for the strong, elastic structure of bread dough. The presence of enough butter or other fat, however, has a "shortening" effect on the flour's gluten, keeping the final product tender and crumbly.

1½ cups hazelnuts (about 5½ ounces), lightly toasted (see page 301)

1 cup butter (2 sticks), at room temperature

1 cup firmly packed brown sugar

1 teaspoon vanilla extract

1¼ cups semisweet or bittersweet chocolate chips (one 8-ounce package)

⅛ teaspoon salt

2 cups sifted all-purpose flour

continued . . .

. . . continued

Heat the oven to 350°F. Put the toasted hazelnuts on a wire rack and rub them to release the excess brown skin. Let cool, and chop the nuts coarsely.

Cream the butter and brown sugar in a large bowl until light and fluffy. Mix in the vanilla and the chocolate chips. Sift the salt and flour together, add to the butter mixture, and blend just until uniform. Press the dough evenly into an 8-by-8-inch pan. Bake for about 25 minutes, or until pale golden brown. With a small, sharp knife, *cut the cookies into bars while warm.* Let cool completely, then remove from the pan.

Pistachio Chocolate Chip Cookies

MAKES ABOUT 4 DOZEN 2-INCH COOKIES
LARGE QUANTITY RECIPE: MAKES ABOUT 8 DOZEN 2-INCH COOKIES

Every member of the nut family has its own special affinity for chocolate, and pistachios are no exception. Here, the lovely green nuts show up among the chocolate chips while the pistachio flavor somehow charms the cookie to a new and elegant realm. You'd love to eat these cookies on New Year's Eve, perhaps made with white chocolate chips.

The base recipe, a classic buttery-sugary American chocolate chip cookie, is delicious featuring other nuts, or with no nuts.

1 cup butter (2 sticks), at room temperature
2 cups butter (1 pound or 4 sticks), at room temperature

¾ cup firmly packed brown sugar
1½ cups firmly packed brown sugar

6 tablespoons granulated (white) sugar
¾ cup granulated (white) sugar

¾ teaspoon vanilla or almond extract
1½ teaspoons vanilla or almond extract

1 egg, at room temperature
2 eggs, at room temperature

2¼ cups sifted all-purpose flour
4½ cups sifted all-purpose flour

½ teaspoon salt
1 teaspoon salt

¾ teaspoon baking powder
1½ teaspoons baking powder

1½ to 2 cups bittersweet, semisweet, or white chocolate chips
3 to 4 cups bittersweet, semisweet, or white chocolate chips

1 to 1½ cups shelled unsalted pistachios (4 to 6 ounces)
2 to 3 cups shelled unsalted pistachios (8 to 12 ounces)

Heat the oven to 350°F. Lightly grease at least 2 baking sheets. Using an electric mixer, cream the butter and both kinds of sugar until fluffy and light in color. Beat in the vanilla and eggs. Sift the flour, salt, and baking powder together. Add to the wet mixture and combine on low speed until there are only a few streaks of dry flour left. Add the chocolate chips and pistachios and combine until the mixture is uniform.

Drop heaping tablespoons of dough onto the baking sheets, and bake for 10 to 12 minutes. If you want soft cookies, bake them just until they are no longer shiny on top. For crisper cookies, bake until they are pale golden brown. Let the cookies rest on the baking sheets out of the oven for a moment, then transfer to a rack to cool. When cooled completely, store in an airtight container.

Pecan Chocolate Chip Cookies

Substitute lightly toasted pecans for the pistachios in the above recipe. I like the nuts left whole, but you may chop them coarsely if you prefer.

Fruit and Nut Cookies

Instead of chocolate chips, use a greater proportion of nuts, and include dried or candied fruit. Often, to let the nut and fruit flavors prevail in such cookies, I use all white sugar, no brown sugar. One of my favorite combinations is almonds and dried cherries, with almond extract added. Also very good are pistachios with chopped candied orange peel.

Sheet Pan Brownies

MAKES ABOUT 4 DOZEN 2-INCH BROWNIES
LARGE QUANTITY RECIPE: MAKES ABOUT 8 DOZEN
2-INCH BROWNIES

This has proven to be *the* brownie recipe for a quantity of brownies. The larger recipe makes enough to fill a restaurant-size 24-by-17-inch sheet pan. Made with cocoa powder and chocolate chips, they are less expensive than brownies made of solid baking chocolate, but they are amazingly rich, chewy, and satisfying. It may seem odd to use brown sugar, but it underscores the deep chocolate flavor. I think these are at their best the day after they're baked.

FOR A 12-BY-17-INCH PAN (WITH AT LEAST A ¾-INCH RIM)
FOR A FULL SHEET PAN (24 BY 17 INCHES)

7 ounces unsweetened cocoa powder (about 1¾ cups; almost a full can)
14 ounces unsweetened cocoa powder (about 3½ cups)

¾ cup canola or other vegetable oil
1½ cups canola or other vegetable oil

2 cups (1 pound or 4 sticks) plus 2 tablespoons butter
4 cups (2 pounds or 8 sticks) plus 4 tablespoons butter

8 large eggs
16 large eggs

4½ cups firmly packed brown sugar
9 cups firmly packed brown sugar

1 tablespoon vanilla extract
2 tablespoons vanilla extract

⅛ teaspoon salt
¼ teaspoon salt

12 ounces all-purpose flour (3 cups sifted)
1½ pounds all-purpose flour (6 cups sifted)

1 pound whole pecans (about 5 cups), lightly toasted (see page 301)
2 pounds whole pecans (about 10 cups), lightly toasted (see page 301)

2 cups bittersweet or semisweet chocolate chips (12 ounces)
4 cups bittersweet or semisweet chocolate chips (1½ pounds)

Heat the oven to 325°F. Butter a 12-by-17-inch pan *(24-by-17-inch sheet pan for large quantity)*, line the bottom with baking parchment, then lightly butter the parchment. Combine a handful of flour with a handful of cocoa powder. Shake this mixture around in the pan, coating the entire greased inner surface. Shake out the excess flour-cocoa mixture, tapping the pan.

Combine the cocoa powder, oil, and butter in a large saucepan and cook over low heat until the butter is melted. Whip together and heat the eggs, brown sugar, vanilla, and salt in the top of a double boiler (I use a large stainless-steel mixing bowl set over, not in, a pot of gently boiling water), stirring frequently, until the mixture reaches 110°F, about the temperature of a warm bath. Combine the two mixtures in a very large bowl and whip with an electric mixer (or by hand with a whisk) for about 5 minutes. Begin to fold in the flour, then add the nuts and chips, continuing to fold just until the batter is uniform. Spoon the batter in globs into the prepared pan, then spread gently with a rubber spatula. The batter will fill the pan to the brim.

Bake, rotating the pan every 10 minutes, until a toothpick comes out clean, 35 to 40 minutes. Let cool completely on a rack. Wrap well and let sit overnight.

To cut, first run a small knife all around the edge of the pan to loosen the edges. Invert the uncut brownies onto a large tray, or onto the back of another sheet pan. Peel off the parchment, then invert onto a cutting board. Cut into squares of the desired size with a long knife.

Peanut Butter Cookies

MAKES ABOUT 5 DOZEN 1½-INCH COOKIES

Traditional recipes for peanut butter cookies use vegetable shortening and processed peanut butter that contains more vegetable shortening and added sugar. This recipe calls for natural peanut butter and butter—less-processed ingredients. They are rich, crumbly, and deeply peanutty. If you are using salted peanut butter, reduce the salt to a pinch.

¾ cup butter (1½ sticks), at room temperature

1 cup natural unsalted peanut butter, chunky or smooth, well stirred

1½ cups firmly packed brown sugar

1 large egg plus 1 egg yolk, beaten

2 teaspoons vanilla extract

¼ teaspoon salt

3 cups sifted all-purpose flour

Heat the oven to 350°F. Lightly grease 2 baking sheets. Cream the butter well in a large bowl. Add the peanut butter and cream well. Add the sugar and cream well. Add the egg, yolk, vanilla, and salt, and whip until smooth. Sift the flour, add it to the bowl, and mix just until the dough is smooth and uniform.

continued . . .

. . . *continued*

Form the dough into 1-inch balls, and place them 1 inch apart on the baking sheets. Press each ball down with a flour-dipped fork, once in each direction to make a grid pattern, to a thickness of about ½ inch. Bake just until slightly puffed, lightly brown on top, and golden brown underneath, 10 to 12 minutes. Let the cookies rest on the baking sheets out of the oven for a moment, then transfer to a rack to cool. When cooled completely, store in an airtight container.

Oatmeal-Coconut Bars

MAKES SIXTEEN 2-INCH BARS

These are very good with vanilla ice cream. My mother saved this recipe decades ago, annotating it with just one word: "Divine."

2½ cups rolled oats

¾ cup sweetened flaked coconut

¼ cup granulated sugar

¼ teaspoon salt

¾ teaspoon baking powder

¾ cup butter (1½ sticks), at room temperature

¼ cup firmly packed brown sugar

Heat the oven to 375°F. Butter an 8-by-8-inch baking pan. Sprinkle 2 tablespoons of the oats evenly into the pan. Combine 2¼ cups of the oats with the coconut in a medium bowl. Combine the granulated sugar, salt, and baking powder in a small bowl. Sift if there are any lumps. Cream the butter with the brown sugar in a large bowl, then add the granulated sugar mixture and cream again. Add the oat mixture and combine with your hands until uniform. Press the dough evenly into the pan without disturbing the coating of butter and sprinkling of oats. Sprinkle the remaining 2 tablespoons oats over the surface of the dough.

Bake for 20 to 25 minutes, or until pale golden brown. For the neatest results, let cool completely and refrigerate for several hours before using a sharp knife to cut the cookies in a 4-by-4 grid into 16 square bars, or whatever shape and size you please. Let the cookies come to room temperature before serving.

Wedding Cookies

MAKES ABOUT 30 SMALL COOKIES

Call these cookies Mexican wedding cakes if you make them with pecans, popular in Texas and the Southwest. If made with walnuts, call them Russian tea biscuits. Made with pistachios and served with hot, strong tea, call them whatever you like; they will be delicious.

> 1 cup unsalted butter (2 sticks), at room temperature
>
> ¼ cup granulated (white) sugar
>
> scant ¼ teaspoon salt
>
> 2 teaspoons vanilla extract
>
> 2 cups unsifted all-purpose flour
>
> 1 cup finely chopped pecans, walnuts, or pistachios (about 3¼ ounces; if salted, reduce the salt to a pinch)
>
> about 2 cups sifted powdered sugar for coating cookies

Heat the oven to 325°F. Cream the butter, sugar, and salt in a large bowl until light in color and fluffy. Add the vanilla, then the flour and nuts. Form into balls the diameter of a bottle cap. Bake on an ungreased baking sheet for 10 to 12 minutes. *Do not let the cookies brown.* Let them sit for a moment, then carefully remove from the baking sheet and roll in sifted powdered sugar while warm. Let cool on a rack. Reroll the cookies in powdered sugar before serving.

Almond Cookies

MAKES ABOUT 4 DOZEN 1½-INCH COOKIES

If you've ever cracked open a peach or nectarine pit, perhaps you've noticed a kernel inside that looks very much like an almond. In fact, all the stone fruits (peaches, apricots, plums, nectarines, and cherries) are in the same botanical family as almonds, and the flavors of those fruits marry well with the singular flavor of almonds. For a simple summer dessert, bring a bowl of assorted fresh stone fruit to the table, accompanied by a platter of these almond cookies.

1 heaping cup whole unblanched almonds (about 5 ounces), lightly toasted (see page 301)

⅔ cup butter (1 stick plus 2⅔ tablespoons), at room temperature

⅓ cup firmly packed brown sugar

⅓ cup granulated sugar

2 large eggs

1½ teaspoons almond extract

¼ teaspoon vanilla extract

1¾ cups sifted all-purpose flour

½ teaspoon salt

1 teaspoon baking powder

Heat the oven to 350°F. Lightly grease 2 baking sheets. When the toasted almonds are completely cool, pulse them in a food processor to a fine meal, or chop finely by hand with a sharp knife.

Cream the butter in a large bowl until smooth and light in color. Add the brown and granulated sugar and beat until creamy again. Add the eggs and extracts and beat until the mixture is uniform. In a medium bowl, sift the flour, salt, and baking powder together, then mix in the ground almonds. Add the dry mixture to the wet mixture and mix just until the dough is uniform. Roll into 1-inch balls and place 1½ inches apart on the baking sheets. Bake for 8 to 10 minutes—the cookies should brown lightly on the bottom, but are tastiest if they remain light on top. Remove to a rack to cool.

If you don't serve these cookies the day you make them, keep them well wrapped in an airtight bag in the freezer.

Sesame Cookies

MAKES ABOUT 200 SMALL COOKIES

These little cookies are loved by everyone. Southern in origin, they still manage, like many Southerners themselves, to feel at home in a variety of settings. They not only admirably conclude a down-home, no-holds-barred meal of Southern barbecue, they taste great after an authentic Asian dinner, a Southwestern fiesta, or a mosaiclike feast of grains and garden vegetables.

1¼ cups sesame seeds

¼ cup butter, melted

1¼ cups firmly packed brown sugar

1 teaspoon vanilla extract

1 large egg

1¼ cups sifted all-purpose flour

¼ teaspoon baking powder

¼ teaspoon salt

Heat the oven to 350°F. Toast the sesame seeds in a shallow baking pan in the oven, stirring and redistributing several times, until they are fragrant and a uniform pale gold, 15 to 20 minutes. Keep in mind that they burn easily. Remove the pan from the oven. The sesame seeds make a very subtle and exquisite crackly sound as they cool. Cool them thoroughly in the pan before you mix the dough.

Raise the oven temperature to 375°F. Lightly grease 2 or more baking sheets. Beat the butter and sugar in a large bowl until light, then beat in the vanilla, egg, and toasted sesame seeds. Sift the flour, baking powder, and salt together, and stir into the butter mixture just until the dough is uniform. Drop *half teaspoonfuls* of dough 1 inch apart on the baking sheets. Bake just until the edges and bottoms are brown, about 5 minutes. Watch carefully; since these cookies are so rich in sugar, they burn easily. Let the cookies set up on the sheet for a moment, then transfer them to racks to cool. Cool the baking sheets between batches.

Variation

For a dramatic effect, use a blend of black sesame seeds and regular sesame seeds, and toast lightly. Don't use all black seeds, or you won't be able to tell when they are toasted.

Cashew Cookies

MAKES ABOUT 3 DOZEN SMALL COOKIES

These cookies are mostly cashew, with just enough cookie to hold them together. If you are feeling bold and daring, add a pinch—or two—of cayenne pepper to the dough.

2 cups roasted, salted cashews

¾ cup sifted all-purpose flour

¾ cup unsalted butter (1½ sticks), at room temperature

½ cup sugar

2 teaspoons finely grated lemon zest

1 large egg

Heat the oven to 350°F. Lightly grease 2 baking sheets. Using a food processor, pulse and grind the cashews to a medium-fine meal, but not to the point that they become cashew butter. Add the flour to the cashews and process for a second or two longer. You could also chop the cashews very finely with a knife—it's a great opportunity to practice patience.

Cream the butter in a large bowl until lightened in color and fluffy. Add the sugar and lemon zest and cream again until light. Add the egg and beat until uniform. Dump in the cashew-flour mixture and mix until you have a uniform dough.

Keeping your hands slightly damp with cold tap water, roll the dough into 1-inch balls and place 1½ inches apart on the baking sheets. (If you like, you may roll them into oblongs about 2 inches long, then bend them into an arc shape when placing them on a baking sheet—the finished cookies will look somewhat like cashews.)

Bake until lightly browned around the edges and on the bottom and cooked through, about 12 minutes. Let the cookies rest on the baking sheets for a moment before removing them to racks to cool. Let them cool completely before arranging or storing. These cookies are quite delicate; they will not withstand much handling.

Walnut Biscotti

MAKES ABOUT 4 DOZEN COOKIES

For walnut lovers, here is a heap of lightly toasted walnuts bound in a light biscotti matrix. In the late afternoon, my Aunt Jean loves to dip walnut biscotti in a glass of pinot noir.

1 pound walnut halves and pieces (about 5 cups), lightly toasted (see page 301)

1 cup minus 2 tablespoons sugar

1 egg

2 egg whites

½ teaspoon vanilla extract

½ teaspoon orange or lemon extract

1½ teaspoons anise seed (optional)

2 cups sifted all-purpose flour

1 teaspoon baking powder

¼ teaspoon salt

Heat the oven to 350°F. Grease a large baking sheet (you can use the baking sheet you toasted the walnuts on). When the toasted walnuts are cool, rub handfuls lightly between both hands to release the excess papery brown skin. Do not chop the walnuts—they should be whole for this recipe.

Using an electric mixer, beat the sugar, egg, and egg whites for about 3 minutes, until fluffy and light in color. Add the extracts and anise seed, if desired. Sift the flour, baking powder, and salt together. Fold the dry ingredients into the egg mixture until just combined, then fold in the walnuts, coating them with dough. It will seem like too many walnuts and not enough dough, but all is well.

Divide the dough in half and shape each portion into a log on the baking sheet, making sure the logs are at least 3 inches apart. The dough will be lumpy from the walnuts. Slightly flatten the top and pat the outer surface of the logs as smooth as possible with your hands. Bake, rotating the pan once, until the loaves are golden, about 35 minutes.

Let the loaves cool for 10 minutes and lower the oven temperature to 325°F. Transfer the loaves to a cutting board. Cut each loaf diagonally into ½-inch slices with a sharp knife. Lay the slices back on the baking sheet, cut side up (you might need to use a second baking sheet), and bake until crisp and lightly gold around the edges, 15 to 20 minutes longer. Cool the biscotti on a rack. When cool, store in an airtight container.

Walnut-Cranberry Biscotti

This is a perfect end to a festive Italian-American holiday meal. Follow the recipe above, adding ¼ cup chopped dried cranberries when mixing the dough.

Lemon-Anise Biscotti

MAKES ABOUT 3 DOZEN COOKIES

These are hard, but not tooth-cracking, true Italian biscotti. The Deep Springs student irrigation team stuffs handfuls of these biscotti into the pockets of their overalls before going out to the alfalfa fields to move the big, unwieldy irrigation lines. Even when the biscotti get soaked, they're still good, and they don't make such a crumbly mess as other cookies.

2 cups sifted all-purpose flour

1 teaspoon baking powder

¼ teaspoon salt

2 large eggs

1 cup minus 2 tablespoons sugar

¼ teaspoon vanilla extract

⅛ teaspoon lemon extract

1 tablespoon finely grated lemon zest

1 tablespoon anise seed

Heat the oven to 350°F. Grease a baking sheet. Sift the flour, baking powder, and salt into a medium bowl. Using an electric mixer, beat the eggs with the sugar for about 3 minutes, until light and lemon-colored, then add the extracts, zest, and anise seed. Fold in the dry ingredients until just combined.

Divide the dough in half and shape each portion into a log, about a foot long and 3 inches wide, on the baking sheet, making sure the logs are at least 3 inches apart. Bake, rotating the pan once, until the loaves are golden and slightly cracked on top, about 35 minutes.

Let the loaves cool for a few minutes and lower the oven temperature to 325°F. Cut each loaf diagonally into ¼-inch slices with a sharp knife. Lay the slices back on the baking sheet, cut side up, about ½ inch apart, and bake until crisp and golden around the edges, about 15 minutes longer. Cool the biscotti on a rack. When cool, store in an airtight container.

Lime Bars

MAKES SIXTEEN 2-INCH BARS

These bars are brownielike in texture, with a deep lime flavor.

⅓ cup butter, melted and hot

2 ounces cream cheese, at room temperature

¾ cup granulated sugar

1 egg

1 egg yolk

1 teaspoon vanilla extract

1 tablespoon finely grated lime zest (from about 3 limes)

¼ cup fresh lime juice (from about 2 limes)

½ cup plus 2 tablespoons sifted all-purpose flour

¼ teaspoon salt

powdered sugar for dusting

Heat the oven to 350°F. Generously butter and flour an 8-by-8-inch pan. Whisk together the hot butter, cream cheese, and sugar in a medium bowl until uniform. Add the egg, egg yolk, vanilla, lime zest, and lime juice, and beat for a full minute. Sift the flour and salt into the wet ingredients and fold to combine, just until uniform. Scrape into the prepared pan and bake for about 25 minutes. Let cool, and cut into bars. Put a few spoonfuls of powdered sugar into a screen sieve and tap the sieve over the lime bars, dusting them generously.

Lemon Slice Cookies

MAKES ABOUT 3 DOZEN 1½-INCH COOKIES

An old recipe from my Aunt Jean, these pale half-moon cookies are wonderfully buttery and lemony.

2 cups *minus* 2 tablespoons all-purpose flour

¼ teaspoon baking powder

¼ teaspoon salt

¾ cup butter (1½ sticks), at room temperature

½ cup granulated sugar, plus more for sprinkling

½ cup powdered sugar

1 tablespoon finely grated lemon zest

3 tablespoons fresh lemon juice

½ teaspoon vanilla extract

EGG YOLK GLAZE (OPTIONAL)

2 teaspoons egg yolk

2 teaspoons sugar

¼ teaspoon fresh lemon juice

2 or 3 drops lemon extract

Sift together the flour, baking powder, and salt. In a large bowl, cream the butter, ½ cup granulated sugar, and powdered sugar. Beat in the lemon zest, lemon juice, and vanilla. Add the dry mixture to the

continued...

. . . continued

wet mixture and combine until you have a uniform dough.

Roll the dough into 2 logs about 6 inches in length, using plastic wrap or waxed paper. If you want perfectly shaped cookies, the logs must be perfectly round. Freeze the logs for at least 1 hour, or chill overnight.

Heat the oven to 350°F. Lightly grease 2 baking sheets. With a sharp knife, carefully slice the frozen logs into even halves lengthwise, then cut ¼-inch-thick slices from each half. Place the half-moons 1 inch apart on the baking sheets. Lightly sprinkle granulated sugar over the surface of each cookie. Bake for about 10 minutes—they will remain pale, as the lemon juice inhibits browning. Let the cookies set on the baking sheets out of the oven for a moment, then carefully remove them to racks to cool.

I almost never have the urge to decorate cookies, but I love to paint the curved outer rim of these with an egg yolk glaze so they resemble half-slices of lemon. Heat the oven to 300°F. Combine the egg yolk, sugar, lemon juice, and extract in a small bowl and stir until the sugar is dissolved. Using a small pastry brush, apply a thick line of glaze to the curved rim of each cookie. There should be just enough glaze to paint all the cookies. To set the glaze, return the cookies to the warm oven for 5 minutes. Let the cookies cool completely before arranging them on a plate.

Italian Orange Cookies

MAKES ABOUT 3 DOZEN 2-INCH COOKIES

These iced, cakelike cookies are perfect with espresso or tea after a big Italian dinner.

¾ cup butter (1½ sticks), at room temperature

½ cup granulated sugar

¼ cup firmly packed brown sugar

3 eggs

1 teaspoon vanilla extract

1 tablespoon finely grated orange zest

¼ cup fresh orange juice

¼ cup orange juice concentrate (undiluted)

3 cups sifted all-purpose flour

2½ teaspoons baking powder

¼ teaspoon baking soda

¼ teaspoon salt

ICING

3 tablespoons orange juice concentrate (undiluted)

¼ teaspoon finely grated orange zest

pinch of salt

½ teaspoon vanilla extract

4 tablespoons butter

2 cups powdered sugar, sifted

Have all ingredients at room temperature. Heat the oven to 350°F. Lightly grease 2 baking sheets. Using an electric mixer, cream the butter, granulated sugar, and brown sugar until fluffy. Add the eggs, one at a time, then add the vanilla, orange zest, orange juice, and orange juice concentrate. Sift the flour, baking powder, baking soda, and salt together, and blend into the wet mixture just until the dough is uniform. Let the dough rest, covered, in the refrigerator for 20 minutes, then drop by neat tablespoonfuls 2 inches apart on the baking sheets.

Bake until the cookies feel springy to the touch and are pale golden brown around the edges, about 8 minutes. Allow the cookies to set on the pan for a few minutes, then remove to racks to cool while making the icing.

To make the icing, combine the orange juice concentrate, orange zest, salt, vanilla, and butter, cut into small pieces, in a small, thick-walled pan. Warm over medium-low heat, stirring occasionally, until the butter is melted. Stir in the powdered sugar and heat the mixture gently, stirring occasionally, for 5 minutes. Remove from the heat and let cool for 5 minutes, stirring a few times as it cools. Ice the cookies, and let the icing dry and harden for an hour or so before arranging the cookies on a platter or stacking them in a tin.

Gingersnaps

MAKES ABOUT 8 DOZEN 2-INCH COOKIES

These gingersnaps are quite snappy, with a hefty, but balanced, dose of spice. Containing only a little butter, they keep well.

¾ cup butter (1½ sticks), at room temperature

2 cups sugar

2 eggs, beaten

½ cup molasses

2 teaspoons apple cider vinegar

3¾ cups sifted all-purpose flour

¾ teaspoon baking soda

¾ teaspoon baking powder

1 tablespoon ground ginger

½ teaspoon ground cinnamon

¼ teaspoon ground cloves

¼ teaspoon black pepper

Cream the butter and sugar in a large bowl. Beat in the eggs, molasses, and vinegar. Sift the flour, baking soda, baking powder, ginger, cinnamon, cloves, and pepper, and add to the butter mixture. Mix just until thoroughly blended. For easiest handling, chill the dough for an hour.

Before baking, heat the oven to 325°F, and lightly grease at least 2 baking sheets. Form the dough into ¾-inch balls and

continued . . .

. . . continued

place 1½ inches apart on the baking sheets. Bake for about 12 minutes, or until crinkled and no longer moist on top. Remove the cookies to racks to cool. As they cool, they will become crisp and snappy. Store in an airtight container.

Gingersnaps, Vanilla Ice Cream, and Boysenberries

When you have perfect sweet boysenberries or blackberries, make Gingersnaps and churn up a quart of Vanilla Ice Cream (page 507). We served this at Deep Springs' graduation one year, following a dinner of grilled pork chops and corn on the cob. If the berries are superlative, this just might be the best summer dessert of all. For every person, generously allow a cup of ice cream, a heaping half-cup of berries, and 5 or 6 cookies. Serve the ice cream in chilled bowls. Heap the berries in a glass bowl, with the cookies on a platter. Give people small plates and let them help themselves to berries and cookies to go with their ice cream. Eat the ice cream using a succession of gingersnaps as a spoon, relieving the sweetness with tart berries now and again.

Ginger Cookies

MAKES ABOUT 4 DOZEN 2-INCH COOKIES

This is your best recipe for soft, chewy ginger cookies—they are more kid friendly than the previous Gingersnaps. In Deep Springs' desert climate, they will harden if left uncovered.

¾ cup (1½ sticks) plus 1 tablespoon butter, at room temperature

1 cup firmly packed brown sugar

¼ cup molasses

1 large egg

1 teaspoon cider vinegar

2⅓ cups sifted all-purpose flour

1 teaspoon baking soda

1 teaspoon baking powder

1½ teaspoons ground ginger

1 teaspoon ground cinnamon

½ teaspoon ground cloves

pinch of salt

granulated sugar for rolling

In a large bowl, cream the butter and brown sugar until fluffy. Add the molasses, egg, and vinegar and beat well, about 1 minute. Sift the flour, baking soda, baking powder, ginger, cinnamon, cloves, and salt, and add to the butter mixture; mix just until thoroughly blended. Chill the dough for 1 hour.

Before baking, heat the oven to 375°F, and lightly grease 2 baking sheets. Form the dough into 1-inch balls and roll in granulated sugar. Place 2 inches apart on the baking sheets. Bake for about 10 minutes—do not overbake. Once they form their crinkly top and are just barely browned, they are done. Remove the cookies to a rack to cool. Keep in an airtight container.

Butter Cookies

MAKES ABOUT 30 SMALL COOKIES

Why are these plain cookies so good, the dough so irresistible? It's the yolk.

1 cup unsalted butter (2 sticks), at room temperature

¾ cup sugar

1 egg yolk

1½ teaspoons vanilla extract

2 cups sifted all-purpose flour

⅛ teaspoon salt

Cream the butter and sugar together in a large bowl until fluffy and light in color. Beat in the yolk and vanilla. Sift in the flour and salt and mix until combined. Roll into logs about 1 inch in diameter, wrap well in plastic wrap, and chill for at least 1 hour.

Before baking, heat the oven to 350°F. Lightly grease 2 baking sheets. Slice the dough into ¼-inch-thick slices and arrange at least 1½ inches apart on the baking sheets. Bake the cookies until they are the palest brown around the edges, about 10 minutes. Transfer to a rack and let cool completely. Store in an airtight container.

continued...

. . . continued

Cardamom Butter Cookies

Remove the inner dark seeds from cardamom pods until you have about 2 teaspoons of seeds. Crush with ¼ cup sugar in a mortar until the seeds are completely powdered. Mix in an additional ½ cup sugar and use this sugar in the recipe above. These make a superb, sophisticated after-dinner digestive.

Bizcochitos

MAKES ABOUT 4 DOZEN SMALL COOKIES

These rich cookies are a traditional Christmas specialty of New Mexico. Made with lots of pork lard, they have a full, creamy flavor. In the more frugal days of our great-grandmothers, many cakes and cookies were made with lard or other animal fats, a practice surviving only in traditional recipes like this. In a diplomatic gesture disclosing the controversial main ingredient, my mother always uses her pig-shaped cookie cutter for bizcochitos, and places a single silver dragée for the pig's eye. Superlative bizcochitos are made with lard rendered from Deep Springs pork (to render your own lard, follow the instructions in the Deep Springs Soap recipe, page 572, for rendering beef tallow, using fresh pork kidney fat instead of beef kidney fat). The anise seeds are controversial—those who dislike them dislike them intensely and might call them *piojos,* Spanish for "head lice," prompting many bizcochito bakers to make two batches, *con piojos* and *sin piojos*, pleasing the whole family. If anise is not to your liking, omit it and add a couple of teaspoons of vanilla extract instead. My sister Diana won a blue ribbon at the county fair for these bizcochitos.

2 teaspoons anise seed (omit if hated, or replace with vanilla extract)

¼ cup dry white wine

2 cups lard, at room temperature

2 cups sugar

3 eggs

6 cups sifted all-purpose flour

4 teaspoons baking powder

1 teaspoon salt

———

TOPPING

1 teaspoon ground cinnamon

¼ cup sugar

Crack the anise seed coarsely in a mortar, or place it in a fold of waxed paper and gently pound with a heavy object. In a small dish, mix the anise seed into the wine and let sit, covered, for several hours or overnight.

Using an electric mixer, beat the lard until creamy and fluffy, until it has become snow-white and opaque. Add the sugar and cream again. Beat in the eggs, one at a time, then beat in the wine-anise mixture. Sift the flour, baking powder, and salt together, and fold into the lard mixture, mixing until the dough is uniform. For easiest rolling, chill the dough for about 2 hours.

Before baking, heat the oven to 350°F, and lightly grease at least 2 baking sheets. On a floured surface, roll the dough into a rectangle about ½ inch thick. For light-textured cookies, avoid overhandling the dough. Using a sharp knife dipped in flour, cut into 1½-inch diamond shapes, or cut into desired shapes with cookie cutters. Place the cookies 1 inch apart on the baking sheets. For the topping, blend together the cinnamon and sugar, and sprinkle some on each cookie. Bake for 10 to 12 minutes, or until pale golden brown on the bottom. Gently transfer the cookies to a rack to cool. Store in an airtight container.

Vanilla Wafers

MAKES ABOUT 4 DOZEN 1½-INCH COOKIES

Plain and simple, these cookies are taken from a cookbook published in 1917—the year Deep Springs was founded. They are good for homemade Banana Pudding (page 454), or for making Mama Nell's Kentucky Bourbon Balls (page 547). Cake flour will give the cookies an especially tender texture.

5 tablespoons butter, at room temperature

1 cup sugar

1 egg

2 teaspoons vanilla extract

¼ cup milk

2 cups sifted all-purpose flour or cake flour

2 teaspoons baking powder

½ teaspoon salt

Heat the oven to 350°F. Grease 2 baking sheets. Cream the butter in a medium bowl; add the sugar and cream again. Beat in the egg, vanilla, and milk. Sift the flour, baking powder, and salt together. Add the dry mixture to the wet mixture and combine until uniform. Drop scant teaspoonfuls of dough about 1½ inches apart on the baking sheets. Or put the dough into a heavy-duty zipper-lock bag, cut a small hole at the corner, and squeeze out evenly shaped wafers. Bake for 12 to 15 minutes, or until brown around the edges and pale gold in the center. Remove to a rack to cool. Store in an airtight container.

Old-Fashioned Vinegar Taffy

MAKES 1 POUND, ABOUT 70 PIECES

For many years when I was a kid, my mother and I made this on the last day of school.

Here are three good candy-making rules:

* For best results, use one of the leading brands consisting of 100 percent pure cane sugar. They are formulated to ensure success.
* Make this or any other candy using very clean equipment, in a kitchen that is otherwise unoccupied. Spattering grease or steam from boiling pots might jeopardize the delicate, controlled crystallization of sugar.
* Choose a dry day for candy making; there is no other kind of day at Deep Springs.

½ cup water

2½ cups granulated pure cane sugar

¼ cup apple cider vinegar

¼ teaspoon salt

1 tablespoon butter

1 teaspoon vanilla extract

cornstarch for pulling

Butter a shallow glass baking dish. Combine the water, sugar, vinegar, salt, and butter in a very clean, medium-sized, heavy saucepan over medium-high heat, stirring constantly until the sugar dissolves. Wipe the sugar crystals from the side of the pan if necessary, using a moistened paper towel. Continue to cook over medium-low heat, *without stirring,* to 272°F, or the soft-crack stage. *Do not let the mixture go above this temperature* or the candy will be too hard. Remove from the heat and add the vanilla extract.

Pour the candy into the buttered baking dish. Let cool for about 30 minutes, turning the edges toward the center several times with a spatula to prevent hardening. When cool enough to handle, dust your hands well with cornstarch. Gather the taffy into a ball and pull and fold, pull and fold, over and over, until it holds its shape. Divide into two parts. Pull and twist each part into a 1-inch rope. Rub a little butter onto your kitchen shears and cut each rope into 1-inch pieces. Place on waxed paper and let harden in a dry place at room temperature for several hours. Wrap each piece in a 4-inch square of waxed paper. Store in an airtight container.

English Toffee with Sea Salt

MAKES ABOUT 2½ POUNDS

This is a deep, dark toffee, with dark chocolate and a light sprinkle of sea salt. Given how extraordinarily good this adult candy is, it is quick and easy to make. Please see the notes about candy making in the previous recipe.

2 cups granulated pure cane sugar

1½ cups butter (3 sticks)

2 tablespoons water

2½ cups whole raw almonds (about 10 ounces)

2 cups semisweet or bittersweet chocolate chips (12 ounces)

¾ teaspoon sea salt

Lightly butter a big flat metal platter or rimmed baking sheet (big enough to allow the candy to spread and not end up too thick; a 12-by-18-inch sheet pan is ideal). If you have baking parchment, line the platter or sheet with lightly buttered parchment.

In a very clean, medium-sized, heavy saucepan, heat the sugar, butter, and water over a medium flame, stirring occasionally. When the butter is melted, stir in the almonds. *Without stirring,* continue to cook the candy over medium heat until the mixture registers a toasty 285° to 290°F on an instant-read thermometer or a candy thermometer (the syrup will be a deep golden color, and the nuts will be toasted). Immediately pour the toffee onto the buttered platter. Let the toffee spread out and set for a few seconds, tilting the pan if necessary, then evenly sprinkle the chocolate chips over the hot toffee. Let the chocolate soften for about 30 seconds, then spread it smooth. While the chocolate is still soft, sprinkle it evenly with sea salt.

Let the toffee harden at room temperature for at least 2 hours, then put the pan in the freezer for several minutes. Secure the pan in a bag and drop the whole thing on the floor to break up the toffee. The toffee should separate easily into lovely, randomly shaped, bite-size pieces.

Mama Nell's Kentucky Bourbon Balls

MAKES 20 TO 30 SMALL COOKIES

I knew my maternal grandmother as Mama Nell. This is perhaps the most treasured old family recipe I have—I always make bourbon balls at Christmas, if only to retell an oft-told family anecdote: when she lived in Texas, Nell once hosted a Ladies' Aid Society luncheon—the most proper, staunch Baptist, teetotaling ladies in town would be in attendance. This was one of her favorite recipes, so she decided to serve them despite their unmistakable whiff of whiskey. The president of the society—the most proper of all—popped one in her mouth and exclaimed, "Nell, these cookies are simply *delicious*; what *is* that familiar flavor?" Without missing a beat, my grandmother replied, "Nutmeg!"

1½ cups pecans (about 5 ounces), very lightly toasted (see page 301)

1 cup vanilla wafers (see page 544 for a recipe), crushed to a powder

1 cup powdered sugar, plus more for coating cookies

2 tablespoons unsweetened cocoa powder

¼ cup Kentucky bourbon

1½ tablespoons cane syrup, golden syrup, or light corn syrup (see the Pecan Pie recipe, page 457)

When the toasted pecans are cool, chop them very finely with a sharp knife—you should end up with 1 cup of chopped pecans.

Combine the pecans with the crushed wafers, 1 cup powdered sugar, and cocoa powder in a medium bowl. Mix in the bourbon and cane syrup. Form into small balls about ½ inch in diameter, and roll them in powdered sugar. Cover tightly and chill for an hour or two. Let them come to room temperature before serving. Store the cookies tightly covered and refrigerated, or else the alcohol will evaporate.

CHAPTER 18

Menus

This is important: a menu is where it all comes together. A menu is not only the list of foods served at a meal, it is the experience of the foods themselves taken as a whole. A good menu is more than the sum of its parts; the various offerings complement and enhance one another. A good menu has a sense of contrast on one hand and balance on the other. A menu may include several courses, or may be as simple and everyday as this:

* grilled cheese sandwich
* tomato soup

Menu writing is its own kind of poetry—I could sit on my couch all afternoon sipping tea and writing menus. However, the trick is to get up from the couch and proceed to cook those lovely-sounding menus, turning out meals that fulfill or exceed every expectation.

This book deals almost exclusively with informal, "family-style" menus, where all the foods appear on the table at the same time and everyone helps themselves. Deep Springs meals are served buffet-style, with the day's menu written on a nearby board. But ambitious cooks may choose to serve a meal in a more formal, restaurant style, sometimes known as French service, where courses are presented already plated, in succession: first an hors d'oeuvre, then maybe a soup, then the main course, then a salad, then dessert. While much more labor is involved in serving a menu of courses, it opens up greater possibilities for the food: risotto is served the moment it's finished; meat or fish is fresh from the pan, still sizzling; the salad has no chance to wilt or the soufflé to fall.

A basic American family-style dinner menu typically consists of a protein; a starch; a vegetable or two, including a salad; sometimes bread; and a dessert. This simple formula may be infinitely varied. Here are some rules for menu making:

Keep it simple. Overambition is the downfall of many a well-intentioned dinner. Very often, less is more. A dinner consisting of only two excellent dishes is far better than a dinner of those same two excellent dishes plus three more not-so-good ones.

Balance the richness. If one course—usually the meat course—is especially rich, make sure the salad and other courses are on the light and refreshing side. Don't follow a goat cheese–laden salad with a steak topped with blue cheese sauce. Both are delicious, but not in the same menu. If the main offerings are rich, a light dessert is welcome. If the main courses are kept light, it's a great opportunity for a rich dessert.

Any composed, complex dish is usually best on its own. Lasagna, pot pie, enchiladas, assorted pizzas, beef stew with potatoes—such dishes are meals in themselves and need only the simplest accompaniments: tossed green salad, vegetables in vinaigrette, a bowl of radishes. . . .

Maintain ethnic continuity. In other words, don't follow barbecued chicken wings with Chinese noodle stir-fry, or sushi with enchiladas. With sufficient experience, however, you can successfully break this rule. Many foods adapt beautifully to other ethnic contexts. Once I slipped a rather European salad of roasted beets, sliced oranges, and tarragon into a Middle Eastern falafel dinner. It tasted right at home. I love menus that contain many ethnic flourishes but where freshness and simplicity define the meal rather than any particular ethnic stamp.

Pay attention to the season and the weather. Hot weather demands the simplest cooking: sliced ripe garden tomatoes with salt, peaches and plums sprinkled with flavored sugars, simple salads of homegrown greens and herbs, boiled fresh corn on the cob, hot chiles and cilantro to cool the body. Cool-weather cooking is more nuanced and complex: long-cooked dishes, braises, beets, hard squash, piquant greens, elaborate starches, spinach, onions, pork, cream, the astonishing brightness of citrus, the precious season of persimmons.

Cooking dinners in the highly unpredictable spring or fall months at Deep Springs can be tricky. Sometimes I commit myself to wintry rib-sticking fare, such as pot roast, before I realize it's going to be a sweltering scorcher of a day. So I heap on the chopped herbs and flavor the gravy with a good splash of vinegar to make a heavy dish taste lighter. Or sometimes I have planned a light, salady menu on a day that starts off sunny but ends up with snow falling at four in the afternoon. So I hustle to throw together a soup and bake the bread late so it's still warm. Cooking, I maintain, is fundamentally an interaction with nature; the good cook must pay attention and respond to the environment to produce soul-satisfying food.

Finally, *consider the sensibilities of your guests*. I say "consider" and not "cater to"; I love to expand, very gently, my guests' comfort zones, to introduce them to new foods or to compel them, with a warm smile, to reconsider foods they thought they hated.

Many sample menus follow; for the dishes marked with an asterisk (*), you will find the recipes in this book. Some of them are from my "archive" of actual meals I've cooked at Deep Springs. Other menus evoke that time, or otherwise suggest especially simple, everyday, home-cooked meals.

Breakfasts

Oatmeal* with Banana and Pecans

Yogurt with Pears

Polenta* with Almonds and
Dried Cherries

Santa Rosa Plums

Maple Yogurt

Soft-Boiled Eggs*

Cornmeal Biscuits*

Tomatoes with Salt*

Scrambled Eggs*

Warm Corn Tortillas

Fresh Salsa*

Pinto Beans* with Sour Cream

Freshly Baked Granola*

Yogurt with Fresh Berries

Baked Bacon*

Scrambled Eggs*

Jack's Buttermilk Pancakes* with
Maple Syrup

Steel-Cut Oats*

Fresh Fruit

Fresh Breakfast Sausage*

Biscuits and Gravy*

Fried Eggs*

Whole-Wheat Pancakes* with
Maple Syrup

Sliced Fruit

Shirred Eggs*

Elaine's Baked Grits*

Ham Slices

Griddle Toast*

Grandma Z.'s Coffeecake*

Lunches

Sweet Potato Cinnamon Rolls*
Ham and Cheese Omelets*
Sliced Oranges

Poached Eggs*
Cream Biscuits*
Griddle-Cooked Sirloin Steak
  with Green Onions
Crispy Breakfast Potatoes

Pumpkin Pie*
Mixed-Grain Porridge with
  Pumpkin Seed Butter
Sliced Pears
Yogurt Smoothies

Egg Salad* Sandwich on Wheaty Bread*
Watercress Soup*

Soupe au Pistou*
Focaccia*
Summer Cucumber Salad*

Grilled Cheese Sandwiches*
Tomato Soup
Green Salad*

Chef's Salad*
Corn Soup*
Tomato Focaccia*

Marinated Steak*
Celery Root Salad*
Minted Iced Tea*

Reatha's Macaroni and Cheese*
Sliced Cold Ham
Green Salad* with Apples

Pasta with Garden Tomatoes, Shell
  Beans,* and Basil
Iceberg Wedge Salad with Blue Cheese
  Dressing* and Bacon

Mama Nell's Chili con Carne*
  CONDIMENTS: sour cream, grated cheese,
  green onions
Skillet Cornbread*
Cut Chilled Vegetables
Limeade*

Green Chile Enchiladas*
Green Salad* with Radishes

Asparagus-Mushroom Frittata*
Leek and Gruyère Frittata
Green Salad*
Soft Wheat Rolls

Sorrel Omelet*
Baby Mixed Green Salad*
Garlic Toast

Gumbo* with Rice
Green Salad* with Shallot Vinaigrette*

Split Pea Soup* with Ham
Warm Wheaty Dinner Bread*
Pickled Winter Vegetables*

Tacos de Carne Asada*
Black Beans* with Sour Cream
Green Salad* with Radishes
  and Oranges
Hibiscus Iced Tea*

Tracy's Caesar Salad*
Cheesecake*

Tortilla Española*
Gazpacho*
Red Onion, Orange, and Olive Salad
Focaccia*

Pepperoni Pizza*
Zucchini and Red Onion Pizza*
Tomato, Basil, and Ricotta Pizza*
Green Salad* with Ranch Dressing*

Pork and White Bean Chili*
Black Bean Chili*
    CONDIMENTS: tomato, chopped white
    onion, sour cream, Jack cheese
Skillet Cornbread*
Chilled Radishes*
Jícama*

Tuna Salad* Melts
Curry Tofu Salad* Melts
Carrot-Raisin Salad*
Green Salad*

Sandwich Bar:
    Freshly Baked Wheaty Dinner Bread*
    Sliced Cold Roast Beef*
    Sliced Cold Roast Pork
    Cheese, Tomato, Shaved Onion, Lettuce,
    Mayonnaise, Mustards
Dill Pickles
Butternut Squash Chips*
Green Salad*
Nettle Broth* Minestrone with Garden
    Leeks and Potatoes

Clam Chowder*
Corn Chowder*
Homemade Crackers*
Green Salad*

Baked Potatoes*
    CONDIMENTS: butter, sour cream, sharp
    Cheddar cheese, sliced green onion, bacon,
    cooked broccoli
Chicken Salad with Tarragon
Green Salad* with Tomatoes

Dinners

Toasted Pasta with Garlic,* Broiled
 Cauliflower,* Tomato, and Toasted
 Breadcrumbs
Winter Lettuce Salad
Sliced Salami

Chicken Soup
Whole-Wheat Cheddar Biscuits*
Shaved Vegetable Salad

Italian Meatballs*
Mushroom "Meat" Balls
White and Brown Rice*
Tomato Sauce* and Parmesan
Tossed Green Salad* with Chopped
 Vegetables

Rico's Tacos* with Avocado and
 Sour Cream
Green Salad* with Red Onion and
 Sweet Balsamic Vinaigrette*

Cayenne-Rubbed Chicken with Potatoes
 and Garlic*
Broccoli* with Garlic and Sesame

Pork Chops Slow-Cooked in Olive Oil*
Polenta*
Greens*

Chicken Paprikash*
Herbed Spaetzle*
Spinach Salad* with Lemon Vinaigrette*

Boiled Shrimp* with Lemon and
Melted Butter

Rice* with Scallions

Cornmeal-Fried Okra*

Big Tossed Salad with Avocado,
Tomatoes, and Croutons*

Roast Lamb*

Potato, Fennel, and Celery Root Gratin*

Escarole, Frisée, and Radicchio Salad

Apple and Candied Orange Pie* with
Cognac Whipped Cream

Artichokes* with Lemon Mayonnaise

Pork Tenderloin*

Minted Rice and Chickpea Salad

Snap Peas*

Broiled Asparagus*

Rhubarb Fool

Vanilla Wafers*

Roasted Eggplant,* Roasted Red Peppers,*
and White Beans with Pesto*

Mixed Green Salad with Shaved
Parmesan and Toasted Pine Nut
Vinaigrette

Tomato Focaccia*

Lemon Ice Cream* with Gingersnaps*

Goulash*

Polenta*

Chicory Salad with Apple Cider
Vinaigrette*

Whipped Cream Cake* with Assorted
Winter Fruit

Baked Salmon* with Meyer
Lemon–Olive Relish*

Sautéed Green Beans* with Toasted
Walnut Olive Oil*

Green Pasta With Sautéed Corn*
and Roasted Peppers

Milk and Honey Cake*

Blackberry Ice Cream*

Wild Mushroom Risotto*

Seared Tuna* with Marinated Beets,*
    Cucumber, and Aioli*

Fennel, Blood Orange, and Toasted
    Almond Salad*

Pear Sherbet* with Sesame Cookies*

Carrot Soup with Ginger*

Turkey with Roasted Grapes*

Brown, White, and Wild Rice Pilaf
    with Mirepoix*

Arugula Salad with Walnuts

Pinky's Jewish Apple Cake*

Roast Beef*

Horseradish-Tomato Relish*

Steamed Red Potatoes

Minty Peas*

Gooseberry Fool*

Butternut Squash Soup with Diced Pear*

Cynthia's Garlic-Studded Milk-Braised
    Pork Loin*

Olive Oil Mashed Potatoes*

Sautéed Rainbow Chard

Kohlrabi-Apple Slaw*

Almond Cream* with Persimmons

Pinto Beans* with Onions and Cilantro

Carne Asada* with Warm Corn Tortillas

Chayote* with Garlic

Fresh Salsa*

Jícama* and Radishes*

Lime Bars*

Fruit with Rosewater

Gin Chicken Liver Pâté* on Thyme
    Crackers*

Olives

Boeuf Bourguignonne* with Parsley
    Potatoes

Red Lettuce Salad with Asparagus*
    and Lemon Vinaigrette*

Currant Cake*

Chicken and Dumplings*

Lettuce Salad with Ranch Dressing*

Lemon Meringue Pie*

Apple-Marinated Pork Chops*

Roasted Potatoes, Apples, and Onions*

Watercress Salad*

Fresh Ginger Cake*

Tarragon-Roasted Chicken with
  Tomatoes*

Wild Mushroom Risotto*

Stuffed Artichokes with Vinegar Butter*

Green Salad* with Blue Cheese Dressing*

Orange Bread Pudding*

Glazed Meatloaf*

Peas

Honey-Glazed Carrots*

Mashed Cauliflower*

Dinner Bread*

Tossed Garden Salad with Creamy
  Dressing

Chocolate-Peanut Cookies*

Braised Chicken in Red Wine with
  Mushrooms*

Parsley Farm Potatoes

Pear and Walnut Salad

Apple Pie* with Whipped Cream

Coffee Ice Cream with Cardamom
  Cookies

Cumin Roast Chicken*

Walnut Couscous*

Sautéed Green Beans* with Bacon and
  Red Onion

Corn Salad*

Mixed Green Salad* with Toasted
  Cumin–Mint-Yogurt Dressing*

Rich Dinner Bread*

Fresh Sliced Peaches and Cherries with
  Almond Cookies*

Gazpacho* of Fire-Roasted Vegetables

Roast Beef*

Horseradish Cream*

Scallion-Buttermilk Potatoes*

Arugula, Mushroom, and Walnut Salad
  with Lemon-Walnut Vinaigrette

Sourdough Bread

Italian Orange Cookies*

Tender Cured Pork Chops* with Fresh
    Sage

Corn on the Cob*

Roasted New Potatoes with Garlic

Fuji Apple Coleslaw*

Tomatoes with Salt,* Feta, and Basil

Sweet Potato Bread*

Gingersnaps, Vanilla Ice Cream, and
    Boysenberries*

Carrot Soup with Ginger*

Cayenne-Rubbed Chicken with Potatoes
    and Garlic*

Fried Parsnip Chips

Garden Salad with Shaved Vegetables

Carbonnade Flamande*

Saffron Risotto*

Rosemary Salt Potatoes

Garden Tomatoes, Summer Squash, and
    Green Beans Tossed with Torn Basil

Olives

Sourdough Bread

Garden Salad with Dijon-Yogurt Dressing*

Ginger Peach Crisp* with Whipped
    Cream

Leek and Vegetable Purée Soup*

Asparagus-Mushroom Frittata*

Red-Leaf Lettuce and Radicchio Salad

Potato Focaccia*

Apples and Oranges*

Falafel*

Hummus*

ACCOMPANIMENTS: tahin sauce,* pita bread,
    cucumbers, tomatoes, red onion, shredded
    lettuce, green salad* with rose petals

Marinated Beets* with Tarragon

Honey–Olive Oil Cake* with Almonds
    and Fresh Citrus

Chicken Cooked Under a Brick*

Scalloped Potatoes*

Sautéed Broccoli and Cauliflower

Mixed Green Salad*

Sourdough Bread

Ginger Cookies*

Skillet Hamburgers* with
Hamburger Buns*

ACCOMPANIMENTS: lettuce, thin-sliced onion,
sliced tomato, mustards, mayonnaise

Potato Chips*

Chopped Vegetable Salad

Tangy Lemon Sour Cream Gelatin*

Russian Borscht*

Sour Cream

Rye Bread

Dill Pickles

Fresh Cucumbers

Poached Pears with Chocolate Sauce*

Goulash*

Polenta*

Dinner Bread*

Mixed Green Salad*

Walnut Biscotti*

Aioli* with Garden Vegetables: beets,
carrots, green onions, green beans,
cherry tomatoes, zucchini, broccoli

Hard-Boiled Eggs*

Crispy Pan-Fried Chicken Strips*

Plum Fool*

Deep Springs Thanksgiving, 1998

Apple- and Rosemary-Scented Roast
Turkey*

Turkey Gravy

Mashed Potatoes*

Clio's Stuffing*

Stuffed Giant Turban Squash with
Cornbread Stuffing

Brussels Sprouts with Brown Butter*

Sweet Potato Purée with Diced Pear

Roasted Garden Carrots with White
Mountain Pine Nuts

Leek and Cabbage Sauté

Sweet Onions Cooked in Cream*

Watercress-Persimmon Salad

Pickled Cauliflower

Pickled Plums*

Cranberry Sauce*

continued . . .

... continued

Cranberry Relish*

Sweet Potato Bread*

Deep Springs Sourdough Bread

Apple and Quince Pie* with Lard
  Piecrust*

Pumpkin Pie*

Pecan Pie*

Pear-Persimmon Crisp

Deep Springs Dairy Whipped Cream

Sparkling Water with Fresh Lime

A Dinner at My House, Passover, 1999

Matzoh Ball Soup*

Roast Leg of Lamb* with Garlic, Lemon,
  and Rosemary

Boiled Artichokes* with Citron
  Mayonnaise

Italian Tzimmes*

Shaved Fennel* Salad

Coconut Macaroons

Strawberries in Sweet Wine

Christmas Eve, 1999

Jícama, Radish, Orange, and
  Pomegranate Salad

Mexican Braised Goat Stew* with Saffron

Goat Tamales

New Mexico Red Chile Sauce*

Lime-Pickled Red Onions*

Refried Beans*

Pico de Gallo, Tomatillo Salsa, Cilantro,
  Limes, Sour Cream

Tortillas

Winter Fruit and Custard Tart

New Year's Eve, 1999

Ginger and Paprika Roast Chicken

Saffron Risotto*

Beet and Carrot Salad

Chickpea Salad with Lemon and Parsley

Potato Bread*

Green Salad with Croutons*

Goose Egg Pound Cake Cinnamon Toast*
  with Vanilla Ice Cream*

Festival of Organ Meats, Fall 2001

Beef Liver with Bacon, Onions, and Mushrooms*

Heart Fritters

Goat Cheese, Spinach, and Green Chile Soufflé*

Mixed Green Salad* and Tomatoes

Sesame Bread*

Chocolate–Chocolate Chip Cookies*

Garden Dinner Offered in Memory of Deep Springs Student Michael Pihos, September 17, 2006

Cucumber-Basil-Yogurt Cooler

Handmade Egg Noodles* with Sautéed Mushrooms,* Garden Greens, and Feta

Chickpeas with Tomatoes, Lemon, and Mint*

Spinach Salad* with Parmesan, Croutons,* Hard-Boiled Egg,* and Lemon Vinaigrette*

Marinated Beets* with Fennel Flowers, Arugula, and Oranges

Warm Bread and Farm Butter*

Chocolate Cream Pie*

CHAPTER 19

Dishes, Stains, and Soap

How to Wash Dishes

Wherever there is good, homemade food, there are dirty dishes. That's just the way it is. Settle into your dishwashing, appreciating the task's meditative simplicity. Every Deep Springs student must perform at least one 2-month tour of duty scrubbing pots and plates in the Boardinghouse kitchen. Here is an excellent, thorough method for washing dishes at home:

1. **De-particleize:** rinse off all visible particles of food and excess grease, using hot water and a nylon scrubber if necessary.

   Be careful of the type of scrubber you use. Some will abrade metals, glass, and glazes. Even softer types can easily abrade plasticware—inexpensive, open-mesh nylon scrubbers are best for most purposes. The mesh bags in which onions and garlic are sometimes packaged make good scrubbers when a cloth or sponge is slipped inside.

2. **Scrub:** put a tablespoon or two of dish detergent in a small basin and fill with about 2 quarts of hot water. Saturate a small dishcloth in your soapy water, and scrub all grease, oil, and any remaining food particles from the dishes. Rinse the cloth frequently in clean water, resaturating it with the soapy water.

   Sponges contain an enormous surface area within their pores and so are traps for bacteria. They are very difficult to clean thoroughly. If you do use sponges, it's a good idea to sterilize them frequently in the microwave (about 1½ minutes) or in boiling water, and replace them at regular intervals. I think small, sturdy cotton dishcloths are better, as they can be thrown in the washing machine.

3. **Rinse:** using hot running water, thoroughly rinse the detergent off the dishes, arranging them in a dish rack. Let dishes air-dry, or thoroughly towel-dry with a clean kitchen towel.

Always wash sharp knives or anything with a blade separately; *never put sharp objects in a basin of soapy water.*

A baking soda solution will sometimes help remove the black residue of badly burned food from the bottom of a pot, depending on the type of food and how badly it was burned. Fill the pot with a few inches of hot water, stir in a couple of heaping spoonfuls of baking soda, and let soak overnight. Bring the water to a boil (watch carefully—don't let it boil over) and cool again to room temperature—the residue should easily scrape off.

In the Deep Springs Boardinghouse and other large-scale kitchens, it's more efficient to use the industrial three-basin method: first, rinse particles off the dishes thoroughly, then immerse them and scrub the grease off in (1) a basin of soapy water (less concentrated than specified on facing page), then (2) in a basin of hot water to rinse, then (3) in a basin of lukewarm water with a glug of bleach added to sterilize. Arrange the dishes on a rack and let air-dry completely.

Laundry Stains

Cooks need to know about stains. Our clothes get stained with food, with grease from various appliances, with soot from the ovens, and with our own blood. Here is everything I've ever needed to know about stain removal from fabric:

Never rinse any protein-based stain (blood, egg, milk) in warm or hot water—always cold.

Use bleach only occasionally if you want your clothes to last. For a large load of white or light-colored clothes, add about ½ cup bleach—a large glug—to the water, *making sure it disperses before adding clothes* (you should do this with detergent, for that matter, too).

If you are away from home and get a stain on an article of clothing you care about, treat the spot as soon as possible with cold water and a little hand soap.

STAIN GUIDE

For most stains: saturate the area of the stain with cold water, then rub well with a bar of Fels-Naptha soap (an antique brand still available in most supermarkets). Rub the soap-saturated fabric vigorously against itself all around the area of the stain. Launder in cold water. Repeat until the stain is gone.

Fresh blood: rinse with cold running water, rubbing the fabric against itself around the area of the stain. On white fabrics, treat any residue as for dried blood—with hydrogen peroxide. On colored fabrics, treat any residue with Fels-Naptha soap.

Dried blood: on white fabrics, saturate the stain with hydrogen peroxide, rub thoroughly, then rinse well with cold water. Repeat until the stain is gone, then launder. On colored fabrics, rinse and rub well under cold running water, then treat with Fels-Naptha soap.

Egg: use cold water to dissolve the egg (even if dried), rubbing under running water until all visible residue is gone, then launder in cold water. Treat any residue with Fels-Naptha soap.

Dirty kitchen towels and chef's jackets: my friend Chef Mona always uses a powdered oxygen-action stain remover on her chef's jackets, soaking the soiled items overnight. This same product, incidentally, is good for removing stains from enameled cookware, coffee cups, or your porcelain kitchen sink.

Handkerchiefs: soak your dirty white hankies for 20 minutes in enough luke-warm water to cover with 2 or 3 glugs of hydrogen peroxide mixed in, then launder in hot water.

Stinky items—socks, washable footwear, nasty bedsheets: wash in hot or warm water, with about ¼ cup baking soda in addition to the detergent.

Ball-point pen ink: rub fabric against itself around the area of the stain with rubbing alcohol, then rinse out the alcohol with cold water. Repeat until the stain is gone.

Deep Springs Soap

MAKES ABOUT 10 POUNDS OF SOAP,
OR 50 BIG BARS

As any Deep Springs student butcher will tell you, a whole cow contains an amazing amount of fat. Beef fat, skillfully rendered, is a splendid medium for deep-frying, and it may be used in place of butter in cookies and cakes, as our ancestors did. But alas, such robustly flavored products taste odd to our modern sensibilities, to say nothing of modern health concerns. So, what do enterprising Deep Springers do with all this fat, besides throw it away? Make soap!

This recipe—one used at Deep Springs for years—yields mild hand and body soap of a quality and purity money just can't buy. All soap is made of fat and lye: the quality and purity of the fat determine the quality of the soap. Often, in commercial soap,

the fat, chemically purified, is of questionable origin. While most soaps contain perfume to hide the smell of the fat, the olive oil in this soap imparts an appealing, clean, naturally soapy scent. We developed this recipe from formulas in an excellent little book published in the 1970s called simply *Soap: Making It, Enjoying It*, by Ann Bramson.

If you require instant gratification in your endeavors, soapmaking is not for you. The ingredients are difficult to find, rendering the tallow takes hours and makes a mess, the temperatures and weights must be exact, the mixing itself requires long, patient stirring, and the soap must cure for at least a month before it's ready to use. Nonetheless, the whole process—including, at last, the satisfying use of the finished soap—offers a fresh appreciation and understanding of an ordinary, every-day product. We use soap constantly, but rarely pay it much attention.

For success, *follow each step precisely;* soap-making is not an improvisatory craft.

Dogs have been known to eat this home-made soap, with very unfortunate, messy after-effects, so keep it out of their reach.

EQUIPMENT/SUPPLIES

meat grinder (or have the butcher grind the fat for you)

large stainless-steel or enamel cooking pot

slow cooker (optional)

screen sieve

cheesecloth or old dish towel

scale accurate to the half-ounce

2-quart glass jar with metal lid (juice jars are ideal; they will withstand the high reaction temperature of the lye)

large wooden spoon (okay to use for cooking afterward—just wash it well)

insulated cooler, about 2-gallon capacity

large plastic garbage bag

2 steel-tipped thermometers with an accurate 60° to 120°F range (1 will suffice, but 2 are more convenient)

large kitchen knife

INGREDIENTS FOR SOAP

6½ pounds fresh, raw beef kidney fat (to make exactly 5.63 pounds, or 5 pounds 10 ounces, or 90 ounces of rendered tallow; a custom butcher will have this; kidney fat is easier to work with than other types of fat)

16½ ounces pure lye crystals (properly known as sodium hydroxide; available by mail order)

48 ounces (by weight) water (3 pounds exactly)

39 ounces (by weight) olive oil (2 pounds 7 ounces; extra-virgin oil is great but not necessary)

½ ounce vitamin E oil (available in body-care stores)

2½ ounces extra-virgin olive oil (added at the end to scent and "superfat" the soap, making it extra mild)

To render the tallow: in a meat grinder, grind the fat, or have the butcher do this for you. Or chop it into small pieces with a large knife. Put it in a large, heavy pot (a slow cooker works well). Set over a very low flame, and allow the fat to render, stirring from time to time. As it renders, the pure fat melts into a clear liquid, and the chunks of solid fat become translucent. After 3 to 4 hours, pour the contents of the pot through a screen sieve set over another pot. Press on the solids left in the sieve to squeeze out more of the liquid fat, then discard the solids.

Now line the sieve with 2 to 3 thicknesses of cheesecloth (or an old dish towel) and place it over a large bowl. Pour the liquid fat through the cheesecloth to filter out any remaining debris. Allow the tallow to cool to room temperature, then refrigerate overnight. Pry the hardened tallow from the bowl. Weigh it—you will need exactly 90 ounces. (Ann Bramson, the soap book author, suggests mixing any leftover tallow with an equal amount of butter and using this blend of fats to make a superlative crust for pecan pie. You may also fry steak in beef tallow; see page 309.)

To mix the lye solution: weigh the lye and water precisely. Put the lye crystals in a 2-quart glass jar with a tight-fitting metal lid. Slowly pour in the water—the reaction will produce a lot of heat. With the handle of a wooden spoon, stir to completely dissolve the crystals in the water. Wash the spoon well afterward.

To prepare the insulated mold: with scissors, cut open one side seam and the bottom seam of the garbage bag, to make one large sheet of plastic. Use this to line the insulated cooler. Drape the flaps of the sheet over the edge of the cooler.

To make the soap: both the lye and the tallow mixture should be within a degree or two of body temperature (98°F). Put the tallow, the 39 ounces of olive oil, and the vitamin E oil together in a large

stainless-steel or enamel pot, and heat over the lowest heat of the stove for just a few minutes, just to begin melting the tallow; the residual heat will melt the rest. Or place the pot in a basin of hot water. If you have just made the lye solution, let it cool for at least 30 minutes, then cool it further, if necessary, by placing the jar in a basin of cold water. Poke 2 holes in the metal lid of the jar for the lye solution (one for the solution to exit, the other for air to enter) so the solution can be dispersed in a thin, even stream.

When both lye and fat are at about 97°F, begin stirring the fat with your large wooden spoon while dispersing the lye into the fat. Keep stirring until all the lye is in the fat and the mixture thickens, keeping the mixture at 97°. If the mixture cools down, place it in a basin of hot water to warm it back up. When you can dribble a stream or droplets of the mixture across its surface and the shape remains for a moment (called tracing), it is ready. Add the 2½ ounces of extra-virgin olive oil to the mixture and stir for about 5 minutes more. Pour the mixture into the prepared mold. Press the flaps of plastic evenly and gently over the surface of the mixture and close the cooler. *Do not open the cooler for 48 hours.*

To finish and cure the soap: After 48 hours, remove the block of solid soap from the cooler, and peel away the plastic. Scrape away any white, powdery residue on the surface. If the soap is still quite soft, let it air-cure on a sheet of plastic on a tray until it firms up—a day or longer. If it seems firm enough to cut, go ahead and cut it into bars with a large kitchen knife. Arrange the bars on a sheet of plastic on a tray to allow for maximum air circulation, and let the soap air-cure in a clean, dry place for about a week. If the bars are still soft to the touch at this point, let them cure for another week, until they are hardened. Wrap each bar individually in butcher paper or waxed paper, and let cure for 3 to 4 more weeks before using.

Cookbooks

These fourteen cookbooks, my idiosyncratic favorites, have all well withstood the vicissitudes of time and trends, have influenced my cooking, and continue to inspire my culinary imagination.

The Betty Crocker Picture Cookbook
published by McGraw-Hill, 1956

This is the first cookbook I used when I was growing up—it was my mother's principal cookbook. A little more approachable than *The Joy of Cooking*, it is a lushly illustrated, encyclopedic treasury of good, mid-century American cooking. It contains many charming "tips" for the "busy housewife," including the admonition to "harbor pleasant thoughts" while scrubbing the kitchen floor.

Charleston Receipts
published by The Junior League of Charleston, 1950

This book is the final word on the cookery of the coastal American South. Most of the recipes (or "receipts") are simple, elegant, and still thoroughly appealing. Though published in 1950, the book vividly evokes earlier ages (for example, a recipe for "Regent's Punch," containing rock sugar candy, green tea [!], champagne, sherry, brandy, and a sliced lemon, notes "As mixed at Lewisfield Plantation, 1783"). Very few convenience foods are called for—virtually everything is from scratch. The "Seafoods" chapter is particularly excellent, as is "Pickles & Relishes."

Chez Panisse Cooking
Paul Bertolli, Random House, 1988

This is among the most beautifully written cookbooks. Of persimmons, he writes, *"There are few things as striking as a persimmon tree in autumn—fruit clinging like Christmas ornaments to the dark arms of the bare tree in the quickening air. Melancholy, fruition, and the close of the circle of seasons are summed up in this image of withering branches and ripening fruit."* Many of the ingredients (rabbit, pigeon, black truffles, walnut oil, Meyer lemons) are hard to find in supermarkets, and many of the recipes have multiple, exacting steps. Nonetheless, each recipe, if followed closely, is a valuable, multifaceted culinary lesson.

Chez Panisse Desserts

Lindsey Shere, Random House, 1985

This collection of elemental, classic, European-inflected preparations has long been my favorite dessert cookbook. These desserts are always thought of in the context of the whole meal—there are virtually no complex showstoppers, just simple preparations—tarts, mousses, compotes, crisps—showcasing the main ingredient's best qualities. Most of the chapters deal with seasonal fruit: "Citrus Fruit," "Apples, Pears, and Quinces," "Berries," "Summer Fruits," "Figs, Melons, and Other Fall Fruits." The ice creams and sherbets are especially wonderful and timeless.

The Chez Panisse Menu Cookbook

Alice Waters, Random House, 1982

When I was a teenager, I discovered this book on my friend Cathleen's kitchen shelf shortly after it was published, sat down, and read the whole thing from cover to cover, like a novel. Duck fat, shallots, fennel, chervil, salt-packed anchovies— I had never encountered such ingredients before. That evening, I successfully made

a carrot soup from it. My imagination was ignited, and the seeds of a culinary career were planted in that moment. The book thoroughly explores the idea of a good, balanced menu (the recipes are arranged in menus, not organized into the usual categories of salads, meats, desserts, and so on) and offers a superb introduction to the idea of cooking seasonally.

English Food

Jane Grigson, Penguin Books, 1974

When the food of the British Isles was still the butt of many jokes, this book quietly and intelligently proved the subtlety, complexity, and overall deliciousness of this cuisine. Celery in cream; Welsh supper herrings; crumpets; steak, kidney, and oyster pie; chicken with mussels; poor knight's pudding; and gooseberry fool are only a few of the book's many unexpected delights.

The Greens Cookbook

Deborah Madison, Bantam Books, 1987

This cookbook broke new ground— it proved that elegant, satisfying, painstakingly crafted food need not contain meat. Madison's clear, poetic enthusiasm for her subject shines from every page. These well-written recipes are more exacting than those in her more recent cookbooks, but each recipe, followed closely, supplies a wealth of culinary information.

Honey from a Weed: Fasting and Feasting in Tuscany, Catalonia, the Cyclades and Apulia

Patience Gray, North Point Press, 1986

A fascinating, erudite compendium of Mediterranean peasant food. The author's life-partner, a sculptor, sought out sources of marble and stone for his work in remote areas around the Mediterranean. While he sculpted in these rural areas of northern and southern Italy, Greece, and Spain, she closely and brilliantly studied the local foodways. Many of the recipes use foraged, fished, or hunted wild ingredients from these places, but a few translate to modern kitchens and tastes, such as ewe's cheese with pears, fried chicken in walnut sauce, "widowed" potatoes, Tuscan loin of pork, and wild peach jam.

The Joy of Cooking

Irma S. Rombauer and Marion Rombauer Becker, 13th edition, Bobbs-Merrill, 1975

By almost anyone's estimation, this is the essential American kitchen reference, written not by a committee, a club, or a corporation, but by a mother and her daughter, over a period of several decades. The recipes themselves are not necessarily unique, but the book contains a staggering amount of information on food and cooking. Cookbook historian Anne Mendelson wrote an absorbing, harrowing biography of Irma, Marion, and their book.

The Moosewood Cookbook

Mollie Katzen, Ten Speed Press, 1977

I heavily relied on this book when I cooked at Deep Springs as an inexperienced Student Cook, and came to trust it as a friend. The hand lettering, the funky illustrations, and the personal conversational nature of the recipes all make for an excellent beginner's cookbook, with many recipes that are still fresh and exciting.

Nothing Fancy

Diana Kennedy, North Point Press, 1984

This is my favorite example of a good, working cookbook that is also highly personal and idiosyncratic. It contains an entire chapter called "Crispy Things." While many of the recipes spring from the author's beloved, adopted Mexico, the teatime and holiday favorites from her native England—hot cross buns, cucumber sandwiches, gingerbread, bitter orange marmalade, lemon curd, rock cakes, barley water, ginger beer—form the spirit and backbone of the book.

Recipes from the Regional Cooks of Mexico

Diana Kennedy, Harper & Row, 1978

Her great, earlier cookbook, *The Cuisines of Mexico*, was one of the first to prove unequivocally the depth and breadth of one of the world's most exciting and intriguing cuisines. This book, focused more on individual cooks and regional specialties, is more personal. It contains a long, wonderful account of an elaborate Oaxacan goat *barbacoa*, full of rich culinary detail.

Summer Cooking

Elizabeth David,
Museum Press/Knopf, 1955

Of the many intelligent, evocative cookbooks on the food of France and the Mediterranean penned by David (*Mediterranean Cooking* [1950], *French Country Cooking* [1951], *Italian Food* [1954], *French Provincial Cooking* [1960]), designed to bring Britons out of their postwar culinary depression, *Summer Cooking* extols, in concise, poetic paragraphs, the culinary virtues of eating appropriately to the season. Ease, lightness, and simplicity prevail. Her work continues to inspire generations of English and American chefs and cooks.

White Trash Cooking

Ernest Matthew Mickler,
Ten Speed Press, 1986

At first glance, this book seems like a joke, but on closer examination, a sensitive, warmhearted cultural document of Southern food emerges. Some of the recipes are great fun to read but not necessarily feasible to cook and eat ("Butt's 'Gator Tail" comes to mind), but many others are genuinely appealing. In the recipes, people's voices are allowed to be just as they are. Haunting, evocative photographs supplement the recipes.

Sources

For the freshest, highest-quality spices and an informative catalog:
Penzey's Spices
800-741-7787
penzeys.com

For truly unrefined sea salt:
Salt Works, Inc.
800-353-SALT (7258)
saltworks.us

For superb flour and an all-around bread-baking resource:
King Arthur Flour
800-827-6836
kingarthurflour.com

For grains of many types, including steel-cut oats and rye flakes:
Bob's Red Mill
800-349-2173
bobsredmill.com

For Southern stone-ground yellow cornmeal:
Louisiana Pride Grist Mill
225-654-6131
louisianapridegristmill.com

For authentic New Mexico ground red chile, whole dried red chile pods, and fresh green chile:
The New Mexican Connection
800-933-2736
newmexicanconnection.com

For food-grade lye, for making Deep Springs Soap:
AAA Chemicals
866-939-CHEM (2436)
aaa-chemicals.com/sodium-hydroxide

For heavy saucepans, omelet pans, instant-read thermometers, and other kitchen equipment and supplies:
CHEFS Catalog
800-338-3232
chefscatalog.com

For a wide selection of high-quality kitchen knives:
Just Knives 101
800-585-1330
justknives101.com

For excellent-quality meat, if there is one in your area, try:
a family-run, locally owned butcher shop

For good, fresh fruits, vegetables, and herbs, or for farm-fresh eggs, investigate:
farmer's markets
roadside farm stands
U-pick places
raising chickens in your backyard
growing a garden

Acknowledgments

* I would like to express my gratitude to the many people who, knowingly or unknowingly, directly or indirectly, helped *The Commonsense Kitchen* through its many incarnations, from "seed" to "tree."

* **Thanks** to the team at Chronicle Books, for their interest in Deep Springs: to Bill LeBlond and Sarah Billingsley, for shepherding us through the publication process; to Rebecca Pepper, for tight, attentive copyediting; and to Katie Heit, for realizing a superb, appropriate design.

* **Thanks** to L. J. "Elge" Bridwell, for delicious friendship, unstinting critical honesty, and intimate involvement with the book over so many years.

* **Thanks** to Charis and Mark Takaro, for countless excellent home-cooked meals and steadfast support.

* **Thanks** to Mona Talbott, for constant inspiration on the culinary path.

* **Thanks** to Deep Springs College community members past and present, including Geoff and Iris Pope, Andy and Heather Jennings, David and Jane Steidel, Jack and Linda Newell, Ross and Kay Peterson, Chuck and Elaine Teel, the Mitchell family, David Neidorf, Justin Kim, Brad Edmondson, Abram Kaplan, Bill Scott, and the Deep Springs Classes of 1986, 1987, 1988, 1989, 1996, 1997, 1998, 1999, 2000, 2001, 2005, 2006, 2007, 2008, and 2009.

* **Thanks** to my friends and family behind many of the recipes, including Carol Adair, Paul Airoldi, Jack Aldworth, Ann Hanchey Applegarth, Diana Applegarth, the Badkar family, Joel Baecker, Mary Nell Brown, the Copelin family, Ann Tracy Drummond, Clay Drummond, Priscilla Freeman, Jean Glover, Nellie Maybelle Hanchey, Iris Ann Hudgens, Michael Thomas Hudgens, Eloise Humphrey, Reatha Jones, David Lebovitz, Cecilia Lopez, Eric "Rico" Luna (*el corazón de mi alma*), Emily Marshall, Scott Miller, Dana Nesbitt, Laura Laylin Nichols, Michael Polek, Linda Rael, Joan Rinaldi, Lela Hanchey Thompson, Amy Toder, Adra Valentine, Ella Vining, Katherine White, Elizabeth "Lee" Zavadil, and Tom Zavadil.

* Finally, **thanks** to all my teachers—transmitters of information, experience, spirit, drive, wisdom, and love—including writing coaches Ruth Lewis, June Wolfe, Pam Perryman, Tim Hunt, and Lydia Fakundiny; science guides Edie Anderson, Carla Scheidlinger, and Gordon Wardlaw; meditation masters Donald Rothberg (a deep bow), Sylvia Boorstein, and Christopher Titmuss; and culinary exemplars Elizabeth Alderson, Catherine Brandel, Kazue Carlson, Eve Felder, Mirka Grbec, Gilbert Pilgram, Cynthia Shea, Peggy Smith, Carole "Cookie" Tam Sing, David Tanis, Alice Waters, and, of course, my mom.

F

G

Galette, Red Onion, 239

Garbanzo beans *see* Chickpeas

Garlic, about, 66–68

Aioli, 427

Cayenne-Rubbed Chicken with Potatoes and Garlic, 350

Cynthia's Garlic-Studded Milk-Braised Pork Loin, 339

Garlic Bread, 394

Garlic Mayonnaise, 426, 427

Garlic Soup, 232

Roasted Garlic, 231

Toasted Pasta with Garlic, 394

Gazpacho, with variations, 287

Gelatin, 512–517

Creamy Orange Gelatin, 514

Fresh Fruit Gelatin, 515

Gelées, 512

Ginger Ale–Lemon-Pear Gelatin, 514

Lemon Sour Cream Gelatin, 514

Lime Yum, 514

Ghee, 63, 177

Gin Chicken Liver Pâté, 363

Ginger

Carrot Soup with Ginger, 223

Elge's Three-Ginger Gingerbread, 490

Fresh Ginger Cake, 491

Ginger Cookies, 540

Ginger-Peach Crisp, 465

Ginger Ale–Lemon-Pear Gelatin, 514

Gingersnaps, 539

Gingersnap Crust for Cheesecake, 463

Gingersnaps, Vanilla Ice Cream, and Boysenberries, 540

Gluten (wheat), 131, 443

Goat Cheese, Spinach and Green Chile Soufflé, 169

Goat Stew, Mexican, 319

Goose Eggs

Goose Egg Pound Cake, 482

Goose Egg Pound Cake Cinnamon Toast, 483

Gooseberry Fool, 506

Goulash, 318

Grains

hot breakfast cereals, 84–86

Polenta, 404

Quinoa, 407

Rice, 398

Grandma Z.'s Coffeecake, 121

Granola, 87

Grapes, Roasted, 367

Gratin

Potato, Fennel, and Celery Root Gratin, 248

White Bean with Fennel Gratin, 199

Gravlax, 374

Gravy

Biscuits and Gravy, 115

Turkey Gravy, 365

Greek Salad, 273

Green Beans, Sautéed, 217

Green Chiles

Green Chile Enchiladas, 172

Green Chile Relish, 423

New Mexico Green Chile Beef Stew, 320

New Mexico Green Chile Sauce, 422

Green Peppercorn Butter Sauce, 425

Green Salad, 269–272

Greens (cooking), varieties of, 232

Greens and Sausage Pizza, 157

Griddle Toast, with variations, 88

Grilled Cheese Sandwich, 45, 159

grinder, meat, for making fresh sausage, 92

Q

R

T

washing dishes, 568–569
Water, how to boil, 47
Watercress
    Watercress Salad, 269, 294
    Watercress Soup, 256
Wedding Cookies, 531
Wheat flour *see* Flour, about
Wheat gluten, in bread, 131
Wheaty Bread, 135
Whey Lemonade, 147
Whipped Cream, 447, 478
    Big Pink Cake, 496
    Blueberry Whipped Cream Cake, 487
    Gooseberry Fool, 506
    Horseradish Cream, 314
    Lemon Cream, 490
    Lemon Curd Cream, 492
    Raspberry Whipped Cream, 496
    Whipped Cream Cake, 486
White Chocolate Chips, Chocolate
    Cookies with, 523
White Beans, about, 186–189, 199
    White Bean and Escarole Soup, 203
    White Bean Chili with Pork, 200
    White Bean Gratin with Fennel, 199
    White Bean Soup with Fried Sage, 202
Whole-Wheat Cheddar Biscuits, 114
Whole-Wheat Crackers, 143
Whole-Wheat Pancakes, 110
Wild Mushroom Risotto, 403
Wild, White, and Brown Rice Pilaf with
    Mirepoix, 400
Wine, red
    Boeuf Bourguignonne, 318
    Red Wine Butter Sauce *(Beurre rouge)*,
    425
    Chicken Braised in Red Wine *(Coq au
    Vin)*, 357

Wine, white
    in dough for Focaccia, 137
    White Wine Butter Sauce *(Beurre blanc)*,
    425
Winter Beef Stew, Elizabeth's, 317
Winter Squash, Stuffed, 408
Worcestershire sauce, about, 73

Y

Yams, about, 139; *See also* Sweet Potatoes
    Roasted Yams, 257
Yeast *see* Breads, yeast
Yogurt
    Cantaloupe–Black Pepper Raita 179
    Cucumber Raita, 179
    Dijon Yogurt Dressing, 299
    Toasted Cumin-Mint-Yogurt Dressing,
    298
    Yogurt-Shallot Sauce, 424
Yorkshire Pudding, 314

Z

Zest, citrus, about, 51, 55
Zucchini squash *see also* Squash, Summer
    Zucchini-Red Onion Pizza, 157

He said: "It is all useless, if the
last landing place can only be the
infernal city, and it is there that, in
ever-narrowing circles, the current
is drawing us."

And Polo said: "The inferno of the
living is not something that will be;
if there is one, it is what is already here,
the inferno where we live every day,
that we form by being together. There
are two ways to escape suffering it. The
first is easy for many: accept the inferno
and become such a part of it that you
can no longer see it. The second is
risky and demands constant vigilance
and apprehension: seek and learn to
recognize who and what, in the midst
of the inferno, are not inferno, then
make them endure, give them space."

—Italo Calvino, *Invisible Cities*